Black Germany

This ground-breaking history traces the development of Germany's black community, from its origins in colonial Africa to its decimation by the Nazis during World War Two. Robbie Aitken and Eve Rosenhaft follow the careers of Africans arriving from the colonies, examining why and where they settled, their working lives and their political activities, and giving unprecedented attention to gender, sexuality and the challenges of 'mixed marriage'. Addressing the networks through which individuals constituted community, Aitken and Rosenhaft explore the ways in which these relationships spread beyond ties of kinship and birthplace to constitute communities as 'black'. The study also follows a number of its protagonists to France and back to Africa, providing new insights into the roots of Francophone black consciousness and post-colonial memory. Including an in-depth account of the impact of Nazism and its aftermath, this book offers a fresh critical perspective on narratives of 'race' in German history.

ROBBIE AITKEN is a Senior Lecturer in Imperial History at Sheffield Hallam University.

EVE ROSENHAFT is Professor of German Historical Studies at the University of Liverpool.

Black Germany

The Making and Unmaking of a Diaspora Community, 1884–1960

Robbie Aitken and Eve Rosenhaft

CAMBRIDGE
UNIVERSITY PRESS

University Printing House, Cambridge CB2 8BS, United Kingdom

Cambridge University Press is part of the University of Cambridge.

It furthers the University's mission by disseminating knowledge in the pursuit of education, learning and research at the highest international levels of excellence.

www.cambridge.org
Information on this title: www.cambridge.org/9781107595392

First published 2013
First paperback edition 2015

A catalogue record for this publication is available from the British Library

Library of Congress Cataloguing in Publication data
Aitken, Robbie John Macvicar.
Black Germany : the making and unmaking of a diaspora community, 1884–1960 / Robbie Aitken and Eve Rosenhaft.
p. cm.
Includes bibliographical references and index.
ISBN 978-1-107-04136-3 (Hardback)
1. Blacks–Germany–History. 2. Blacks–Germany–Social conditions. 3. Cameroonians–Germany–History. 4. Africans–Germany–History. 5. Germany–Race relations–History. 6. Germany–Emigration and immigration. 7. Germany–Colonies–Africa–Emigration and immigration. 8. Cameroon–Emigration and immigration. I. Rosenhaft, Eve, 1951– II. Title.
DD78.B55A48 2013
305.896043–dc23 2013009484

ISBN 978-1-107-04136-3 Hardback
ISBN 978-1-107-59539-2 Paperback

For Ella, Alec and Daniel – cosmopolitans all

Contents

Illustrations

Maps

Acknowledgements

This book has been a long time in the making, and each of the authors has their own memory of where it began. For Robbie it started in 1998 with the discovery of an article in the London *Times* about the trial of the Cameroonians Wilhelm Munumé and Peter Makembe, and its reference to a larger black community present in the courtroom. Eve's engagement with this history grew out of a collaboration with Susan Pennybacker and Jim Miller that explored the international dimensions of the Scottsboro case and the meanings of transnational black activism in the 1930s; she is waving from the bridge as the last of three 'Scottsboro books' arrives in its berth.

This is by way of saying that the book is in multiple senses the product of conversations and collaborations among scholars. It draws on the research of others that has gone before, and while we hoped in developing it to add a new depth and dimensions to our understanding of Black German history, we acknowledge here the achievement of a generation of historians and activists engaged since the 1980s in excavating a past largely buried in the archives and in popular memory. We're grateful to have been able to draw on their findings, and especially to those who have shared their data and ideas with us, some of whom are named below.

Carrying out a project of this scale would have been unthinkable without the help and support of many individuals and institutions, in particular the interviewees in both Cameroon and Europe who were willing to share their knowledge and experiences with us and who are named in the bibliography. We are greatly indebted to a grant from the Arts and Humanities Research Council (grant number 112228), which enabled us to carry out the bulk of the archival research in Europe and Cameroon, and to our respective departments at the Universities of Liverpool and Sheffield Hallam for continuing supplementary financial and infrastructural support. Similarly the hard work of numerous archivists and librarians in retrieving material in an array of local, state and national archives and libraries has been key to building the research base of the project. Help on specific matters is acknowledged in our footnotes, but in particular we should like to thank Gisela Erler and Bianca Welzing-Bräutigam of the Landesarchiv Berlin, Volker Reismann and Julia Wannagat at Staatsarchiv Hamburg, Monika Marschalck at Staatsarchiv Bremen, Sergey Belov at the Russian State Archive of Socio-Political History and the staff at the National Archives in Yaoundé for their unflagging patience in dealing with our continued requests.

Guy Thomas and his undergraduate seminar group at the University of Basel in 2006 kindly enabled Robbie to accompany them on a first research trip to Cameroon. In Douala Anja Michels, Chantal Nina Kuoh and Ngando Mackay provided invaluable help in the organising and carrying out of interviews and the locating of material. Carl Ebobissè, Valère Epee, Emilien Joseph Manga Douala Bell and Ngosso Isidore all offered a wealth of support and advice on the project. Special thanks are due to the Ebongue family in Yaoundé, particularly Nestor and Stéphane, who took good care of Robbie during research trips in the city and to Albert Gouaffo who not only organised lodgings in Dschang, but has also been of great assistance on many aspects of our work. Whether in Cameroon or in Switzerland Anna Sommer has been a dedicated and expert research assistant and Maria Hermes has provided similar valuable assistance in Germany.

Colleagues and friends Barbara Bush, Dmitri van den Bersselaar, Jonathan Derrick, Elisa von Joeden-Forgey, Patrick Harries, Christoph Laucht, Eveline Meister, Susan Pennybacker, Niels Petersson, Matthew Stibbe, Andrew Zimmerman and Kate Marsh have all read or heard parts of this project and their constructive comments have greatly contributed to its development, as have the comments of anonymous reviewers. Caroline Authaler, Gesine Krüger, Susann Lewerenz, Peter Martin, Stefanie Michels, Sara Pugach, Peter Schick, Holger Stoecker, Pastor Dietrich Sonnenberger and Woodford McClellan provided archive tips and generously shared their research findings with us as did the late Heiko Möhle. Victor Dicka Akwa in Douala kindly provided access to photographic material. Pastor Martin Grawert of the Evangelisch-Freikirchliche Gemeinde Eberswalde and Pastor Reinhard Assmann of the Evangelisch-Freikirchliche Gemeinde Zoar Prenzlauer Berg (Berlin) were welcome collaborators in unearthing the role of Baptist hospitality in the early history of our subjects. Silke Betscher, Manuela Bauche, Katharina Müller and Ulrika Schaper assisted in hunting down documents. Without Brian Murphy's expert and enthusiastic translation of yards of Comintern files we should not have had access to key elements of our story, while Dhanavadee Underwood's transcriptions of French-language interviews helped us to understand what we were hearing. Sandra Mather was an expert and patient collaborator in the production of maps. Nicholas Stargardt gave us the title for the book, though it took us some time to realise it and he has probably forgotten. Last, and certainly not least, the completion of this book would not have been possible without the support, encouragement and patience of Nigel, Daniel, Alec, Eveline and Ella.

Abbreviations

AAKA	Auswärtiges Amt – Kolonialabteilung (Colonial Department of the Foreign Office)
AH	Afrikanischer Hilfsverein (African Welfare Association)
ANCB	Archives Nationales de Cameroun, Buea
ANCY	Archives Nationales de Cameroun, Yaoundé
BArch	Bundesarchiv, Berlin
BHstAM	Bayerisches Hauptstaatsarchiv, Munich
CAC	Archives Nationales de France, Centre des Archives Contemporaines, Fontainebleau
CADN	Archives Nationales de France, Centre des Archives Diplomatiques, Nantes
CAI	Service de Contrôle et Assistance en France des Indigènes des Colonies (Office of Control and Assistance for the Indigenous People in the Colonies)
CDJC	Centre de Documentation Juive Contemporaine, Paris
CNDIC	Comité National pour la Défense des Interêts du Cameroun (National Committee for the Defence of the Interests of Cameroon)
DGfE	Deutsche Gesellschaft für Eingeborenenkunde (German Society for the Study of Native Cultures)
DKB	Deutsches Kolonialblatt
DKG	Deutsche Kolonialgesellschaft (German Colonial Society)
FR ANOM	Archives Nationales de France, Centre d'Archives d'Outre-Mer, Aix-en-Provence
GDR	German Democratic Republic
GStA	Geheimes Staatsarchiv Preußischer Kulturbesitz, Dahlem

HHStAW	Hessisches Hauptstaatsarchiv, Wiesbaden
ITS	International Tracing Service, Bad Arolsen
ITUCNW	International Trade Union Committee of Negro Workers
KEDGV	Kamerun Eingeborenen Deutsch Gesinnten Verein (Association of German-Spirited Cameroon Natives)
KPA	Kolonialpolitisches Amt der NSDAP (Nazi Office of Colonial Policy)
KPD	Kommunistische Partei Deutschlands (Communist Party of Germany)
KUTV	Communist University for the Toilers of the East
LAB	Landesarchiv, Berlin
LABO	Landesamt für Bürger- und Ordnungsangelegenheiten Abt. I Entschädigungsbehörde, Berlin
LAI	League against Imperialism
LDRN	Ligue de Défense de la Race Nègre (League for the Defence of the Negro Race)
LICA	Ligue Internationale Contre l'Antisemitisme (International League against Antisemitism)
LzVN	Liga zur Verteidigung der Negerrasse (League for the Defence of the Negro Race)
MASCH	Marxistische Arbeiterschule (Marxist Workers' School)
NAK	National Archives Kew
NSDAP	Nationalsozialistische Deutsche Arbeiterpartei (National Socialist German Workers' Party)
Onckenarchiv	Onckenarchiv des Bundes Evangelisch-Freikirchlicher Gemeinden in Deutschland, Elstal
PAAA	Politisches Archiv des Auswärtigen Amtes (German Foreign Office Archives), Berlin
PCF	Parti Communiste Français (French Communist Party)
Pol. X	Politische Abteilung X (Political Department X, Colonial Affairs Section of the Foreign Office)
RGASPI	Russian State Archives of Socio-Political History, Moscow
RGBl	*Reichsgesetzblatt*
RKA	Reichskolonialamt (Reich Colonial Office)
RKM	Reichskolonialministerium (Reich Colonial Ministry)
RKPA	Reichskriminalpolizeiamt (Reich Criminal Police Bureau)

RSHA	Reichssicherheitshauptamt (Reich Security Main Office)
StABremen	Staatsarchiv Bremen
StAHam	Staatsarchiv Hamburg
StAWürzburg	Staatsarchiv Würzburg
UC	Union Camerounaise (Cameroonian Union)
UTN	Union des travailleurs nègres (Union of Negro Workers)
VfdSW	Vereinigung für Deutsche Siedlung und Wanderung (Association for German Settlement and Migration)

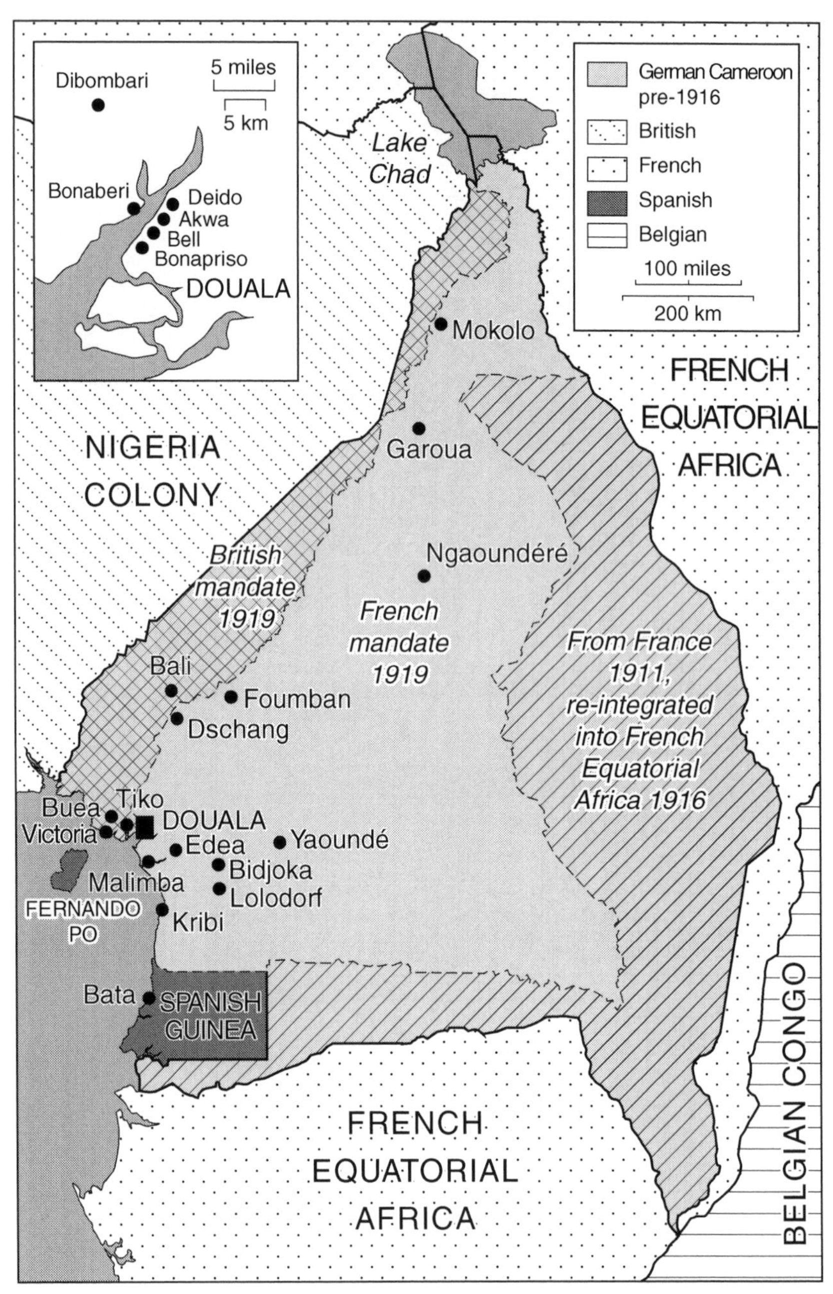

1.1 Cameroon as protectorate and mandate

Introduction

In April 1885 a brief article in the *Teltower Kreisblatt* reported the return to Berlin of the German Consul in Cameroon, Eduard Schmidt.[1] Accompanying Schmidt for the duration of his home leave was a young Cameroonian prince, who was said to have been brought up in the Christian faith and was able to understand German. According to the article the pair drew considerable attention (particularly female) as they took a carriage through the city centre. Later reports named the prince as Ebobse Dido, the then youngest son of Epee Ekwalla Deido (Jim Ekwalla), the traditional leader of the Deido quarter in the coastal town of Douala.[2] Only ten months after the proclamation of German protection over Cameroon, the newspaper speculated that this was the first Cameroonian to visit the 'Fatherland'. Dido was certainly one of the first German colonial subjects to reach Germany, but a mobile population of Africans and African Americans was already becoming visible and increasingly attracting public attention. As early as April 1882 the same newspaper had reported that Berlin had a '*Neger* colony' of sixty people from both the United States and Africa.[3] According to the article many of them were not only fluent in German, but even spoke in Berlin dialect; three men were married to 'white girls' and their children were said to be doing well at school. While Dido's brief stay in Berlin received little press coverage, two years later news of the arrival of another Cameroonian, Alfred Bell (Belle Ndumbe), to undertake an apprenticeship in Altona featured in a number of regional and local newspapers throughout

[1] 'Konsul Schmidt aus Kamerun', *Teltower Kreisblatt,* 21 April 1885, p. 3.

[2] Section 'Steglitz', *Teltower Kreisblatt,* 4 July 1885, p. 4. For Cameroonian place-names we use the current, French, spellings throughout.

[3] 'Die Berliner Negerkolonie', *Teltower Kreisblatt,* 11 March 1882, p. 2. The story was picked up in the United States, see 'Minor Doings across the Sea', *New York Times,* 1 April 1882, p. 4. An article in the same newspaper some five years later suggested that there were now twenty-three men of African heritage in the city: 'Berlin's Negro Colony', *New York Times,* 12 November 1887, p. 4.

Germany.[4] By 1890 147 Africans were registered in Hamburg and in 1903 the *New York Times* remarked that there were around 200 residents of African origin in Berlin.[5] In 1902 the *Berliner Illustrirte* newspaper reported: 'Everyday here in Berlin new dark faces appear, some of whom indeed come from the German colonies.'[6]

Young men with dark faces who hailed from Germany's new African colonies became the founding generation for a substantial black presence in Germany. For two centuries or more, individual Blacks had sojourned at German courts and universities or in German cities as exceptional individuals (though of widely ranging status and provenance).[7] Once a German nation state was formed in 1871, its emergence as a maritime and colonial power generated a metropolitan black population that displayed the potential for continuous growth. Coming mainly from Cameroon, Togo and East Africa, and very occasionally from South West Africa, colonial subjects formed the core of this population, which saw several thousand passing through Germany before 1914 and probably numbered up to 1,000 at any one time. And at the same time, the popular media which flourished under the very conditions of rapid economic and social development that fuelled Germany's maritime project articulated metropolitan interest in and curiosity about these new neighbours. These media produced and reproduced in print the vision of a collective black presence as well as refining visual and verbal stereotypes of Blacks themselves.[8]

Up to this point, the story of Germany's black population is not very different from that of the black presence in other European states that had African colonies. France and Britain, Germany's principal comparators and competitors, had larger empires that had been channelling people of colour into their metropolitan territories for a much longer time – not least through their massive and direct involvement in the transatlantic slave trade and colonial slave economies. But in both countries the arrival of people from sub-Saharan Africa in the wake of the late colonial settlement opened a new chapter in the history of the black presence. Numbers grew, fed simultaneously by continuous in-migration

[4] See press clippings in BArch R1001 4297, p. 31.

[5] Möhle, 'Von Duala nach Altona', p. 17; 'Stories of American Lynchings Inspire Assaults on Negroes in German Capital', *New York Times*, 4 October 1903, p. 4. The *Times* article reported that a 'Black and White Society (Schwartz [*sic*]-Weiss Verein)' protested against attacks on Blacks in Berlin inspired by reports from the US.

[6] 'Dunkle Existenzen: Aus dem Berufsleben der Berliner Neger', *Berliner Illustrirte Zeitung*, 13 June 1902, p. 40.

[7] For an early and still authoritative overview, see Martin, *Schwarze Teufel, edle Mohren.*

[8] On the dissemination of visual stereotypes in the print media, see Ciarlo, *Advertising Empire.*

and natural increase, and forms of collective life evolved as physical and occupational proximity (often the result of white racist exclusionary practices) threw together people who had different origins but who shared the fact of being identified as black by metropolitan society. Successive waves or major episodes of black immigration, like the arrival of the Windrush generation of West Indians in post-war Britain or the post-colonial influx of legal and illegal migrants, refugees and asylum-seekers since the 1960s, have added new (and often conflictual) dimensions to this history without breaking a continuity that can be traced in the public archives and in family memories, as well as being asserted and celebrated in the writings of black activists and intellectuals. Indeed one of the features of the black experience in the British and French imperial contexts has been the emergence of 'organic intellectuals' speaking as and for black people in the respective metropolitan societies and building institutional and discursive bridges between black people in different parts of the world.[9]

This continuity is what seems to be missing from the black German experience. Rather, the modern history of black people in Germany is notoriously *discontinuous*. The colonial generation and their families were dispersed, reduced in numbers and largely forgotten by the 1950s. Of the pre-World War Two generations, the 'black Germans' whose experience left traces in public memory and historiography were the several hundred children fathered by Africans among the French troops that occupied the Rhineland following World War One; they are remembered as the victims of Nazi Germany's first measure of mass sterilisation.[10] In the wake of the American occupation of Germany after World War Two some 5,000 children were born to German women and African-American soldiers. Those among these *Besatzungskinder* who were not adopted by African-American families grew up in white families or in children's homes in West Germany, often in relative isolation from other black people.[11] From the 1960s onwards the international interests of both West and East Germany encouraged the presence of new cohorts of African professionals and students, and East Germany also recruited

[9] On the growth of African populations in Britain see among others, Fryer, *Staying Power*; Killingray (ed.), *Africans in Britain*; Green, *Black Edwardians*; Frost, *Work and Community*; Tabili, *'We Ask for British Justice'*, esp. pp. 135–60. Historical writing on Black France has given less attention to the fabric of everyday life and local community; for some approaches see Fletcher, 'City, Nation and Empire'; Boittin, *Colonial Metropolis*; Boittin, '"Among them complicit"?'; Blanchard, Deroo and Manceran, *Le Paris noir*.

[10] Pommerin, *Sterilisierung der Rheinlandbastarde*.

[11] Lemke Muniz de Faria, *Zwischen Fürsorge und Ausgrenzung*; Fehrenbach, *Race after Hitler*.

thousands of contract workers from Mozambique and Angola – on the assumption in both Germanies that their presence would be temporary.[12] In 2010 the Federal Statistical Office reported that there were some 500,000 people of African origin in Germany, of whom nearly 300,000 (mainly adults) had not acquired German citizenship.[13]

A key moment in the construction of this series of arrivals and departures as a coherent history was the publication in 1986 of *Farbe bekennen* (translated as *Showing Our Colors*) – a volume of narratives, critical essays and interviews on the experience of being black in Germany. Its making is characteristic equally of the diffuse heritage to which black Germans lay claim and of the hunger for collective narrative that accompanied the coming to consciousness of a generation. It documents an encounter between women of the post-World War Two generation whose fathers were variously African and African-American and who define themselves in the subtitle of the German edition as 'Afro-German women on the trail of their history'. The phrase 'Afro-German', with its explicit echo of 'Afro-American', signalled the beginning of a black German political movement; the 1980s also witnessed the creation of the first associations of black Germans, and this movement itself depended on and worked to reproduce through argument and practice the sense of a common interest rooted in history.[14] *Farbe bekennen* not only offered the first outline history of Blacks and colour-based racism in modern Germany, but it also reinstated retrospectively an interrupted genealogy, through interviews with the daughters of two men of the first, colonial generation. That book can thus be seen as the foundational text for a generation of empirical historical research on the black presence in Germany.[15]

Black Germany builds on that research, our own and others', but it aims to do more than synthesise what has already been done, and that has everything to do with the questions of internal cohesion and potential continuity that the work of the 1980s opened up. Our title is both assertive and interrogative. It invokes the Black Britain and Black France (and indeed the Black Atlantic) of recent activist and critical historiography, in order to raise the possibility of a Black Germany and to ask what

[12] Döring and Rüchel (eds.), *Freundschaftsbande und Beziehungskisten*; Schmelz, *Bildungsmigranten*; Kuck, '"Für den sozialistischen Aufbau ihrer Heimat"?'; Dennis, 'Asian and African Workers in the Niches of Society'.

[13] Statistisches Bundesamt, *Bevölkerung und Erwerbstätigkeit*.

[14] On the actual and imaginative dialectic between African-American and African-German identities, see Campt, 'African German/African American'. The African-American poet Audre Lorde contributed an essay to *Farbe bekennen*.

[15] This began with the publication of the master's thesis of one of its authors: Oguntoye, *Eine Afro-Deutsche Geschichte*.

became of it. Evidence of connections among individuals over space and time seems critical to the vision of a black history, and it is striking that three decades of meticulous and imaginative research with black German subjects at its centre has achieved a *collective* account largely by accumulating individual case studies in anthologies or monographic biographies.[16] One of the aims of the research underpinning this book, then, was to fill what we saw to be a gap in the historiography by asking how these individuals related to one another – and in that sense to see whether we could see German Blacks as a living collective rather than a collection of lives. At the centre of the book is an effort to make visible the relationships among them and between them and other Germans – ties of kinship, affinity, neighbourhood and association – that should enable us to understand what *might have* grown from the founding presence of the colonial generation, as well as to gain a more rounded understanding of individual lives and actions. That is, where up to now we have taken a broken history as read, this book looks at the sources of possible continuity in the connected lives of individuals in order to better understand *how* it was broken.

As our subtitle indicates, in asking after connections, relationships and collective trajectories, and with the social history of other black immigrant populations in mind, we were seeking to test whether it is possible to characterise the undeniable black presence in Germany in terms of community. 'Community' is a word that does not translate easily into German (or even French);[17] as applied to the lives of black people in Europe it invokes an ideal type. It draws heavily on features of the African-American experience and the way it has been narrated since the 1960s, when the vision of an embattled but cohesive urban neighbourhood emerged as a response to discourses of social pathology in public and academic discussion of urban riots. In Britain, the discussion of black communities can be dated from a comparable moment of contest, following the riots of the early 1980s in English cities. Critical thinking about the parameters of black community intersected with a scholarly interest in the relevance of community to the politics and culture of the working class, and in particular in the ways in which

[16] Even the recent monographic study by Peter Martin and Christina Alonzo, *Im Netz der Moderne*, offers a collage rather than an in-depth study, placing heavy emphasis on the dramatic and relatively well-rehearsed themes of political mobilisation and persecution under National Socialism. Other representative monographs, articles and edited volumes are cited below in individual chapters and in the bibliography.

[17] 'Community' is increasingly used untranslated in Afro-German activist circles; AntiDiskriminierungsBüro (ADB) (ed.), *TheBlackBook*, has a section on political and cultural initiatives headed 'Schwarze Community'.

'community' could act as a basis for or even the object of progressive social movements, reinforcing class consciousness or serving as an alternative point of reference for solidarity and self-defence. In Britain it also coincided with a critical approach to public anxieties about street crime in which discourses of race and racialised urban space played a significant role.[18] Following Anthony Cohen's characterisation of community as a 'largely mental construct, whose "objective" manifestations in locality or ethnicity give it credibility', Paul Gilroy's 1987 breakthrough study *'There Ain't No Black in the Union Jack'* argued in detail for its salience as a social reality among British Blacks. His account starts from the 'mental' phenomenon – the self-conscious deployment of a rhetoric of community in the riots and their aftermath – but also observes that the idea of community is rooted in the materialities of neighbourhood, daily experiences of face-to-face communication and involvement in kinship and associational networks.

As Gilroy pointed out then, communities however articulated can be divided and contested in practice. 'Black' is a social construct that comprehends people with a variety of backgrounds and interests, and the idea of a *black* community that emerged in the crisis is a political one. It is at least as much an acknowledgement of antagonism between Blacks as a group and the majority white society as it is a statement of internal solidarity.[19] Accordingly, work on black immigrant history which has used the term 'community' to signal both everyday networks and associations and their expression in collective identities often distinguishes – as Diane Frost does in her study of Kru seafarers who settled in Liverpool – between historic ethnic and occupational communities and a wider 'black community' which is structured by external perceptions of 'blackness' as well as by internal practices and articulations of identity.[20] The inherently political sense of this use of 'community' means that it can take on a normative character; it excludes as well as includes, and when paired with 'black' it may be used as a measure of who is really black or whose black experience counts.[21] The possibility of articulating new and

[18] See Centre for Contemporary Cultural Studies (ed.), *The Empire Strikes Back.*

[19] Gilroy, *'There Ain't No Black in the Union Jack'*, pp. 223–50. The quote from Cohen, *The Symbolic Construction of Community*, p. 109, is on p. 235.

[20] Frost, *Work and Community*, pp. 187–96. See Lawless, *From Ta'izz to Tyneside*; Chessum, *From Immigrants to Ethnic Minority.*

[21] Brown, *Dropping Anchor, Setting Sail*, explores the ways in which the assertion of community undercut solidarity in practice in a city where self-identification as 'black' in the face of institutionalised white racism has a long history. On the ambivalence of 'black community' for individuals – especially those of 'mixed' heritage – who are perceived as 'not black enough', see also Tate, 'Translating Melancholia'.

more inclusive models of black community has been the object of critical work since the 1990s.[22]

We use the term here not in a normative but in a descriptive manner. We take the model sketched above in relation to Britain and France, of a dynamic set in motion by high colonialism that involves an interplay of demographic growth, geographical concentration, social networks and sustained interactions, self-articulation as black and address to a global black population, as a starting point for asking whether we can find the traces in Germany of a comparable evolution from presence to community and from black identity to black politics. Approaching black German history with this comparative question about the prospects for continuity also allows us to reflect from a new angle on the features and peculiarities that perplex and preoccupy us as students of German national history (or of the society made largely by white Germans).

In order to do this, we have adopted the strategy of tracing the careers and experiences of a particular group among the founding generation, between the time of their arrival in the metropole and roughly the 1960s. Our study focuses on those, like Ebobse Dido and Alfred Bell, introduced at the beginning of this introduction, who were born or grew up in Cameroon when it was a German colony. Cameroon, a territory extending some 300 miles east and over 500 miles north from the port city of Douala on Africa's west coast, was one of four African territories where German control was formally acknowledged by international treaty in 1885. In that year the Berlin Conference, seeking to bring some order to the 'scramble for Africa' in which the European powers were engaged, ratified a set of treaties that had been made in the previous year between Germany's representatives and native leaders in the coastal settlements of what then came to be called Cameroon, Togo, German South West Africa (now Namibia) and German East Africa (now Tanzania). Echoing the terms of the original treaties, the General Act that concluded the Conference gave each of these territories the status of protectorate; Germany's continued right to rule was contingent on the 'protector' power maintaining a local administration. 'Native tribes' were to be preserved, and the 'improvement of the conditions of their moral and material well-being' to be attended to. The promotion of the economic development of the territory was also envisaged. In the case of Cameroon this meant modernising the port and shipping facilities, increasing the production of plant-based raw materials, especially palm oil, and opening up the hinterlands to exploitation through infrastructure

22 Stovall, 'Harlem-sur-Seine', provides an excellent summary of this discussion.

developments. The terms of the Conference licensed the exercise of military and police powers, as German administration was extended inland from the coastal trading posts and the building of a railway into the interior called for the forcible recruitment of labour.[23]

Because of the size of the territory, its opening to the western oceans and the ambitions of a cosmopolitan elite which we discuss below, natives of Cameroon constituted the largest single group among colonial Africans present in Germany in the early twentieth century. They were also prominent in the associational and political initiatives that were among the first documented manifestations of the black presence in modern Germany to come to scholarly attention.[24] We have been able to identify 285 individuals who made the journey from the Cameroon territory to Germany; the 70 whom we know to have stayed for an extended period and to have been present in Germany after 1914 make up the core of our narrative.

The decision to focus on Cameroonians may require explanation in the light of our claim to be writing about 'Black Germany'. The strategy of following the fortunes of a particular group of people presented itself as a way both to direct the search for elusive data and to limit and structure what turned out to be a very large body of information about individuals. More important, it makes it possible to trace the growth and extension over time of the networks of association that both define individual horizons of survival and identity and enable collective action. Finding and understanding the connections between individuals as they existed at any one point and developed over time calls for exploring individual lives in some depth and detail; the everyday forms of association and sociability that are self-evident to the subjects often elude observers (whether contemporaries or historians) more interested in their public personas and actions. This only works, though, insofar as we understand where our subjects were coming from in the most precise possible terms, and that dictated the choice of individuals who had generation and point of origin in common.

To return to our title, the notion of Black Germany (or black Germans, or German Blacks) hypothesises that our subjects have 'become black' and raises the question of how this happened.[25] The starting focus on

23 On the colonial history of Cameroon see Ardener, *Kingdom on Mount Cameroon*; Austen and Derrick, *Middlemen*.

24 See Chapter 6. The earliest scholarship on African-German political movements was produced in the GDR – notably by Adolf Rüger – largely because the Colonial Office files were held in archives there.

25 The phrase is borrowed from Michelle Wright, *Becoming Black*, which shares our comparative interest, though her work focuses on textual evidence for subjectivity rather than social and material processes.

Cameroonians – a particular group – allows us to trace in some detail the incomplete and contested process through which individuals of varied backgrounds, languages and religions, who shared little apart from their African origins, came to be 'black' – or to be seen by others and to articulate themselves in terms of the skin colour they shared with people who had come from quite different places with quite distinct expectations. Even 'Cameroonian' is a problematic category. Our subjects arrived in Germany as Christians or Muslims, speakers of Duala or Beti or Ewondo or Batanga, from the coastal towns or the up-country sultanates (though not in equal numbers). At the point where our narrative begins it was Europeans who identified them with a single territory, 'Kamerun', created by a combination of German military force and international treaties and with a name deriving from the Portuguese.[26] But by the end of World War One we find them speaking of and for Cameroon, at the same time as we observe them associating and politicking with Africans and people of African descent from other parts of the world. Over subsequent decades the distinctions between their situation and forms of self-articulation and those of other people of African descent become increasingly insignificant, so that occasionally, and more often as the narrative progresses, we widen the lens to take in the experiences of Blacks who were not of Cameroonian or even German colonial origin.

Forms of public self-articulation are central to our use of a second key term: we use the terms 'diaspora' and 'diasporic' in this book in the sense of a self-consciously transformative identification with other people of colour around the world. This definition structures the account of politics in Chapter 6, whose title invokes Brent Hayes Edwards' emphasis on the construction of a diasporic vision of the world through practices of translation.[27] But 'becoming black' in this sense is always part of a dialogic engagement not only with other Blacks but with racialising discourses in society at large, and that can involve active processes of appropriation and answering back. One index of the process of racialisation on which we comment further below is the use of the term *Neger* in everyday and official language to characterise people of African descent irrespective of their origins; the parallel term in French, which would become an enforced second language for some of our subjects, is *nègre*. Cognate with both 'negro' and 'nigger', these words had complex national histories and could be deployed in relatively neutral, descriptive

[26] For historical studies of the conquest, settlement and geography of Cameroon: Ardener, *Kingdom on Mount Cameroon*.

[27] Edwards, *Practice of Diaspora*.

ways; *Neger* was particularly ambiguous, since in Germany the use of 'Black' (*Schwarze/r*) as a noun was practically unknown before the late twentieth century (while *noir* was established as a neutral or philanthropic usage in France by the late eighteenth). By the 1920s the pejorative or abusive sense of the terms had become sufficiently well established that it was an acutely political gesture when first a French anti-colonial and anti-racist organisation and then its German sister organisation adopted *nègre/Neger* into their names to signal the common oppression and common interest of all people of African descent.[28]

That said, a developed political consciousness of this kind constitutes only one, and by no means the only possible or plausible outcome of the process of becoming black or even building community in a majority white society. There is another way of understanding 'diaspora' that informs this book. In complementary approaches to the history of black Europeans that reflect the impact of feminism and gender studies on black studies since the 1980s, Jacqueline Nassy Brown and Tina Campt have elaborated a vision of diaspora that draws our attention away from global interactions. They offer a critical perspective on James Clifford's challenge to understand comparatively 'the specific dynamics of dwelling/traveling' in migrant lives, and his characterisation (following Gilroy) of diaspora discourse as something that 'maintain[s] identifications outside the national time/space in order to live inside, with a difference' and the celebratory refiguring of mobility that has followed the reception of Gilroy's *Black Atlantic*, inasmuch as they explore in different ways the implications of finding oneself in one place. Brown, who has done ethnographic work on the Liverpool black community, invites us to think about diaspora in terms of both location and wanting, writing of 'situated encounters in which people actually express a desire for connection', a desire which is based on the acknowledgement of difference as well as what they have in common.[29] A pioneer in the historical study of gendered subjectivities among black Germans, Tina Campt has most recently offered the terms 'diasporic dwelling' and

[28] The Comité / Ligue de défense de la race nègre and the Liga zur Verteidigung der Negerrasse are discussed at length in Chapter 6. On discussions of the use of the term *nègre* among Francophone black activists, see Boittin, 'Black in France'; Miller, *Nationalists and Nomads*, pp. 30–41 (with particular reference to Lamine and Léopold Sédar Senghor). While individual Africans testify to the shock of being called *Neger* for the first time, once settled in Germany members of the first generation used it routinely as a descriptive term, at least in dealings with the authorities. See for example Mandenga Diek's characterisation of Bruno Ekwe Ngando as *Neger* in a letter to the Berlin police confirming his status as a Cameroonian native: Mandenga Diek to AAKA, 30 March 1904, BArch R1001 5149, p. 13.

[29] Brown, 'Black Europe and the African Diaspora', p. 201.

'diasporic home-making', asking us to look again at what can be gained from studying evidence for the textures of everyday life and the labour of families in maintaining them, or the business of living with (a) difference.[30]

As Campt proposes, this is a strategy that recommends itself in the case of black Germans, given the peculiarities of their history and the fragmentary nature of the sources. It is also a reading that takes necessary account of a key feature of the black experience in Europe, namely the formation of mixed families. The lives of mixed couples and their children stand at the centre of the empirical work of both Brown and Campt, and they are also part of our story. They are an index of the dual dimension of displacement into Europe that creates diasporic subjects: the inevitability of relationships with both white and black 'others' and the construction of self and networks of affinity (or community) in the field of tension that this generates even in intimate spaces. Black Germans of the first generation were certainly travellers, and one of the central themes of this book is the ways in which their lives were characterised by a transnational condition, or by successive border-crossings both voluntary and unwilled. Attention to the fabric of 'dwelling', or the materials of family life, reveals some specific ways in which home-making could preclude moving back or moving on and dynamise the articulation of community. Chapter 3, which examines the evidence for family life, sets out how the occasion of marriage brought the question of men's status, or formal affiliation to the metropole, to a critical point and also the obstacles that were placed in the way of men's return to Africa once they had white wives and children. The exploration of 'politics' in Chapter 6 shows how challenges to family life informed the articulation of associational and political programmes on the part of Africans in Germany from a very early stage.

The experience of these families confirms the intimate relationship between constructions of race and sexuality that is well established in the historiography of modern Europe.[31] At the same time it reminds us that colour-based apperceptions of 'race' had different valences in different contexts. If it was black men's conjugal relations with white women that made blackness visible and problematic to the extent of constraining individual freedom, this was as much a consequence of the socio-political

[30] Campt, 'Family Matters', p. 88; Campt, 'Pictures of "US"?', p. 75. See most recently Campt, *Image Matters*. Cf. Clifford, *Routes*, pp. 24–5 and 251; Gilroy, *The Black Atlantic*. A key moment in the reception of *The Black Atlantic* in the context of black German studies is Campt and Gilroy (eds.), *Der Black Atlantic*.

[31] For example Stoler, *Carnal Knowledge*; Fletcher, 'Unsettling Settlers'.

logic of colonialism as of the independent workings of 'racial ideology'. Where colonial relations were new, as for nineteenth-century Germans, the salient colour line was the global one, a construct that divided a white Europe from the rest of the world and rationalised the former's conquest of the latter.[32] Once Germans were in the position of constructing dominion in their own colonies, the enforcement of racial difference became functional to the maintenance of orderly rule as well as to its legitimation; it was on the grounds of public order that the return of mixed families to the colonies was blocked by all colonial powers. But within the German colonial empire the elaboration of racial categories and their enforcement in laws against miscegenation was a feature only of some settler colonies (notably German South West Africa, and not including Cameroon) and was by no means complete by the turn of the century.[33] And in contrast, laws and regulations enforcing the separation of whites and Blacks or codifying a racial hierarchy were not introduced in Germany itself before the establishment in power of the Nazi regime. For our first generation, then, it was their transgression of the global colour line in travelling from Africa to Germany that challenged both them and metropolitan Germans to negotiate the terms of their difference and of their presence in the metropole.

In considering the wider experiences of that generation, we accordingly resist taking either the extent to which they were racialised or the character of their difference in the eyes of white society as read. This is to argue against the grain of the now extensive and sophisticated literature on the development of ideas about 'race' in late nineteenth-century Germany and Europe, which has traced the institutionalisation of scientific racism as well as the popularisation of negative or comic stereotypes of Blacks to the colonial encounter which carried our subjects to Germany. The fact that around the turn of the century German South West Africa was both a test-bed for the theories of racial eugenists like Eugen Fischer and the site of a genocidal war adds plausibility to a narrative that traces a straight line from the imperial contact zone to the Nazi 'racial state' in the realm of ideology.[34] Even in terms of the sources of a German racial imaginary, this narrative has recently been complicated by Andrew Zimmerman's work on reciprocal readings of race, labour and economic development in the United States and Germany's Togo

[32] See Lake and Reynolds, *Drawing the Global Colour Line*.

[33] Becker (ed.), *Rassenmischehen*; Wildenthal, *German Women for Empire*; Aitken, *Exclusion and Inclusion*.

[34] For some recent contributions to this scholarship see Perraudin and Zimmerer (eds.), *German Colonialism and National Identity*; Moses and Stone (eds.), *Colonialism and Genocide*.

colony.[35] His work underlines the importance of America as a uniquely resonant third term or point of reference for Germans, black and white, at all periods (including under National Socialism).[36] It also draws our attention to the extent to which the colonial project involved Germans in a *process* of experimentation, constructing and coming to terms with orders of racial difference in both global and local contexts. Our subjects arrived in Germany at the beginning of that process. The interest and surprise registered by the Berlin press of the 1880s reminds us that the extent to which skin colour 'trumped' other features of the background and personality of Africans in the minds of white Germans varied and shifted in these decades. We want to keep this processual element in view, not least because the question of whether (or when) our subjects were to be seen respectively as Blacks – *Neger* – or colonial subjects persisted in governmental and administrative practices that shaped their daily lives, outliving Germany's colonial empire itself.

For Africans who settled in Germany, becoming black was part of another process: becoming German. They inserted themselves and were inserted into a complex social order defined by structures and categories that pre-dated the colonial empire. Accordingly, we find the structuring categories of gender and class, too, inflected by the African origins of our subjects, while the question of how these relate to 'race' remains open in sometimes unexpected ways. The members of the founding generation of Africans in Germany were not born into racial hierarchy. They had grown up in a society in which people like them were the visible majority, and the orders of inequality that did exist were not based on skin colour. At the same time, it was true of many Cameroonians that they had considerable experience of encountering white Europeans on terms of equality. For centuries before the arrival of German administration, West Africans had been dealing with Europeans as trading partners, and this was notably true of the ethnic Duala elite, who dominated Douala and its immediate surroundings. With a long history as middlemen both between hinterland and coast and between Africans and Europeans, many Duala were literate in English before the Germans arrived thanks to the efforts of the British Baptist Missionary Society which had entered Cameroon around the middle of the nineteenth century.[37] There was already a tradition in some families of sending their sons to Europe to be educated as a means of heightening their own prestige and political

[35] Zimmerman, *Alabama in Africa*. [36] Rosenhaft, 'Afrikaner und "Afrikaner"'.

[37] On the presence of the British Baptist Missionary Society in Cameroon, see Messina and van Slageren, *Histoire du christianisme*, pp. 27–36; Johnson, *Schwarze Missionare – Weiße Missionare!*

influence at home. Ndumbe Lobe (better known as King Bell), the Bell paramount chief who signed the treaty with Germany in 1884, made it clear that he would have preferred taking on the British as protectors; his eldest son August Manga Ndumbe Bell (August Manga) had spent two years at a school in Bristol from 1867 to 1868 and been baptised there at St Mary Redcliffe.[38] These families were also accustomed to social interaction with European businessmen, visitors, missionaries and settlers, up to and including marriage. From this point of view, we may liken the Duala to the Atlantic Creoles described by Ira Berlin, who in his terms constituted the 'charter generation' for emergent black communities in the Americas: originating in Africa but highly mobile, bearers of a complex cultural heritage and intercultural experience, middlemen between Europe and Africa. With reference to the Duala proper, Stefanie Michels prefers to use the term 'cosmopolitanised West African elite'.[39]

Typically it was the children of the Duala and to a lesser extent other regional elites who now travelled to Germany, and they took both this cosmopolitanism and this sense of privilege with them. Educated by Europeans in mission schools or, after the German takeover, in German government schools, they made the journey at the behest of their parents or on their own initiative, and in the first decade or so after the founding of the protectorate they travelled with the encouragement of German officialdom in Cameroon and Berlin. As Chapter 1 explains, they came to be educated or trained or to seek their fortune, usually in the expectation that they would return to the same position they had left behind, or possibly a better one. In the late nineteenth century, high-status visitors from Germany's colonies could be greeted and celebrated in German cities as 'princes' or semi-diplomatic representatives of 'our new colonial brothers'. The young people who came as pupils or apprentices were under the eye of the authorities, their names and careers the object of correspondence between governors, ministers and chancellors, and they sometimes intervened directly in that correspondence. At the same time, the caricature of the *Hosenneger* – the 'nigger in trousers', too 'civilised' to be authentic but not able to do more than mimic true civilisation – emerged as a powerful counter-reading of the colonial subjects' claim to moral and civil equality and a reminder of the risks involved in crossing the global colour line.

38 Information from Bristol City Council Archive. A Jim William Bell from Cameroon attended St Mary Redcliffe school from 1863 onwards: Bristol Records Office 40477/R/1. For the practice among other West African elites, see Killingray, 'Africans in the United Kingdom', pp. 7–9.

39 Berlin, 'From Creole to African'; Michels, *Schwarze deutsche Kolonialsoldaten*, pp. 31–2.

Once settled in the metropole, colonial subjects had to find their way in a modernising industrial society already structured by class (and the politics of class). Chapter 4, which focuses on the ways in which they made their livings, has as one of its themes the challenge that new forms of subordination and dependency posed to their own sense of status, particularly after World War One. On the one hand – partly as a result of their own political efforts – they became the privileged recipients of financial support from semi-governmental agencies. This parodic extension of the patronage relations of the 1880s made them clients of men who were willing to support them because they were colonials but who had no interest in countering an encroaching process of proletarianisation. On the other hand, the process of de-classing left most of our subjects not in the industrial working class (or even in the maritime trades that underpinned significant British and French black communities), but increasingly in liminal occupations, including petty trading, hustling and stage performance of various kinds. These called simultaneously for the deployment of their cosmopolitanism and mediating skills and for the assertion and display of what made them different – exotic at best. Chapter 6 explores how that paradox played out in a key moment in the development of diasporic consciousness – when it was the workers' international (Comintern) that offered the most welcoming context for the incubation of a critical black politics in the early 1930s. A close reading of the sources for the career of Joseph Bilé, who was trained among black revolutionaries in Moscow, also allows us to see some of our subjects through the eyes of other activists, black, white and brown, who found their Africanness and their Germanness troubling by turns.

For the years from the foundation of the Cameroon protectorate in 1884 to the National Socialist takeover in 1933, then, Chapters 1 and 4 trace a broad and broadly collective narrative from arrival through the shifting material conditions for survival – work, welfare and mutual aid – while Chapter 6 recapitulates the chronology giving particular attention to forms of political activity. Chapter 2 sets out the formal conditions that governed both the presence of colonial subjects in Germany and their capacity to return to Africa; it outlines the legal and administrative practices that defined their status in relation to the German states, in order to explain the concrete ways in which their daily lives were shaped by shifting documentation regimes.[40] While it ranges over the half-century between 1884 and 1933, it focuses centrally on the defining shift in conditions brought about by Germany's defeat in World War One.

[40] See Grosse, 'Koloniale Lebenswelten', on the constraints inherent in the fragile civil status of Africans in Germany.

The question of access to German nationality and citizenship and the mobility accorded by a passport, unresolved before World War One, was critically complicated by the war's outcome. Control of Germany's colonies passed to the victorious powers or their allies, nominally exercising a League of Nations mandate. Most of Cameroon came under French control, with authority over a section near the border with Nigeria passing to Britain; Togo, too, came under French, East Africa under British control. 'Nobody's people' (in Elisa von Joeden-Forgey's telling phrase), former German colonial subjects found that among other things the transfer of sovereignty exacerbated the obstacles faced by all colonial subjects (including French and British ones) who sought to return to the colonies with European wives and children. In Chapter 3 we tell the story of one man, Martin Dibobe, who managed to circumvent this system. But most of our subjects who did not return to Africa before 1914 found themselves 'stuck' in Europe after 1914, and one reason for that was precisely a choice of marriage partner that in the event turned out to be a choice between Europe and Africa.

Chapter 3 explores marriage and family as key elements of settling down or 'diasporic dwelling'. Following some family stories beyond 1933 and even into the post-World War Two years, it sets out not only the institutional constraints under which marital relationships operated but also what we can learn of their internal dynamics. In all cases but one, when the men of our 'founding generation' married, they married white German women, and most of them had children born in Germany. In examining how these partnerships were formed, sustained and challenged we have sought to identify – often through the eyes of the second generation – some constituent elements of a settled community; these include personal ties operating between these families and those that bound the men, through their wives and children, neighbours and friends into networks that transcended racial and ethnic difference. There is also evidence that in the absence of colonies the discourse of 'race' came to be more insistently applied to challenges to the colour line on German soil.

In anatomising marriages we can begin to observe the combined workings of gender and pressure on social status expectations at the intimate level – including the clash between expectations of the marriage partners and examples of mutual adaptation. Chapter 5 focuses more directly on issues of gender and sexuality. Most of the Cameroonian travellers, and (as far as we know) all the ones who remained, were men, and they had been socialised in a particular set of patriarchal relations. Chapter 5 allows us to consider the handful of mainly elite women who travelled to Germany but did not stay there. They serve as exemplars for the impact of the metropolitan sojourn on their gendered identities and not least as foils for their male compatriots. They were also 'middlewomen' in their own right, one of whom, Maria Diop née Mandessi Bell, returned to Europe to play an important facilitating role in the development of Francophone diasporic cultural politics after 1945. The chapter opens, however, with an exploration of the ways in which the men of that generation constructed and enacted gender identities under metropolitan conditions. We approach their articulations of masculinity initially through the lens of problematic sexual behaviour, in order to open out the discussion to other key aspects of masculine *habitus*, such as dress, and link them to the ways in which these men verbalised their qualities as men. Often entangled with values of status and prestige, expressions of masculinity provide another register of the tensions involved in survival in the metropole, particularly since post-World War One Germany witnessed the crystallisation of particularly virulent political discourses linking black masculinity with sexual transgression. The extent to which individuals were able to negotiate these tensions productively was bound to depend on the extent to which they could develop new forms of practice or arguments for their existing practices in dialogue with other black men. Here, too, then, the question of these people's capacity to build community is relevant.

What, then, of community? Each chapter provides some evidence of patterns of association and cooperation among our subjects. These patterns extend from instances of individuals offering moral and material support to one another on the basis of kinship or regional affinity, through the sharing of accommodation, to cases of families joining other families in urban neighbourhoods where children and adults interacted on a regular basis. Individual leadership figures like the businessman Mandenga Diek, who both mentored newly arrived countrymen and was prompted to marry off his daughters to them, emerged relatively early, and there is also evidence that informal networks could be mobilised in actions of solidarity and mutual support. Networks expanded as people socialised informally, often in the context of performance work. The particular concerns of immigrant Africans, growing out of the pressing need to support themselves and their families in Germany and not to lose touch with their kin back in the old colony, inspired formal associations that appealed beyond the circle of Cameroonian-born men to all Africans. And (as noted above) the concern with mutual aid and ameliorating the conditions that made personal fulfilment and family life difficult remained a persistent feature even of the more explicitly political initiatives that they developed between the wars; that is, the preconditions of community were an explicit object of struggle. By 1933, the tendential existence of a *black* community articulated in terms of an ideal of internal solidarity (not always realised) and diasporic connectedness is apparent not only in organisational life and the adoption of black internationalist rhetoric by key political activists but also in the extension of their range of contacts to include British and Francophone black activists and, more significantly, African Americans.

That said, what we have are often no more than traces and hints, which we think allow us to say that by 1933 there was a black German community in the making. This has something to do with the nature of the sources. They are heavily dominated by official and administrative documents, and even where it is possible to hear our subjects' voices the occasions of their speaking are rarely of the kind that would deliver the sort of ethnographic detail that social historians dream of. The distance in time means that it has not been possible to ask our subjects about the aspects of everyday life that were self-evident to them and remain opaque to us, though the testimony of their children and grandchildren has proved illuminating when the right questions were put to it.

More important – and part of the explanation for the paucity of source material – is the fact that that community really was interrupted in its growth before anybody could begin to articulate it as a historical formation. Germany's loss of control of its colonies in 1919 brought an end to the flow of colonial visitors and migrants, though African Americans and other mainly Anglophone Blacks continued to visit and to settle in Germany. It also meant that former colonial subjects ceased to be in any formal sense German (with the exception of the handful of naturalised Africans and their children); whatever their allegiance, and even when leaving Germany proved difficult in practice, the extent to which black Germans could count on remaining settled there was open to very particular challenges. They became subjects of France and Britain, and this limited the prospects for assimilation in Germany – or indeed anywhere, given that what it meant to be the subject of a mandate power remained undefined, and that post-war Europe was transfixed by anxieties about immigration.

At the same time the post-war settlement gave them a point of reference outside of Germany that was meaningful in two respects. On the one hand, we can see Cameroonians in the interwar period as peculiarly subject to the competing pulls of the transnational and the local. Transnational connections are characteristic of most migrant groups; even community rooted in the intimacy of family and neighbourhood comprehends (and sometimes depends on) interaction with kin back home (and sometimes also in other countries of emigration).[41] For our

[41] Clifford, *Routes*, pp. 245–7, is a key point of reference for the use of 'transnational' to characterise the multiple attachments of immigrant groups.

subjects, direct communication with 'back home' was severely disrupted by post-war conditions, not least because German-educated natives were regarded with intense suspicion by the French authorities. At the same time, the change of sovereignty promoted the growth of a Cameroonian population in France. This population was engaged in its own process of community building, which saw its members poised between mobilising around regional identities and colonial grievances that remained critical for them as first-generation migrants and assimilating to a wider black population that was older, larger, more diverse, better organised and politically more articulate than the first Germanophone generation had encountered.

What the consequences of this for the growth of a black community in Germany might have been had it not been for the rise of Nazism and World War Two is difficult to project; unsurprisingly, there is evidence of contact between Africans in Germany and France at all points in our story (to an extent that has not been acknowledged in either Francophone or German black studies), including after 1945, so that the growth of parallel but connected communities seems a likely outcome. In the event, the deterioration of the political and economic conditions for black life in Germany in the Depression and the Nazi takeover of power revealed the advantages of this particular transnational condition, when France, bound under the terms of its mandate in Cameroon to protect the territory's natives, became a place of refuge and a base from which to raise the alarm about the situation of Blacks under National Socialism. One cost of this for the German community was the intensified dispersal of individuals and families. Chapter 8, which follows some of our subjects and their children to France, shows how connections made in Germany were reconstituted and new ones established, though the refugee condition often threw people back on specifically Cameroonian networks in the first instance. Following our subjects to France also allows us to explore the French black experience as a counter-example to the German, since even under the pressures of war and German occupation Francophone Africans enjoyed a degree of political and cultural freedom and Black Paris continued to evolve. For most of our subjects, though, the experience of official racism, both French and German, was inflected by the fact of being – or sounding – German.

Key to this development was of course the rise to power of National Socialism, whose impact on Blacks who remained in Germany is explored in Chapter 7. An early consequence of the Nazi takeover was to stifle the development of black politics in Germany. Considered in the light of 'community', the defining feature of those Nazi policies towards black people was the project of breaking the ties that bound them into

German society. Pressures on mixed couples to separate which pursued them into emigration in France and the practice – less than systematic, more than opportunistic – of sterilising the adult children of the first generation have emerged as persistent themes in the testimony of survivors. The Nazi demonisation of the 'mongrel' (*Mischling*) expressed a rejection of the kind of society in which a black community might grow, and inspired practical measures designed to make the existence of black Germans literally impossible. In one sense this can be read as the outcome of a process of racialisation that Nazism brought to its climax when it introduced the categories *Neger* and *Negermischling* into legislation. And there is evidence of a radicalisation of policy and police practice during the war that suggests that in the longer term all Blacks would have been rounded up and eliminated, had the war continued or been won by Germany.

The years of dictatorship and particularly the war years were for most black Germans a time of intensified everyday racism and abuse, ever-narrower opportunities to earn a living, and physical terror in the face of the threat of sterilisation and the prospect of arbitrary internment and forced labour. Families were broken, and individuals forced into hiding. But most of our subjects survived, and among them were families that remained more or less intact. Community was undermined but continued to reproduce itself. Our subjects' experiences typically reflected the effects of internal policy debates and inconsistencies of everyday practice that challenge the proposition that the Nazi system succeeded in instituting a coherent vision of 'race'.[42] In particular many continued to be protected by their status as colonial subjects as long as the regime fostered hopes of recovering a colonial empire. The travelling spectacle the Deutsche Afrika-Schau – which developed as a means to keep Blacks under control and surveillance while exploiting them to keep colonial irredentism alive – had the paradoxical tendency to assimilate all Blacks to the status of colonials rather than the other way around. And the Afrika-Schau while it lasted and the film studios that also served as a way of both containing and showcasing Blacks under German domination formed a context in which black people could continue to socialise, communicate and hear about each other's situations. Even under conditions of active persecution, people went on networking, listening and exercising forms of practical solidarity.

The Epilogue sketches the challenges that faced people trying to rebuild individual lives and connections after the war, in both Germany

[42] See also Rosenhaft, 'Blacks and Gypsies in Nazi Germany'.

and France. The situation was one of new beginnings, often enforced though sometimes offering new prospects, for example of emigration to France or the United States. The evidence of their post-war activities, including their mobilisation to claim compensation for their sufferings under National Socialism, bespeaks the continuity of contacts and networks formed before the war, the basis for recovering community in spite of small numbers. At the same time, the process of claiming compensation exposed their relative isolation as a group, as well as official and public ignorance of their history and circumstances. While Nazi racism was increasingly reduced to antisemitism and its consequences in public and official discourse, the racist tropes of a persistent but objectless colonial memory reappeared in the media to represent black subjects as ahistorical exotics. These blocked the articulation of any continuous narrative, or memory of community, and left the 'founding generation' and their children to be rediscovered by a new generation of activists in the 1980s.

Even in this condensed form, the story we tell here is complex and contradictory and often doubles back on itself. It is also fragmentary and speculative in parts. At the same time the chapters that follow are crowded with people and incident. While we approached our study with the question of community in mind and in a spirit of putting what we thought we knew about German history and black Germans to the test of implicit comparison, we also see our work as a project of recovery. Some of the stories that the sources threw up do not fit easily into an argumentative narrative, and we choose to pursue them *because* they take us in unexpected directions or shed light in unanticipated corners, often illuminating topics that merit further research. None of them, we hope, is irrelevant to understanding the first Black Germany – what made Blacks German and what particular historical conditions made their experience in Germany what it was. At the core of that understanding must be Germany's frustrated engagement with the colonial project: it brought Africans to Europe as German subjects, but its abrupt end at the point where members of the first generation had begun to construct a way of 'dwelling' between Germany and Africa locked them into a liminal status defined as much by their colonial origins, association with a lost empire and unsought affiliation with the competing colonial power France as by 'race'. The loss of colonies became part of a national trauma that took political expression in the rise of Nazism, avenging itself on the bodies of black people with a violence proportional to the extent to which they had made themselves at home.

1 The first generation: from presence to community

The beginnings of a black community in Germany lay in Africans' travel to Germany in the colonial period. That development was largely unanticipated by either the colonial authorities or the Africans themselves. This chapter traces the experiences of the first generation of travellers from the protectorate, most of whom did not remain, and sets out the conditions for settlement of those who did stay. Before 1914 three main traits characterised this population. First, black people were scattered throughout the country. Second, this was a male-dominated population. Third, this was a population in constant flux. Most arrivals were transients, though as the relationship between protectorate and metropole became established it became possible for individuals to envisage seeking their fortune in Germany. The nature of the black presence was a reflection of the reasons and routes that brought black people to Germany as well as of the efforts of the German authorities to manage migration. And the experiences of the first generation, not only in Germany but in their return to Cameroon, in many ways established the terms on which those who became residents would be accommodated by the authorities and with which they would have to contend in constructing their lives and identities. That is, the increasingly visible presence of Africans in German towns and cities challenged both the

In the text and notes, reference is made to a series of German state agencies that had responsibility for colonial affairs. Before 1 April 1890 the responsible office was the Inspectorate for German Overseas Interests (Dezernat für die deutschen überseeischen Interessen) in the Foreign Office (Auswärtiges Amt). On 1 April 1890 a Colonial Department was established within the Foreign Office (Auswärtiges Amt – Kolonialabteilung, AAKA). This was succeeded in May 1907 by a Reich Colonial Office (Reichs-Kolonialamt, RKA), directly responsible to the Chancellor. Between 20 February 1919 and 1 April 1920 a Reich Colonial Ministry (Reichskolonialministerium, RKM) replaced the RKA; the Department for Colonial Administration (Abteilung Kolonial-Zentralverwaltung) in a new Reich Ministry for Reconstruction then took over responsibility for winding up Germany's colonial interests in the wake of the Versailles Treaty. In 1924 a new Colonial Section was established in the Foreign Office, with responsibility for pursuing opportunities for the recovery of the colonies lost in 1919; it was known as Section III – Colonial Policy, and later as Political Department X (Politische Abteilung X, Pol. X).

authorities and the majority population to respond. This resulted in the implementation of travel restrictions from the protectorates and helped feed into racial stereotypes such as the *Hosenneger*, which outlasted the colonial period and continued to impact upon the lives of metropolitan Blacks after World War One. Cameroonians who arrived as elite visitors would remain as something rather different.

Education and migration

Multiple factors brought Cameroonians to Germany. Personal servants accompanied colonial officials, missionaries or private individuals on home leave, while others were participants in ethnological exhibitions. A handful of Cameroonians taught as language instructors at the Hamburg Colonial Institute or the Berlin Seminar for Oriental Languages. Others arrived at German ports as members of the increasingly international workforce in the German merchant fleet. Although the German merchant fleet (unlike the French and the British) preferred to do without Africans as regular seamen before 1914, the Woermann Company's establishment of direct shipping links to the protectorates from 1890 helped to ease mobility.[1] Central to this mobility, however, was travel for educational or training purposes. Around a quarter of Cameroonians who arrived before 1914 (over sixty people) came to undertake formal schooling and/or to begin an apprenticeship. The vast majority of these were both male and Duala.

The initiative in sending their children to Germany was taken by the elite Duala families themselves, in keeping with their history of strategic cosmopolitanism. A number of Duala notables whose children would study in Germany, including Ndumbe Lobe Bell, his son August Manga, Jim Ekwalla and David Mandessi Bell, were also active in encouraging and promoting European education in Douala itself through financial support or gifts of land to the missions or the administration.[2] Often young people who travelled to Germany had spent some time attending mission or government schools in Cameroon where they had gained at least a basic knowledge of German before they departed. As early as 1885 Ndumbe Lobe, one of the two foremost traditional Duala leaders, and the Akwa government translator David Meetom (Mwange Ngondo)

[1] Küttner, *Farbige Seeleute*, pp. 27–8.

[2] Contract between the Governor and the Headman Epea Kwala (*sic*), 29 September 1889, BArch R1001 4073, p. 95; Rudin, *Germans in the Cameroons*, p. 354; Report of the Middle School, Bethel 1890, 28 January 1891, Mission 21, E-2.3 1890, no. 103; Deibol, Mandessi Bell, Diboko a Mongo and Bismarck Bell to Bohner, 10 January 1893, Mission 21, E-2.5 1892, no. 109.

approached the governor of Cameroon Julius von Soden to request that their sons be educated in Germany. Governor Soden responded positively, writing to the State Secretary for Foreign Affairs, Herbert von Bismarck: 'By the very fact of their birth the sons of these men (Bell and Meetom) are bound to play a certain role in the colony and the education that they enjoy should not be a matter of indifference to us.'[3]

Soden believed that this provided an opportunity to tie such prominent families closer to the colonial system and to integrate their children into the administrative structure upon their return. He was also worried that the few Africans already in Germany had arrived in the company of young European traders, who did little for the moral and practical education of their charges. According to Soden these Africans often ended up in servitude as exotic curiosities or as objects of advertising campaigns. His primary concern was to control as far as possible the exposure of young Africans to everyday life in the metropole. He was accordingly willing to support a policy of taking on some from elite backgrounds as long as a guarantee of strict supervision was imposed over their upbringing. This he believed was best achieved by placing them in smaller towns in state-run facilities or with government-vetted families. Soden argued that alongside mastering basic German language skills it would be advantageous were pupils also to be instructed in practical skills such as agricultural work and gardening. In particular he emphasised the importance of the moral education of African visitors. This was in keeping with the notion of the colonisers' civilising mission that was inscribed in the documents of the Berlin Conference (though the vision of Africans' moral inferiority could also be an excuse for colonial brutality), and those charged with educating or looking after young Africans were always expected to provide them with moral guidance. The German authorities in Berlin were initially approving of Soden's suggestions, although it would take time before the first Cameroonians arrived in Germany to be educated or trained with the support of the administration.[4]

Alfred Bell

The experience of the apprentice Alfred Bell is one of the best documented and exemplifies the possibilities and pressures that characterised

[3] Soden to Bismarck, 8 August 1885, BArch R1001 4297, pp. 3–5. Evidence suggests that elite families in Togo similarly sought to arrange their children's education in Germany; see individual cases in BArch 5571–6.

[4] Ministry for Religious, Educational and Medical Affairs to Bismarck, 3 October 1885, BArch R1001 4297, pp. 8–10.

sojourns in Germany in the high colonial period.[5] Bell's own awareness of himself as the representative of an elite in his homeland generated cultural and political challenges for both him and the watchful German authorities which set a pattern for those who would come later. He was the nephew of Ndumbe Lobe and it was with the latter's blessing as well as that of the Cameroonian administration that he departed for Germany. He arrived in June 1887 accompanied by three other Duala from the quarter of Deido, Etame Mungu, Etuman Ekwalla and Ekwa Money. The four youths were trained at the Altona branch of the architecture and construction firm F. H. Schmidt. Ndumbe Lobe had been impressed by the firm's work on the prison and the administration buildings in Douala and had reached an agreement with the colonial authorities to send his nephew to Germany.[6] Alfred spent less than a year and a half as an apprentice metal worker (*Schlosser*), rather than a carpenter. As part of his training he received no pay, but instead the costs of his accommodation, food and clothing were covered by the firm and he received a gift of 10 Marks at Christmas. In autumn 1888 he left Schmidt to begin a further apprenticeship as a machinist in the repair workshop of the shipping line Norddeutscher Lloyd in Bremerhaven. Here he stayed on similar terms, although Soden provided him with a small amount of pocket money. Alfred received positive reports from his employers and appears to have been well liked by his fellow workers.

Despite the positive feedback the authorities received concerning Alfred's development they were increasingly worried about his behaviour outside of the workplace. Alfred, whose training and movements were meant to be under strict control, had been to Berlin on several occasions and had let himself be photographed a number of times. More worrying for the colonial authorities were the contents of several intercepted letters that Alfred had sent to a close friend and to his brother Joseph Bell (Bebe Ndumbe) in Douala. In these he made numerous critical comments about German society, German colonial rule and, in particular, Soden, who he claimed was soon to be recalled on account of his maltreatment of the Duala. Similarly, in an interview with London's *Pall Mall Gazette*

[5] Unless otherwise indicated, the account that follows is based on correspondence in BArch R1001 4297 and 4298. See also Mehnert, 'Schulpolitik', pp. 125–34.

[6] *Kölnische Zeitung*, 27 June 1887, in BArch R1001 4297, p. 31. Little is known about the boys who accompanied Alfred, though it is likely that they also came from an elite background: draft contract between the company F. H. Schmidt and Etame Mungu, Etuman Ekwalla, Ekwa Money and Alfred Bell, 8 May 1887, BArch R1001 5571, pp. 119–21. Of Alfred's three companions there is only evidence of Ekwalla having returned to Douala. A 1914 document refers to him as a Bonabela leader: Notes on Natives' Meeting, 20 April 1914, BArch R1001 4430, pp. 126–30, here p. 129.

he commented on the German presence in Cameroon. His words were reproduced in a South African English-language newspaper and were brought to the attention of the colonial authorities: 'Yes, it belongs to them [the Germans] in a way. They have money and guns, and an army and therefore having might they have the right. But do not imagine that the natives, from my uncle Bell downwards to his humblest subject, feel that the Germans are the masters.'[7]

The tone and content of such comments fuelled the authorities' belief that Alfred was being led astray in Germany. In particular they were suspicious that he had come under the influence of the ideas of Social Democracy which he had likely encountered at his place of work. This is hinted at in one of his letters to his brother where he commented, 'Day after day many men show me the way to solving all questions.'[8] These suspicions appear to have been public knowledge; the satirical magazine *Kladderadatsch* mockingly suggested that Alfred was soon to be leader of the Social Democratic Party, while rumours of his involvement with the Socialists or indeed with anarchist groups were even picked up in the foreign press.[9]

Some of Bell's written remarks at least suggest an empathy with the German working classes. He described the short-lived liberal Emperor Friedrich III in positive terms as a friend of the poor, but observed to his brother: 'Joe believe me it is true the poor people here in Europe are not better than slaves ... our slaves in Cameroon are much more than the poor people or workmen in Europe the European rich people look down to the work people not more than a beast.'[10] In using the language of a society of masters and slaves in which his was the voice of a master, he signalled his qualification to assess the performance of the Germans in both the colony and the metropole, and his remarks articulate an awareness that the image German colonisers projected in the protectorate as '*Herrenmenschen*' was simply an illusion.[11] The content of the messages that he was sending to Cameroon was accordingly seen by the colonial administration as an implicit challenge to Soden's authority. Their potential influence on local politics was underscored when he reported to his

7 'An African Prince on German West Africa', in *Pall Mall Gazette*, 16 April 1890, p. 1, reprinted in *African Times*, 1 May 1890, p. 68, in BArch R1001 5571, p. 70.

8 Alfred Bell to Joseph Bell, 30 April 1889, BArch R1001 4298, pp. 46–9, here p. 47.

9 'Ein schwarzer Sozialdemokrat', *Kladderadatsch*, 8 June 1890, p. 98; 'Foreign News and Gossip', *Daily Evening Bulletin* (San Francisco), 1 July 1890, p. 4.

10 Alfred Bell to Joseph Bell, 31 October 1888, BArch R1001 4297, pp. 88–9, here p. 89.

11 On the practices of slavery in coastal Cameroon with which Alfred Bell would have been familiar, see Austen, 'Slavery and the Slave Trade'. On the impact of the slave trade in the western interior of the protectorate, see Argenti, *The Intestines of the State*, pp. 93–120.

cousin August Manga Bell in Douala that the government school-teacher Theodor Christaller had made disparaging remarks about King Bell in a German newspaper. Protests against Christaller in the Bell quarter of Douala followed and numerous parents withdrew their children from his school.[12] The resultant increased tension in the city coincided with August Manga being arrested and then exiled to Togo.

By the circumstances of his presence in Germany Alfred became a middleman through whom members of the Bell family hoped to protest against the colonial administration. He thus became the first of a number of Cameroonians who actively sought to defend Cameroonian and African interests in Germany as well as to criticise German rule in Africa. The correspondence he received from home included letters apparently from Ndumbe Lobe which he then sent on to Herbert von Bismarck with the help of German friends.[13] In a letter of September 1888 a list of ten points of complaint was drawn up against German officials in Douala. Among other things Soden was accused of treating Ndumbe Lobe with a lack of respect, breaking agreements over land use, and not intervening in local disputes. Although the letter was signed by Ndumbe Lobe and bore his seal Soden believed it had been written by Joseph Bell and that Alfred was its 'intellectual initiator', probably under the influence of friends in Germany. The two brothers together with August Manga were singled out as the main instigators of discontent in the Bell quarter.[14] The administration was aware that Joseph was a member of a breakaway indigenous Baptist movement in Douala which was challenging the authority of the European Basel Mission. Alfred, meanwhile, was in correspondence with the Jamaican-born Baptist missionary Joseph Jackson Fuller, who was similarly suspected of being involved in passing on letters of complaint from the Bells to the German government.[15]

Soden's reaction was to impose yet tighter control over Alfred's education and movements, and in autumn 1888 he refused to allow him to return to Cameroon for fear of greater political unrest. Alfred's letters from and about this period convey a strong sense of distress at his economic situation, especially after Soden stopped his pocket money. In particular winter 1888–9 in Bremerhaven proved to be a difficult time since his supervisors at Lloyd provided no financial support. His clothes

12 Böckheler, *Theodor Christaller*, p. 64. See also Alfred Bell to Bismarck, 25 December 1888, BArch R1001 4297, pp. 61–3.
13 Alfred Bell to Joseph Bell, 31 October 1888, pp. 88–9.
14 King Bell (Ndumbe Lobe Bell) to Bismarck and the Reichstag, 23 September 1888; Soden to Bismarck, 23 December 1888 and 16 April 1889: BArch R1001 4297, pp. 36–9, 85–96 and 39–40.
15 King Bell to Bismarck, 15 November 1888, BArch R1001 4297, p. 81.

and boots were in a state of disrepair and he had no money to pay for coal to heat his three-room apartment. As a consequence he fell ill. Alfred pleaded with relatives in Douala to provide him with funds; he was relying on the help of a German friend who provided him with the not insubstantial sum of 80 Marks to keep him over the winter. This was one of several debts Alfred ran up in Germany which Soden put down to the 'scandalous' treatment he had received from his employers. Eventually the colonial authorities decided that controlling his actions with Lloyd was too difficult and relocated Alfred to Berlin to continue his training under the strict supervision of the Railway Engine Inspector Garbe. At the same time Soden stopped all letters sent from Cameroon to Alfred reaching their destination. Cut off from his family in Douala, Alfred complained that his life in Germany was like being held in a fortress.

Alfred's intervention on behalf of his kin in Douala appears to have prompted action from the German authorities. Soden was asked to explain the Bell protests to Bismarck and in June 1889 a government minister visited Alfred to discuss the situation in Douala.[16] Months later Alfred was at the Foreign Office and also claimed to have spent forty-five minutes visiting Bismarck himself in the Prince's house. He was now allowed to both write and receive letters again. In Berlin his movements and friendships continued to be monitored, but this did not prevent him from making contact with the Berlin-Bethel Baptist congregation.[17] He had been schooled by the English Baptist Mission in Douala before arriving in Germany (his letters home were written in English) and in Berlin he became a member of the Bethel congregation. He even held a public lecture there on life in Cameroon.[18] Eventually Alfred was baptised by its founder, Eduard Scheve, an incident that helped persuade Scheve to establish a German Baptist Mission in Cameroon. Later African migrants would also seek to contact the Cameroonian missions in times of trouble.

In spite of the progress Alfred was now making Soden deemed it desirable to return him to Cameroon on the grounds that outside parties continued to be a bad influence on him. The tension in the Bell quarter had eased and August Manga had since returned from exile. In May 1890 Alfred left for Douala together with another Duala student,

[16] Soden wrote to Bismarck in April 1889 to explain the unrest in Douala. Alfred claimed to have been visited by a government minister in June of the same year to discuss the situation in Douala: Soden to Bismarck, 16 April 1889; Alfred Bell to Joseph Bell, 8 June 1889, BArch R175f 81939.

[17] Eduard Scheve, 'Die Baptisten-Mission in Kamerun, West-Afrika', conference paper presented to the Brüderkonferenz in Hamburg, 24 August 1891, p. 5, copy in Onckenarchiv.

[18] 'Chit Chat from the Continent', *Pall Mall Gazette*, 30 January 1890, p. 1.

Ndumbe Elokan, who had been in Wiesbaden for three years.[19] Ironically, once back in Cameroon Alfred was found a job on board a liner named *Soden*, where the administration could continue to monitor him.[20] They could not, however, prevent Alfred from becoming involved in a further short-lived anti-colonial endeavour in 1893, the revolt of the soldiers recruited from Dahomey to serve under German command in Cameroon.[21]

Alfred Bell's experiences in Germany were of central importance to the evolution of official attitudes to the presence of Africans in Germany. It had proven impossible to keep him under observation and just over a year after his arrival Soden and others within the colonial administration were forced to question the wisdom of encouraging such visits.[22] Reference was frequently made to his case in discussions concerning future educational visits. Similarly some Duala seeking permission to travel referred in their applications to Alfred's alleged misbehaviour with promises of acting differently.[23] On account of the troubles encountered with Alfred a proposal made by Christaller and originally backed by Soden to send gifted students at the administration's school in Douala to Germany for a further year of training as teachers, clerks or translators was dropped. Disappointed at the simultaneous refusal of funding to bring his own African protégé, Konrad Deibold, to Germany, Christaller now reversed his own position and became a vocal opponent of educational visits.[24] In a swipe probably aimed at Alfred he remarked:

> But if one of them (a young African) comes to Germany and wants to be a carpenter, he immediately becomes a prince, never mind how naked he went around before and how hungry he was. Then he is taught that he is meant for higher things, he has business cards and large-scale photographs made for himself; the fool is then complete and Cameroon is one more good-for-nothing richer.[25]

Christaller's remark bespeaks not only cultural arrogance but also a genuine clash of expectations which would become a leitmotif in relations

[19] Soden to Caprivi, 9 July 1890, BArch R1001 4299, pp. 8–9.

[20] Norberg, machinist on board the steamer *Soden*, to Administration in Cameroon, 7 September 1890, R1001 4299, p. 25.

[21] On the revolt of the Dahomey soldiers, see Rüger, 'Aufstand der Polizeisoldaten'.

[22] See Soden to Bismarck, 29 October 1888, BArch R1001 4297, pp. 52–4; Foreign Office (?) to Maybach, 29 April 1889, BArch R1001 4298, pp. 15–17.

[23] Wilhelm Bell to Governor, 29 April 1891, BArch R175f 81939, p. 186.

[24] Soden to Bismarck, 30 June 1888, BArch R1001 4071, pp. 99–102; Bismarck to Soden, 23 January 1889, and Soden to Bismarck, 10 June 1889, BArch R1001 4072, pp. 12–16 and 62–3; Report of School-Teacher Christaller, in Soden to Bismarck, 27 October 1888, BArch R1001 4297, pp. 45–51; Böckheler, *Theodor Christaller*, pp. 65–71. See also Mehnert, 'Schulpolitik', p. 126.

[25] Böckheler, *Theodor Christaller*, p. 68.

between Africans and their German 'handlers'. Nonetheless, the colonial authorities did not completely abandon official involvement in African education in Germany. Rather, they continued to facilitate educational visits and resolved to avoid the 'mistakes' made in training Alfred.

Schoolchildren and apprentices

The German administration's role in supporting the educational visits of young Africans to Germany was that of a mediator between the elite families and the educational institutions or German firms in Europe. This involved little or no cost to the administration. Instead it was travellers' parents who financed their children's education. Although in 1885 the costs of this were estimated by government officials at upwards of 2,000 Marks, in reality it appears that in this first decade they were closer to 1,000 Marks.[26] This included the costs of schooling, clothing, food and accommodation. This was a significant sum at a time when the average German worker earned a yearly wage of just over 580 Marks.[27] Consequently it was almost exclusively children of Duala leaders, notables, religious figures or wealthy traders that were educated in Germany. At the same time it is remarkable just how many children from such families born between the mid 1870s and the mid 1890s spent time there before 1914. These included young men who would later assume positions at the forefront of the Duala traditional political elite. Foremost among these were the first-born sons of the Akwa and Bell paramounts Ludwig Mpundu Akwa, future anti-colonial activist and son of Dika Akwa (King Akwa), and the future Bell paramount and anti-colonial martyr Rudolf Duala Manga Bell (Duala Manga), son of August Manga.[28] Mpundu's cousin Manga Akwa also spent time in Germany as did at least four of Duala Manga's brothers. In addition, men of local importance such as Jim Ekwalla and Ekoko Mukumbulan, a Bonaberi notable, sent their children to Germany as did wealthy and influential

[26] This is the yearly sum that Christaller had anticipated it would cost to educate Africans in Germany: Bismarck to Soden, 23 January 1889, p. 15. This is also the sum that the parents of Mpundu Akwa and Tube Meetom were paying in 1889 and 1895 respectively: Vandenesch to Pilgrim, 8 August 1889, BArch R1001 5571, pp. 26–9, here p. 27; Pahl to Caprivi, 7 November 1891, BArch R1001 5571, pp. 112–13; Dean Knapp to Basel Mission, 23 January 1895, Mission 21, Q-3-4, Mixed correspondence.

[27] Figure from Hohorst, Kocka and Ritter, *Sozialgeschichtliches Arbeitsbuch II*, p. 107.

[28] Little has been written about their schooling in Germany, but there is a large secondary literature on their subsequent careers. On Rudolf Duala Manga Bell see Kala Lobé, *Douala Manga Bell*; Eyoum, Michels and Zeller, 'Bonamanga'. On Ludwig Mpundu Akwa see among others, von Joeden-Forgey, 'Nobody's People', pp. 269–307; Eckert, '"Der beleidigte Negerprinz"'. On Rudolf's 'martyrdom', see Chapters 5 and 6.

businessmen like the planter David Mandessi Bell and trader James Bilé a M'bule.[29] What is significant in the cases of Mandessi Bell and Bilé is that their first-born children were daughters and they would be among the very few Cameroonian women to travel to Germany.[30]

Young Duala, whose ages ranged from six to early twenties, were usually accompanied on their nineteen-day voyage to Germany by a supervising European, a returning civil servant, colonial businessman or missionary.[31] Once in Germany, as Soden requested, they were placed in smaller towns usually in the care of a watchful host family or institution. These guardians were to provide the colonial authorities with regular updates on the progress and behaviour of their charges. The schooling they received depended to some extent upon the institution that they attended and the denominational background of the school. Rudolf Duala Manga and Tube Meetom, son of David Meetom, for example, attended the Protestant boys' primary school in Aalen before both going on to the local vocational secondary school. Later Duala Manga studied at the Gymnasium in Ulm while Tube began an apprenticeship as a cook in an officers' mess in the same town. Typically, however, Cameroonian boys received instruction in a range of subjects that included German language skills, mathematics and a foreign language.

These pupils generally received positive school reports.[32] In particular their diligence, ability and behaviour during lessons were praised. Yet, in spite of their progress there was little or no opportunity for them to go on to a university education. The colonial authorities' educational policy aimed to produce amenable, dependent and loyal colonial subjects rather than highly educated, free-thinking individuals who might question the Germans' right to rule. In all the years before World War Two fewer than half a dozen Africans ever attended a German university, one of them Duala Manga's son Alexander Douala Manga Bell. He enrolled to study medicine at the Christian-Albrechts-Universität at Kiel in the immediate aftermath of World War One.[33] Duala Manga himself appears to have sat

[29] Lobe, son of Ekoko Mukumbulan, was sent to Germany before 1914: interview, Suzanne Ebokulu Mukumbulan, Bonaberi, March 2006.

[30] See Chapter 5.

[31] Two boats a month sailed from Cameroon to Germany: Seidel, *Deutschlands Kolonien*, p. 154.

[32] For examples see reports in the Bundesarchiv files R1001 5571–6. These include reports on Rudolf Duala Manga Bell, on the four trainees with Schmidt in Hamburg, on Jeremias Burnley, on Mpundu Akwa, on Tube Meetom and on Josef Timba and Andreas Mbange.

[33] Landesarchiv Schleswig-Holstein, Amtliches Verzeichnis der Studierenden der Christian-Albrechts-Universität zu Kiel für das Winter-Halbjahr 1918/19. Stephan Dualla Misipo claimed to have studied medicine at the University of Frankfurt in the

in on lectures for one semester at the University of Tübingen, making him the only Cameroonian to have experienced higher education before 1914.[34] Suggestions that Tube Meetom, who regularly received positive reports, could go on to study medicine at university were dismissed out of hand by the new Cameroon Governor Eugen von Zimmerer.[35] Zimmerer stated that an African doctor would never replace a white one within the colonial administration; he argued that indigenous African doctors would never be able to keep up to date with the latest medical advances, which he assumed would take place outside of Africa. At best he envisaged a role for the likes of Meetom as an assistant in a military hospital in the protectorate.

Cameroonian apprentices similarly received a basic education. Private tuition was provided in German language skills, to accompany their practical training in trades geared towards their future participation in the development of the protectorate. These included construction skills such as carpentry, joinery, masonry and mechanical trades as well as crafts like tailoring, cooking and shoemaking. A contract drafted between the colonial administration and a Berlin construction firm responsible for work on administration buildings in the protectorate gives an insight into some of the obligations placed upon firms training Africans.[36] The firm's manager, Karl Wüsten, was charged with finding a young Duala to undertake a three-year apprenticeship in Berlin and chose M'bende Epo. According to the contract of June 1892, the company would meet all costs of his apprenticeship, including his accommodation and clothing. Additionally the company was to finance elementary education in reading, writing and mathematics for Epo, who had already been receiving such lessons in Douala. For its part the administration committed itself to paying the travel costs to and from Germany, while Zimmerer agreed to pay for two suits and other clothes for Epo for the outward journey out of private funds. It is likely that this charitable gesture was made because Epo was an orphan. Finally, the contract stipulated that Epo had to follow the orders of his teacher and that should he show signs of 'immoral behaviour' such as laziness or recalcitrance then the company was at liberty to send him back to Cameroon.

1920s, but there is no record of his matriculation: information from the Johann Wolfgang Goethe University Archive, Frankfurt. The Togolese Peter Olympio studied medicine at the Friedrich Wilhelm University in Bonn in 1922 before transferring to the Ludwig Maximilian University in Munich from 1922 until 1925: correspondence with Ursula Lochner, Ludwig Maximilian University Archive, January 2006.

34 Alfred Scheve, 'Vier Generationen', *Unsere Heidenmission*, 2 (1902), 12–14, here p. 13.

35 Zimmerer to Caprivi, 11 May 1894, BArch R1001 5572, pp. 105–6.

36 Contract for the Education of the Duala M'bende Epo, 25 June 1892, BArch R1001 5571, pp. 134–5.

Other German firms active in the protectorate such as Schmidt were similarly keen to recruit indigenous apprentices and finance their training in Germany. Undoubtedly part of the reason for this was the shortage of skilled European craftsmen in Cameroon during the first decade of colonisation. In its report for the period from August 1892 to July 1893 the *Deutsches Kolonialblatt* put the entire European population at 215.[37] Out of this number there were only 4 carpenters, 3 machinists and 1 metal worker. In the light of debates over the ability of Europeans to work in tropical regions there appeared a growing need to develop a skilled class of indigenous craftsmen.[38]

The available documents provide only a brief insight into the experiences of these young Cameroonians and their reception in Germany; it appears that much depended on their situational context. Although it was not unknown for them to be sent to Europe in pairs, young Cameroonians in Germany tended to live in relative isolation and had little or no contact with other Africans. Most of them were all too aware of the various reactions that their presence and skin colour elicited from sections of the German public not accustomed to seeing Africans on German streets. This was an often unsettling experience that all Africans were confronted with at some point. Unwanted attention ranged from the curious to the abusive.[39] A keen and critical observer, Alfred Bell was not inclined to treat this as a private matter. During his interview with the *Pall Mall Gazette* he remarked: 'Did you see that fellow who passed us just now, and did you hear the vulgar remarks he made about me?' The reporter confirmed that he had and that this had not been the first comment he had heard aimed at Alfred. Alfred dismissed the incident and put it down to the public's general lack of first-hand knowledge of Africans:

> Well they might think themselves highly civilized and refined, but they have not yet learned, what we Africans even might teach them, although we make no boast of our culture, that it is coarse and unmanly to laugh at a person or to insult him because his skin happens to be dark. But there again . . . you have to make allowances. We have always been represented as such wild cannibals and

[37] 'Bericht über den Zustand und die Entwicklung des Schutzgebietes von Kamerun während des Zeitraums vom 1. August 1892 bis 31. Juli 1893', *DKB*, 20 (1893), Supplement, 1–13, here p. 1.

[38] For more on the question of European acclimatisation, see Grosse, *Kolonialismus*, pp. 53–95.

[39] Similar experiences were reported by Togolese Martin Aku (Westermann, *Afrikaner erzählen ihr Leben*, pp. 269–71) and Bernhard Epassi (Paula Karsten, 'Kamerun in Berlin und deutsche Briefe von Kamerun', *Globus: Illustrierte Zeitschrift für Länder- und Völkerkunde*, 6/72 (1897), 97–9, here p. 98).

savages, that as yet they have had neither time nor opportunities to learn that intellectually, at all events we are not quite as black as we are painted.[40]

More threatening was the attitude of the Berlin crowd which gathered around two people, 'simply because one was of a different colour and dressed not quite in fashion', and hounded them down the Brunnenstraße amid cries of 'Eene aus Kamerun!'[41] In general visitors, particularly early arrivals, were the focus of much local interest and local newspapers kept the public up to date with stories about their arrival, baptism and departure. In some cases this publicity could be overwhelming and intrusive. Thus, in Aalen Rudolf Duala Manga was distraught when his school reports, which compared unfavourably to Tube Meetom's, appeared in the local newspaper.[42]

Integration into local communities was a process fraught with difficulties, but was not always unsuccessful. Upon their arrival in Aalen Meetom and Duala Manga were greeted by the town's brass band and according to a former schoolmate the two were popular among their fellow pupils: 'There was out-and-out competition for their friendship, because both were physically very fit, good runners and swimmers. Rudolf was immensely strong; whoever had him as a friend was well protected.'[43] By contrast in Görlitz Alfons Demba and Richard Lukenje were subjected to the taunts of fellow pupils and their ability to resist this provocation was praised in a school report. They also developed a strong relationship to their host mother who financed their education and helped to find them an apprenticeship.[44] Others like Mpundu Akwa experienced difficulties with their host family or institution and eventually changed families. In particular Soden felt that Mpundu, like Alfred Bell before him, was being unduly influenced by outside forces as evidenced by the alleged 'nonsense' expressed in his letters home, and that stronger control needed to be exercised over his education.[45] His school-teachers at

[40] 'An African Prince on German West Africa', p. 1.

[41] 'Eene aus Kamerun!', *Teltower Kreisblatt*, 30 May 1891, p. 2. Intriguingly, the object of the crowd's hostile interest was clearly an African woman.

[42] School-teacher Oesterle to AAKA, 1 April 1894, BArch R1001 5572, pp. 99–100.

[43] Hermann Stützel quoted in Henning Petershagen, 'Afro-Aristokrat in Aalen ausgebildet', *Südwest Presse*, 31 May 1997, in Stadtarchiv Ulm.

[44] Report on Lukenje and Demba, Realschule-Director Baron, 20 November 1893, BArch R1001 5572, p. 65. On their relationship with their host mother Frederika Dörfling, see von Joeden-Forgey, 'Nobody's People', pp. 352–69.

[45] Soden to Humbert, 10 September 1889, BArch R1001 5571, p. 31. Mpundu complained bitterly about his period of stay with the teacher Reismann in Paderborn and asked his father to arrange for him to stay elsewhere; see Soden to Bismarck, 7 November 1889, BArch R1001 4298, pp. 90–3. Two apprentices with Schmidt in Altona, Andreas Ekame Sale and Isaak Tube, changed host family three times in just over a year: F. H. Schmidt to AAKA, 8 April 1893, BArch R1001 5572, pp. 14–15.

the Catholic Reismann School in Paderborn attributed his unhappiness there to his own haughtiness and arrogance.[46] This they suggested had developed after he had spent time in the company of the family of Graf von Westphalen zu Fürstenberg, which had allegedly given him a false sense of his own importance. The idea was dismissed, however, by a teacher in his new school in Rheindahlen, who markedly praised Mpundu's behaviour and ability and argued that his previous teachers had been too quick to judge him. In this new environment Mpundu appears to have flourished.[47]

In at least one case the colonial administrators in Cameroon struggled to find a home for their charges. In 1888 they were unable to find a master in Paderborn willing to take on Josef Timba and Andreas Mbange, who had travelled to Germany with Mpundu.[48] Instead the two were sent to the Catholic institution St Ottilien at Türkenfeld near Munich. There they were trained alongside two other youths, Leo Dagwe from Liberia and Hassi from Sudan, and like most educational migrants received religious instruction. Although the colonial authorities were determined to limit the contact Africans had with Europeans in Germany, religious instruction and observance provided a means through which young Cameroonians interacted with local communities. In particular a large number of them received confirmation or were baptised. Mbange's baptismal ceremony was such a well-attended event that it had to be moved from the institution's own chapel to the larger church nearby. Among those in attendance were the writer Emilie Ringseis, Mbange's godmother, and Ludwig Windthorst, head of the Catholic Centre Party who had taken on the role of godfather to the two Cameroonians.[49] Mbange was baptised Andreas Ludwig Maria Johann, taking on the names of the founder of St Ottilien, Andreas Amrhein, Windhorst's Christian name and the name of Ringseis' father, along with the name of Mary, mother of God. Upon his baptism he received a letter of congratulation from his cousin Mpundu, who was also later baptised. For some, baptism or confirmation was the beginning of a lifelong religious commitment. Mbange, for example, dedicated his life to the

[46] Vandenesch to Pilgrim, 27 December 1889, BArch R1001 5571, pp. 41–2.

[47] Schulte to Ministry for Religious, Educational and Medical Affairs, 21 April and 5 November 1890, BArch R1001 5571, pp. 77–80, 100.

[48] Vandenesch to Pilgrim, 8 August 1889, p. 26.

[49] A picture of Windthorst and his two godchildren can be found in Hüsgen, *Ludwig Windthorst*, p. 296. Timba's baptism alongside Dagwe and Hassi is reported in 'Die Taufe dreier Neger in St. Ottilien', *Missionsblätter St. Ottilien*, 1 (1888/1889), 586–91. We are grateful to Brother David at the St Ottilien archive for providing copies of this material.

dissemination of the Catholic message. Following his return to Cameroon in 1891 he was appointed assistant teacher at the Roman Catholic Pallottine Mission station in Marienberg and he later worked as a teacher and catechist in Edea and Duala under first German and then French missionaries.[50]

Adapting to the climate in Germany and often related bouts of ill health were also typically part of Africans' metropolitan experience. Reports sent to the colonial authorities about the progress of schoolchildren or apprentices frequently made reference to their health. Respiratory diseases like tuberculosis and pneumonia afflicted a number of Cameroonians, just as they continued to affect the German public at large despite improvements in public health. Illness was naturally a cause of great concern to the Africans themselves. The Ewondo language assistant Paul Messi expressed his misery at being ill in a letter sent from Hamburg to a relative in Yaoundé during the war.[51] 'Since I have been in this land there has not been even five days that I have been well. Since I arrived I have been ill four times without knowing whether I would survive or not.' Several like Messi sought help from their sponsors, the colonial authorities or the missions to return home after having fallen ill.[52] In Messi's case the state of war made it impossible for him to return to Cameroon until 1920, by which time he had fully recovered. Others were not so fortunate. Vinzenz Tsala, from Yaoundé, was employed as a language assistant at Berlin Seminar for Oriental Languages in 1913, having been recruited by the Pallottine missionary Hermann Nekes.[53] Within weeks of arrival in Berlin he had fallen ill with tuberculosis. Under the terms of his contract he was committed to spending at least three years working at the Seminar and if he were to return to Cameroon early he would be liable for the travel costs.[54] The Seminar was willing to

[50] Hermann Nekes, 'Vierzig Jahre im Dienste der Kamerunmission. Zum Tode des schwarzen Lehrers Andreas Mbange', *Stern der Heiden*, 39/12 (1932), 317–23.

[51] Paul Messi to Johann Zungi, 3 June (1915?), reprinted in Atangana and Messi, *Jaunde-Texte*, pp. 271–2. The other source of misery for Messi in Germany was having to pay tax (p. 274).

[52] Gottfried Manga Bell sought help from the Foreign Office to return to Cameroon. He was deemed too ill to travel and died in Berlin weeks later: report, 30 December 1910, BArch R1001 4443, pp. 19–20. Johannes Malapi (Julius Manga) asked a missionary in Berlin to help him to return: Pastor Vogel to Basel Mission Society, 4 July 1912, Mission 21, Q-3-4 Mixed Correspondence. Eduard Scheve tried to help Soppo Elame to return after the latter experienced financial and health problems: Scheve to AAKA, 1 August 1899, BArch R1001 5575, p. 62.

[53] Nekes to Sachau (Seminar), 14 August 1912, GStA Rep. 208A, no. 89, p. 10. We are grateful to Sarah Pugach for drawing our attention to these documents.

[54] Für die Vereinbarung mit einem Jaunde-Mann, 31 March 1912, GStA Rep. 208A, no. 89, p. 8.

forgo this and finance the return trip, but Tsala was never deemed well enough to undertake the journey and died in Berlin just under five months after having been diagnosed. Similarly, in 1892 F. H. Schmidt selected a further four Duala youths to train at its Altona branch in anticipation of them later working in the ship-repair workshop under construction in Cameroon.[55] Within a year the apprentice carpenter Isaak Tube had died of pneumonia and around a year later two of his compatriots, Johannes Fuller and Joki Dikonge, had asked to be allowed to return home early following prolonged bouts of ill health.[56] As well as Tube and Tsala, at least nine other Cameroonians are known to have suffered from respiratory disease before 1914, with six eventually succumbing to their illness. Four other Cameroonian men died in this period from unknown causes.

Returning migrants and travel restrictions

In facilitating educational visits to Germany it was never the intention of the colonial authorities that the visitors should stay on a long-term basis. Once their education or training was completed they were expected to return to Cameroon and put their skills to work. This meant that only a handful of those who reached Germany before 1900 for educational purposes were still resident there in 1914. The experiences of returnees, however, were central to shaping administrative policy towards later arrivals and in the introduction of policies and practices that effectively sought to obstruct the development of a permanent black presence in Germany.

Often employment within the colonial administration or with European firms was arranged for returning Cameroonians. Josef Timba, who had trained as a shoemaker, was provided with basic materials and equipment on account in order to set up a shoemaking workshop, and he worked as both shoemaker and clerk to the administration.[57] Ndumbe Elokan was taken on by the government teacher Friedrich Flad, with whom he stayed, and others like Dikonge, Fuller, Demba, Lukenje and Meetom were given positions working either for the authorities or for firms connected to the administration. This allowed the administration to keep returning migrants under observation; Meetom was separated

[55] 'Ausbildung von Negern als Handwerker', *DKB*, 3/7 (1892), 215.

[56] F. H. Schmidt to AAKA, 8 April 1893 and 10 February 1894, Joki Dikonge to Schmidt, 24 June 1894, BArch R1001 5572, pp. 26, 79, 136.

[57] 'Ein eingeborener Neger als Kanzlist und Schuhmachermeister in Kamerun', *DKB*, 3/1 (1892), 23.

from family and friends in Douala who were said to be exercising a bad influence on him and sent to work in Buea.[58] Re-adjusting to life in Cameroon brought a number of difficulties. Elokan, returning to Douala aged twelve after his time in Wiesbaden, was greeted by his father at the port only to find that he was no longer able to communicate in his native language, and he was not unique in this.[59]

Greater problems resulted from difficulties in reintegrating into the hierarchical social structure of colonial society. Cameroonians whose progress as schoolchildren or apprentices had been praised by teachers, masters and host parents in Germany often found that their skills and European experience were dismissed by the authorities and European employers in Cameroon. An administrative report argued that after six years in Germany Meetom had learnt little more than German language skills and that his cooking skills were inferior to those of any unskilled young Togolese.[60] He was to retrain as a clerk. Similarly, after an initial positive report on their progress, Governor Seitz wrote that Demba and Lukenje were not as able as Duala who had been trained in workshops in Cameroon and that they were falling into bad habits such as laziness.[61] He concluded that this was a further example of how little of a lasting impression a carefully organised period of education or training left on Africans sent to Europe. As workshops were established in Cameroon the necessity of training Africans in Europe decreased.

It was in this context that derogatory terms such as 'Half Europeanised' *Neger* or 'nigger in trousers' (*Hosenneger* or *Hosen-Nigger*) emerged in colonial discourse to describe returning migrants or assimilated Africans. These epithets mocked as inauthentic those whose adoption of European manners and customs challenged notions of the fundamental difference between Europeans and non-Europeans that legitimised colonial rule.[62] Advertising and the pages of satirical magazines increasingly featured half naked Africans, particularly Cameroonians, in trousers and sporting top hats. At this stage, the imagery contained an element of ambivalence. Cover pages from *Kladderadatsch* of the 1880s feature typical *Hosenneger*, but also satirise the dress sense of Cameroonian women – a knowing

[58] Soden to Caprivi, 9 July 1890, pp. 8–9; Zimmerer to Caprivi, 12 October 1894, BArch R1001 5572, p. 155; Seitz to Hohenlohe-Schillingsfürst, 7 October 1895, BArch R1001 5573, p. 69; Puttkamer to AAKA, 24 December 1897, BArch R1001 5574, pp. 147–8.

[59] Soden to Caprivi, 9 July 1890, pp. 8–9. The Togolese Johannes Mansa Arra similarly lost the ability to speak his native language. See correspondence in BArch R1001 5574, pp. 115, 116, 132.

[60] Puttkamer to AAKA, 24 December 1897, pp. 147–8.

[61] Seitz to Hohenlohe-Schillingsfürst, 1 August 1896, BArch R1001 5573, p. 165.

[62] For an example of the use of this term, see Buchner, *Aurora colonialis*, p. 40. See also O'Donnell, 'Home, Nation, Empire', pp. 49–52.

comment on the actual preference of both men and women for European clothing (on which we have more to say in Chapter 5).[63] In the pages of *Kladderadatsch* Cameroonians, especially students, featured as typical Berlin 'characters' (Figure 1.1).[64] These knowing and sympathetic representations contrast significantly with the approach of the generally less critical *Fliegende Blätter*, which represented Cameroonians as ignorant savages wrestling with the trappings of 'civilisation'.[65] From that point of view they are an index of the range of possible attitudes to visitors, at least in the early years.

The *Hosenneger* appeared as a purely negative figure where there were doubts about the desirability of exposing Africans to Europe. The Basel missionary Mader remarked in 1892 that 'some Africans, when they are sent by the administration to Europe, arrive in an Eldorado'.[66] Zimmerer calculated that the ratio of negative to positive experiences in training young Africans was ten to one. He argued that while they would begin to return to their natural state again (*vernegern* used here in a positive sense) once back in Cameroon, their European experience had spoiled them for deployment in the protectorate.[67] Equally scathing were the comments of the head of the Pallottine mission Heinrich Vieter, reproduced in the *National-Zeitung* in 1898:

> Here in Cameroon one finds a large number of *Neger* who were in Germany for educational purposes. On the whole one must say that this has brought no happiness to those educated, or better 'spoiled', there. The results are largely discontent with their situation [and] demands that will not be satisfied. They were treated in Germany as something special, even as Princes.[68]

The last comment is a reminder that especially in the first years of migration a handful of Cameroonians, like Alfred Bell and Mpundu Akwa, were granted audiences with members of Germany's royal families and ruling elite.[69] Like the ambivalent imagery, it hints at a processual

63 'Weihnachten', *Kladderadatsch*, 23 December 1888; 'Sonntagsvergnügen in Kamerun', *Kladderadatsch*, 19 July 1885; 'Unsere Marine', *Kladderadatsch*, 17 April 1887. On advertising, see Ciarlo, *Advertising Empire*.

64 See also an advertisement for a beer-mug in the form of a Cameroonian student in evening dress with a fraternity sash: *Kladderadatsch*, 4 April 1886, 158

65 'Ein schwarzer Corpsbruder aus Kamerun', *Fliegende Blätter*, 82 (1885), 180; 'Erster Export deutscher Ölgemälde in Kamerun', *Fliegende Blätter*, 82 (1885), 152; 'Einführung der ersten Modeartikel in Kamerun', *Fliegende Blätter*, 84 (1886), 43.

66 Annual Report of the Middle School, Bethel 1892, 2 February 1893, Mission 21, E-2.5 1892, no. 137.

67 Zimmerer to Caprivi, 30 August 1894, BArch R1001 5572, pp. 144–5.

68 *National-Zeitung*, 25 August 1898, in BArch R1001 5575, p. 13.

69 See e.g. Gouaffo, 'Prince Dido'; Wei, *Le Paradis tabou*, p. 173; interview with Valère Epée, Douala, March 2006.

Figure 1.1 '15 Degrees below Zero', *Kladderadatsch*, 29 January 1888

shift from the curiosity and, in some cases, respect shown by sections of German society to early travellers like Ebobse Dido and demonstrated in newspaper coverage, to a more hardened and dismissive stance, and at the way this was driven by colonial interests in the protectorate. Colonial administrators in particular were incensed at African visitors mixing socially with the German elite, and their references to visitors being spoiled reflected experience with returners who did resist accommodating to the colonial order.[70] The Basel Mission student Heinrich Eugen Ndine (Dinne Dumbe) who had spent several years at Langenau in Württemberg was accused of helping to stir up discontent at the Mission's school in Bethel.[71] Ekame Sale's request for higher wages on account of his European experience was dismissed as greedy and unwarranted.[72] Timba temporarily broke with the Catholic Mission on arrival in Douala and allegedly fell in with a bad crowd of Europeans and ended up in prison.[73] Both Dikonge and Meetom were dismissed from their administrative jobs after being convicted of stealing, and Dikonge's actions were blamed on his European experience.[74] In Meetom's case the evidence suggests that his dismissal was occasioned by his protest to the Basel Mission against the way he was treated by the colonial administration under Governor Puttkamer; he had committed himself to serve in the administration for at least four years in return for the opportunity to train in Germany.[75] Demba and Lukenje also encountered difficulties back in the protectorate. Their host mother in Görlitz, upset by the letters she was receiving from them in which they complained of abusive treatment, requested that they be allowed to return to her care.[76] Permission was denied by the authorities.

The idea that returners were disappointed, discontented or somehow 'spoiled' by their metropolitan experience glossed over the real problems and frustration that these young people encountered when faced with the developing racial hierarchy of the colonial arena. It was not until 1896 that the first measures were taken towards codifying the relationship between colonised and colonisers in German law, but what prompted the move towards legislation was the public scandal over abuses of power

70 Soden to Bismarck, 7 December 1886, BArch R1001 4297, pp. 64–6; Report of School-Teacher Christaller, 27 October 1888, pp. 49–51.
71 Annual Report of the Middle School, Bethel, 1892.
72 Seitz to Hohenlohe-Schillingsfürst, 7 February 1896, BArch R1001 5573, p. 106.
73 Hermann Nekes, 'Andreas Mbange und seine Gefährten', *Stern der Heiden*, 40/1 (1933), 4–14, here, p. 12.
74 On Dikonge: Zimmerer to Caprivi, 12 October 1894, p. 155. On Meetom: Notice, 28 August 1898, BArch R1001 5575, p. 12.
75 Tube Meetom to Brother Spellenberg, 14 August 1898, Mission 21, E-10, 43.18, no. 2.
76 Von Joeden-Forgey, 'Nobody's People', p. 364.

and police violence in Cameroon.[77] As Elisa von Joeden-Forgey has astutely observed, '[e]xposure to ridicule, floggings, expropriations, and other harassments were hidden and redescribed as their own "dissatisfactions" with their own "position"'.[78]

For their part, the authorities increasingly questioned the benefits of educating Africans in Europe. This was part of a larger debate in both Germany and the overseas protectorates about the presence of colonial subjects in Europe. It was clear that the colonial authorities' educational policies were failing to produce the loyal, docile subjects that they had been hoping for. Moreover, some, like Alfred Bell and Rudolf Duala Manga, had run up considerable debts in Germany which the Cameroon administration feared it would have to carry.[79] A further concern was that British Reverend Hughes at the Colwyn Bay African Training Institute in Wales was attempting to recruit young Cameroonians to be trained for British colonial projects. While the colonial administrators were disappointed with the results achieved by the metropolitan educational policy, they were loath to allow the rival colonial power to benefit from training German colonial subjects.[80]

Their solution was to introduce restrictions upon the ability of Cameroonians to leave the territory. A travel ban was issued in December 1893 just three months after the German governor of the Marshall Islands had introduced similar legislation in the South Seas protectorate. Cameroonians who wanted to leave now required the governor's permission to do so. They had to fill out a complicated application form and pay a 10 Mark fee. The penalty for breaching the restrictions was that the travellers themselves, members of their family or the person who encouraged them to leave faced a potential 1,000 Mark fine. By 1900 similar travel restrictions were implemented in several of Germany's other overseas protectorates.[81]

The effect of these measures was that the flow from the protectorate steadily decreased. Nonetheless, between the introduction of these travel restrictions and the outbreak of World War One migration for educational purposes remained a powerful pull factor in drawing Cameroonians to Germany and elite Duala families remained insistent on sending

[77] Martin Schröder, *Prügelstrafe und Züchtigungsrecht*, pp. 35–41.
[78] Von Joeden-Forgey, 'Nobody's People', p. 338.
[79] Soden to Bismarck, 7 November 1889, pp. 90–3; Puttkamer to Hohnelohe-Schillingsfürst, 8 December 1896, BArch R1001 5574, p. 24.
[80] 'Auswanderung Eingeborener aus Kamerun', *DKB*, 5 (1894), 111–12; Leist to AAKA, 8 August 1893, BArch R1001 5572, pp. 47–8.
[81] *DKB*, 5 (1894), 105. Legislation for other territories at BArch R1001 5576, p. 31 (Togo); Riebow *et al.* (eds.), *Die deutsche Kolonial-Gesetzgebung*, vol. II, p. 214 (East Africa).

their children to Europe. As a result more than two dozen further young people arrived in Germany to be schooled or undertake apprenticeships. This now included children from a handful of elite non-Duala families based in other parts of the protectorate. Thus, three sons of the Batanga paramount Malapa Madéviné from the coastal town Kribi left for Germany and the Grassland paramount Fonyonga II arranged for one of his sons to go to school in southern Germany.[82] Evidence suggests that a son of the Ngumba leader in Bidjoka was schooled in Hamburg, while members of the Baptist elite in Victoria (now Limbé) also spent time in Germany.[83] Although there was a relative decrease in the number of those travelling, it is striking that several of these later visitors did receive official permission to leave. Notable among those allowed to travel was the eighteen-year-old Soppo Elame from Akwa, who entirely financed his own trip. His ability to raise the necessary funds and his strong desire to leave for Germany impressed the governor, who helped arrange an apprenticeship for him.[84] Yet in Germany he fell ill and was unable to pay for his return journey to Douala. The authorities reluctantly agreed to bear the cost.[85] Less information is available about the educational experiences of those who left Cameroon after the mid 1890s. They seem to have been older on average than those who went before them, and because the government was no longer sponsoring their travel it took no responsibility for monitoring their success. Similarly it remains unclear how these visits were organised by the families and institutions involved. Certainly one means open to parents was to approach the European missions for help, and the missions gradually became involved in sponsoring travel.

Mission-sponsored travel

In Cameroon it was the various religious mission societies, principally the Basel Evangelical Mission, the Baptist Mission, the Catholic Pallottine Mission and the American Presbyterian Church, and not the German government, that played the dominant role in the education of the indigenous population groups. By 1911 the missions were running a combined total of 525 schools with more than 26,000 pupils, while the colonial

[82] 'Paul Malapa Décryptage', p. 4. On Noah Sosiga, son of Fonyonga II, see below.
[83] Governor of Colonies to Minister of Colonies, 19 January 1919, FR ANOM 2300 COL 30/268. On Stephan Wilson and Carl Steane from Victoria, see below.
[84] Seitz to Hohenlohe-Schillingsfürst, 17 February 1897, BArch R1001 5574, p. 55.
[85] AAKA to Remittance Department, 20 October 1899, BArch R1001 5575, p. 92.

administration had just 6 schools attended by around 900 pupils.[86] Unlike the Bremen-based North German Mission which was active in Togo and sent around twenty Togolese to be trained as preachers at its seminaries in Württemberg, the European-based Cameroon missions initially placed little importance on the training of Africans in Europe.[87] It was partly through accident and in some cases with a great deal of reluctance that they found themselves involved in supervising educational visits to Germany.

The Baptist Mission

The Baptist Mission, and in particular the founder of its Berlin-Bethel community Eduard Scheve, was the most active in promoting the education of young Cameroonians in Germany. Scheve had played a central role in building a German Baptist Mission in Cameroon to continue the work of the British Baptist Mission once the latter had withdrawn from the territory following the establishment of German administrative control. His interest in Cameroon was influenced by his meeting with Alfred Bell, who provided Scheve with information about the indigenous Baptist congregation. One of the men Scheve corresponded with while researching the situation in Cameroon and who had responded positively to Scheve's plans to send Baptist preachers to the protectorate was the indigenous pastor Joseph Wilson, head of the Baptist church in Victoria. Acting on a request from Wilson, in May 1893 the Foreign Office approached the Baptist Mission to ask whether it would be willing to supervise the education in Germany of Wilson's son, Stephan, who was to be trained as a German teacher. The committee of the Baptist Mission unanimously agreed to look after Stephan in order to increase its influence within the Baptist community in Victoria.[88] Several months before his arrival, however, another young Cameroonian turned up unexpectedly on the doorstep of the Mission's headquarters in Friedrichshain. Dressed in a sailor suit, with a walking stick in one hand and a letter of introduction in the other, this was the fourteen-year-old Duala, Richard Edube Mbene. The Baptist missionary August Steffens, author of the note, had arranged for Mbene to accompany a returning European to Germany and to be brought to Scheve. Like Stephan Wilson, Mbene was

[86] Günther, 'Mission im kolonialen Kontext', p. 61. On missionary education in Cameroon, see also Orosz, *Religious Conflict*.

[87] On Togolese at the North German Mission's seminaries in Germany, see Bazlen, 'Die Mohren von Westheim'; Debrunner, *Presence and Prestige*, pp. 355–8.

[88] Scheve, *Die Mission der deutschen Baptisten*, pp. 9–10, 26; Johnson, *Schwarze Missionare – Weiße Missionare!*, p. 138.

part of the Cameroonian elite and he was connected to the Baptist Mission through his father who had been an assistant to the British Baptists. Steffens' expectation was that Mbene would be trained to work for the Mission back home. Although taken by surprise by this newcomer, Scheve welcomed Mbene into his household. He later remarked of these arrivals: 'without our planning, indeed, in part against our will, a beginning to the training in Germany of suitable natives for the mission had been made'.[89]

Scheve not only provided a home to young Cameroonians in Germany; his houses, first in the Gubener Straße 11 and from 1900 at Emdener Straße 15 in Moabit, were also places of welcome for Cameroonian Baptists and those associated with the Mission who were visiting Berlin. Visitors including participants in the 1896 Colonial Exhibition, and young Cameroonians working and training in and around Berlin, attended services at the Mission and were received as guests in Scheve's home.[90] He provided hospitality to members of the Bell delegation visiting Germany in 1902 (Figure 1.2). The delegation, composed of leading Duala notables, including the Bell paramount August Manga Bell and his son Rudolf Duala Manga, was in Germany to protest at the actions of the colonial government. Eleven of the Duala representatives spent six weeks with Scheve and their visit was positively reported on in one of the Mission's main publications.[91] In turn August Manga expressed his thanks for Scheve's hospitality in the pastor's guest book: 'Sango Scheve is a man, although light coloured in appearance, whose heart in my opinion is dedicated to God and with all his heart he stands by the Africans. Only God can repay him for the kindness that he has shown me and my family.'[92]

Such was August Manga's confidence in Scheve that before his return to Douala, both he and Duala Manga entrusted their respective sons, Richard and Alexander, into Scheve's care. They stayed with the pastor from 1903 to 1908, at their parents' expense. The Deido paramount

[89] Scheve, *Die Mission der deutschen Baptisten*, p. 26. Like many travelling Cameroonians, Mbene had a native name (Edube) and a baptismal name (Richard) as well as his family name. Throughout this book, we have adopted the practice of giving individuals both their native and German names the first time they are mentioned and then using the given names by which they most often appear in the sources; this is usually, though not always, the German name.

[90] Scheve to Graf Schweinitz, President of the German Colonial Exhibition, 22 September 1896, Onckenarchiv, Nachlass Scheve, Mappe 15, no. 429.

[91] Scheve, 'Vier Generationen'.

[92] Translation into German from the original Duala of the entry in Scheve's Guest Book in Balders, '100 Jahre Beteiligung', pp. 9–10.

Figure 1.2 Duala visiting Eduard Scheve in Berlin, 1902

Jim Ekwalla, who was also part of the delegation, similarly left his son, Otto, to be looked after by Scheve.[93]

Mbene and Wilson became the first of a series of young Cameroonians to live with Scheve and his family over a period of around sixteen years. In the case of these first two, the Mission agreed to cover the costs of their upbringing and education as well as their passage to Germany.[94] All of the Cameroonians who followed them came from either Douala or Victoria, the main centres of Baptist missionary activity. In Berlin they shared rooms with Scheve's own children and were treated and schooled in a similar manner, and they seem to have developed a strong relationship

[93] On daughters, see Chapter 5. On Otto Ekwalla, see Scheve, 'Vier Generationen', 13–14. Stoecker, *Afrikawissenschaft*, p. 318, lists him as a language assistant or informant in Berlin in 1904. Jim Ekwalla had previously sent his first-born son, Songue Epeye Ekuala, to be schooled in Mülheim on the Ruhr around 1890: Sonnenberger, 'Der Prinz von Holthausen'; Michels, 'Mülheim an der Ruhr'; Aitken, 'Education and Migration'.

[94] *Blüthen und Früchte aus unserem Arbeitsfelde für unsere Freunde* (1894), 7; Alberts, Secretary of the German Baptist Committee to Foreign Office, 1 June 1893, BArch R1001 4073, p. 68; Leist to AAKA, 20 June 1893, BArch R1001 4073, p. 77.

with him. Mbene referred to him as 'father' Scheve and the Privy Counsellor Rose wrote of the 'veneration' that Richard and Alexander showed towards the pastor.[95] The length of time these Cameroonians stayed in Germany depended largely upon their age upon arrival, and they attended a variety of schools. In general, however, the training they received was geared towards them later working as teachers or teaching assistants in the Mission's schools. Mbene, for example, stayed four and a half years in Berlin and attended the primary school across the road from the Scheves' home before qualifying with positive reports at the city's Teachers' Training School.[96] Wilson was six years with Scheve and also attended both the primary school and then the Teachers' Training School before his untimely death in 1899. Following this, another Victoria native Carl Steane arrived in Berlin and spent around seven years in the city, also attending the Teachers' Training School, before returning to teach in northern Cameroon at the government school in Garoua.[97]

The return experience of Richard Mbene shows that even within the ostensibly supportive and nominally egalitarian ambit of the Mission the transition between metropolitan and colonial cultures could prove problematic. One reason for his return in 1897 was his mother's desire to see him again. Cameroonian families were known to be very child-centred, and there is ample testimony to the fact that the departure of a child or young person to Europe, however desirable, was a wrench for both parents and children.[98] In Mbene's case, events in Cameroon also called him back: following the death of several of the Baptists' European and German-American workers, the Mission committee decided to send him to Cameroon to teach in the boys' school and the attached Mission school in Bonaku, as well as to instruct new missionaries in the Duala language.[99] Later he also gave lessons in Duala in the girls' school.[100] But he did not settle in well. White Baptist missionary workers, particularly German Americans accustomed to systematic racial discrimination in the United States, appear to have been hostile towards their African

95 Günther, 'Mission im kolonialen Kontext', p. 66.

96 Scheve to Brother Schunke, 18 January 1897, Onckenarchiv, Nachlass Scheve, Mappe 16, no. 32; Scheve, 'Richard Edube Mbene', *Unsere Heidenmission*, (1907), 36–7, here p. 36.

97 Lyonga, Breitinger and Butake, *Anglophone Cameroon Writing*, p. 28; Scheve, *Die Mission der deutschen Baptisten*, p. 102. Steane was responsible for producing a grammar of the Fula language: Steane, *Kleine Fullah Grammatik*.

98 See for example Misipo, *Der Junge aus Duala*, p. 14. For an outsider's view: Plehn, *Die Malaria der afrikanischen Negerbevölkerung*, p. 4.

99 Scheve to Brothers Wedel, Ems and Schwester Steffens, 28 June 1897, Onckenarchiv, Nachlass Scheve, Mappe 16, no. 134–8.

100 Marie Bechler, 'Unsere Mädchenschule und ihre Bewohner', *Unsere Heidenmission* (1902), 20–2, here p. 22.

co-workers. Mbene's presence in the Mission house soon upset the established racial hierarchy; he was accused of showing a lack of respect when he referred to the Mission doctor as 'Brother' and not 'Doctor' Schauffler.[101] Scheve, who had visited the United States and had been appalled by the relationship between white Americans and African Americans, appealed to his colleagues in Cameroon not to let Mbene feel hurt by the 'differences between black and white'.[102] That his request had little impact is hinted at in a further letter sent six months later: 'With respect to Richard, there is no need for any special instructions; it must be a requirement for you and the other brothers and sisters in the mission's house to always treat Richard as though he were an equal partner in our mission.'[103]

Scheve felt it important that Mbene be involved in all deliberations held by the missionaries and that they should show him love and support. At the same time he asked Mbene not to take it personally when his co-workers treated him with disrespect. In spite of these difficulties and developing health problems he continued to serve the Mission and became engaged to marry a daughter of August Manga Bell. His close relationship to his mentor was demonstrated by his brief return to Berlin in 1903 to 1904 in order to convalesce following a serious liver complaint. Richard's life, however, was brought to a premature end when he drowned following a boating accident in 1907. In his obituary, Scheve's son Alfred praised Mbene's service to the Baptists, but hinted at the continuing difficulties between Richard and the other missionaries – possibly with reference to critical comments Mbene was said to have made about the Mission's role in supporting colonial oppression. In doing so, Alfred Scheve deployed the familiar trope of the 'spoilt' native:

> It is true that our dear Cameroonians in Germany are placed, both internally and externally, in a completely different situation than in their homeland, and this means that they are so easily spoilt that afterwards it is unbelievably difficult for them to re-accustom themselves to the old relationships and to work successfully. Sadly, this also proved to be the case in the work of our friend Richard.[104]

The Basel Mission

A second, and much larger, missionary enterprise active in Cameroon was the Protestant interdenominational Basel Evangelical Mission,

[101] Günther, 'Mission im kolonialen Kontext', p. 65.
[102] Scheve to Wedel, 6 August 1897, Onckenarchiv, Nachlass Scheve, Mappe 15, no. 177–8.
[103] Scheve to Schwarz, 7 January 1898, Onckenarchiv, Nachlass Scheve, Mappe 15, no. 242–3.
[104] Scheve, 'Richard Edube Mbene', 37.

which had been present there since 1886. In contrast to the Baptists the Basel Mission was resolutely against Africans being brought to Europe. Its committee took the popular view that a stay in Europe usually led to the moral corruption of African migrants.[105] Despite several requests from Cameroonian notables – James Bilé a M'bule among them – asking for mission support for the education of their children in Germany the committee held to this principle.[106] Indeed in 1896 in order to dissuade a Duala Christian from sending his son to Germany the committee formally ordered that no missionary should return to Europe with the child.[107] At the same time the views of its missionaries on the ground in Cameroon helped shape those of the administration and the missionary Bohner produced a damning report on the prospects of African education in Europe for Governor Zimmerer.[108]

The Mission made a notable exception, however, in the case of a son of the influential Bali-Nyonga leader Fonyonga II. Fonyonga II enjoyed a flourishing relationship with the Basel missionary Ferdinand Ernst and he was a keen supporter of the Mission's educational efforts. He commanded that local children, including three of his sons, attend the Mission's school in Bali while he himself received private lessons from Ernst. His soldiers and wives were sent to the Sunday service, which he also often attended.[109] As a sign of their developing friendship Fonyonga II handed over one of his sons, Noah Sosiga, to the care of Ernst, who baptised him as one of the first Mission converts. When Ernst was due to return to Germany on leave in summer 1909, Fonyonga II asked that Noah go with him. The committee in Basel was reluctant to breach its policy, but the missionaries in Cameroon impressed upon them the importance of maintaining good relations with Fonyonga II in order for the Mission to have success in the region.[110] Ernst reached an agreement with Fonyonga II, whereby the latter was to provide the Mission with 3,000 Marks' worth of ivory to fund his son's education.[111]

Noah left Cameroon with Ernst for the village of Spöck near Karlsruhe – with fewer than 1,700 inhabitants, considerably smaller than Bali. Here he was to live with Ernst and his relatives and to be trained in agricultural

105 Committee Minutes §406, 8 April 1888, Mission 21.
106 See for example Committee Minutes §1057, 9 November 1904, Mission 21, 27 June.
107 Committee Minutes §4, 3 January 1896, Mission 21.
108 Bohner to Zimmerer, May 1892 (exact date unknown), BArch R1001 5571, pp. 141–8. See also Zimmerer's reply, 18 May 1892, Mission 21, E-2.5, no. 42.
109 Annual Report, Bali 1908, 2 January 1909, Mission 21, E-2.28 III, no. 63.
110 Keller to Committee, 25 October 1909, Mission 21, E-2.29 1909, no. unclear.
111 Committee Minutes §735, 5 July 1909, Mission 21. Above the figure the sum 1,700 M is written in pencil.

skills. Within weeks of arriving, however, Ernst died suddenly and Noah came under the 'influence' of a local teacher and the local minister in Spöck. This proved to be a short-term solution, and the Mission was unable to find a suitable family to take care of him. As a result, by November 1909, less than half a year after he had originally left, he was returned to Cameroon. It is likely that this state of affairs, coupled with Ernst's death, heightened the already deteriorating relations between the Mission and Fonyonga II.[112] At the same time it signalled the end to the Basel Mission's involvement in sponsoring the education of Cameroonians in Europe.

Nonetheless at least four other Cameroonians accompanied Basel missionaries to Germany or Switzerland as language assistants. They did so with the express permission of the committee only because the purpose of their stay was to help to translate the Bible or other texts into Duala. Work in the native language was a key feature of the Mission's proselytising practice, and this consideration overrode anxieties about the corrupting effects of European life on the four men. The young Duala involved, Daniel Akwa, Eduard Doo, Joseph Ekollo and Samuel Jenge were not only baptised members of the Basel Mission in Cameroon, but three were employed by the Mission in a teaching capacity and Doo was a talented older student at one of the Mission's schools. In Europe they stayed with the missionaries whom they were to assist; Jenge and Ekollo lived at different times in Kirchheim near Munich and Akwa was based in Riehen near Basel, while Doo's location remains unknown. Doo was the first to leave for Germany (1891) and Akwa the last (1911). The length of their stay ranged from one to three years, during which they received no payment, only food and accommodation.

While little is known of the metropolitan experiences of Akwa, Doo and Jenge, Ekollo's impressions of Germany were published some years later by the Mission under the title: *Wie ein Schwarzer das Land der Weißen ansieht*.[113] Before the German takeover of the protectorate Ekollo, the son of a Duala trader, had enjoyed an apprenticeship as a merchant under an English trader and then become a student of the Baptist preachers Joseph Jackson Fuller and then Joseph Wilson.[114] With the arrival of the Germans and the Basel Mission he attended the Mission

[112] Committee Minutes §735, 5 July 1909; Committee Minutes §879, 1 September 1909, Mission 21; Hauß, *Der Pionier der Balimission*. On the relationship between the Basel Mission and Fonyonga II, see also O'Neil, 'Imperialisms at the Century's End', p. 95.

[113] Ekollo, *Wie ein Schwarzer*. See also the autobiography of Amur bin Nasur ilOmeiri from Zanzibar: bin Nasur, 'Leben des Herrn Amur bin Nasur'.

[114] See Ekollo's Curriculum Vitae, Mission 21, E-2.33 1911, no. 141, and his son's account in Ekollo, *Mémoires*, pp. 13–26.

school in Douala and eventually helped to translate lessons from English into Duala, before being appointed a teacher in his own right. In 1896 he accompanied the missionary Schüler to Germany. His short book, which appeared in a German translation from the original Duala in 1908, is one of the first known pieces of published literature to have been written by a Cameroonian.

Ekollo's account of his year-long stay in Kirchheim eschews any reference to negative experiences. He presents German society as a model to which Cameroon and Cameroonians should aspire. Germany appears as a harmonious utopia in which rich and poor live peacefully together, the rules of government are respected, and religion and education are key to creating a civil society. Yet, despite the idealistic tone of the book, it still offers some insight into Ekollo's impressions of everyday life. European weather in particular fascinated him and he outlines the four seasons of the year, taking time in particular to discuss winter, snow and ice before concluding that 'winter in Europe is terrible'. He expresses a sense of wonder at physical manifestations of Germany's rapid modernisation in a section entitled 'Wonderful things that the Whites have made'. These included the train and tram systems, department stores, street lighting and urbanisation in general. The sheer scale of the buildings in Europe impressed him, especially the Mission house in Basel, an indication that his experience of Europe was not limited to Kirchheim. Ekollo was also taken with the German penchant for politeness, the use of 'please' and 'thank you', addressing people by formal titles, and simple greetings. These he saw as examples of 'fine' European customs. He concludes the book with a discussion of the life of Christians, the work of the Mission and religion which he sees as playing a central role in German society.[115]

After his year in Kirchheim was over Ekollo, like the other language assistants, returned to Douala. In keeping with the discretion he displayed in his account of the metropole, he made a successful career as one of the Basel Mission's first ordained indigenous preachers. He continued to play an important role in Cameroonian Protestantism until his death in 1946.[116] Ekollo, Doo and Jenge were appointed as teachers in mission schools while Akwa's fate after his return is unknown. As in the case of Mbene, reintegration into mission life and work after a sojourn in Germany was not always easy. Doo was twice released from

[115] Ekollo, *Wie ein Schwarzer*, pp. 8–9; 10–14; 21–2; 25–31. For similar observations about urban life in Germany by a visitor from Yaoundé around 1912, see Atangana and Messi, *Jaunde-Texte*, pp. 242–3.

[116] On Ekollo's role in the early church in Cameroon, see Messina and van Slageren, *Histoire du christianisme*, pp. 46–7; Ekollo, *Mémoires*, pp. 6–7, 20–6.

teaching positions, the first dismissal coming less than six months after his return. He was alleged to have made negative comments about the missionary Bizer with whom he had travelled to Europe, asking permission to leave Bizer's care and return home early.[117] On the second occasion the grounds for dismissal was 'insubordination'.[118] The committee agreed to employ him again only on the condition that it was in a place where nobody could have heard of his 'fall from grace'.[119] While he was eventually taken on in Nyasoso in 1902, it appears that here too he did not stay long.[120]

Catholic missions

Catholic missionaries were also active in promoting the education of Africans, in Germany as in Cameroon. Something over a dozen Cameroonians, primarily from Douala or Yaoundé, spent time in Limburg an der Lahn. Seven of these can be directly connected to the Pallottine Mission, whose mother house was in Limburg. As yet, little more than the names of these individuals has been recovered from the documentary evidence available. The first group to arrive in Limburg in 1893 included the ten-year-old Mundi ma Lobe, Josef Mandene, Peter Mungeli and Andreas Toko, all of whom were later baptised. Toko, the son of a local leader, King Toko from Toko, was later sent to Ehrenbreitstein in order to train for the priesthood. Pupils in Limburg undertook an apprenticeship as well as educational and religious instruction.[121]

The missions played a not insignificant role in offering an alternative route to Europe particularly after the colonial authorities had retreated from doing so, and it was also partly under the aegis of the missions that members of the non-Duala elite reached Germany. Like the colonial administration none of the mission societies envisaged their charges taking up permanent residence, and few sought to do so. Indeed, the majority of mission-sponsored visitors returned to Africa before the outbreak of war

[117] Bohner, 'Ein Blick in die Arbeit eines Kameruner Missionars', unpublished notes, April 1895, Mission 21, E-2.8a 1895, no. 119.

[118] Brother Bohner to Inspector Oehler, 23 October 1895, Mission 21, E-2, 8a 1895, no. 57.

[119] Annual Report, Bethel 1892, 16 March 1893, Mission 21, E-2.5 1892, no. 136; Mission 21, Committee Minutes §173, 27 March 1895; Change in Native Personnel, 3 September 1902, Mission 21, E-2.15 1902, no. 69.

[120] Annual Report, Nyasoso 1902, 26 January 1903, Mission 21, E-2.15 1902, no. 207.

[121] Holzbach, 'Kamerun, Limburg und die Pallottiner'. Information on Mundi ma Lobe from Diözesanarchiv Limburg. See also 'Unser Bild', *Echo aus Afrika: katholische Monatsschrift zur Förderung der afrikanischen Antisklavenbewegung und der afrikanischen Missionstätigkeit*, 5–6/9 (1893), 85, 91; 'Notice, Kamerun', *Pädagogische Blätter* (1897), 447. Toko's life would be cut short when he drowned in the Sanaga River.

and several of them, like Richard Mbene, Joseph Ekollo and Andreas Mbange became important members of the developing Christian church in Cameroon. At the same time a handful of others broke with the European missions and their paternalistic support upon their return.[122] In Germany the missions remained an important point of connection for African migrants whether they were seeking religious or financial help or had encountered any number of problems adapting to life in Europe. At the same time the missions were concerned about the context in which some Africans arrived in Europe. In particular they were critical of ethnological exhibitions, which put Africans on show and often asked them to perform their 'heathen practices'.[123] Such exhibitions, however, provided a further means by which Africans could reach and potentially remain in Europe should they choose to do so.

Völkerschauen and the Berlin Colonial Exhibition 1896

From the late eighteenth century, ethnological shows had begun to take off in Germany and Europe at large and by the end of the nineteenth century they were being staged on a regular basis in larger German cities. Even before the onset of German colonialism increasing numbers of non-Western European individuals and groups were recruited to appear in exhibitions and to perform in German zoos; a 'Nubian Caravan' was put on display in Berlin's zoological garden in 1878 and 1879. Such events were often well managed and framed with the help of anthropologists to 'replicate and reinforce the dynamics of the unequal relationship that had existed between coloniser and colonised, master and slave'.[124] Participants performed elements of their 'own' customs and traditions, although it was frequently European anthropologists and exhibition impresarios who not only determined what was authentic, but on occasion also 'coached' participants as to how to perform practices that were not actually their own.[125]

Impresarios such as the Hamburg zoo manager Carl Hagenbeck were responsible for bringing groups of people from all over the globe to

122 Konrad Deibold fled from the controlling influence of the missionary Theodor Christaller after returning from Germany and working briefly at the administration's school in Bonebela: Böckheler, *Theodor Christaller*, pp. 65–71. Peter Mungeli, trained in Limburg, left the Pallottine Mission once back in Cameroon: Vieter, *Les premiers pas de l'Église*, p. 60.

123 Van der Heyden, 'Die Kolonial- und die Transvaal-Ausstellung 1896/97', pp. 136–7.

124 Lindfors, 'Introduction', p. x.

125 Zimmerman, *Anthropology and Antihumanism*, p. 30. See also Thode-Arora, 'Völkerschauen in Berlin'.

perform in Germany. Yet it was relatively uncommon for people from the German colonies to be put on display. Hagenbeck had organised the four-and-a-half-month visit of Samson Dido and seven other Duala to Germany in 1886, but it was the First German Colonial Exhibition ten years later that brought metropolitan Germans into contact with Germany's colonial population on a new scale.[126] Mounted in Berlin from May to October 1896, the Colonial Exhibition was a celebration of German colonialism and an attempt to inspire more public enthusiasm for the Reich's imperial possessions at a time when the colonial project was beset by mismanagement and scandal.[127] The exhibition was part of the larger Berlin Trade Fair and was situated in the east of the city on the grounds of the soon-to-be-completed Treptow Park. Large crowds flocked to see recreated African villages populated by 103 people from various ethnic groups and representing various regions of the German Empire from West Africa, East Africa, Southwest Africa and the South Seas colony of New Guinea. Among the participants were twenty Cameroonians under the leadership of Bismarck Bell (Kwelle Ndumbe), a son of Ndumbe Lobe – eighteen men and two women, from the coastal towns of Douala and Kribi. The four Batanga from Kribi were Catholic while a number of the Duala were baptised members of the Baptist or the Basel missions. They had been recruited for the exhibition by officers of the colonial administration including Governor Theodor Seitz.[128]

In return for free passage, free housing in Berlin (on the site of the exhibition), pay for the duration of the exhibition and warm clothes to combat the Berlin weather and an unusually cold summer, the Cameroonian participants were expected to perform 'authentic' Cameroonian customs and traditions. Over the twenty-four weeks of the exhibition they were daily asked to dance, play examples of the Cameroonian drum language (*Trommelsprache*) or race canoes over the site's carp pond while wearing something approximating traditional dress.[129] Evenings, away from the prying eyes of the daily audiences, they spent their time playing dice games and singing.

126 On Dido, see Thode-Arora, '"Charakteristische Gestalten des Volkslebens"'; Gouaffo, *Wissens- und Kulturtransfer*, pp. 201–25.

127 Meinecke and Hellgrewe (eds.), *Deutschland und seine Kolonien*; Zimmerman, *Anthropology and Antihumanism*, pp. 24–36; van der Heyden, 'Afrikaner in der Reichs (kolonial)hauptstadt'.

128 Official efforts to persuade members of population groups from the interior of the protectorate to participate were unsuccessful, largely because of hostility to the authorities resulting from policies of enforced labour recruitment and plantation building: Zimmerman, *Anthropology and Antihumanism*, p. 27.

129 Neisser, 'Deutschland und seine Kolonien', pp. 34–5.

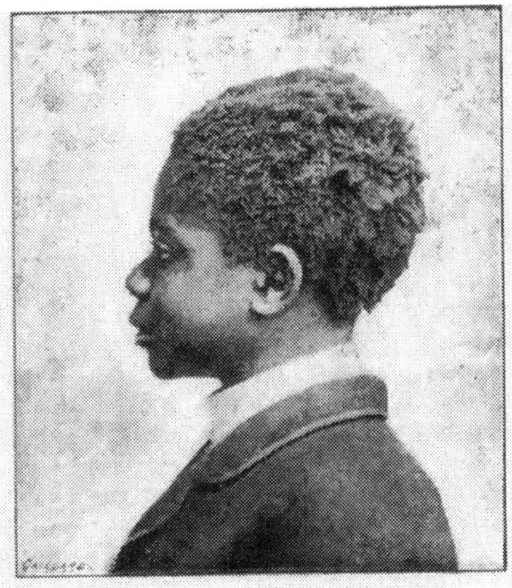

Figure 1.3 Image of Tongo reproduced in *Verhandlungen der Berliner Gesellschaft für Anthropologie, Ethnologie und Urgeschichte*, 1891

They were also subjected to a range of inspections and anthropometric examinations by the exhibition's resident anthropologist Felix von Luschan. Some years earlier a handful of young men from the protectorates had been brought by their European supervisors to see the Head of the Berlin Anthropological Society Rudolf Virchow. He had them photographed in 'European' and 'native' dress, took their measurements, and on at least one occasion presented them to the rest of the Society during one of the group's meetings (Figure 1.3).[130]

While the language Virchow employs in his published descriptions of the younger men is largely neutral and in some places positive, there is no indication of how willing his 'research subjects' were to cooperate. In contrast it is clear that a number of the older participants at the Colonial Exhibition protested and refused to let themselves be measured or photographed in non-Western clothes, much to the annoyance of Luschan. The anthropologist exacted his revenge by berating those who did not comply with his requests in his published account of the project. Much of his anger was directed towards Bismarck Bell who only allowed von Luschan to photograph him when dressed in a jacket and tie. He dismissed Bell and two other Duala, August Djemba Ewane (who

[130] *Verhandlungen der Berliner Gesellschaft für Anthropologie, Ethnologie und Urgeschichte*, 21 (1889), 541–5 and 23 (1891), 280–2.

had also insisted on wearing a suit to be photographed) and Martin Quane Dibobe, as 'Hosen-Nigger'.[131]

The exhibition organisers used the event not simply to entertain and educate its German audience about the supposed differences between the colonisers and the colonised, but also to impress upon the participating colonial subjects a sense of their own inferiority. The performers were taken around Berlin and shown the sights of the city, from museums to the zoological gardens and theatres. Equally, they were allowed to be present at military parades. The aim of these outings was as follows: 'Those returning later to their homelands should recount to their fellow-tribesmen their impressions of Berlin, thus spreading reverence and subservience before the "clever white man".'[132] Aside from these official visits the performers were locked inside the exhibition arena and not allowed to leave it by themselves. Whether the visitors really were impressed with what they saw is impossible to reconstruct from the surviving documents. Certainly at the conclusion of the exhibition a number of the African performers asked to be allowed to remain in Germany.

Twenty-one of the African participants, one from East Africa, eight from Togo and twelve from Cameroon, were granted permission to stay.[133] The Togolese J. C. Bruce set up his own performing troupe which included two of his wives, the only women to remain behind, while Gaula, a young Maasai, returned to East Africa before the end of the year.[134] The remaining seventeen Africans were placed under the care of the Working Party which had organised the Colonial Exhibition and its three-man committee composed of the businessman Bruno Antelmann, the pastor Martin Schall and the butcher Ahlert. It was the responsibility of the committee to supervise the Africans' stay and to look after the money that had been set aside for their eventual return.[135] The Africans themselves, likely with help from the committee, placed advertisements in the *Berliner Lokalanzeiger* in which they solicited local

[131] Von Luschan, *Beiträge zur Völkerkunde.*

[132] Neisser, 'Deutschland und seine Kolonien', p. 42. Similarly, Tube Meetom and Rudolf Duala Manga were taken to see a military parade while living in Aalen to impress upon them Germany's military might: Oesterle to AAKA, 14 September 1893, BArch R1001 5572, p. 40.

[133] List of the Natives Remaining, no date, and Rudolf Joss to AAKA, 17 July 1898, BArch R1001 6350, pp. 50 and 56–7.

[134] See also Brändle, *Nayo Bruce.*

[135] Schall to AAKA, 26 July 1898, BArch R1001 6350, pp. 59–60. The Kladow-based Schall had previously hosted Julius Attang and Martin-Paul Samba, the personal servants of the colonial officers Hans Dominik and Kurt von Morgen, respectively: Dominik, *Sechs Kriegs- und Friedensjahre*, p. 169.

businessmen to take them on as apprentices.[136] Eventually positions were found for all of them. With the exception of Josef Garber who was employed by a tailor, Antelmann took on the Togolese in his trading company. This was the German Colonial House, based in Berlin, but eventually with six other branches throughout Germany, selling goods imported from the German colonies.[137] Antelmann realised the potential commercial pulling power of employing colonial migrants as exotic attractions in his store. He also assumed guardianship of J. C. Bruce's three-and-a-half-year-old son Kwassi, who had been present at the Colonial Exhibition.

The twelve Cameroonians, eight Duala and four Batanga, were in their mid teens to early twenties. They were placed in a variety of apprenticeships. Two were found positions in towns to the east of the capital, in Straußberg and Danzig respectively, while the others were to be trained in Berlin, in the primarily working-class districts of Kreuzberg and Neukölln, often not far from one another. Karl Boimbo, who was employed by Graf von Schweinitz, President of the Colonial Exhibition, probably worked as a house servant. His compatriots were trained in a range of crafts including butchery, shoemaking, tailoring, engineering and working with amber.[138] At least two of them gave up their first apprenticeships, and the two on whom we have information went on to train with photographers – evidence perhaps of an awareness of where the future lay in metropolitan consumer culture. Like Schmidt and similar firms that were earlier involved in the training of Africans, the masters to whom these young men were apprenticed were expected to provide moral and religious guidance for their charges. In contrast to Schmidt and Antelmann, though, none of these masters had a connection to the German colonial project and they were running small-scale operations. The masters agreed to provide their charges with food, clothes and accommodation within their own homes or on their own premises. By the end of the nineteenth century such conditions of training were exceptional; it was no longer customary for apprentices to live with their masters in Berlin or to be clothed by them, and the educational aspect of apprenticeships was also no longer commonplace.[139] Indeed, the expenses involved in training and looking after their Cameroonian apprentices placed a considerable burden on the employers, many of whom lived in straitened circumstances themselves.

[136] Karsten, 'Kamerun in Berlin', 97–9. [137] Zeller, 'Das Deutsche Kolonialhaus'.
[138] List of the Natives Remaining.
[139] Volkov, *The Rise of Popular Antimodernism*, p. 111.

The consequence for Rudolf Massako Joss, a trainee with the photographer Carl Seegert in Große Frankfurter Straße 71, was that he was reduced to living in poverty. In spring 1897 Joss sought financial help from the Basel Mission, of which he had been a member in Douala. The committee was concerned that Joss in his time of need might be tempted to turn to the rival Baptist Mission which, as we have seen, already provided a home for several Cameroonian students. It agreed to give him 50 Marks. The committee, however, resisted suggestions that Joss be paid a regular subvention for fear that he would settle in Berlin, as he apparently hoped to.[140] Six months later, when his situation had still not improved, Joss wrote to the Colonial Department in the Foreign Office (AAKA) comparing his experiences with those of his cousin August Ewane, now an apprentice photographer with Witte in the Skalitzer Straße not far from Joss' own place of work. Within weeks of beginning his training Ewane had already been working in the photography lab and studio. In contrast Joss complained that: 'In the year and a half I have been there I have learnt next to nothing of photography. Instead the whole day I am being used to run errands, etc.' The meagre 6 Marks a week he was earning was clearly not enough to survive on. He had unsuccessfully tried to find a new apprenticeship for himself and was now totally penniless and soon to be homeless. Schall, who was responsible for supervising Joss' stay, reported to the AAKA that Seegert was only the most extreme case among a number of masters who were having trouble meeting their responsibilities to their apprentices; he could neither feed nor house his apprentice, and Joss was having to live several doors down from his place of work. Schall himself had to secure private funds and a one-off payment from the German Colonial Society (DKG) to support his charge. He stressed that the apprentices were showing signs of good progress in their training, but added that funding was desperately needed to help them. The AAKA, reluctant to release funds, responded by asking whether it was not more advisable to transport Joss back to Cameroon with the next steamer. Joss, however, was determined to remain in Germany and complete his apprenticeship with another master. The surviving documentation does not reveal whether he was successful, but in 1900 he was living in Bautzen, over 200 kilometres away from Berlin, and ready to return to Douala. His financial situation had improved to such an extent that he offered to put money towards the costs of the return journey himself.[141]

[140] Committee Minutes §469 and §545, 2 June and 23 June 1897, Mission 21.

[141] Correspondence between Rudolf Joss, the mission and the AAKA, July 1898–July 1900, in BArch R1001 6350, pp. 56–61, 83. From the available documentation it is unclear whether Joss did return to Cameroon.

Joss' negative experience as an apprentice was far from exceptional. Others such as Anton M'bonga Egiomue and Franz Ekwe showed their dissatisfaction by changing or running away from their apprenticeships.[142] Egiomue changed master at least once and Ekwe complained that a second master treated him as little more than a glorified house servant. Authoritarian supervision by masters was a further source of conflict. Sixteen-year-old Bernhard Epassi, another participant at the Colonial Exhibition, was identified as a problem case. At his own request his master gladly handed him over to the care of Antelmann, for whom Epassi worked during the day before attending classes at a primary school in the evening.[143] Antelmann reported to the Foreign Office: 'Through strong discipline I endeavoured to teach the extremely hot headed boy something of the way of life and orderly circumstances of a European upbringing.'[144] By contrast, Epassi's tutor, the colonial author Paula Karsten, described him as being well brought up, polite, friendly and with a thirst for knowledge.[145] Within a year he requested a change and was sent to a branch of the Colonial House in Kassel. From here he fled to Lübeck against Antelmann's wishes only to return several months later. Incensed to find knuckledusters, photographs and numerous love letters from German women in Epassi's possession, Antelmann resolved to enforce discipline and moral improvement upon Epassi. Again Epassi fled, and this time he began working in a wine bar in Berlin. Antelmann reported this to the AAKA with the request that the young man be transported back to Kribi. Just over a month later Epassi was given a police escort on board the steamer *Aline Woermann* heading for Cameroon.[146] A police report concluded: 'He found so much enjoyment in the life in Berlin that after the end of the exhibition he stayed behind, [but] he was not in a position to adapt to the ways of civilisation.'[147]

The official records concentrate on those Africans who encountered problems, but several of the Cameroonian participants at the Colonial Exhibition, like many other African apprentices, successfully completed their training. Instead of returning to Cameroon at least half of the exhibition participants further prolonged their stay in Germany. Anton

142 For Egiomue, see Conrad Beck to Privy Councillor Schmidt Dargitz, 7 October 1903, BArch R1001 6350, p. 92. For Ekwe, see Missionary C. H. Schwarz to Mission's Administration, 26 January 1912, Mission 21, Q-3-4.

143 Beck to Bruno Antelmann, 8 May 1900, BArch R1001 6350, p. 80.

144 Antelmann to AAKA, 7 May 1900, BArch R1001 6350, pp. 71–2.

145 Karsten, 'Kamerun in Berlin', 97.

146 Police Commissioner, Berlin to AAKA, 26 July 1900, BArch R1001 6350, p. 79.

147 Memorandum on the Question of the Exportation of Natives from the German Colonies for the Purpose of Display, no date, BArch R1001 5576, pp. 27–9, here p. 28. On Epassi, see also Bowersox, 'Kolonial-Lehrling wider Willen'.

Egiomue, Josef Bohinge Boholle, Bruno Ekwe Ngando and Martin Dibobe all remained at least into the 1920s as did the Togolese tailor Josef Garber. It remains unclear why the colonial authorities allowed these individuals to stay. Masters were at least initially required to keep the authorities updated on the progress of their apprentices, but it is quite possible that the authorities simply lost track of them. An exchange of correspondence between Antelmann and the AAKA perhaps offers a different explanation. Antelmann wrote in 1907 that one of the Togolese participants now wished to return home, but the cost of the crossing would be considerably more than originally anticipated. When Antelmann asked the Colonial Department to meet the estimated difference of upwards of 60 Marks per person, the request was politely declined.[148]

The policy of avoiding the further growth of an African presence was reinforced. In keeping with the general retreat from sponsoring any kind of mobility of Africans from the protectorates, the regulation of ethnological exhibitions was tightened. By 1901 the individual administrations of Germany's four African territories had introduced bans on the transportation of Africans for the purpose of display. Displays of people from places other than the German colonies now required the permission of the Colonial Department and in some cases a deposit had to be paid guaranteeing the wages and cost of returning the participants to their homelands.[149]

Abandoned servants and new travel restrictions

Over a quarter of Cameroonians who entered Germany before 1914 did so in the service of returning colonial civil servants, entrepreneurs or private individuals. Variously referred to as 'Boy', 'Hausbursche' or 'Diener', nearly all of these personal servants were male and under twenty years of age. Typically, their experience of Germany was fleeting; only in rare cases did they stay more than a few months before returning with their masters to the protectorates. Some of them would, however, re-enter Germany on one or more further occasions with or without their masters. In cases when they remained on a longer-term basis it was likely that their masters intended to put them through an apprenticeship or that they had been abandoned and left to fend for themselves. Notably in the

148 Antelmann to AAKA, 27 September 1907 and AAKA to Antelmann, 5 October 1907, BArch R1001 6350, pp. 105, 108–9.

149 Thode-Arora, '"Charakteristische Gestalten des Volkslebens"', p. 114; Sippel, 'Rassismus, Protektionismus oder Humanität?'

early 1890s Tongo, a nephew of the Ngila paramount (Figure 1.3), and Zampa, better known as the nationalist hero Martin-Paul Samba (Mebenga m'Ebono), enjoyed a military education in Potsdam thanks to the sponsorship of the Cameroon explorer Lieutenant Kurt von Morgen.[150] Naturally, the Colonial Office (RKA) was more concerned about the frequency of servants being abandoned by their masters and the Department left to bear the cost of returning them. In August 1899 it sent a circular to the various colonial administrations asking that they review thoroughly requests from Europeans to return to Germany with African servants in the light of recent incidents.[151]

Abandonment was likely when ill health or poverty befell the master. The Basel Mission received several letters asking for support from former colonial civil servants and private individuals who were no longer willing or able to look after African children or adolescents whom they had brought to Europe.[152] Just under a year later a further circular was sent, this time to German officers stationed in the protectorates, stressing that it was preferable that they not bring their personal servants to Europe with them. This followed newspaper criticism of a member of the colonial forces who had physically abused a young African in his care in Germany. The circular suggested that 'the usual methods' of educating young people in Africa were not appropriate in Europe.[153]

Among those abandoned by their masters was Johannes Mbida from Yaoundé. In 1909 Mbida was brought to Germany by a certain Mittelstadt and left to wander around Berlin by himself with no source of employment. Mittelstadt explained to the RKA that he no longer had the money to send Mbida back to Cameroon and argued that because Mbida had been granted administrative permission to travel there was no legal prerogative for him to be returned. Nonetheless arrangements were made for Mbida's transportation to the protectorate

[150] On Tongo, see *Verhandlungen der Berliner Gesellschaft für Anthropologie, Ethnologie und Urgeschichte*, 23 (1891), 280–2; Lieutenant Morgen to AAKA, 20 April 1895, BArch R1001 5573, p. 14. Tongo died unexpectedly before he could start training. On Martin-Paul Samba, see Zeller and Michels, 'Kamerunischer Nationalheld'; von Morgen, *Durch Kamerun von Süd nach Nord*.

[151] Hellwig to Puttkamer, 16 August 1899, BArch R1001 5576, p. 30. A similar letter was sent on the same date to the Colonial Governors in German East Africa, German Southwest Africa, Togo and New Guinea. See also von Joeden-Forgey, 'Nobody's People', p. 339.

[152] For examples of abandonment, see District President of Lower Alsace to Committee of the Basel Mission, 4 February 1891; Friedrich to Directorate of the Basel Mission, 16 November 1897; Kies to Oehler, 15 June 1898: all Mission 21, Q-3-4.

[153] Riebow *et al.* (eds.), *Die deutsche Kolonial-Gesetzgebung*, vol. v, pp. 73–4.

at the express request of Governor Seitz.[154] On the date of his intended departure, however, Mbida failed to show at the port in Hamburg. By this time he had found a job with the Bergmann Electrical Works in Berlin earning 20.24 Marks a week and he insisted on being allowed to stay. His cause was helped by a positive reference from his employer and a report filed by the Berlin Police Commissioner which questioned the correctness as well as the legality of forcibly returning Mbida, and the RKA was persuaded to allow him to remain in Germany.[155]

Although Johannes Mbida was permitted to prolong his stay, Seitz was in the process of introducing new measures to prevent such a situation from ever arising again. On 15 October 1910 new Regulations for the Control of the Natives came into force. Would-be travellers still required the permission of the governor before they would be allowed to leave and now a fixed limit was set on the length of their stay outside of Cameroon. Successful applicants were to be placed under the direct care and supervision of a European for the duration of their visit and a deposit of at least 500 Marks had to be left with the administration before departure, as security for any costs of the journey falling to the public charge. Seitz also attempted to initiate the return from Germany of several other Africans, as did the Governor of Togo.[156]

Seitz's policy was certainly influenced by the case of Mbida, but it was also linked to events in Douala. Several months before the introduction of these new restrictions he had refused permission for Ebonge Ndumbe and his father Joseph Bell, brother of Alfred, to travel to Germany. This was partly because of a belief that the men wanted to bring protests against the actions of the colonial administration.[157] Of equal concern to Seitz was a fear of a potential mass migration of Duala to Germany. He believed this was a possibility because many Duala, in return for relinquishing their land to the administration as part of the construction of the *Mittellandbahn* railway line, were now in possession of large amounts of ready money and thus in a position to finance their travel.

[154] Seitz to RKA, 18 August 1909; Mittelstadt to Seitz, 19 August 1909; Mittelstadt to State Secretary of the RKA, 23 August 1909: BArch R1001 4457/6, pp. 18, 25–6, 28.

[155] Graf, Woermann Line, to RKA, 26 August 1909; Police Commissioner Berlin to State Secretary of the RKA, 29 September 1909; RKA to Seitz, 14 October 1909: BArch R1001 4457/6, pp. 23, 29, 30.

[156] Decree of the Governor of Cameroon Concerning Measures for the Control of the Natives, 15 October 1910, BArch R100 4457/6, pp. 53–5. On Togo, see the case of James Emanuel in StAHam, 132-1 I, I 2679 Ausweisung von Schwarzafrikanern aus Hamburg, 1903–12.

[157] Seitz also questioned the benefit of someone of Bell's age, said to be between 45 and 47, being allowed to migrate. Seitz to State Secretary of the RKA, 1 April 1910, BArch R1001 4293, pp. 262–3.

Were Seitz to allow Joseph Bell to leave he feared that many others would soon follow. In the event, the flow of colonial travellers to the metropole was further reduced, but like the 1893 legislation these new restrictions failed to stop Cameroonians coming to Germany. Over three dozen of those on whom we have information arrived between the enactment of Seitz's new restrictions and the outbreak of World War One. Not only were Cameroonians continuing to arrive in Germany, a growing number, like Mbida, were set on making their stay more permanent.

The beginnings of community

Few Africans who arrived in Germany during the colonial period actively sought to take up residence. Of those who reached Europe before 1914 the vast majority returned to Africa before the onset of war. Official controls on travel, themselves a consequence of the experience of the early visitors in both Germany and Cameroon, slowed the growth of the black population though it was unable entirely to put an end to the mobility that fed it. In the event it was not legislation, but the outbreak of war in 1914 that effectively ended travel from the protectorates. By the same token, the war contributed to the crystallisation of elements of community by stabilising the black presence. Africans living in Germany at this time generally had no means of returning home whether they wanted to or not. Instead they were stranded there for at least the duration of the fighting.

Those affected included many who under other circumstances would have remained merely visitors. Among the 'stayers' who feature in subsequent chapters of this book was the (then) schoolboy Stephan Dualla (henceforth Dualla) Misipo, who had only arrived in 1913. But other names that will recur in our story belong to men who had arrived as young adults and were often neither brought nor sent, and of whom we might say they were seeking their fortune in Germany if not necessarily intending to settle. Mandenga Diek was twenty when he arrived 1891 to study medicine at his father's behest; instead he chose to train as a shoemaker, and by the turn of the century he was a successful businessman with a family in Hamburg. Theophilus Wonja Michael was thirty-five and had been living in Germany for at least ten years at the outbreak of war; he told his children he had made his way to Germany working on a ship after being disowned by his father. At seventeen, Anton Egiomue was the youngest of the men who stayed on after the Colonial Exhibition; Martin Dibobe and Bruno Ngando were twenty, Josef Boholle twenty-six, and none of them showed any sign of wanting to leave Germany before the war. Having trained as a mechanic, Dibobe made a successful career as a conductor on the Berlin transport system and became a recognised Berlin 'character'. Joseph Ekwe Bilé and his brother Robert Ebolo assuredly travelled with the approval and support of their father, but when they arrived, each at twenty, to train respectively as an engineer and a teacher, Robert at least was looking forward to working in Germany after his training. Gottlieb Kala (henceforth Kala) Kinger arrived in Germany to train as a teacher but fell in love and decided to stay. Paul Bulu (henceforth Bulu) Malapa was sent to school in Germany at the age of sixteen, but was still there ten years later in 1913. Josef Mambingo, Peter Mukuri Makembe, Wilhelm Edimo Munumé and Joseph Soppo Muange had in common that they were born in the 1890s, after the establishment of the protectorate. Mambingo arrived at twenty-two and started work as a carpenter. Muange arrived in Hamburg as a nineteen-year-old stowaway, Makembe to take up an apprenticeship, Munumé as a servant 'boy' – but by the outbreak of the war they had all struck out on their own in the metropole.

Through men like these, what started at the beginning of the period as a transient population composed of often isolated individuals, their lives to a greater or lesser degree regulated by the colonial and metropolitan authorities, was already developing into clusters of people who could build on relationships they brought with them from home to develop new networks. In fact, the lives of adults among our subjects suggest that to some extent the vision of the lone African at large in Germany was always a product of wishful thinking on the part of the authorities. Most of them kept in contact with family and friends back in Cameroon and it is highly likely that through this correspondence they were informed about other arriving travellers. The missions also acted as nodal points for maintaining communication among Africans in Germany and between Germany and Africa. We have already suggested that Scheve's house was a meeting-place for a range of visitors of varied age and status and of both sexes. Even in wartime, Dualla Misipo, who was at school in Herborn, was sent letters by family in Douala to pass on to his relative Alexander Douala Manga Bell in Neumünster, and this correspondence was facilitated by the Basel Mission.[158] Many of the Duala migrants and some from other regions (especially Kribi) were related to one another and came from similar social backgrounds. Not surprisingly family and friendship networks remained important in Germany itself. Doo Dayas, who went to school in Mannheim, made the not inconsiderable journey to Berlin to meet Alexander, to whom he was related through marriage.

[158] Mixed letters, 1916, Mission 21, E-4.4 Kriegsakten: Briefe von Einheimischen.

Mpundu Akwa remained in written contact with his cousin Andreas Mbange with whom he had travelled to Germany, while among the prize possessions that adorned Alfred Bell's wall in his Bremerhaven apartment was a photograph of the Deido youths with whom he had trained in Hamburg.

In the colonial period there is evidence of the growth of new networks and forms of mutual support and representation developing in the metropolitan context. In 1903 and 1904 Mandenga Diek, who by this time had attained Hamburg citizenship and had considerable experience of dealing with the German authorities, wrote in German to the Colonial Department in Berlin on behalf of first Bruno Ngando and then later David Ibon Dowo, both from Douala. He presented himself as the representative of his two compatriots and formulated their requests for copies of identity papers.[159] Diek also stood as godfather to Ngando when he was baptised in 1900.[160] Similarly the Duala man Victor Bell (Dei Ndumbe) and Paul Mukeke from Malimba visited the Foreign Office on behalf of their friend Gottfried Manga Bell to request that the latter, who was dying of tuberculosis, be provided with help to return to Cameroon.[161] Mukeke and Victor Bell had both arrived in Germany as independent travellers from Lagos in 1909 and London in 1908 respectively, while Gottfried Manga had entered as a seaman in 1909. Men who arrived independently of one another, at different times and in different contexts, had established contact and used these connections for their mutual benefit in dealings with the authorities. Just how exactly people made these contacts remains unclear. In all likelihood Gottfried Manga and Victor Bell would have already known one another in Douala. Gottfried was a son of August Manga Bell, while Victor was an adopted son of August Manga's father. Participation in events such as the Colonial Exhibition also provided a context in which new acquaintances and connections could be established among Africans that cut across family and even ethnic and regional affiliations. In Berlin Bernhard Epassi continued to socialise with at least one of his fellow exhibition participants while he also remained in correspondence with another who was based in Danzig.[162] As will be explored in Chapter 4, as the African population stabilised certain metropolitan centres developed in which migrants were increasingly visible to each other as well as to outside

[159] Mandenga Diek to AAKA, 30 March 1904, BArch R1001 5149, p. 13; Diek to AAKA, 2 October 1903, BArch R1001 6350, p. 94. Dowo had been brought to Germany as a servant in 1903 and was living in Hanover.

[160] D. Nagl, *Grenzfälle*, p. 155.

[161] Report, 30 December 1912, BArch R1001 4443, pp. 19–20.

[162] Karsten, 'Kamerun in Berlin', 98.

observers, often living and working close to one another, in an environment and under circumstances that fostered association both informal and formal.

For Cameroonians who chose to remain numerous impediments still had to be overcome in order for them to be able to establish roots in Germany. As we shall see in the next chapter foremost among these was their status as German colonial subjects rather than citizens, which could impinge upon all aspects of their lives. The sometimes paradoxical consequences of this status were a continuing legacy of the fact that it had not been anticipated that Africans from the protectorates would ever take up permanent residence in Germany.

2 Should I stay and can I go? Status and mobility in the institutional net

On 27 September 1914 the British army captured Douala, a key strategic point in the German protectorate of Cameroon. By February 1916 the German colonial authorities, powerless to stop the advance of French and British troops, had effectively surrendered control of the protectorate, although fighting continued in the far north until the end of the year.[1] The Germans suffered similar setbacks in their other overseas territories and were forced to cede control over them to the Allies by the end of the war. The war had been lost, and under Article 22 of the League of Nations Covenant, which was incorporated into the Versailles Treaty, control of Germany's colonies passed to various of the Allied states. They exercised a mandate with powers delegated by the League and were answerable to the League for their execution of that mandate. The lands in East and West Africa were designated Mandate B territories, 'inhabited by peoples not yet able to stand by themselves under the strenuous conditions of the modern world', and the mandate powers were charged with creating the conditions for modernisation there. (Territories in the former Ottoman Empire considered provisionally fit for self-government and requiring only the transitional support of the mandate powers came under the rubric Mandate A.) The majority of the old Cameroon protectorate, including Douala and the adjacent littoral, came under the control of France, a strip in the northwest adjacent to Nigeria under British control, reflecting and confirming the disposition of the respective armies in the territory since 1916.

The immediate consequence of the outbreak of war was that migration from the German protectorates to Europe effectively ended, and the ending of the protectorate status meant that it could not resume. Very few individuals were able to return from Germany to Africa. Just over a dozen new arrivals appear to have reached Germany after 1914; those who did so arrived either during the war, finding a way to flee

[1] Strachan, *The First World War in Africa*, pp. 19–60.

Cameroon with German colonists, or in the immediate post-war period when travel controls were still in flux. The Abo man N'Seke Nkoti, for example, successfully travelled to Germany in 1916 with a German missionary while three members of the Bell family left the territory in 1920 and arrived in Munich, where they joined a circus.[2]

No reliable figures exist as to the exact size of the German African population in these years. At the beginning of 1919 German Foreign Office officials were seeking Africans willing to declare their loyalty to Germany as part of their agitation against the loss of the colonies.[3] To their disappointment they were only able to find evidence of twenty-five to thirty men from the African protectorates living in the country. In contrast the French colonial authorities, relying partly on information provided by Alexander Douala Manga Bell, believed that there were some 3,000 people from Germany's former African territories still in Germany in 1919.[4] Alexander claimed to know around fifty Cameroonians living in Berlin alone. The true size of this population is more likely to have been closer to the first figure. Of the Cameroonians on whom we have data who arrived in Germany before the outbreak of war, just over fifty men are known to have still been there at the war's end. About a dozen second- and third-generation children had been born by 1914, and around four dozen more children were born before 1933.

Under these conditions, the developing black community was stabilised in the sense at least of being immobilised, and (even if we consider only Cameroonian families) it was beginning to grow and put down roots through the birth of new generations. At the same time, expansion through new in-migration was no longer possible. Moreover, the extent to which any black community would also be German – or to which there were real prospects of settling down and settling in – was also called into doubt by the post-war settlement. Most of our subjects continued to be outsiders in terms of their formal civil status alone – terms distinct from those of 'race' though always inflected by it in practice. In the colonial period, they had been subjects of the German state without rights of

[2] On Nkoti, FR ANOM 110COL 1003/3551. The three Bells are named as Esebou Bell, Ndoumbe Bonny and Rudolphe Mandenge Bell. The former was the uncle of Alexander Bell and the latter two were cousins of Alexander: Foreign Minister to Minister of Colonies, 5 January 1921, FR ANOM 2300 COL 31/289. Mandenge Bell, who was married to a German woman, had been living in Düsseldorf up until 1920 at the latest, when he briefly returned to Cameroon: Governor of the Colonies to Minister of Colonies, 29 March 1920, ANCY APA 10222.

[3] Rüger, 'Imperialismus, Sozialreformismus und antikoloniale demokratische Alternative', 1294.

[4] Note on Interview with Alexander Douala Manga Bell and Elong Ngando, Minister of Colonies, 14 October 1919, FR ANOM 2300 COL 31/289.

nationality or citizenship. In the post-war years, they remained subject *to* the German state, and as a result of the legacy of colonialism their relationship to political authority was different in crucial ways from that of their native-born neighbours. Individuals and agencies which fostered the project of recovering Germany's colonies took a special interest in them. The RKA was wound up in 1919, but a Ministry for Reconstruction took responsibility for prosecuting the colonial interest and dealing with ex-colonial subjects in Germany, and in April 1924 a Colonial Department was created within the Foreign Office.[5] Government agencies in turn worked together with colonialist interest groups and associations. The most significant of these for the daily lives of Africans in Germany was the German Society for the Study of Native Cultures (DGfE), which channelled funds to support individual ex-colonial subjects in Germany.[6] The DKG also continued to involve itself in the affairs of ex-colonials. The attentions of these agencies provided some protection to Africans, but they also constrained their scope for action in ways that will become apparent in subsequent chapters. At the same time, after 1919 the status of Africans and others who had been German colonial subjects was complicated by the fact that they became *actual* subjects of the mandate powers. What that meant in practical terms remained uncertain in many respects; at the very least it meant that most Cameroonians living in Germany who wished to return to Africa, or even travel freely in Europe, had to learn to deal with a foreign power.

At all periods in the lives of Cameroonians in Germany, then, managing everyday life required negotiating complex and shifting webs of formal and informal policy and documentation regimes, and this was the case whether they sought to return to Africa or determined to live as Germans. Moreover the presumption and possibility of return never entirely disappeared, though it meant different things to the authorities and the Cameroonian subjects and was subject to many permutations. If even before 1918 they had been 'nobody's people', the post-war situation was one in which they were simultaneously everywhere and nowhere, their material circumstances as well as their imaginative lives dictated by the new triangulation Germany – Africa – France (or Britain). This chapter sets out in some detail the regulations on nationality status and the documentation regimes that governed their lives both before and after World War One and the ways in which these were applied by the authorities, as well as some examples of how individual Cameroonians managed within them.

[5] Ruppenthal, 'Die Kolonialabteilung', pp. 22–8.
[6] On the origins of the DGfE, see Chapter 4.

Staying I: subjects and citizens

As outlined in Chapter 1, shifting attitudes and expectations on the part of the Wilhelmine colonial authorities meant that before 1918 the conditions of travel for Cameroonian natives varied, and this affected the terms of their presence in the metropole and their visibility to the authorities. In the first twenty-five years of German rule what policies there were focussed on the question of who might leave the protectorate rather than conditions of entry into Germany, and most practice seems to have been premised on the expectation that not the travelling African but his or her host, sponsor or employer was the subject of the journey. The regulations of October 1910 that set out the limitations on travel of Africans from Cameroon provided for the African traveller to be issued with a Native Passport (*Eingeborenen-Reisepaß*) – but as set out in the regulations this document would have provided very little information of the kind that would have been meaningful outside the protectorate. It was to contain the bearer's name, tribal affiliation, last place of residence, current employment (where relevant to the journey), destination and purpose of journey, date of departure and length of time permitted to remain away from the protectorate.[7] Dualla Misipo, who left Cameroon for Germany in 1913 aged twelve, was still using his *Eingeborenen-Reisepaß* as valid proof of his identity in 1939.[8]

For Africans who entered Germany before this requirement was introduced, there was a strong presumption that they were not there as subjects in their own right, and no consistent form of documentation appears to have been in force. In any case, in Wilhelmine Germany there was no requirement on anyone to carry a passport or to present one when crossing the borders of the Reich or any of its constituent federal states. The law did stipulate that every person must be able to present proof of their identity if asked to do so by the authorities, and the respective federal states could issue passports to their 'nationals' who wished to travel to countries requiring a passport for entry.[9] In this period it was not the fact of travel but a change of circumstances within the metropolitan state that meant that a necessity arose for colonial subjects to document their status. In this sense, the 'border' was not the geographical dividing line (or space) between nations and continents, but the point at which the travelling individual came into contact with the machinery of metropolitan

[7] Decree of the Governor of Cameroon Concerning Measures for the Control of the Natives, 15 October 1910, pp. 53–5. See also *RGBl* (1900), 813 and 1908, 397, *DKB*, 13 (1902), 389.

[8] Copy of an *Eingeborenen-Reisepaß* for Dualla Misipo, FR ANOM 110COL 1003/3554.

[9] Torpey, *Invention of the Passport*, pp. 75–92, 108–11.

society in a relatively formal way. In Germany, one such contact point was the requirement to register with the local police at each address. According to his teacher, sixteen-year-old Hans Bell arrived without papers at Dömitz (Mecklenburg) in May 1907 to study music. He had travelled from Cameroon to England and then on to Hamburg as a houseboy, presumably legitimated where necessary by his employer. While he was formally registered at a lodging house on arrival in Hamburg, once he struck out on his own and reached Dömitz the police there refused to register him without documentary evidence of his identity and status. His teacher wrote in some uncertainty to the Colonial Office requesting that an 'identity document and/or passport' be provided – or advice on who else might provide one.[10]

As Bell's case suggests, the consistency with which local police investigated the details of residents for the purposes of registration varied, as did the ways and means of being registered (in person, through one's landlord or host and so on), and many residents, particularly in the big cities, managed to evade the registration system entirely.[11] But those who sought to live a respectable life, to regularise or periodically change their circumstances, could not long avoid the need for identity documents. Marriage was a key event of this kind, and in many, probably most cases it was the intention to marry that precipitated a quest for legitimate civil status on the part of African men. What they generally sought was a *Staatsangehörigkeitsausweis* or certificate of nationality. After 1881, like any indigenous German, a colonial subject would need a *Staatsangehörigkeitsausweis* if he or she changed residence from one federal state to another, or a *Heimatschein* if he or she wanted to travel abroad with a prospect of return.[12] In the case of a colonial subject, either of these documents would identify the bearer as a *Schutzgebietsangehörige(r)* – native of a German protectorate – or *Landesangehörige(r)* of a named protectorate. That is, while a *Staatsangehörigkeitsausweis could* indicate that the bearer was a citizen or a full German national (*Reichsangehöriger*), in the case of a *Schutzgebietsangehörige(r)* it certified no more than that the bearer was subject to German sovereignty. It did not document or confer citizenship rights, and this was in keeping with the general thrust of German legal practice in respect of colonial natives, which denied them the status of legal subjects in either colonial or metropolitan jurisdictions.

10 Franz Rösicke, Dömitz, to Reich Colonial Office, 13 June 1907, BArch R1001 4457/6, p. 12; StAHam 741-4 Fotoarchiv K4222 (Meldewesen).

11 Hochstadt, *Mobility and Modernity*, pp. 59–60.

12 Gosewinkel, *Einbürgern und Ausschließen*, p. 247. For the following discussion of the situation of colonial subjects, see D. Nagl, *Grenzfälle*.

The possibility that *Schutzgebietsangehörigkeit* might be legally stabilised in the direction of full nationality remained open to discussion, but the situation was not settled before World War One, and among the African colonies Cameroon was the one in which there was the least movement in this area. The only way for a native man to attain German citizenship in the protectorate was naturalisation.[13] Under colonial legislation this would depend on his demonstrating a level of 'civilisation' equivalent to that of a European; the presumption was against this being possible, and there is evidence of only one successful application before 1914 (from the Marianna Islands). But the ambiguity of the terminology almost certainly contributed to confusion on all sides, both before and after 1918, and it seems likely that many Cameroonians assumed that they held a status equivalent to that of native-born Germans when they asked for a *Staatsangehörigkeitsausweis*.

For an African resident in Germany who sought naturalisation, the procedure was the same as for any other resident: he or she needed to acquire citizenship in one of the federal states, a status which would automatically confer Reich citizenship under the constitution of 1871.[14] Migrants' civil status, and hence their life course, depended for better as well as for worse on the attitudes of individuals, local institutional cultures and effective networking, and this was particularly true as long as the power of decision remained in local hands. Mandenga Diek, naturalised in 1896, was one of the very few Africans to succeed in acquiring citizenship, and the process was eased by the fact that only local authorities needed to be involved. He made a point of being baptised into the Hamburg Protestant community in one of the city's oldest churches. It was not only this public gesture of assimilation, but positive references from his employer and the Hamburg Police Commissioner that helped to make his application successful.[15]

By contrast, when Robert Bilé applied to be naturalised in Württemberg in 1912, the authorities in Stuttgart sought the advice of the Colonial Office, and this case exemplifies the way in which 'race' – or the systematic distinction between Black and White – gained relevance specifically in relation to the maintenance of political order in the protectorate. The governor in Cameroon shared the view of the Basel Mission, of which Bilé was a member, that he was politically unreliable. He was more

[13] A woman could gain German nationality by marrying a German national, where mixed marriages were not banned. For further discussion of marriage and family, see Chapter 3.

[14] Gosewinkel, *Einbürgern und Ausschließen*, pp. 233–4; Nathans, *The Politics of Citizenship*, pp. 139–67.

[15] StAHam 332-7 Staatsangehörigkeitsaufsicht BIII 51606 Mandenga Diek.

worried, however, about the potential repercussions should Bilé return to the protectorate as a German citizen.[16] His viewpoint informed that of State Secretary Solf who advised against naturalisation. Solf replied to Stuttgart, adopting the governor's wording, that up to then no native of Cameroon had been granted 'Reich nationality and thus the legal status of a White'.[17] In light of Mandenga Diek's experience, this bespoke a wilful ignorance on the part of the Colonial Office, reinforced by the policy preoccupations of the administration in Cameroon. It was a phrase – and a prejudice – that would haunt subsequent cases. At about the same time as Bilé made his application, Thoy Esomber was issued a German passport in Karlsruhe; after the war the authorities in Stuttgart replaced this with a Württemberg passport. In 1925, this passport was confiscated in turn by the Munich police, on the grounds that the original decision to certify his German nationality must have been an error.[18]

The actions of the Munich police against Esomber were based on a reading of the 1913 Nationality Act. The 1913 act introduced the category of 'immediate Reich national' (*unmittelbarer Reichsangehöriger*) for those unable to attain German nationality through citizenship of one of the federal states, and natives of German protectorates *resident in the protectorate* were named among those to whom this status could be granted. For Africans living in Germany, the route to citizenship still went through the federal state. The act introduced a new complication, though; any application, once approved in principle by the local and regional authorities, had to be circulated to all the other federal states for consideration. If substantive objections were raised at this level, the case was to be referred to the Reichsrat, the upper house of the national parliament in both the Wilhelmine and Weimar periods, in which each of the states was represented. Once naturalisation required approval above the local level and an application was likely to be scrutinised by less liberal authorities and those less interested in the personal qualifications of the applicant than in 'principles' of population or racial policy, the chances for success were slim. After 1919, applications for naturalisation from individuals of problematic origin which had been accepted in progressive and urban jurisdictions repeatedly foundered on the objections of more conservative states, notably Bavaria. This was true in particular of Eastern European Jews; public and official anxieties about Germany being 'swamped' by foreigners in the wake of the post-World

16 Governor Cameroon to State Secretary Solf, 16 March 1912, BArch R1001 5149, p. 92.

17 D. Nagl, *Grenzfälle*, p. 156.

18 Fehn to Foreign Office, 15 April 1925, BArch R1001 4457/6, p. 173. Esomber was also known as Thomas Sommern or Thomas Atoy.

War One refugee crisis focussed on this familiar outsider group.[19] But Africans were also affected. Of our first-generation Cameroonians, over the whole period 1890–1933, two (Mandenga Diek and Josef Boholle) certainly acquired German citizenship and two were treated by the authorities as citizens for a time, four are on record as having been refused naturalisation, five were explicitly stated not to be German nationals, and in twenty-five cases the grant of protected person status or freedom to return to Cameroon after 1919 constitutes evidence that they were not German nationals. There are also cases of men being named in official documents as German nationals when there is no evidence and little likelihood of their having been formally naturalised – evidence of the actual fluidity of circumstances and variable attitudes and punctiliousness of local officialdom.

It seems likely that the prospects for naturalisation became slimmer as the reasons for seeking it multiplied. The consequences of statelessness were most keenly felt in the case of marriages between African men and German women, and will be discussed in Chapter 3. A number of requests for naturalisation in the late 1920s were prompted by economic considerations; among other things, it was difficult (though not impossible) for a stateless person to engage in work that required international travel. When Thoy Esomber asked a prominent German for his assistance in recovering German nationality in November 1929, it was to enable him to regain work in a circus. The men who were directly party to the correspondence around Esomber's case were not optimistic, both because Esomber was dependent on public assistance and because his initial application would be made in conservative Bavaria. But Esomber was emboldened in his application by what he knew of other Africans, Josef Boholle and the Togolese Johannes Kohl, who had recently (and he believed successfully) applied for naturalisation.[20]

Josef Boholle's naturalisation, to which Esomber referred, was itself most likely the result of an economically motivated application. In 1928 he, his wife, their two teenage sons and his twenty-one-year-old daughter Josefa were granted Prussian and German citizenship. Josefa was a successful dancer, and proof of her substantial income along with evidence of her father's respectability contributed to the success of their applications, even over the predictable objections of the conservative Thuringian

[19] See Gosewinkel, *Einbürgern und Ausschließen*, pp. 249–77; Oltmer, *Migration und Politik*; Sammartino, 'Culture, Belonging and the Law', pp. 57–72; Nathans, *The Politics of Citizenship*, p. 208.

[20] Fehn to Eltester, 21 November 1929, BArch R1001 4457/7, pp. 182–3; Eltester to Fehn, 17 January 1930, BArch R1001 5149, p. 152. Esomber was mistaken about Johannes Kohl, whose application for naturalisation is discussed in Chapter 3.

Interior Ministry.[21] Since she had argued that she needed German nationality in order to be able to travel freely for professional purposes, it seems possible that the application was made at her suggestion.[22]

Staying II: documentation regimes

Regularising one's civil status was thus less about actualising a sentimental allegiance than about acquiring the freedom to act associated with status, and that freedom was certified by the possession of identity documents. Changing forms of documentation and management regimes accordingly had real meaning for the everyday lives of African subjects. The promulgation of the 1913 Nationality Act was one of three changes between 1900 and the 1920s that tended to make naturalisation more problematic. The other two were consequences of World War One and its messy conclusion. The war itself led to closer controls on the movement of people across borders throughout Europe and the colonial world. The end of the war and the Versailles Treaty set people in motion across Europe, with the consequence that the German authorities were particularly vigilant and suspicious of foreigners of all kinds. Moreover, the elimination of Germany's sovereignty over its former colonial subjects closed down any prospect of automatic access to German nationality and undermined the presumption that they had any claim to the goodwill of the German state.

The beginning of World War One in 1914 brought with it the introduction of compulsory passports, first for anyone entering German territory and then for anyone leaving or entering the country. Foreigners resident in Germany were also obliged to carry passports. For those who were unable to qualify for a passport, other forms of identification such as the *Staatsangehörigkeitsausweis* or *Heimatschein* could be accepted. The passport was to carry a physical description of the bearer, a photograph, the bearer's signature and confirmation by the local police authorities of the bearer's identity. It appears that these stipulations were also applied to alternative identity papers where that was not already the practice. In mid 1916 a form was prescribed for the issue of new identity papers that would be valid for travel for anybody unable to acquire a valid passport, under the term *Personalausweis* (personal identity document).

[21] Thuringian Interior Ministry to Reich Interior Minister, 14 November 1927, BArch R1001 4457/7, p. 64.

[22] LAB A Pr Br Rep 030-06, No. 6473 Einbürgerungsantrag Josef Boholle. On Josefa see also Robert S. Abbott, 'My Trip Abroad. VIII: The Negro in Berlin', *Chicago Defender*, 28 December 1929, p. 8.

Figure 2.1 Identity papers, Gottlieb Kala Kinger, 1922

This was the document that German colonial subjects and after 1919 former colonials would need to carry, as long as they possessed neither German nationality nor the nationality of any other state empowered to issue passports. A *Personalausweis*, like a passport, could be endorsed for travel only within the Reich, apparently at the discretion of the issuing authority. It had to be renewed regularly, at a passport office operated by the local police authorities in Germany or a consular office abroad, and a fee was charged on each occasion. Kala Kinger's *Personalausweis* of 1922 saw plenty of use, since his work as a performer meant that he travelled around northern and central Europe; it shows renewals at roughly three-monthly intervals over the year, mainly at consular offices abroad (Figure 2.1). Under a 1924 decree, issued in association with the League of Nations deliberations on the status of stateless persons and refugees, the *Personalausweis* was valid for a year and could be extended once before a new one had to be issued.[23]

[23] Gosewinkel, *Einbürgern und Ausschließen*, p. 247; Torpey, *Invention of the Passport*, pp. 113–14; relevant legislation in *RGBl* (1914), 1:264–5 and 521–2; *RGBl* (1916), 1:601–9; *RGBl* (1924), 1:616–17.

Changes in the documentation regime had an impact on daily life without necessarily affecting status. The more often a document needed to be renewed, the greater the inconvenience and the greater the danger that the bearer might fail to renew it. Infringement of passport regulations – not having one's papers when challenged by the police or presenting papers that were out of date – was in principle a punishable offence, and the more visibly 'foreign' an individual was the more likely they were to be challenged.[24] The need to renew one's papers regularly also increased opportunities for police surveillance and for the interference of unsympathetic officials, as Thoy Esomber found in 1925.

In June 1932, the *Personalausweis* as surrogate passport was done away with. Instead stateless persons were to carry a *Fremdenpaß*, or Alien's Passport, renewable annually for up to five years.[25] It is not clear what the motivation behind this move was. It was enacted by the arch-conservative government that was appointed that month with the tacit support of the Nazi Party. The new government simultaneously brought in new measures to rationalise unemployment and welfare support in the face of the deepening Depression, and this may have been intended to make it easier to identify quickly those who were ineligible for benefits. The *Fremdenpaß* was issued to all stateless persons regardless of race or national origin, but for former colonial subjects, like others who thought of themselves as German, the new documentation enforced a new and hurtful regime of discrimination. Before the war *Personalausweis* was a generic term for identity documents issued by the federal states, and even after the war and the introduction of passports German nationals continued to carry them. By contrast, the *Fremdenpaß* immediately and emphatically identified its bearer as an outsider to the national community. The heading 'surrogate passport' which the *Personalausweis* had carried disappeared, and was replaced by the explicit statement that 'the bearer does not possess German nationality'. There was no longer space to indicate that the bearer had any positive connection to the Reich, whether as former national or as former colonial subject. Under 'distinguishing characteristics' the word *Neger* was routinely entered.

[24] Examples of prosecutions include Thomas Manga Akwa 1932, BArch R1001 5149, p. 128; Mohamed Husen 1935, Bechhaus-Gerst, *Treu bis in den Tod*, p. 78. For examples of Africans challenged by the police to present identity papers to legitimate themselves before World War One: Same Tobi, BArch R1001 5149, pp. 32–3; Bruno Ngando, BArch R1001 6350, p. 89.

[25] *RGBl* (1932), 1:257–61.

Being in two places at the same time: 'protected persons'

The documentation that definitively declared these people 'alien' raised by implication the question of what might be done with them. In the case of undesirable aliens, the local police enjoyed considerable powers to enforce arbitrary deportations, and their readiness to do so during the 1920s is well documented.[26] But colonial subjects were not so easily dealt with, because before 1919 they were not quite foreigners, and after 1919 it was not immediately clear what kind of foreigners they were.

The post-war transfer of sovereignty over Germany's protectorates precipitated a change in the nationality status of the natives who had formerly been *Schutzangehörige* of the Reich. Article 127 of the Versailles Treaty stipulated that 'the native inhabitants of the former German possessions shall be entitled to the diplomatic protection of the governments exercising authority over those territories'. In 1921 the League's Permanent Mandates Commission undertook to investigate and regularise the status of natives, in consultation with the British and French governments.[27] The British agreed to extend to mandate subjects the status of 'British Protected Person'. This category already existed in British law to designate natives of territories under British protectorate who were neither colonial subjects nor British; as such they did not enjoy the rights or status of British subjects. They carried travel documents identifying them as British Protected Persons (and still do), but just what claims they had on the British state beyond diplomatic protection remained uncertain and contested. The question became more vexed as the 1919 mandates extended to black Africans a status which had up to then been enjoyed mainly by the natives of formerly self-governing principalities in the middle east and Asia.[28] The Colonial Office in London had already concluded that the term 'native inhabitant' in the Treaty – and hence the scope of those eligible for diplomatic protection – covered natives 'whose domicile of origin was within the territory in question and who [have] not acquired a different domicile'. This raised the question of what constituted a different domicile, and on the whole the British authorities were uneasy about extending protection to natives who appeared to have settled in Europe.[29]

26 Oltmer, *Migration und Politik*, pp. 64–5, 489.

27 Callahan, *Mandates and Empire*, p. 111 – also for what follows.

28 Tabili, *'We Ask for British Justice'*, pp. 33–6.

29 Colonial Office (London) correspondence August–September 1920, in NAK CO 649-21 Cameroons 42787. The correspondence was prompted by an enquiry from the Cameroonian Alfred Köhler to the British Consulate in Venice.

France also had its category of 'protected person' (*protégé*) inherited from pre-war protectorates over Morocco and Tunisia, but the French resisted extending this term to their new charges. The tendency of French policy was to apply in the mandate territories of Cameroon and Togo the practice that applied in France's own African colonies; this envisaged the assimilation of colonial subjects to French culture as part of a general process of incorporating the overseas territories into a unitary empire. In black Africa French administration distinguished between indigenous subjects (*sujets*) governed directly under special regulations and *évolués* who were sufficiently acculturated to qualify for rights equivalent to those of French citizens. (The exception to this was the 'Four Communes' of Senegal – Saint Louis, Gorée, Dakar and Rufisque – whose inhabitants, like the natives of Guadeloupe and Martinique, enjoyed a form of French citizenship.)[30] Under pressure from the Permanent Mandates Commission, the phrase 'administered persons [*administrés*] under mandate' was adopted in 1922; 'natives of Togo/Cameroon, protected persons [*protégés*] under French mandate' was adopted in 1923.[31] In the same year a League of Nations resolution confirmed that the natives of mandate territories did not and should not enjoy the nationality of the mandate power, although individuals could be naturalised subject to appropriate metropolitan legislation. Natives of France's sub-Saharan African colonies also did not have a nationality of their own, but their relationship to the French state was at least better established than that of the *protégés*.[32]

The Cameroonians living in Europe were entitled to no more, but no less, than diplomatic protection, and they were clearly aware of this. The records of French consulates in Germany show Cameroonians and their family members registering there as persons eligible for French protection and being issued with French passports as early as 1921.[33] What this protection meant in practice remained unclear. In 1923 Thomas Ngambi ul Kuo escaped an expulsion order from Strasbourg because the local court held that as a protected person he was not subject to the laws controlling the residence of aliens in France. The French Foreign Ministry rejected this position and insisted that Ngambi's entitlement to diplomatic protection *outside of* France did not imply that

[30] Conklin, *A Mission to Civilize*, pp. 166–9.
[31] Callahan, *Mandates and Empire*, pp. 110–13.
[32] Bruschi, 'La Nationalité dans le droit colonial'.
[33] Registrations and passport applications are recorded in French consular records in CADN.

he could not be treated as a foreigner *in* the metropolis. This left open the question of where Ngambi might have been expelled *to*.[34]

Leaving: repatriation

The extent to which either the French or the German authorities showed awareness of the responsibilities the transfer from German to French control incurred, and the way in which mandate protection was exercised, depended very largely on the policy concerns of the respective powers. The attitudes of successive post-war German administrations to Africans in Germany reflected a preoccupation with maintaining order (social, political and increasingly 'racial') in Germany, while continuing to promote the colonialist project that had brought Africans to Europe in the first place. For the French, the principal policy concern was maintaining order in the mandate territories while they decided how they fitted into the wider French imperium. The practice of the authorities in the mandate powers was shaped by tensions of various kinds among the respective Interior, Foreign and Colonial Offices and the administrators in the mandate territories. Typically the interior and foreign officers were more alert to wider policy issues, including those of international treaties and human rights, while the administrators on the ground in Africa were concerned about public order in the territory, and the colonial officers in the metropole were poised between them, articulating a paternalist vision of how to handle Africans. In Germany, the ex-colonial administrators in the Colonial Department and the DGfE, some of whom had known the Cameroonians with whose cases they had had to deal since before the war, displayed some grounded knowledge of their circumstances and sometimes acted as advocates in the face of metropolitan bureaucracy and prejudice. The tensions generated by these configurations impacted directly on the lives of individuals especially where return to Cameroon – voluntary or forced – was at issue.

Return to the old protectorate was now dependent on the approval of the new protectors. As early as August 1919 the French consul in Berlin reported to the Foreign Ministry in Paris that numerous Cameroonians had approached him asking for permission to return home and to be provided with the necessary documents to allow them to do so.[35] Other French consulates throughout Germany received similar queries.[36]

[34] Correspondence in FR ANOM 2300 COL 30/259.
[35] Consul Berlin to Foreign Minister, 18 August 1919, FR ANOM 2300 COL 25/218.
[36] Foreign Minister to Minister of Colonies, 6 September 1920, FR ANOM 2300 COL 31/284.

The archives contain information on fourteen Cameroonians who requested repatriation from the French authorities in the first five years following the end of the war.[37] In several cases the explicit reason given for seeking repatriation was unemployment or poverty; post-war economic and political turmoil meant that Germany was not a particularly comfortable place.[38] It is likely, however, that there was also a pull-factor behind authentic requests for repatriation, given that the travellers had always expected to return home at some point. Most of these men had spent more time in Germany than they had originally intended and had been effectively disconnected from their families in Cameroon during the war. Theodor Michael said of his father Theophilus that the years after the end of the German empire were 'a very difficult time for him because he had become disoriented. His longing was always: to return home, home.'[39] Theophilus, along with Anton Egiomue and Martin Dibobe, requested help from old Colonial Office contacts to take their families back to Cameroon, and would continue to seek repatriation throughout the 1920s.[40] For some, the dream of return combined present hopes for economic improvement with nostalgia for a world in which they had been valued members of elite families.

Not least because of their potential influence back home, German-speaking Cameroonians were viewed by the French as a potentially

[37] Martin Dibobe, Bello Naue, Theophilus Michael, Thomas Manga Akwa, Mandenga Diek, Peter Makembe, Wilhelm Munumé, Joseph Bilé, Gottlieb Kala Kinger, Josef Mambingo, Heipold Jansen, Subeiru bin Adamu, Kassan Ndanke and Paul Messi. Another three, Reinhold Elong Ngando, Rudolphe Njo Bell and Harry Thomson Mandenge, made their way back to Cameroon by other means; none of them remained there. The further case of Alexander Douala Manga Bell is *sui generis* because of its political character: As heir to the martyred Rudolf Duala Manga Bell and presumptive head of the Bell clan and political leader of the Duala, Alexander was allowed to travel to Paris and settled there with his young family – and briefly his mother and sisters – while the French authorities decided when and how he should be allowed to return: see Joseph, 'The Royal Pretender'. The repatriation case of the Beti chief Karl Atangana was similarly political, though different in its geography: see Chapter 3.

[38] For examples see the case of Josef Mambingo, Repatriation Demand, 7 April 1921, FR ANOM 2300 COL 25/218; Political Department to Minister of Colonies, 29 January 1921, FR ANOM 2300 COL 31/284; documents on Joseph Bilé's request in BArch R1001 4457/6.

[39] Theodor Michael, interviewed in 'Die erste Erfahrung'. For Theophilus Michael's attempts to return, see Chapter 3. Not all applicants for French passports wanted to leave Europe; Wilhelm Munumé applied for a passport in October 1920 in order, he said to visit France to learn French: Foreign Minister to Minister of Colonies, 31 October 1920, FR ANOM 2300 COL 31/294.

[40] Mansfeld, Association for German Settlement and Migration (VfdSW), to British Passport Control Office Berlin, 5 May 1920, and associated correspondence, NAK CO 649-21 Cameroons no. 24858. On Alfred Mansfeld, see Chapter 5. He wrote requesting British permission for the families to travel via Lagos.

subversive element and their return was generally deemed to be undesirable. This was particularly true of the Duala, who had a record of political fractiousness in dealing with the German authorities that showed no sign of abating under French control. It was also feared right from the start that even if their instincts were not anti-colonial they were likely to be pro-German and anti-French, and the actions of Duala spokesmen in both Cameroon and Germany at the end of the war went some way to confirming those suspicions. As a result background checks were carried out on all Cameroonians who requested repatriation for evidence of continuing loyalty to Germany. The French Commissioner in Cameroon made a direct reference to Kala Kinger's association with Martin Dibobe, by now a known political activist, as a reason for refusing Kinger permission to return to Cameroon.[41]

While the French Minister of Colonies and the Commissioner in Cameroon investigated the possibilities of preventing the return of individuals they considered to be of dubious character, the French Foreign Ministry was convinced from the start that repatriation requests could not be denied under the terms of the Versailles Treaty.[42] As a result eleven of the fourteen Cameroonians known to have asked to return were granted safe passage to sail from Bordeaux or Marseilles to Africa. Of the three other applications, two outcomes remain unknown and one applicant, Bello Naue, was advised to contact the British authorities.[43] In spite of the reservations of the British Colonial Office, Naue, working as a hawker in the Netherlands after spending the war in Germany, was granted a British Protected Person passport in 1921.[44] It was not until 1926, however, that the British consulate in Berlin formally declared itself willing to help former colonial subjects from the British mandate

41 Commissioner Cameroon to Minister of Colonies, 30 October 1923, FR ANOM 1 AFFPOL 613/1071. On Dibobe's activism, see Chapter 6.

42 Much of this discussion developed around the case of Peter Makembe discussed in Chapter 4. See Minister of Colonies to Foreign Minister, 18 September 1920, FR ANOM 2300 COL 31/284; Telegram, Minister of Colonies to Commissioner Cameroon, 4 September 1920, FR ANOM 2300 COL 31/280; Foreign Minister to Minister of Colonies, 6 September 1920, and Minister of Colonies to Foreign Minister, 18 September 1920, FR ANOM 2300 COL 31/284; Foreign Minister to Minister of Colonies, 22 September 1920, FR ANOM 2300 COL 25/218.

43 French archival sources contain no answer to Kassan Ndanke's 1920 request to return to Cameroon contained in FR ANOM 2300 COL 31/282. Similarly, no answer was received to a repatriation request on behalf of Joseph Bilé: Kümpel to Minister for Reconstruction, 22 July 1921, BArch R1001 4457/6, p. 154.

44 Colonial Office (London) note, 1 February 1933 and other correspondence, NAK CO 554/89/12; Bello Naue to Ministry of Colonies (Paris), 8 August 1920, FR ANOM 2300 COL 31/281.

territory to return.[45] In contrast residents of Germany who originated from the French mandate territory were not only allowed to travel back to Cameroon in the early years, but in most cases they were provided with funds to travel to France and to sustain themselves while they waited to leave as well as to pay for their passage.[46]

It appears that only half of these men ever left for Africa. The career of the Duala Heipold Jansen suggests that some of them did not intend to – at least not immediately. What counted was having a valid passport that would give them freedom to seek their fortunes. Jansen received permission to travel from Berlin to Cameroon via France in December 1920.[47] However, he disappeared from his hotel in Paris and never appeared at Bordeaux to catch his boat. Instead, he turned up two years later at the Colonial Service office in Marseille, now asking to be allowed to go to Italy. When challenged as to why he had not previously left for Cameroon, Jansen responded that he did not believe that he would be able to find employment there in his chosen profession of chauffeur. He claimed to have left France and taken up a job with the British navy as a machinist on board a boat that was heading for Cuba. Later he returned to Berlin via Holland, and he had in his possession a certificate stating that he had worked for nine months as a chauffeur in the German capital. Eventually, Jansen explained, he had headed to Switzerland, Luxembourg and finally France. The French authorities were suspicious, and resolved to investigate further to ensure that he was not a German agent.[48] Before they could do so Jansen disappeared once more. He resurfaced in Germany in the late 1920s as a jazz musician and again requested help to return to Cameroon, this time from the German authorities.[49] By the late 1930s he had illegally managed to procure a British passport which he had been using to travel both outside and inside of Germany until stopped by the

[45] This is referred to in Report from D. A. W. Schreiber, The Tasks of the DGfE, 9 September 1927, BArch R8023 1077a, pp. 34–8, here p. 35. The French Commissioner in Cameroon was aware of British policy regarding repatriation and suggested that the French adopt a similar policy: Commissioner Cameroon to Minister of Colonies, 23 November 1920, FR ANOM 2300 COL 25/218.

[46] For examples see the cases of: Subeiru bin Adamu, FR ANOM 2300 COL 31/285; Manga Akwa, FR ANOM 2300 COL 31/284; Josef Mambingo, FR ANOM 2300 COL 25/218.

[47] Telegram, Consulate Berlin to Foreign Minister, 18 December 1920, FR ANOM 2300 COL 31/286.

[48] Interim Minister for the Liberated Territories to Interior Ministry (Sûreté Générale), 18 January 1923, FR ANOM 2300 COL 31/286.

[49] Eifler (DGfE) to Foreign Office, 16 January 1930, BArch R1001 4457/7, p. 234. Just under 300 Marks were to be provided towards the costs of repatriating Jansen: DGfE to Foreign Office, 27 January 1930, BArch R1001 4457/7, p. 236.

police in Saarbrücken. He was subsequently declared stateless by the German foreign office.[50]

When men did return their refusal to cooperate with the authorities often served to confirm French anxieties.[51] The problems of accommodation to the colonial order that had faced returning migrants before 1914 were also experienced by those re-entering the territory in the early 1920s. The mandate authorities kept detailed lists of suspected Germanophiles who were then kept under observation by the local authorities. Typically these were men who had profited from German rule, who had worked for the administration or German firms before World War One, or who had protested against the arrival of the French. Cameroonians who had spent time in Germany also automatically came under suspicion, regardless of when they had returned to Cameroon. The former interpreter for the German postal service in Lolodorf, Namalui Schwamme, who had spent several years in Germany before 1914, featured on a list of suspected German sympathisers in Kribi and was described as being 'extremely devoted to Germany'.[52] Ekwe Bell, brother of Rudolf Duala Manga, Paul Messi and Awoudi were named as hostile elements in Yaoundé, all on account of the fact that they had spent time in Germany.[53] Mandate officials were not averse to using physical violence, ransacking houses, imprisoning or deporting to the north of the territory individuals they suspected of undermining their authority. There is no evidence that such an extreme fate awaited returnees, but a handful of them chose not to remain in Cameroon and managed to return to Germany. Harry Thomson Mandenge left for Germany after having spent six months back in Douala in 1920 because, according to the French Commissioner, he had become too accustomed to life in Europe.[54]

Thomas Manga Akwa (Figure 2.2), on the other hand, was forced to flee Douala after coming into conflict with the mandate authorities. Manga Akwa, nephew of the former Akwa leader Dika Akwa, returned to Douala at the beginning of 1921 after eleven years in Berlin. In Germany he had trained in agricultural-machine building with the

50 Bielfeld (Department X) to State Police, Berlin, 29 March 1939, BArch R1001 6383, p. 312.

51 Commissioner Cameroon to Minister of Colonies, 30 October 1923.

52 Head of District, Kribi to Commissioner Cameroon, 16 November 1922, ANCY APA 10222.

53 Head of District, Yaoundé to Commissioner Cameroon, 30 December 1922, ANCY APA 10222, and lists of undesirables in the same files.

54 Commissioner Cameroon to Minister of Colonies, 18 February 1929, FR ANOM 1 AFFPOL 613/1073.

Figure 2.2 Thomas Manga Akwa, date unknown

firm Richard Heike based in Alt-Hohenschönhausen, before working in a munitions factory during the war.[55] Unable to find employment after the

[55] Political Department to Minister of Colonies, 29 January 1921, FR ANOM 2300 COL 31/284.

war he sought repatriation. According to his version of events, shortly after arrival in Cameroon he held a pro-German talk to Duala elders that was discovered by the French authorities.[56] As a result he was accused of being a German spy and forced to flee the territory. The report of the French Head of District in Douala tells a slightly different story. He wrote that Manga Akwa had been involved in provocative activities such as planning the erection of a monument in the Akwa quarter of the city that was to serve as a meeting place for the local population.[57] Construction of the monument was prohibited as were all planned meetings and Manga Akwa was accused of embezzling funds already raised for the project by his fellow Duala. He was said to have disappeared from Cameroon in a canoe heading for the island of Fernando Po; from there he managed to return to Germany. Manga Akwa was now confirmed as a German agent in the eyes of the French authorities. In 1930, when he was unemployed and largely destitute in Berlin, the German authorities requested on his behalf that he be returned to Cameroon. The request was denied, as was a request he submitted in his own name a few months later.[58]

Such incidents may have led to a hardening of French attitudes; French and German archival material for the years 1924–7 contains only one further repatriation decision. In October 1923 the Commissioner in Cameroon reiterated his desire to prevent migrants from returning because of the problems they caused local authorities.[59] In June 1927, however, the Foreign Ministry still issued a positive response to Joseph Muange's request for safe passage.[60] It is thus possible that the dip in the volume of correspondence around repatriation reflects a genuine decline in the numbers of Cameroonians wishing to leave during a period of relative economic prosperity in Germany, though the state of the archives does not allow any certain conclusions.

By the late 1920s the German authorities in their turn were increasing their efforts to repatriate former colonial subjects. Throughout the interwar period German policy towards former colonial subjects still in

[56] Manga Akwa to [Theodor Seitz] [transcript copy], 15 June 1929, BArch R1001 4457/7, pp. 144–5.

[57] See 1921 report quoted in District Head, Douala to Commissioner Cameroon, 17 September 1930, ANCY APA 10226.

[58] Correspondence of 1930 in ANCY APA 10226; Minister of Colonies to Foreign Minister, 18 August 1930, and Manga Akwa to Minister of Colonies, 4 February 1931, FR ANOM 1 AFFPOL 613/1062.

[59] These views were expressed in reference to an application for repatriation from Kala Kinger, which eventually received a positive response: Commissioner Cameroon to Minister of Colonies, 30 October 1923.

[60] See the case of Joseph Muange in FR ANOM 1 AFFPOL 613/1073.

Germany was largely shaped by lingering hopes that Germany would one day recover control over its former protectorates. This meant that the African presence was to be tolerated for fear of negative publicity and accusations of mistreatment. The long-term goal of ensuring the return of all former colonial subjects to Africa, however, remained unchanged. In October 1926 it was still the understanding of the German Foreign Office that a Cameroonian who had remained resident in Germany after the war rather than returning to Cameroon did *not* enjoy protected person status under the terms of the mandate.[61] But in the following years the difficulties that Africans were facing in finding work focussed the minds of the DGfE and the Foreign Office. By May 1928 at the latest Foreign Office staff had agreed to an initiative whereby all ex-colonial natives who could not support themselves should be returned to Africa. They knew that this would require insisting that the mandate powers acknowledge their responsibilities towards their protected persons, but also that that was realistic: following the evidence of British willingness to accept repatriates, in 1927 the French consulate in Berlin had formally confirmed that natives of Cameroon who registered with the consulate would be deemed to be French subjects and provided with passports enabling them to return to Cameroon.[62] Two problems remained from the point of view of the German authorities. First, by no means all former colonial subjects had registered, and second, the Commissioner in Cameroon now apparently had the final say as to whether or not migrants could return. The Commissioner could, and did, as in the case of Manga Akwa, refuse requests for safe conduct or he could simply ignore them, leaving those concerned effectively stranded in Germany. This was a source of frustration to the German authorities; for Cameroonians, it presented an existential challenge as the economic and political climate began to turn against them. By this time, men's desire to leave Germany was often informed by the fact of having a wife and children – the family which had originally provided the rationale for settling and seeking citizenship.

[61] Certificate issued by the Foreign Office for Jakob Mandenge, 5 October 1926, StAWürzburg, Regierung Unterfranken Einbürgerung 982, p. 19.

[62] Report from Schreiber, The Tasks of the DGfE, p. 35; DGfE to Foreign Office, 25 April 1927 and 15 May 1928, BArch R1001 4457/7, pp. 30, 121–2.

3 Settling down: marriage and family

The vicissitudes of civil status and the way in which it was managed not only affected the freedom of movement of Africans in Europe; they shaped their private lives as well. This chapter begins an examination of what we can learn about the quest for self-fulfilment in sexuality and parenthood and its implications for both community and individual identity, which we continue in Chapter 5. Those who did not return permanently to Cameroon, whether through choice or misadventure, needed to construct a life worth living in Germany, and a key feature of this was establishing sexual partnerships, marrying and building families. These were all 'mixed' relationships in terms of the nationality of the partners, and nearly all in terms of their 'race'. This was in turn a reflection of the gender imbalance among travellers from Africa to Germany. Our whole sample group of Cameroonians comprises eleven women certainly of the first generation. By contrast, eighty-two men who arrived in the first generation stayed on in Germany for at least four years. What this meant was that they were bound to seek partners for both casual liaisons and long-term relationships among native-born Germans. For forty-three men of that generation records have survived that give some indication of their family circumstances. All but two of their partnerships were with white women, and in all but three of these cases the couple either married or documented an intention to marry. In addition, two women of the second generation had relationships with African-born men, both Cameroonian and non-Cameroonian. Marriage, then, meant not only putting down roots in Germany (for a time at least), but also making new connections both with white Germans and with other Blacks. This chapter focuses on those families, considering when, why and how people married and the challenges they faced in building and sustaining households. Among those challenges was a creeping racialisation of official language and attitudes after World War One. If the loss of empire had made it all the more imperative for administrators trained in the colonialist ethos to hold the colour line at home, mixed families were by definition a problem of a particular kind. And at the same time those families were finding their way to 'domestic dwelling' into the second and even the third generation.

Meeting and courtship

It is difficult to reconstruct the specific circumstances under which African men met and formed relationships with women in Germany. The sources for the details of private life, rare at the best of times, are particularly limited in this case. The most detailed account we have of the sexual and emotional life of one of our subjects takes the form of an autobiographical novel, *Der Junge aus Duala* by Dualla Misipo. That text records a first encounter between lovers in which the (German) woman watches the (African) man competing in and winning a student track event and introduces herself to him in the canteen afterwards.[1] This is almost certainly invented, but Misipo may well have met his wife, Luise Dutine, in the Frankfurt student circles that he frequented in the 1920s; by coincidence, her father, like his father back in Cameroon, was a post office employee and she was working as a typist.[2]

There are other cases where we may presume that the couple met each other in a shared occupational or neighbourhood milieu: Bruno Ngando seems to have met his wife when they were both working in a restaurant in Hanover.[3] The first wife of shoemaker Anton Egiomue, Alice Henke, was a dressmaker, the daughter of a roofer whose family had been in Berlin for at least two generations. Mathias Ndonge's wife Johanna was a shop assistant, the daughter of a labourer and his wife who had migrated to Hamburg from the Prussian East; a Dora Ndumbe lived in the same apartment block as Johanna's widowed mother at the beginning of World War One, and it is possible that Johanna and Mathias (who married in 1921) met through her. Jakob Mandenge's wife Barbara was a milliner, daughter of a lithographer. Georg Soppo Ekambi Menzel's wife Charlotte was officially registered as a 'worker'.[4]

1 Misipo, *Der Junge aus Duala*, pp. 29–30.

2 Compensation claims Dualla Misipo and Luise Misipo née Dutine, 1954–60, Hessisches Hauptstaatsarchiv, Wiesbaden (HHStAW) 518/40437 and 518/2469/22.

3 On Ngando, see D. Nagl, *Grenzfälle*, p. 155.

4 On Egiomue, information from Bianca Welzing Landesarchiv Berlin; *Berliner Adressbuch* 1875–1904; on Mandenge, Betty (*sic*) Mandenge to Landratsamt Würzburg, 7 July 1958, StAWürzburg, LRA Würzburg 377; on Ndonge, Malapa and Menzel, StAHam 741-4 Fotoarchiv K7006, K6509, K4172. On Dora Ndumbe and Johanna, StAHam 332-8 K7006; *Hamburger Adressbuch* 1913, 1914. The blacksmith Jakob Ndumbe's wife signed herself Dora, but the Ndumbes lived in Berlin and it is not possible to state with any certainty that the Hamburg Dora was Jakob's wife. The name certainly suggests a Cameroonian connection.

That said, the fragments of lives that make up the 'official' record often compose no more than a snapshot whose pre-history remains obscure. When Kala Kinger married Bertha Brühl in 1923 they were both working as entertainers, but according to family lore they had met while he was still training to be a teacher – as much as ten years earlier. It was their meeting that had decided him to stay in Germany, and at that point they had embarked together on a career as stage dancers. Bertha was four years older than Kinger and had been married before. The witnesses at their wedding included their neighbour, a brushmaker, and Bertha's brother, a musician. This was clearly a strong relationship which enjoyed the support of Bertha's family and which survived both National Socialism (in spite of Bertha's family being Jewish) and Kinger's wartime relationship with another woman. After the war the child of that relationship lived with Kinger, Bertha and Bertha's mother and sister.[5]

Relationships in the metropole could also be rooted in transoceanic networks built up in the colonial period. The ties between African travellers and their missionary patrons and hosts could be close, emotionally charged and persistent, and similar lasting ties developed between some individual Cameroonians and colonial officers and administrators.[6] There is a hint of this in what we know of the relationship between Joseph Bilé and Helene Lück. When she bore their daughter in 1929, he had been associated with the family for several years. As early as 1921 he was lodging at Helene Lück's address in the Goltzstraße in Berlin, where her widowed mother was also living. Helene's father, a furniture polisher, had been living in Berlin since 1912, but there is evidence of a Lück family settled in Cameroon and travelling between Berlin and Douala in the same years, so it is possible that Bilé got to know the Berlin Lücks through mutual acquaintances.[7]

Transoceanic links of another kind came into play in late 1923, when the French colonial authorities began monitoring the mail of Joseph Ekwé Dick, now resident in Cameroon. He was suspected of being a Germanophile on account of his recent trip to Germany and his family history; the attention of the Douala authorities was drawn to him by a

[5] Berger, '"Sind Sie nicht froh...?"'; marriage certificate, FR ANOM 1 AFFPOL 613/1071.

[6] The best example of this is the relationship between Karl Atangana and Captain Dominik cited in Chapter 5, but there are examples throughout of Cameroonians appealing directly to former colonial officials at times of need.

[7] *Berliner Adressbuch* 1912–14, 1921; see DKB 1903, p. 543 and the Hamburg passenger lists, StAHam 373-7 I, VIII A 1, vol. 142, p. 853 for the travels of a farmer named Arthur Lück between Hamburg and Douala. In 1912 a Helene Luck, from Berlin, sailed for Duala, though in light of her age this is unlikely to have been Bilé's partner: StAHam 373-7 I, VIII A 1, vol. 250, p. 2296.

denunciation which probably originated in a dispute with his wife's family. In the course of a brief visit to Germany in 1922 he had visited Hamburg. There he had met with the lawyer Friedrich Rosenhaft to discuss the possibility of settling in Germany, and befriended the lawyer's daughter to whom he sent photographs and an ivory necklace on his return. He had also made contact with a marriage broker in Leipzig, who was willing to provide him with the names of possible wives and arranged accommodation for him there. He never visited Leipzig and a year later had not settled his bill with the marriage broker, nor did he ever return to Germany, but the episode may explain why his in-laws in Douala were sufficiently put out to want to detach him from the family. Although nothing positive seems to have come from Dick's visit, the image that this story offers of a relatively open 'border' between the metropole and the ex-colony, which could be seen as providing opportunities for parties on both sides in hard times, is reinforced by a letter from the brother of the Leipzig marriage broker, asking Dick to find him a position in Cameroon.[8]

In other cases, the evidence for living arrangements suggests some possible trajectories for individual relationships and also the extent to which couples retained ties to the wife's family. In 1900 Martin Dibobe was lodging in the family home of his fiancée, Helene Noster, a flat in Berlin Mitte. The head of the household, presumably Helene's father, had recently taken over a sewing-machine business nearby. Although the business operated primarily as a shop, the previous tenant had manufactured sewing machines and Noster may have continued to repair and maintain them. It is thus possible that Dibobe met his bride's father in the course of his training as a mechanic, though equally possible that they first met through his renting a room or even that the Nosters first made house-room for Dibobe after he and Helene had become engaged. This would have been characteristic for working families, and by Dibobe's own account the couple were unable to set up house independently in lodgings he had already signed for because they were not yet married.[9]

There is more than fragmentary evidence for the two marriages of Mandenga Diek. He met his first wife, Friederike Schöning, in early 1895 at the latest; their daughter Erika Mandenga was born in November of that year. They married in August 1897 and three months

[8] Correspondence in ANCY APA 11295. Dick's wife was a member of the Mandessi Bell family, and Dick himself was a nephew of Mandenga Diek.

[9] Martin Dibobe to AAKA, 16 October 1900, BArch R1001 5576, pp. 15–16; *Berliner Adressbuch* 1899–1901. For details on living arrangements in the contemporary urban working class, see Hagemann, *Frauenalltag und Männerpolitik*, pp. 173–4. For more detail on housing patterns and living arrangements, see Chapter 4.

later Friederike's divorced mother was lodging with them in the Glashüttenstraße in Hamburg. After she moved out, there were two subsequent occasions when the Dieks lodged with her, in 1900 and 1903. After Mandenga and Friederike divorced and Diek moved to Danzig, their daughter continued to lodge with her grandmother (and probably her mother as well) periodically into the 1920s.[10] Diek remarried in Danzig. By his daughters' account, he met his second wife, Emilie Wiedelinski, at the home of mutual friends. They report that there were mixed feelings in Emilie's family about her marriage to an African.[11] Their memory that her brother took an enlightened view and proved an affectionate uncle is echoed in the archives by Diek's request to the French authorities in 1920 that he be allowed to take his brother-in-law with him as an assistant when setting up an export business in Cameroon.[12] By contrast, Emilie's mother, from a small town in the country, only got used to the idea once the children had been born, and her sister remained ambivalent. Dualla Misipo's first child was born out of wedlock in 1926. His partner Luise and the child continued to live at the same address as her parents and three of Luise's five brothers and sisters. Luise's mother died at the end of 1928, and her father remarried and moved away the following August, leaving Luise alone in the flat with her son. The sources do not reveal whether this represented an opportunity to legalise a relationship that Luise's parents had opposed or made marriage a material necessity for mother and child. The couple married in August 1930.[13] Hermann Muna Kessern and his partner Anna Martin postponed marriage for over twenty years after meeting in 1927. Anna was a professional artist (they met when she was designing costumes for Kessern's circus troupe), but as the mother of an illegitimate child from an earlier relationship she depended on her parents for support, and they opposed a marriage to Kessern. The decision not to marry was accordingly a considered one, even before the Nazi takeover made it safer to remain unmarried.[14]

It is noteworthy that Hermann and Anna did not have any children of their own, and this may reflect an awareness that having a child would precipitate the marriage they could not afford. The simple demographics of what we know of first-generation marriages suggests that African men

[10] Richter to Ministry of the Interior, 20 September 1936, StAHam 332-7 Staatsangehörigkeitsaufsicht B IV 1993, no. 138 (Erika Mandenga Diek); StAHam 332-8 K4365 and K6914.

[11] [Reiprich and Ngambi ul Kuo,] 'Unser Vater war Kameruner', pp. 66–8.

[12] Diek to French Minister of Colonies, 21 December 1920, FR ANOM 1 AFFPOL 614/2.

[13] Household registration records, Institut für Stadtgeschichte, Frankfurt a.M.

[14] Firla, *Der kameruner Artist*, pp. 90–3. On marriages under National Socialism, see Chapter 7.

faced particular obstacles in formalising relationships once they had found partners, and that children served both as an occasion for marriage and as the reason for its postponement. The age of our subjects at first marriage is one clue. With an average age of 32.4, first-generation African men married relatively late, while their wives – on average 25.6 – matched the profile of the general population, in relation to one available comparator, namely all Hamburg marriages in the 1920s.[15] The age gap between husband and wife also displays a significant pattern. In the twenty-six first marriages for which we have data, the wife was at least five years younger than the husband in sixteen cases (with five being more than ten years younger). This is more than double the proportion of Hamburg marriages showing a similar age gap. The largest difference was that of twenty-two years between the forty-six-year-old Louis Mbebe Mpesa (henceforth known by his stage name Louis Brody) and the daughter of Mandenga Diek – a relatively exceptional arrangement. But gaps of fifteen and sixteen years in other cases bespeak the difficulties not only of finding partners and maintaining relationships but in particular of fulfilling the conditions for placing partnerships on a legal basis. Another indicator of this is the number of cases where children were born before a couple married. Among our subjects, twenty-nine first-generation partnerships (including both first and second marriages) are on record as having produced children. In eight of these cases, one or more children were born before the marriage, and in two more the bride was in advanced pregnancy when the couple married.[16] Around the turn of the century it was common in Germany's urban working classes, from which most of the wives were drawn, for the approaching birth of a child to be the occasion for wedlock.[17] Where couples waited to marry for between eight months and six years *after* the birth of a child, even when the father signalled his continuing attachment by acknowledging the child, exceptional circumstances were clearly at work.

The story of the marriage of Bulu Malapa and Frida Lexow was narrated by their son as one blighted from the start by colonialist racism.[18] In 1913 Bulu was twenty-six-years old and working as waiter

[15] For comparative figures, see Hagemann, *Frauenalltag*, p. 170.

[16] In the case of Joseph Bilé, who did not marry the mother of his German-born children, 1932 is taken as the latest date at which a marriage might have been possible, since he left Germany at that point and was unable to return.

[17] Hagemann, *Frauenalltag*, pp. 172–6; the legitimacy of premarital sex if based on a promise of marriage was inscribed in the Civil Code, para. 1300.

[18] This account is based on 'Paul Malapa Décryptage' and Interview with Benny Malapa, Paris, July 2010. These put flesh on the bones of a story that left its traces in the official records: StAHam 332-8 K6509 (Rudolfine Lexow, Emma Therese Lexow née Hamann; Wilhelm Friedrich Lexow), StAHam 741-4 K4494 and K6556 (Paul Bulu

in a Hamburg beer-garden; Frida was seventeen and regularly visited the beer-garden with her schoolmates. There she began to pay attention to Bulu, and one Saturday when she had missed her train home she spent the night in his lodgings nearby. Frida's father Wilhem Lexow, a tailor by trade, had spent time in Cameroon himself working on the construction of the railway. When it became clear that his daughter was pregnant he disowned her and brought a prosecution against Bulu. Frida, now under the supervision of the youth-welfare authorities, bore their son Rudolf Paul (henceforth Paul) in the spring of 1914. He was immediately placed in an orphanage. Frida spent World War One working in munitions factories in Hamburg, living sometimes with a sympathetic relative and sometimes in furnished lodgings; she was twice jailed for pilfering in the last months of the war. Bulu remained in Hamburg at the beginning of the war, lodging with African friends on several occasions. In 1915 a second son was born, but did not survive. Bulu was away from Hamburg for most of 1917–18, probably engaged in war work himself. He and Frida married in April 1920; at that point Bulu was hoping to find his feet in an import-export business set up by Peter Makembe. Paul was only released into their care two years later, when he was aged eight.

This is more or less the story that Paul repeated to his son after both his parents had died. His version included details that are not borne out by the documentary evidence, making his parents younger and their forced separation more dramatic. His narrative constructed his own father, Bulu, as victim and hero, while he represented his mother Frida both as an injured Juliet figure and, in later life, as a loose woman undeserving of his respect. Told and retold within the family – at any rate among the men – this narrative serves to explain to speakers and listeners a central feature of this family's life: the fact that both Bulu and Paul had explosive tempers and frequently used physical violence or the threat of violence towards members of their family as well as towards those who threatened it. Paul Malapa thought that his mother's experience had made him more sensitive to racism than other 'mulattoes' of his acquaintance. Paul's son Benny said of Bulu simply, 'He was a victim of racism, racial insults and all that. He beat her a lot.'

Delaying marriage: institutional obstacles and the cost of statelessness

Bulu and Frida Malapa's marriage was blocked by the racism of her father, which the welfare authorities were bound to enforce as long as

Malapa, Rudolf Ernst Malapa); StAHam 373-7 I, VIII A 1, vol. 224, p. 1567; Hopkins, 'Einbürgerungsakte 1154', p. 165.

she was a legal minor. There is substantial evidence in other cases of administrative delays and obstacles arising from the husbands' status as African colonial subjects. The question of mixed marriage provoked a lively debate in the colonial period, after marriages between natives of the colonial territories and Germans had been banned by the local administrations in German South West Africa, East Africa and Samoa between 1905 and 1912, but public and parliamentary opinion prevented any extension of the ban to the metropole.[19] The views of the colonial authorities still carried some weight in 1916, when Wilhelm Solf, head of the Colonial Office, enquired of the Prussian Ministry of the Interior whether it might not be possible after all for marriages between natives of the German colonies and 'white women' to be prevented. He argued with reference to the reservations of the German administrators in the colonies and offered as possible legal grounds the inherently 'immoral' quality of a union between a German and someone who was too uncivilised to understand the nature of Christian marriage.[20] Nothing came of this, however, and before 1933 there was no legal basis on which unions between whites and Blacks as such could be prevented. From the beginning, though, becoming a couple in the eyes of the state also put the very legitimacy of an African's presence 'to the test'.

In purely practical terms, getting married required formal interactions with the authorities one of whose functions was to establish a civic status which might have remained unclear or negotiable up to then. German marriages were normally enacted by a registrar – a civil servant of the federal state in which the marriage took place – and this required at the minimum that the marriage partners be able to prove their identities. The Civil Code of 1900 prescribed that proof of legal capacity for marriage (*Ehefähigkeitszeugnis*) and/or proof that both partners were single (*Ledigkeitszeugnis*) should be provided to the registrar. In the case of stateless persons or foreigners, the police authorities in the German locality where the person was resident were empowered to issue an *Ehefähigkeitszeugnis* or the equivalent if necessary.[21] In principle, then, any application to marry would provoke an inquiry into the groom's

[19] The best account of this is still Wildenthal, *German Women for Empire*, pp. 79–130. There is evidence that officials in the Foreign Office in the 1920s believed that a marriage ban had been in force in all the colonies; see for example a manuscript note of June 1927 in the case of Theophilus Michael, BArch R1001 4457/7, p. 34.

[20] Colonial Office to Prussian Interior Ministry, June 1916, BArch R1001 4457/6, pp. 121–3.

[21] The procedure in respect of foreigners was covered by para. 1315 of the Civil Code, and article 29 of the Introductory Law for the Civil Code framed the application of the law to stateless persons.

nationality status. But it is clear that many couples understood the advantages of establishing the husband's Germanness: A German woman marrying a foreigner lost her nationality and children inherited the nationality of their legitimate father. It is probable that in many cases the bride or her family made clarification of the groom's status a precondition for marriage.

Certainly it was family concerns that prompted most of the requests for confirmation or change of nationality by Cameroonians that reached the authorities. Mandenga Diek's application for citizenship was made at the point at which the impending birth of his first child made marriage a priority. The Dieks provide an example of why marriages might have been delayed, in two respects. They were among those who chose not to marry before their nationality status was regularised. Their daughter was born in December 1895, but Diek did not acknowledge her as his legitimate child until the marriage had been solemnised. This suggests that he was aware that had he done so before his naturalisation his daughter (who retained her mother's nationality as long as she was illegitimate) would have lost her German nationality even if he and Friederike had not married. And there was further cause for delay in the length of the naturalisation process itself; the application was submitted during 1895 and Mandenga Diek became a citizen of Hamburg in December 1896. The Dieks married in August 1897.[22]

It was just such requests that prompted Solf's 1916 proposal that mixed marriages be banned in Germany. Solf reported that one Manga Bell had requested written confirmation of his status, in order 'to prove his identity for a German family and their daughter in Berlin'. The letter cited a second case, that of Max Same Bell, who had applied for proof of German nationality, which he (and his former commanding officer in the colonial police force) believed he held. The Colonial Office had denied him even confirmation that he was a native of a German protectorate. This case is a reminder that as far as the colonial authorities were concerned the crux of the issue when it came to mixed marriages was not nationality but race – and also that colonial subjects in the metropole were well aware of their rights and/or had access to expert advice. According to Solf, Same Bell's was one of an unspecified number of cases in which the aspiring bridegroom had frustrated the Colonial Office's plans: he had requested and received an *Ehefähigkeitszeugnis* from the local registrar so that he could marry as a foreigner or stateless

[22] This was not peculiar to African immigrants: see Nathans, *The Politics of Citizenship*, pp. 154–6, 181–4.

person, even though the Colonial Office had expressly refused to provide positive certification of his status.[23]

Acquiring the necessary documentation was rarely simple. Martin Dibobe's quest for the proofs he needed to marry Helene Noster in 1900 reveals an absence of clear procedures, where even the goodwill of the bureaucrats could have negative consequences for the couple. Dibobe had been working in Berlin for four years when he and Helene decided to marry. But he still had nothing to prove to the registrar that he was who he claimed to be. He wrote to the Colonial Office to request documentation confirming his date and place of birth and civil status, and followed the letter up with a visit when he had heard nothing for a month. The Colonial Office told Dibobe to go back to the registrar for a letter confirming what documentation was needed, but the registrar sent him back with the advice that 'they should take [Dibobe's] word for it' and all that was needed was something from the Colonial Office confirming his details. A further letter from Dibobe moved the Foreign Office to write to former Governor Seitz, who was acquainted with Dibobe and then (probably at Seitz's suggestion) direct to the office of the Governor in Cameroon. The Cameroonian authorities appealed in turn to the Basel Mission, under whose auspices Dibobe had been educated and baptised. On the basis of information received, the Colonial Office was able to produce a document confirming Dibobe's date of birth, baptism, address and occupation and identifying him as a 'Native [*Landesangehöriger*] of the German Protectorate Cameroon' – nearly six months after he had first written to the Colonial Office.[24]

After 1918 the sentimental links between Germany and its former colonials became attenuated and it became clear that most of them were foreign or worse (stateless). Naturalisation, always the safest way to 'normalise' the status of their wives and children, was now the only way. As we observed in Chapter 2, naturalisation was more difficult after 1913 than it had been before, because of the way in which the nationality law enabled ideological objections to overrule local knowledge. Similarly, with the removal of colonial subjecthood as a defining quality of Africans in Germany after 1919, racial terminology often came more easily to the lips and pens of German officials, and all the more as a post-war economy in permanent crisis generated competition for scarce resources.

[23] Colonial Office to Prussian Interior Ministry, June 1916; D. Nagl, *Grenzfälle*, p. 159. This was most likely a son of August Manga Bell.

[24] Dibobe to AAKA, 16 October and 5 December 1900, and reply 28 March 1901, BArch R1001 5576, pp. 15–16, 54, 59.

Peter Makembe's situation is in many ways characteristic. He was significantly older than his first wife, whom he married in 1937. But this was not his first relationship or his first attempt at marriage. In 1924 he was intending to marry a divorcee by the name of Olli Dose, and his marriage plans became part of an application for housing. Under the tight controls on housing in force since the war, transfers of tenancy even in privately owned flats were subject to the approval of the local housing authority.[25] Makembe applied through a lawyer for permission to take over the flat in which he had been lodging – two rooms, a windowless sleeping alcove and a kitchen overlooking a rear court – at the point at which his landlady was due to be evicted for non-payment of rent. Makembe had formally moved away from Hamburg in 1921 and later returned, and the lawyer acknowledged that he did not have a strong claim to preferential treatment where there was a waiting list for a vacant flat. He argued for treating Makembe as a special case both on the grounds of his forthcoming marriage and because it was 'in the public interest' in view of Germany's continuing colonial interests that natives of the former protectorates be treated generously. The Foreign Office civil servant who responded to the lawyer's request for a reference contradicted Makembe's account of his own career, characterising him as one of those 'half civilised *Neger* who are bumming around Germany' and a likely Francophile, and ended by declaring that he had 'not the slightest reason to facilitate his marriage to a German woman or to recommend ... that he be given preference over Germans looking for accommodation'.[26]

In the Foreign Office draft, 'German' replaced 'white', which the civil servant had struck out. He would have been aware that there was nothing in law or policy to justify discouraging mixed marriages. The presumption remained a negative one, however. At the end of 1929, while the musician Alfred Mangundo Köhler was out of the country either working or looking for work, his wife applied to the DGfE for help to keep herself and her three children going. The officer in the Foreign Office who was responsible for advising on such payments, Paul Eltester, took the view that in times when funding was limited it was 'not possible to extend the circle of those receiving support to include the wives of natives'.[27]

25 On post-World War One housing controls, see Führer, *Mieter, Hausbesitzer, Staat und Wohnungsmarkt*.

26 Walter Burmeister to Foreign Office, 20 November 1924 and draft response of Otto Losch, 25 November 1924, BArch R1001 4037, pp. 9–14. The name of Olli Dose does not appear again in the records, so we may presume the couple did not marry.

27 Handwritten note by Eltester 29 December 1929, and Eltester to DGfE, 7 January 1931, BArch R1001 7562, pp. 78–9.

Without explicit reference to the question of race, though almost certainly in the awareness that the wife of any African 'native' was likely to be white, Eltester articulated here a powerful vision of the African as an individual isolated in German society and destined to remain so, with no rightful claim to family life. Founding a family in the majority white community was thus increasingly an act of resistance in itself.

The family history of Togo-born Johannes Kohl provides an example of how urgent and contentious the question of citizenship could be under post-1913, post-war conditions as well as another well-documented insight into the dynamics of mixed relationships.[28] Kohl had arrived in Germany as a ten-year-old in 1904, probably as a servant to a German officer. In 1921, he was working as a musician and variety performer when he met and had a brief relationship with the seventeen-year-old singer Luise Hoffmann. They had parted by the time it became clear she was pregnant; her son Fritz was born on 23 May 1922. She immediately placed Fritz in care in Bremen, where she continued to live with her parents. Kohl only learned of the boy's existence when the Bremen Youth Bureau tracked him down; it had taken a year to find Kohl because Luise Hoffmann knew him only by his stage name. Determined to look after his child, Kohl moved to Bremen at the beginning of 1924 and tried to persuade Hoffmann to marry him. She refused to have anything to do with him or Fritz. At this point, Kohl determined to marry his current partner Veronika Meiners and take over the care of his son, which he did in September 1925. But Kohl wanted to go further and formally declare the child his legitimate son, thereby establishing himself as his legal guardian. The Bremen authorities believed that he needed to be a German national to do this. Enquiries about Kohl's status began in October 1927, and by the following September a formal application for naturalisation had been made in his name. This precipitated a lengthy and complicated legal process at local and national level, in which discussion centred on issues of skin colour as well as of formal nationality. The Bremen Youth Bureau was particularly emphatic in support of Kohl's application. Reporting that Fritz was thriving in the care of his father and stepmother, the youth officers argued that Kohl's 'decency in standing up for his illegitimate child deserves to be acknowledged' by facilitating the legitimation. The Bremen Welfare Bureau objected, primarily because of fears that the family of a travelling performer would

[28] Kohl does not figure among our subjects for the purpose of statistical analysis. The sources for the case are in StABremen B.6. no. 374, Senatsregister 4,13/5. See also PAAA Inland I-Partei R99166, betr. Sterilisierung der Rheinlandbastarde v. 1934 bis 1942, pp. 185–6, and Chapter 7 for the subsequent history of the Kohl family.

be liable to become a public charge; from 1926 onwards, the family was indeed reliant on welfare benefits, and between February 1927 and February 1928 Kohl worked at six different locations and took on shift work at the docks in Bremen in order to support his family. The Welfare Bureau was finally persuaded by the arguments of the youth workers that 'because the child is of mixed race and on account of the ... mother's rejection is entirely dependent on his black father, [a] refusal of naturalisation would simply result in great disadvantage to the child without bringing any financial relief to the state'.

This seemed to remove the last obstacle to the application's approval in Bremen, where the local and federal state authority were identical, but the process was slowed once approval was sought from the other states, as the Nationality Law of 1913 still required. Two of them expressed formal reservations. An official in the Munich Interior Ministry observed, 'Kohl is a *Neger*. In my view there must be fundamental reservations against naturalising coloureds.' This view was shared by the Thuringian Interior Ministry, whose representative commented that no natives in the colonies had been naturalised because they had not reached the moral, educational and economic level necessary to warrant them receiving German citizenship and that the same principles ought still to apply. At this point the Reich Interior Ministry could have referred the case directly to the Reichsrat for adjudication. Instead, the Ministry took advice from the Foreign Office and the Ministry of Justice. Foreign Office officials endorsed the Thuringian position, adding that irrespective of the colonial history 'it hardly needs saying that the naturalisation of coloureds is undesirable' from the point of view of population policy. The Bremen authorities now responded that Kohl's case should be regarded as exceptional: 'The fact that the child's white mother has completely failed while the black father has shown decency and devotion in carrying out his duty under quite difficult circumstances gives this case its particular quality.' But the lawyers at the Ministry of Justice introduced a new consideration, concluding that nationality was a red herring and that it was possible for a stateless man to be declared the legitimate father of a child. Jurisdiction was thereby returned to the Bremen authorities, and the process of legitimation itself initiated in 1930.

Veronika Kohl played a key role at this stage. By contrast with Luise Hoffmann, Veronika clearly had no reservations about her relationship with Johannes and his child; a social worker commented that she was largely responsible for the good care that Fritz was receiving. She further demonstrated her commitment by appearing in person at the Bremen registry office to argue for Fritz's legitimation. Now the registrar raised the objection that as the legitimate child of a stateless man Fritz would lose the citizenship conferred on him by being born to a German woman, and that statelessness would be a considerably greater handicap than the stain of illegitimacy. As a final way out of the dilemma, and in acknowledgement of Veronika's role as primary carer, it was suggested that the couple could jointly adopt Fritz; although Fritz would remain stateless, adoption would tie him more closely to his mother and reinforce his Germanness. With her agreement the contract of adoption was concluded in March 1932.

The cost of continued statelessness for the wives and children of Africans became apparent when a marriage broke down, when the husband died, or when – as during World War Two – the family was split up for other reasons. Mandenga Diek's daughters inherited his citizenship status. His first born, Erika Mandenga Diek, lost her citizenship in 1919 when she married Bonifatius Folli, a native of Togo who had not been naturalised, and she remained formally stateless even after their divorce in 1923. Ten years later, when she applied to be re-naturalised, she claimed that she had not been aware of this before. The occasion for the application was very likely the fact that she had been dismissed from her post in a public agency on the basis of the Nazi Law for Restoration of the Professional Civil Service, a process in which her race was at issue but which would certainly have made her conscious of her liminal civil status as well. At this stage in what would become a protracted campaign on her part for restoration and maintenance of her civil rights, the Hamburg and Prussian authorities acknowledged her absolute right, as someone born with German nationality, to have her citizenship restored.[29]

The situation of the Diek family after 1933, which is set out in detail in Chapter 7, is an example of how being fully German could prove a disadvantage once a regime was established in which racial considerations entirely overrode legal rights. Under those circumstances the presumption or fact of foreign nationality accorded by the status of 'protected person' might provide a cushion against arbitrary treatment, possibly strengthening the hand of a white mother in protecting a black child. Once the war was over, however, being a foreigner in one's native land lost any advantages it might have had in troubled times. In 1955 Barbara Mandenge was caring for her granddaughter. She had married Jakob Mandenge in Würzburg in 1920 and their two daughters had been born in 1921 and 1922 respectively. The elder daughter, Mathilde, had died in 1946, just over a year after the birth of her own daughter. Jakob was never naturalised, and some time before his death in

[29] StAHam 332-7 B IV 1993, no. 138.

Vienna in 1940 – probably in 1939 – he had been granted a French passport. After the war Barbara and her two daughters were accordingly regarded as having French nationality. Barbara applied for naturalisation for herself and her granddaughter. Her reasons were compelling: as a foreigner she had to apply annually for permission to reside in her home town and every two years for permission to work. This was not only inconvenient but expensive; the 4 DM fee charged in 1958 for the residency permit seemed to her substantial in light of her weekly wage of 50 DM and the costs of transport and supporting her granddaughter.[30] The account of her life that she submitted as part of her application is eloquent, not least in that it reveals her own imperfect grasp of the legal background to her predicament:

> In 1920 I married the then performer Jakob Mandenge. He was formerly a subject of the German protectorate in Duala in Cameroon. As a result of his many trips abroad with various shows, such as the Circus Krone, Sarrani, Gleich etc he lost his German nationality and travelled with a passport for stateless persons. During the NS regime he was forbidden by the local authorities in Höchberg to travel with that passport and had to get a passport showing some nationality [*einen bodenständigen Pass*]. Since he had lost his German nationality he was forced to turn to his home country, whereupon he came under French protection. Now, 18 years after my husband's death, I would like to put an end to this situation, since up to now it has led to nothing but constant unnecessary expense year after year. Besides, my home was always in Würzburg, and since 1936 in Höchberg, so always with my parents, and consequently I regard myself only as German . . . I feel myself to be German and by language and habits, just as German as my parents were. The same is true for my grandchild, whose education is in my hands.[31]

The processing of Barbara Mandenge's application was complicated by the fact that Mathilde had not formally acknowledged her daughter, born out of wedlock, as her own, so that under French law the child could not acquire her mother's nationality and remained stateless.[32] But they were both granted German citizenship in April 1960.

Staying married: challenges

The kinds of challenges that forced couples to delay marriage did not disappear once their relationships were legalised. Of fifty-three marriages or established relationships which are recorded for first-generation men

[30] Betty (*sic*) Mandenge to Landratsamt Würzburg, 7 July 1958. On Mandenge's death and funeral, which Hermann Kessern paid for: Firla, *Der kameruner Artist*, p. 171.

[31] Barbara Mandenge to Landratsamt Würzburg, 3 February 1959, StAWürzburg, Regierung Unterfranken Einbürgerung 982, p. 24.

[32] The father was probably a Liberian national whom Mathilde had met in Hanover.

among our subjects, twenty are known to have ended in separation or divorce, including seven within five years and a further five within ten years. This is a relatively high proportion.[33] It is not clear whether Martin Dibobe did marry his fiancée of 1900, Helene Noster. In March 1919 he married Alma Rodmann, a thirty-five-year-old widow with three children of her own, who seems to have been his landlady.[34] The timing here may reflect the pressures of wartime: when Anton Egiomue made his first application for repatriation in May 1920, he named not Alice Henke, whom he had married before the war, but thirty-year-old Anna Wolle as his partner; she had three children, two who were probably her children from her first marriage and a daughter, born in September 1918, who was certainly his. This was a family to which he was sufficiently committed that he gave his own surname to all the children, but by 1921 he had married again.[35]

Dibobe's and Egiomue's serial relationships seem characteristic of the determination of this generation of men not to remain single for long, and also of a willingness to assume responsibility for their children which is apparent also in the cases of Kala Kinger and Johannes Kohl. Heinrich Dibonge married in Cameroon after returning there from his first sojourn in Germany in 1903. He left a wife and three children behind when he sailed again for Hamburg. His son Sam was born in Hamburg in 1908; it is characteristic that Sam took his father's name, although his mother's name remains unknown. Dibonge's first wife died during a second visit back to Cameroon, and in 1911 he returned to Hamburg, where he married Wally Blumenthal, a Jewish woman, in 1919.[36] Alice Egiomue continued to live in the same Berlin neighbourhood as her ex-husband into the 1940s.[37] For the majority of our subjects we know or must suppose that the marriage was successful, and the evidence of private archives confirms this. In particular, surviving family photographs are a reminder of the everyday successes of this generation in what

[33] The national divorce rate in the late 1920s fluctuated around 3 per 1,000 population; in Hamburg, it reached nearly 8 in 1925, while the proportion of dissolved marriages to new marriages in Hamburg in the late 1920s was roughly 1 to 5: Hagemann, *Frauenalltag*, pp. 171, 325; Blasius, *Ehescheidung in Deutschland*, pp. 157–8.

[34] Marriage certificate and associated documentation, NAK CO 649-21 Cameroons no. 24858.

[35] List of Cameroonians seeking repatriation, May 1920, NAK CO 649-21 Cameroons no. 24858; French Consul, Berlin, to Office of Political Affairs, 2 May 1928, FR ANOM 1 AFFPOL 614/2.

[36] Dibonge remarried in Munich after World War Two: registration cards and passenger lists in StAHam; StAHam 332-7 Staatsangehörigkeitsaufsicht B VI 1930 Nr.132 Heinrich Dibonge; compensation claims in StAHam 351-11 1175, 20514.

[37] *Berliner Adressbuch* 1921–43.

Tina Campt has described as 'producing domestic subjects in the places where diaspora eventually arrives and takes root'.[38] It remains the case that the processes by which 'domestic subjects' of either generation were produced were subject to extraordinary stresses in the decades that followed World War One.

The increasing difficulty of finding a steady source of income, which is discussed in detail in Chapter 4, was a source of domestic stress in itself, and from 1924 the rules governing support for the unemployed excluded foreigners from locally administered welfare benefits. In 1925 Thoy Esomber, having had his citizenship papers revoked, was denied unemployment support in Munich with the remark that 'we don't have any colonies any more, and he should ask in Berlin'; the best the local authorities, charged with the support of families, could do for him was take his two children into care.[39] Thomas Manga Akwa reported in June 1929 that his straitened circumstances meant that he was 'hardly capable of continuing to live with [his] family' – a wife and nine-year-old child – and on at least two previous occasions he had had to move out of the family home (in 1929, a furnished room) for financial reasons; by January 1930 he and his wife had separated for good.[40]

Even in relatively good times, the actual and potential mobility of African men, including continuing material and emotional ties to Cameroon and the hope and possibility of return, was in tension with the principle of settling down. Not all of them were permanently present in Germany. Even after World War One and the decline of Germany's shipping links to the colonies, there were African and Afro-Caribbean seamen who made occasional visits to port cities like Hamburg and were regular enough visitors to retain family and friendship links there. The singer Marie Nejar's grandfather was a Francophone West Indian who married and settled down with a middle-class Hamburg woman; her father was a Ghanaian seaman who never lived with her mother. Her memoir of growing up in Germany in the 1930s reports on visits by her father and by black friends of her father and grandfather stretching into the post-war years, which attest as much to the maintenance of networks of a kind under conditions of extreme mobility as to the uncertain status of this kind of 'family' for the wife and children left behind.[41] This kind of travelling life seems to have remained possible

[38] Campt, 'Pictures of "US"?', p. 75.

[39] Fehn to Foreign Office, 25 March and 15 April 1925, BArch R1001 4557/6, pp. 169–70, 173.

[40] Akwa to [Seitz] [transcript copy], 15 June 1929, pp. 144–5; Mansfeld to Foreign Office, 9 June 1926, BArch R1001 4457/6, p. 230.

[41] Nejar, *Mach nicht so traurige Augen*.

for Cameroonians in the early 1920s. A Manga Bell, who may have been the one looking to marry in 1916, shipped into Hamburg from London in 1920 and stayed there with fellow Cameroonians for short periods during 1920–2 before disappearing again.[42] Jonas N'Doki, the son of a small farmer, did not have occasion to leave Cameroon until after World War One, and made his way to Europe working as steward and trimmer on British ships. After first registering in Hamburg he continued to ship out until 1926, when he took up a career as a performer, punctuated by casual work of various kinds.[43] Other kinds of travel necessitated by the difficulty of finding steady work could put strains on family life. There were few performing couples like the Kingers, and travelling performers were sometimes away from their families for extended periods.[44] Barbara Mandenge spent most of her married life at home with her parents while her husband was on his travels, but the family remained intact for the twenty years until his death. In other cases, once families had been established the husband's travels could constitute effective abandonment, though it is rarely clear what intentions or negotiations lay behind the move. Wilhelm Anumu sailed from Hamburg for his native Togo in 1926, leaving behind a wife and two children whom he had consigned to the care of the youth welfare bureau because he was unable to support them and who were described in 1930 as 'completely neglected'. When his wife asked him for a divorce so that she could remarry, he continued to insist that he was going to return to Germany; in spite of the intercession of a native pastor the situation was still unresolved in 1933.[45]

Travel trajectories were not always a matter of choice. When Joseph Bilé, now a Comintern activist, left Germany to be trained in Moscow in 1932 he remained aware of the situation of Helene Lück and their three-year-old daughter Gertrud, and of his responsibilities to them. In Moscow he asked that 50 Marks be sent to Helene for Gertrud's support. The child was being cared for in another household, but Bilé asked that the money be sent to Helene, 'so that she can oversee the child's care,

[42] StAHam 741-4 K4222.

[43] Record of 1941 Prosecution, StAHam 213-11 Staatsanwaltschaft Landgericht Strafsachen 4807/42. For more on N'Doki, see Chapters 5 and 7.

[44] See the cases of Alfred Köhler and Johannes Kohl. On Köhler, see note, Eltester, December 1930, BArch R1001 7562, p. 78; Eltester to DGfE, 7 January 1931, p. 79. On Kohl, see City Registrar I, Bremen to Commissioner for Civil Registries, 29 June 1931, StABremen B.6 no. 374, 4, 13/5, p. 44.

[45] Unknown to Heinrich Waltz, 30 January 1933, enclosing Robert Baetà to Pastor Stoevesandt, Lome, 14 June 1930, University of Hamburg Archives, Seminar für afrikanische Sprachen, Afrikanistik CIIIb me, pp. 4–5. Thanks to Heiko Möhle for sharing this information with us.

and for conspiratorial reasons' – the latter phrase suggesting that the care arrangements may have been made via the Party or with a political contact. Once it was clear that he could not return to Germany after the Nazi takeover, and he found himself in Paris, Bilé made no mention of his German family in his appeals to the French and international publics for funds to take him back to Cameroon.[46] Bulu Malapa spent some time at sea in the 1920s, but his long-term career presents an example of another kind of constraint; after a series of convictions for assault and damage to property he was deported to Cameroon in March 1929 and never returned to his family. They remained aware of each other's whereabouts, but when his son petitioned the French authorities to be allowed to join him in Cameroon Malapa was unwilling to welcome him.[47]

For a good many others, voluntary return to Africa remained a plausible option, if only in their imaginations, and this, too, may have militated against permanent partnerships. Where return was feasible, life in the metropole might prove to have been less than real for the African partner. In June 1925 Lisbet Elong Ngando wrote to the French consul in Douala seeking a divorce from her husband of eight years. He had left for Cameroon in September 1919, after just over two years of marriage, selling her furniture to raise money (the 'elegant flat' they shared was apparently hers) and promising to return the following spring. He had begun to send small amounts of money back to her and their five-year-old son in March 1920, but had not reappeared until August 1922, when he had spent a week with them. When he had visited again in January 1923 he was on his way back to Cameroon; he had explained to her that his family back home disapproved of his marriage to her and he needed to find an African wife. Since June 1923 her letters to him had remained unanswered; she implied that she had attempted to contact members of his family in Douala (he was related to the Bells), without success. Her conclusion was that he genuinely wanted to be rid of her, and she was ready to regularise her situation by seeking divorce herself, 'though I would still insist on compensation for my furniture'.[48]

[46] Morris [Bilé] to Special Section, 26 September 1932, and statements of payments to Helene Lück, RGASPI 532/1/149, pp. 70, 71, 79. The connection was not entirely broken, however; Bilé's German family reportedly tried to locate him in Cameroon after World War Two.

[47] Truitard, Director of AGEFOM, to Commissioner Cameroon, 5 February 1932 and reply of May 1932, FR ANOM 110COL 1003/3526. See also Chapter 8.

[48] Lisbet Elong Ngando to French Consul, Douala, 30 June 1925 [French translation of a lost German original], ANCY APA 11295. The irregularity of her situation extended to uncertainty about her nationality, since as she pointed out her Cameroonian husband was no longer a German but a French subject; she might have added that her home town, Graudenz, was no longer German but Polish.

The 'white wife problem'

There were also men who assumed that if they did return to Africa they would take their families with them. Just as the African man's 'entry' into German society through marriage precipitated the demand that his status be fixed and documented, it was often the effort to leave Europe that exposed the racism of the European authorities. In 1905 the authorities in German East Africa refused to permit the German-born wife of the Swahili tutor Mtoro bin Mwinyi Bakari to disembark with him, and this episode remained a touchstone and a model even after the colonies were lost.[49] If marriage could not be prevented, the presence of a mixed couple in the protectorate was nevertheless regarded by the authorities as inherently scandalous and dangerous to public order. In this view, the Germans were at one with the post-war mandate powers, and as long as the German authorities retained both some control over the movements of their former colonial subjects and a conviction that they had some responsibility for the reputation and morale of white Germans in Africa, they would make life difficult for couples seeking repatriation. The fates of both Martin Dibobe and Theophilus Michael were shaped by the need to negotiate the interactions between their former and current European 'protectors', though with varying results – comic in Dibobe's case and tragic in that of Michael.

Martin Dibobe's campaign to return to Cameroon began in May 1919, when he wrote the first of a series of letters to leading figures in the Reich administration; by November he had contacted the Minister for Colonial Affairs (Bell), the Foreign Minister (Müller) and the Army Minister (Noske). He offered himself as an agent for German interests in Cameroon, as someone well qualified by his own political experience to represent to his countrymen the advantages of a continued connection with newly republican and progressive Germany. This was in keeping with the political activities he was engaged in at the time (discussed in Chapter 6) but in his letter to Noske he made clear that he had family reasons for wanting to return to Africa; there were problems with the disposition of some family property. Moreover, he had lost his position with the Berlin Transport Authority and his health was poor. It appears that he had first thought of working his passage to Cameroon, probably as a lone traveller, but now he requested a loan to enable him to take his new wife and two of her children with him. In early 1920 he was advised that he could expect no help from the

[49] Wimmelbücker, *Mtoro bin Mwinyi Bakari*, pp. 45–8.

German authorities.[50] He apparently determined to raise the fare himself and applied to the French authorities for safe passage to Douala via Liberia; in June 1921 the French were prepared to approve his return subject to keeping him under close surveillance at all times, since he was seriously suspected of being a German spy. The expectation was that he would sail from Hamburg, but by his own account he was blocked from sailing from a German port on the grounds that he was taking his white wife and children with him. Instead, to the considerable surprise of the French authorities, he made his way to Rotterdam with his family at his own expense, where he presented himself to the consul with a ticket to Las Palmas and the request that he be given money to pay his onward fare. On 11 August the Minister of Colonies in Paris declared himself prepared to fund Dibobe's passage as long as he travelled direct from Bordeaux to Douala – only to be advised that the Dibobes had already arrived in Monrovia on 8 August. They had clearly got tired of waiting for official decisions, and at nearly every point Dibobe was able to move faster than communications between the ministries in Paris did. Once arrived in Monrovia, Dibobe really was penniless, claiming to have exhausted his own funds in the amount of 57,000 Marks (the equivalent of between £3,000 and £4,000 today); his baggage was impounded by the shipping line until friends were able to raise the cost of his tickets, which the French Consulate in Lisbon had estimated to be the equivalent of another 14,000 Marks (£900 today), and he continued to depend on the help of friends until he could cable his brother in Douala for money. The Minister of Colonies was once again inclined to subsidise Dibobe's onward travel, for the sake of keeping him under control, and in this context it becomes clear that race remained an issue; he explicitly authorised extension of the subsidy to 'German wife and two white children accompanying him if they are his legitimate family'. In November 1921 the Dibobes still had not left Monrovia, and seemed to have settled into the Cameroonian community there. Asked why he had insisted on stopping in Liberia, Dibobe explained that he had a nephew there whom he wanted to visit – and neatly turned the colonial discourse back on its inventors by saying that he also wanted to be sure that his wife and children would be able to tolerate the African climate.[51]

[50] Dibobe to Reich Colonial Minister Bell, 22 May 1919, BArch R1001 7220, pp. 130–1; Dibobe to Reich Government, 13 September 1919, Dibobe to Noske, 25 November 1919, Dibobe to Müller, 18 December 1919, BArch R1001 3930, pp. 226–7, 269–70, 300–1 and marginalia.

[51] French ministerial and consular correspondence June 1920–November 1921, FR ANOM 2300 COL 31/287.

Dibobe's odyssey reflects a conjuncture of his own circumstances and the political conditions. Clearly he was not entirely dependent on metropolitan agencies for resources; once the situation in Germany had become less welcoming, the ties to friends and family 'back home' which both called him back and offered an escape route also provided a realistic hope that he and his family would be able to manage the journey and its aftermath. And while the German, British and French authorities were hardly sympathetic, the fluidity of the post-war situation, their mutual suspicion and in the case of the French their relative inexperience with managing determined migrants eased the business of multiple border-crossings.

By the time Theophilus Michael thought again of returning to Cameroon, the conditions were less favourable in every respect, and there was more scope for the prejudices of the authorities to play a role. Having failed in his 1920 request for repatriation, he tried again in 1922, when his family was dependent on public assistance; his first wife Martha Wegner was still living and he had three small children. On this occasion Eltester commented that even if Martha were to be permitted to disembark in Cameroon, which he doubted, her presence would do serious damage to Germany's international standing.[52] Michael's last concerted attempt to get home came in 1927. At this stage, both the DGfE and the Foreign Office were in favour of his departure; his situation had not improved, and his wife had died. But the news that he was intending to marry again and that his fiancée Marta Lehmann had applied for a German passport to travel to Cameroon set a number of processes in motion. Michael was a native of Victoria, now under British mandate. Alfred Mansfeld, head of the DGfE, reported back from a visit to the British consulate that if the couple were not married, the British would certainly not issue a visa to Marta, so that 'in this case the Berlin police could go ahead and give her a passport, but she wouldn't be able to depart'. If, on the other hand, they wanted to marry, Michael – a British Protected Person – would need to meet the requirement for a foreigner wishing to marry: a German authority would need to issue him with an *Ehefähigkeitszeugnis*.

> Should he get a certificate, in the view of [the British vice-consul], it would take several months before the English authorities would recognise the marriage as valid ... If the marriage were declared valid, then the wife couldn't be denied a British passport. [The vice-consul] stated in so many words however that the English authorities are completely opposed to *Neger* taking whites with them when they travel.

[52] District Superintendent, 227th District, Berlin, to Foreign Office, 13 December 1922 and manuscript note by Eltester, 8 January 1923, BArch R1001 4457/7, pp. 159–60.

This was indeed the consensus view among British colonial officials, though each of them had his own rationale for the ban.[53] In view of the unlikelihood of anything ever coming of Michael's application, Mansfeld suggested that the Foreign Office let it run its course, but advise the Prussian authorities responsible for certifying Michael's marriageability what problematic consequences it might have. Eltester in turn reminded the officials who were considering the passport application, 'Since 1925 nearly all the plantations in British Cameroon are again in German hands. For the Germans who live there, especially the German women, it would naturally be particularly unpleasant to see a fellow-countrywoman together with a *Neger*.'[54]

Some days later Marta Lehmann visited Mansfeld to talk through her situation. She reported that Michael had promised her that once they were in Cameroon she would be a respected person with a European house and servants, and that they would travel together as missionaries. But recently she had received warnings 'from several quarters' and was beginning to have doubts. Mansfeld 'outlined for her all the conditions she has to look forward to' – and she declared that she would not after all marry Michael. Mansfeld told the Foreign Office, 'Since there is no longer any question of a marriage, we may assume that we will be granted [Foreign Office] funds to pay for the passage of Michael and his four children.'[55] His optimism proved at first to be misplaced; the couple married just six weeks after the interview, in August 1927, and applied for entry to British Cameroon as a family. By the middle of March it was apparent that the British authorities in Africa would not grant them entry, and Michael declared that he was willing to travel without his wife. The DGfE was prepared once again to support his repatriation, but the British continued to resist. The outcome was that Theophilus and Marta divorced and Theophilus remained in Germany until his death in 1934.[56]

[53] Memorandum by Mr Maclennan on the position of white wives of natives. Wives of natives desirous of entering West Africa [*sic*] [1936–8], NAK CO 554/105/6. See the extensive discussion of this in Ray, '"The White Wife Problem"', pp. 628–46.

[54] Mansfeld to Foreign Office, 10 June 1927, and Eltester to Berlin Police Commissioner, 24 June 1927, BArch R1001 4457/7, pp. 33, 36–7.

[55] Mansfeld to Foreign Office, 12 July 1927, BArch R1001 4457/7, p. 44. There is no other evidence of the German authorities warning women not to marry colonial subjects; it was common practice in France: Saada, *Les Enfants de la colonie*, p. 45. In October 1936 the prospective mother-in-law of the German-educated Nkoti N'zegue/N'Seke, now living in Paris, was invited to an interview by officers of the French General Agency for the Colonies and warned against letting her daughter marry an African: FR ANOM 110COL 1003/3551.

[56] Mansfeld to Foreign Office, 13 September 1927, 14 March 1928, 20 March 1928, 16 May 1928, BArch R1001 4457/7, pp. 49, 105, 107, 121–2. The Foreign Office expressed

Popular racism

The authorities' objections to repatriating mixed couples were informed by a familiar preoccupation with the racial underpinnings of colonial order, but we have also seen notions of race whose roots were in the colonies being transferred to the domestic scene in German official practice. Accordingly, it might be expected that everyday racism was a source of pressure on African-German couples and their children. Black visitors from the United States, where the colour bar was more rigid and of longer standing, tended rather to be impressed by an absence of racial discrimination and the scope for action of black Germans, and this extended to the visual evidence that in some milieus at least black men and white women could socialise without sanction. The editor of the *Chicago Defender* Robert S. Abbott, who visited Germany in 1929 and published a series of enthusiastic vignettes, commented: 'In other race relations there seemed to be no prejudice, and wherever a Negro is seen with a woman she was invariably white.' His compatriot J. A. Rogers, also reporting for the American Negro press in 1927, had put it more dramatically; his article had as its sub-headline 'German Women Find Delight in Associating with Negroes; Unlike Americans, Couples Appear in Daylight Rather Than After Dark.'[57] W. E. B. Du Bois set his romance of anti-colonialism, *The Dark Princess* (1928), in a Berlin in which he could imagine an African-American man wooing an Indian woman whom he had defended against American racists. Interracial sociability was celebrated in the jazz imagery of the period. It was also addressed in high culture. Claire Goll's 1926 novel, *Der Neger Jupiter raubt Europa*, is a reworking of Othello, though one in which the wife is made actually culpable by the workings of racial difference. While it traces the destructive dynamics of a mixed marriage, the novel displays considerable

similar reservations about supporting the return to Cameroon with white wives in the cases of Thomas Manga Akwa (March 1928) and Thoy Esomber (January 1930), in spite of the fact that their material circumstances would otherwise have recommended it: Brückner to DKG, 16 March 1928, BArch R1001 4457/7, p. 102; Eltester to Fehn, 17 January 1930, p. 152. It was the Cameroon authorities that blocked Kala Kinger's return to Cameroon with his wife in 1923: Foreign Minister to Minister of Colonies, 10 November 1923, Minister of Colonies to Commissioner Cameroon, 19 November 1923, Commissioner Cameroon to Minister of Colonies, 30 October 1923, all FR ANOM 1 AFFPOL 613/1071.

57 Abbott, 'My Trip Abroad. VIII', p. 8; J. Rogers, 'Negro Colonies Lost, Germany is Fast Losing Former Interest in Negroes', *Philadelphia Tribune*, 29 December 1927, p. 9. See also Lewis McMillan, 'Superior attitude of native German not essentially race discrimination', *Philadelphia Tribune*, 3 October 1929, p. 9. Robert Abbott's stepfather, John H. Sengstacke, was himself the son of a (white) German immigrant and a slave woman who had been married in South Carolina in 1847, and Robert had cousins in Germany: Ottley, *The Lonely Warrior*.

sympathy for the African husband, not least in its delineation of the contradiction between the humiliations he suffers as a *Neger* and his sense of himself as a high-status African. (Goll highlights this conflict by setting the action in Paris, which makes it possible for the protagonist to be a senior civil servant as well as an African prince.)[58]

Foreign observers, of course, only saw what happened in respectable public spaces. Single black men had difficulty finding and keeping accommodation because of the hostility of potential landlords, and there is reason to suppose that the same applied once they were married. There is *ex-negativo* evidence for this in the cases where African men lodged successively with the same white families and married into them. These include Anton Egiomue, who seems to have taken over the Berlin flat of his partner's widowed mother in 1904, Rudolf Walter Steinberg, and the Andritzkis, whose daughter married Georg Menzel, but who also accommodated Joseph Bell briefly in 1922.[59]

The extent to which hostility to mixed couples was expressed more openly in the community at large seems to have varied from place to place. More especially, it seems to have been dependent on particular political conjunctures. A first wave of intensified hostility to Blacks, which arose in the early 1920s, was in fact prompted by agitation around sexual relationships. This was the propaganda campaign against the presence of African soldiers among the French troops who occupied the Rhineland under the terms of the Versailles Treaty. The campaign against the 'Black Horror' (*schwarze Schmach*) crystallised resentment against the whole of the post-war settlement and legitimate doubts about its fairness in the accusation that white German women were the victims of sexual violence and abuse on the part of the Africans. It involved the dissemination of sensational rumours and visual and verbal representations of the stereotype of the oversexed and predatory black man. That this campaign had a direct impact on other Africans resident in Germany is well attested. Alfred Köhler reported being spat on in the street in Dresden.[60] In May of 1921 Louis Brody protested: 'The ... Blacks who are resident in Germany today have had to suffer a lot in the wake of the accounts of the "Black Horror" published in certain newspapers.' He added that the protest had been occasioned by the fact that '[a]bout two weeks ago one of our compatriots was attacked and

58 On *Der Neger Jupiter raubt Europa*, see among others McGowan, 'Black and White?'.

59 *Berliner Adressbuch* 1903, 1904 (Egiomue), StAHam 741-4 Fotoarchiv K4490 (Menzel), K4560 (Steinberg), K4222 and K4386 (Joseph Bell). For a similar case of an East African migrant, see Wimmelbücker, *Mtoro bin Mwini Bakari*, p. 42.

60 T. Nagl, *Die unheimliche Maschine*, pp. 155–6.

seriously beaten by passersby on the street, because they took him for a Black from the occupied territory.'[61] In 1922, the sole political expression of a short-lived (and possibly non-existent) Verband deutscher Neger, founded by Dualla Misipo, was a protest against the *schwarze Schmach* propaganda.[62] The impact the experience had on him personally is recorded in his novel, *Der Junge aus Duala*, whose core theme is the racism of metropolitan society. During the years of the *schwarze Schmach* campaign Misipo was living in southern Hessen east of the Rhine, not far from the zone of occupation itself. He characterises the atmosphere in which his protagonists meet and fall in love with the sentence: 'Now the war against the *Neger* is unleashed.' At their first meeting the protagonist predicts that his partner will suffer condemnation and ostracism and that expectation is soon fulfilled:

> At the sight of me they seem mildly disturbed. But [when I am] in the company of Marianne they start behaving like a bunch of ants whose anthill has been kicked over. Ladies' indignant glances are turned sharply in her direction. Dull grumbling and angry disapproval on the part of the Gentlemen! A '*Neger*' has the audacity to go for a walk with a well-born lady, to sit with her, to drink, to dance, to talk with her in a café – creating 'a public nuisance' ... Marianne is despised ... Intellectuals and semi-intellectuals outdo each other with explanations, exhortations and warnings ... 'You ought to have realised by now,' they say to Marianne when she isn't with me, 'that you have to give up consorting with this "*Neger*"!'[63]

Misipo's own marriage survived everyday racism and official harassment under the Nazi regime, but the struggle clearly left its mark on him.[64] There is evidence, too, that more than the beginnings of this relationship were challenging. In *Der Junge aus Duala*, the courtship ends with their engagement, to which 'Marianne's' parents are reluctantly reconciled – but the reconciliation scene closes with a reflection on the problems faced by the children of mixed marriages. And according to his son's autobiographical account, Luise remained cautious when twenty years later her son in his turn brought home a white fiancée, remembering 'the vicissitudes of the past'.[65]

[61] Louis Brody, 'Die deutschen Neger und die "schwarze Schmach"', *BZ am Mittag*, 24 May 1921, cited in T. Nagl, '"Sieh mal den schwarzen Mann da!"', p. 85. The extensive literature on the Rhineland campaign has most recently been summarised by Maß, *Weiße Helden – schwarze Krieger*, pp. 71–120.

[62] Eltester to Information Office for Emigrants and Returnees, 30 October 1922, and reply: BArch R8023 1077/a, pp. 192, 195.

[63] D. Misipo, *Der Junge aus Duala*, pp. 120, 161–3.

[64] See Chapter 7.

[65] E. Misipo, *Métissages contemporains*, p. 81.

A second wave of public hostility to mixed couples and their children came in the Depression years. Mandenga Diek's daughters recalled that their family was 'very popular' in Danzig, but things started to change as early as 1932, though it was not until the Nazis were fully in power that their aunt declared that she would no longer welcome her sister's husband and children in her house.[66] This development was associated with a general intensification of racist sentiment which we consider further in Chapters 4 and 7. It can be accounted for by the anxieties unleashed by the economic crisis and also by the rising public profile and political presence of the National Socialist movement. As early as March 1930 the Nazi Reichstag delegation proposed an amendment to a public order bill which called for the criminal prosecution of anybody 'who contributes to the racial deterioration or subversion of the German people by mixing with people of Jewish blood or members of the coloured races'. The amendment was voted down without debate; even the Nazi delegates did not speak to it in the Reichstag.[67] But it was sufficiently notorious to be picked up by the American press, and alongside other episodes of verbal and physical abuse by Nazis will have poisoned the atmosphere and emboldened less militant racists.[68]

Internal tensions

Among the possible internal sources of friction in a marriage was the risk of differing expectations rooted in differences of upbringing and culture. There is a hint of this even – perhaps most markedly – in relationships between black partners. The marriage of Alexander Douala Manga Bell to Hamburg-born Andrea Jimenez-Berroa was notoriously troubled. Andrea was the daughter of a German woman and an Afro-Cuban classical musician who had settled in Hamburg after touring Europe with his brothers. It seems likely that she met Alexander in the Baltic resort Zoppot, where Alexander was staying with his Duala 'minder' Reinhold Elong Ngando (husband of the aggrieved Lisbet) following a period of military service in the war, and Alexander followed her to Hamburg.[69]

[66] [Reiprich and Ngambi ul Kuo,] 'Unser Vater war Kameruner', pp. 65, 68, 69.

[67] *Verhandlungen des Reichstags* 1930, vol. 440, item 1741; vol. 427, p. 4476; vol. 428, p. 5567.

[68] 'Attempt Made to Ban German Intermarriage', *Philadelphia Tribune*, 17 April 1930; 'German Fascists Riot over Negro Play', *New York Times*, 20 October 1930, p. 9. Discussion in the African-American press about how seriously to take the Nazi initiative collided with an ongoing debate about the politics of black and white sexuality: '"Charm of Negro Men Over German Women Idle Chatter," Says McMillan in Article', *Pittsburgh Courier*, 24 May 1930, p. 10.

[69] Reinhold Ngando accompanied the couple to Paris in 1919, where he acted as escort and sometime interpreter to Alexander.

They married in June 1919; she was seventeen and he was nineteen. Between then and the summer of 1921 the couple were nominally settled in the Paris suburbs at the invitation of the French authorities, and their son José Manuel (Manga Duala) and their daughter Andrea Emma (Tüke) were born there in 1920 and 1921 respectively. With the ambivalent encouragement of the French, Alexander learned to cast himself as leader of the Duala destined to assume power and authority. He returned to Douala for the first time in November 1919 and once back in France he pursued a lifestyle well beyond his means, to the acute embarrassment of those around him. By the time he returned permanently to Cameroon in spring 1922, Andrea had already taken the children back to Hamburg, where they were raised by her mother. Andrea and Alexander were never reunited, although they remained married at least until 1939, when Andrea was accorded French citizenship in respect of Alexander's naturalisation; Andrea later reported that Alexander had refused to divorce her unless she gave him custody of the children. She received no financial support from him while the children were growing up, and worked as a performer, graphic artist and secretary. In 1929 she met the novelist Joseph Roth, with whom she lived from 1931 (when the children joined them in Berlin) until 1936; she accompanied him into exile in France in 1933. Alexander resumed contact with his family in Paris after the war, and provided his daughter with a large dowry. On a visit to Douala in August 1947, Manga was shot and killed by Alexander. The circumstances of the killing were unclear, but Andrea explained it as the natural outcome of Alexander's early neglect of his son. She never forgave him, although in later life she began to identify herself with the rebel heritage of his father Rudolf, hanged by the Germans in 1914.[70]

The copious documentation that was generated around the Manga Bells offers only limited insight into the internal dynamics of their relationship. Certainly the marriage of these two very young people, one of whom had been separated from his own family since early childhood and lost his father to political murder, and who were subject to close

[70] Documentation on the Manga Bells in France 1919–22 in FR ANOM 2300 COL 31/ 289; Andrea Manga Bell's registrations at the Hamburg Consulate CADN 261PO/A/ 49 and 52; documentation on Andrea Manga Bell and her children in Paris, FR ANOM 110COL 1003/3517; Andrea Manga Bell to Karl Retzlaw, 10 April 1967, 15 and 25 April 1978, Deutsches Exilarchiv Frankfurt a.M., Karl Retzlaw Papers, I.A.288, no. 2, 56, 57; 'Weißer Mann immer schlecht', pp. 19–22, an account of the marriage occasioned by Manga's shooting, purports to be based on interviews with Andrea. For Andrea's relationship with Roth, see Bronsen, *Joseph Roth*, pp. 369–73. For an apologetic view of Alexander, see Douala Manga Bell, *Le Prince Alexandre*. On the hanging of Rudolf Duala Manga Bell, see Chapters 5 and 6.

surveillance by the political authorities, was under exceptional pressure while they were together. Andrea later reported that Alexander was physically violent towards her. For Alexander, as for Reinhold Ngando, one source – or manifestation – of incompatibility was the style of life that his class position in Cameroon led him to take for granted.

The Manga Bells were unusual among black couples in being roughly the same age. In most other cases, there was a difference of generation, and there is ample evidence in relations between immigrant parents and their children of the sources of friction that arise from the fact of differential acculturation. Among our subjects there are hints of this particularly in relations among men: when James, the older of Theophilus Michael's two sons, thought about his father (who handed him over to the manager of a troupe of acrobats at the age of twelve when Theophilus became too ill to support the family), the first term that occurred to him was 'despot'.[71] Paul Malapa resented the mercurial self-absorption with which Bulu coped with the frustrations of racism and de-classing, though in later life he himself grew into the role of the African prince in exile, with similar consequences for his own family. The ambivalence towards his mother cited above also points to the sources of tension particular to relationships between dual-heritage children and their white or black parents.[72]

In the case of the relationships between first-generation men and second-generation women that we know of, we can only guess that similar tensions may have arisen. Interviewed in the 1980s, Dorothea Diek recalled that other African men of her father's generation showed so much interest in his daughters that he was impelled to declare that he was not a marriage bureau.[73] This suggests that where black partners were available men of the first generation sought them out, at any rate when they were respectable parties. We know of five cases of liaisons or marriages between first-generation men and second-generation women. Of these, four were in Mandenga Diek's family.[74] When Erika Mandenga married Bonifatius Folli in 1919, she already had a four-year-old son fathered by the Sierra Leonean Joseph Metziger; she had been engaged to Metziger when she was sixteen or seventeen, though they never

[71] Reed-Anderson, *Eine Geschichte von mehr als 100 Jahren*, p. 44.

[72] The ethnographic work of Jacqueline Nassy Brown on Liverpool is richly suggestive on this: see Brown, *Dropping Anchor, Setting Sail.*

[73] [Reiprich and Ngambi ul Kuo,] 'Unser Vater war Kameruner', p. 72.

[74] The fifth is Benedikt Gambe, whose partner in 1935 was his fellow performer Charlotte Rettig, a German-born 'mulatto': Gunzert to Interior Ministry, 18 September 1935, BArch R1001 7562, pp. 114–16, here p. 116.

married, and the baby had been born when she was eighteen. The older of Diek's daughters by his second marriage, Erika, married Louis Brody in 1938 and, following a divorce, Thomas Ngambi ul Kuo in 1947. These relationships bespeak the existence of milieus in which black people of different backgrounds encountered one another, though the experiences of the two Erikas, almost a generation apart, also point to important shifts in the conditions for community. Metziger, ten years Erika Mandenga's senior, was a familiar figure on the Hamburg maritime scene, and like Folli he was associated with Mandenga Diek in the first German African Welfare Association (AH). This was the port city milieu that drew Blacks from all over and in which her father had already established himself as a community leader. Of the younger Erika's husbands, Louis Brody was also a member of the AH and Thomas Ngambi ul Kuo had started his career in Germany in Hamburg. Either of them might have known Erika as a baby. But it seems likely that these relationships arose in the performance milieu in which black people were thrown together willy-nilly under National Socialism and in the immediate post-war years.[75]

All of these relationships broke up, though we have no direct testimony as to why. The memoirs of a third-generation Afro-German woman testify to the possibilities for intercultural conflict between German-born Blacks and native Africans. Marie Nejar writes of her brief relationship with a Ghanaian man in the late 1950s after two affairs with white men had foundered on the racist attitudes of friends and relatives:

> Now for the first time I had a black boyfriend, a boyfriend from Ghana, my father's homeland. But after nine months I saw ever more clearly that we just didn't fit together, our attitudes were too different. I just wasn't an African, and this was proved time and again by everyday things.

Following a contretemps at a dinner party where all the other guests were African, he challenged her with 'You're not white', to which she responded, 'I am white, born in Germany, and I can't get out of my own skin.'[76] Nejar had transgressed by refusing to stay with the women

[75] StAHam 332-7 B IV 1993, no. 138; Landesamt für Bürger- und Ordnungsangelegenheiten Abt. I – Entschädigungsbehörde, Berlin (LABO) 400/770, Erika Ngambi ul Kuo; StAHam 741-4 K6665 (Ngambi ul Kuo); Stoecker, 'Sprachlehrer, Informant, Küchenchef'; Martin, 'Der Afrikanische Hilfsverein', p. 78. See also [Reiprich and Ngambi ul Kuo,] 'Unser Vater war Kameruner', pp. 77–8. On the AH, see Chapter 4. On performance milieus under National Socialism, see Chapter 7.

[76] Nejar, *Mach nicht so traurige Augen*, pp. 236, 238.

while the men carried on their conversation in another room. Here the difference between African and European – articulated paradoxically in terms of 'race' or skin colour – was problematic because it was implicated in gendered practices and identities, or in what it meant to the individuals involved to be a man or a woman. The ways in which masculinity and femininity were expressed and enacted in the lives of Cameroonians are explored further in Chapter 5. The material conditions for their survival and self-expression once settled in Germany are the subject of the next chapter.

4 Surviving in Germany: work, welfare and community

In the years immediately after World War One some opportunities existed for Cameroonians to return to Africa, but few did so. Instead, along with other ex-colonial subjects they increasingly set down roots in Germany where they formed families and established working lives. This chapter explores the ways in which they and their children met the challenges of carving out space and a living for themselves in post-war German society, considering their material circumstances, employment patterns and survival strategies. It begins by looking at the development of key centres of settlement and the evidence for the creation of friendship and associational networks at local and supra-regional levels within Germany. In both Imperial and Weimar Germany African men and women lived all over the country. It was not uncommon for them to move around, often as a result of their search for employment or because of work they carried out as touring performers. But even before World War One small clusters of Africans who had established contact with one another were emerging. During and after the war these developed into networks of contacts that took in Africans of different origins and that took on a formal character in the AH. There was also a degree of geographic concentration. While pockets of former colonial subjects were to be found in cities such as Hanover, Munich and Cologne, the majority of Cameroonians and other black residents gravitated to Germany's two largest cities, Berlin and Hamburg, where not only black single men but now families lived near one another.

The evidence of association, mutual aid and social solidarity is often to be found in sources that document primarily the precarious employment situation of our subjects. The multifarious ways in which they made a living are characterised by a central paradox: getting on in Germany often depended on exploiting the things that made them different from other Germans. The fact of being former colonial subjects won them the patronage of state and non-state agencies, though at the cost of dependency and surveillance. The fact of being black meant that they were sought after as performers, though often in roles that reinforced

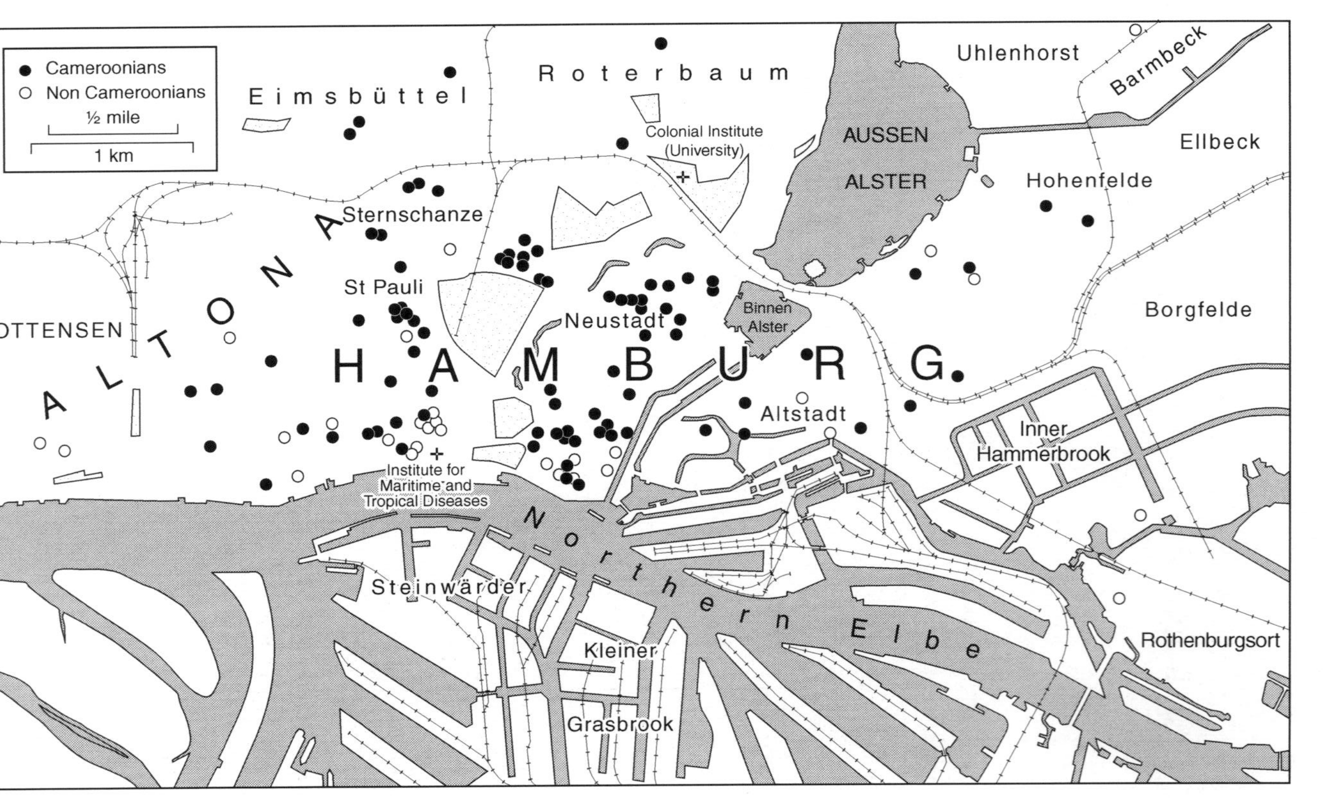

4.1 Africans in Hamburg 1884–1917

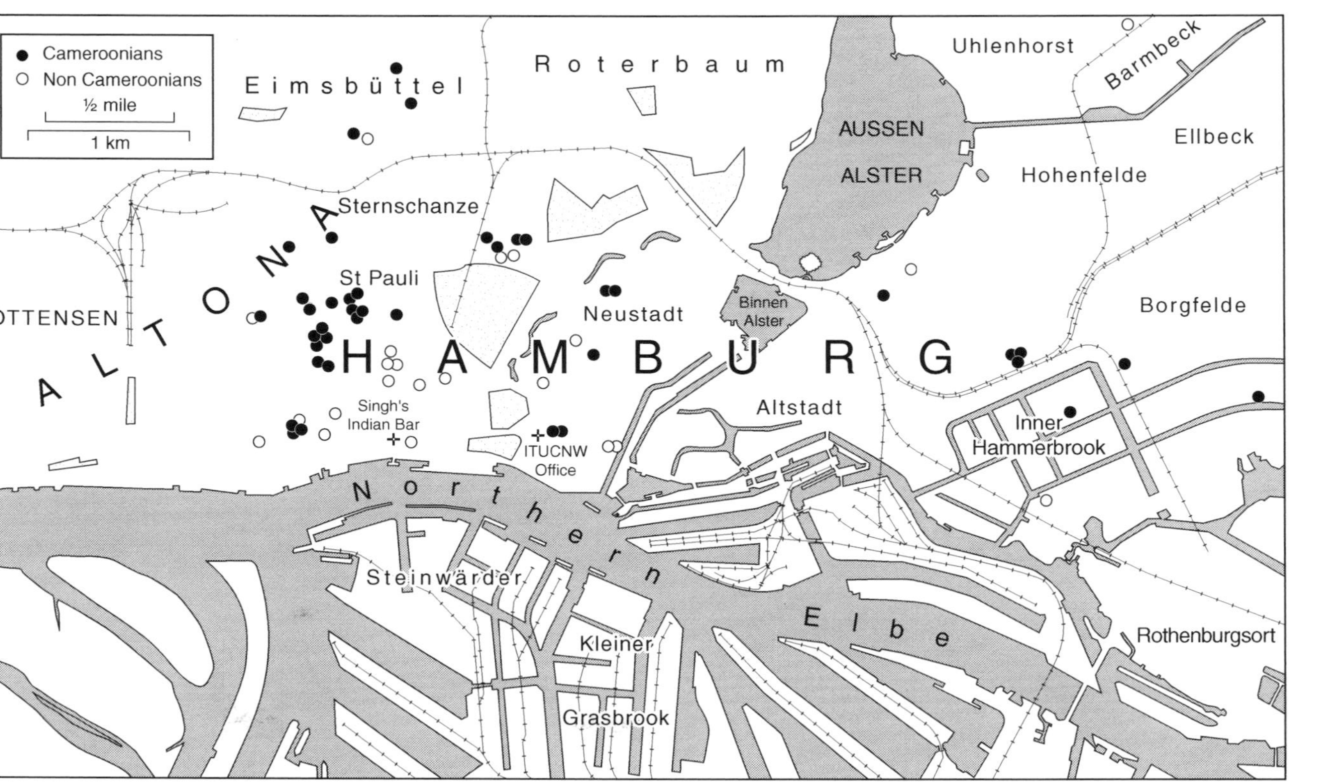

4.2 Africans in Hamburg 1918–39

their liminal status. Some of them found other ways to exploit the stereotypes to their own purposes, while at the same time the performance milieu itself became a space where community could be cultivated.

Centres of settlement

Hamburg, including the then independent city of Altona, was an attractive base for African men and women for a number of reasons. The city's harbour was the point of entry into Germany for most Africans arriving from overseas and men who had become ill during the voyage might spend their first days in Germany in the city's Institute for Maritime and Tropical Diseases.[1] The docks also provided a place of work for many African and Asian seamen which meant that it was home to a fluid, heterogeneous population of non-Europeans. Both before and after World War One, most of the city's Africans were to be found living in close proximity to one another in the inner city districts of St Pauli and Neustadt, as well as Altona Altstadt, all located close to the docks (see Maps 4.1 and 4.2).[2] All three districts had large working-class populations and black residents typically rented accommodation in the poorest areas, like the eastern parts of Altona Altstadt where population density was high and rents were low. St Pauli, in particular, with its sailors' bars and cheap entertainment and commercialised sex and leisure scene provided places of work and accommodation for all types of migrants.[3] There in the late 1920s a number of jazz bands playing on the Reeperbahn featured black performers.[4] The Jamaican writer Claude McKay, who briefly visited Hamburg in 1923, recalled spending 'three days among the docks and the Negroes of different nationalities and languages'.[5] In this milieu from the mid 1920s, the 'Indian Bar' at Bernhardstraße 63 (see Figure 4.1) established itself as a favourite haunt of African men. Located in St Pauli, near the ferry terminal and within sight of the Institute for Maritime and Tropical Diseases as well as a host of other bars, it was run by the Indian Hardas Singh. Part of the

[1] For example, see StAHam 741-4 K5765 (Mohamed bin Abdullah); Stoecker, *Afrikawissenschaften*, p. 62.

[2] These maps include all known places of residence of Cameroonians and their families, and include multiple entries for some individuals. They accordingly do not record the number of black households at any point, but are a guide to where those households found housing in each of these two periods.

[3] McElligott, *Contested City*, p. 57.

[4] Robert S. Abbott, 'My Trip Abroad. VII: Sojourning in Germany', *Chicago Defender*, 21 December 1929, p. 10.

[5] McKay, *A Long Way from Home*, p. 237.

Figure 4.1 The 'Indian' Bar, Hamburg, *c.* 1925

bar's attraction was said to be two 'Negro' waitresses, who served Köm (caraway schnapps) to customers.[6]

It was Berlin, however, that housed Germany's largest concentration of people of African heritage (see Maps 4.3 and 4.4). By 1925 the capital was a cosmopolitan city of over four million, many of whom were not native Berliners, but migrants particularly from the East. The pre-war flow from Germany's overseas territories had brought numerous Africans to the city. Like Hamburg, Berlin featured a university department of African languages, a source of employment for African men.[7] After the war others were attracted to Berlin by hopes of finding work, especially in the film and entertainment industry that was flourishing in and around the city. As the seat of the German Foreign Office and its Colonial Department the city was an increasingly important reference point for ex-colonial subjects needing administrative or financial support. In 1929 an African-American visitor estimated the size of Berlin's resident 'coloured' population at around two hundred and fifty, and described

[6] Abbott, 'My Trip Abroad. VII', p. 10; Heinz Liepmann, 'Häfen, Mädchen und Seeleute', *Velhagen und Klasings Monatshefte*, 47 (1932), 283–5, here 285.

[7] For more on the Hamburg Colonial Institute, see Meyer-Bahlburg and Wolff, *Afrikanische Sprachen*; Pugach, *Africa in Translation*. On the Berlin Seminar for Oriental Languages, see Stoecker, *Afrikawissenschaften*.

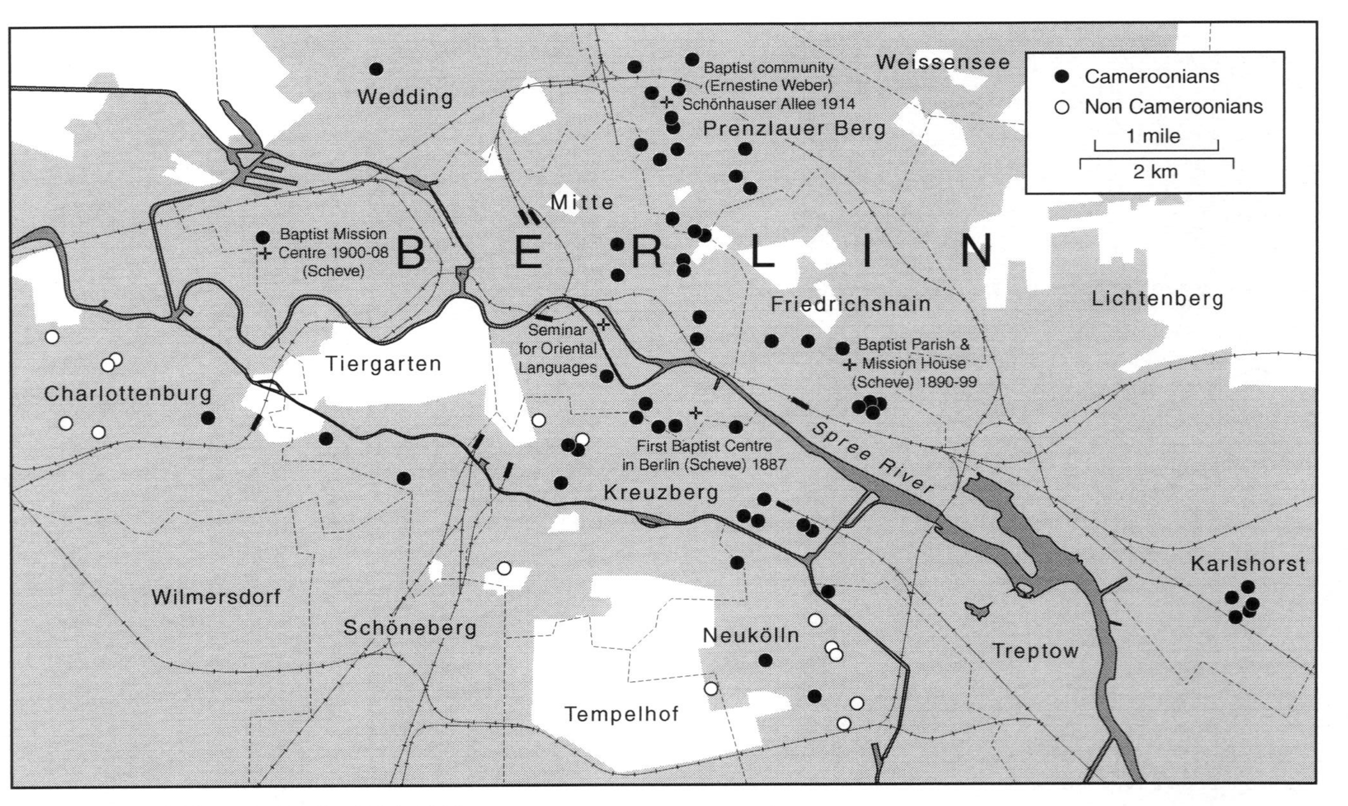

4.3 Africans in Berlin 1884–1918

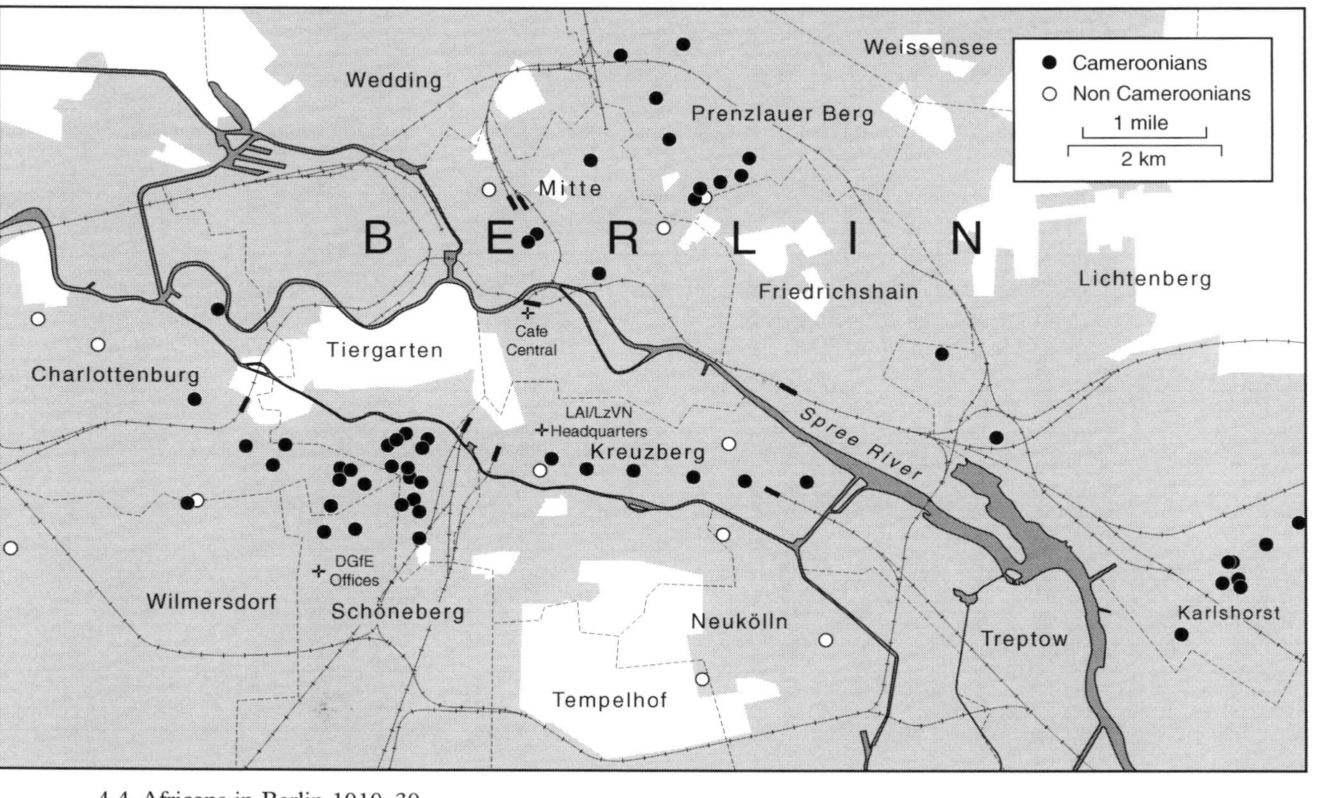

4.4 Africans in Berlin 1919–39

it as made up primarily of Cameroonians and their German-born children. Interviewed in the 1990s Theophilus Michael's daughter Juliana, born in Berlin in 1921, similarly suggested that around two hundred Cameroonians lived in the city between the wars.[8]

Residential patterns in both cities provide clear evidence of an evolving black community, with Cameroonians and other Africans tending to be concentrated in a small number of areas. In post-war Berlin, the majority of Cameroonians lived in the west of the city largely in the newly incorporated districts of Charlottenburg and Schöneberg. Although both districts were relatively affluent, Africans tended to live in the poorer parts. At various times thirteen Cameroonians and their families lived within a two-mile radius of Nollendorfplatz, all within walking distance of stations on the *Stammstrecke*, Berlin's first underground train line which could take passengers from Charlottenburg in the west of the city all the way across to Friedrichshain in the east.[9] The area around the Potsdamer Straße and Bülowstraße formed the core of Schöneberg's amusement and sex district.[10] It was here in the side streets where prostitution thrived that Cameroonian migrants found rented accommodation and in the 1930s a number were still based on or near the Augsburger Straße. An explanation for the concentration of migrants in Berlin's West End is provided by Wilhelm Munumé's comment that he and his compatriots were treated better in the west of the city than in more solidly proletarian northern districts, where their rights were abused by landlords and they often had to move out.[11] The element of prejudice underlying landlords' attitudes is made clearer in a police report concerning another Duala, Richard Dinn.[12] The report's author noted that Dinn frequently had to move apartment because his 'habits and customs' were deemed incompatible with those expected by his landlords. In both Berlin and Hamburg many Africans lived an almost nomadic lifestyle, constantly moving from one apartment to the next. In Hamburg, for example, the language assistant Paul Messi changed accommodation twelve times between 1914 and 1920, while in Berlin Thomas Manga Akwa moved at least six times

8 Abbott, 'My Trip Abroad. VIII', p. 1. Reed-Anderson, *Eine Geschichte von mehr als 100 Jahren*, p. 43. Another African-American visitor at the time estimated the size of Berlin's black population to be around sixty to eighty. Lewis K. McMillan, 'Berlin receives Negro with Open Arms', *New Journal and Guide*, 5 October 1929, p. 1.

9 For more on the U1, see Karwelat, 'Bitte einsteigen', pp. 107–10.

10 Röblitz and Schmiedecke (eds.), *Berlin-Schöneberg*, p. 8.

11 Alfred Mansfeld to Foreign Office, 9 June 1926, p. 230. See also Mansfeld to Foreign Office, Department III, 24 November 1925, BArch R1001 7562, pp. 44–5, here p. 44.

12 Berlin Police Commissioner to Foreign Office, 9 March 1927, BArch R1001 4457/7, p. 18.

between 1916 and 1925.[13] In part this mobility was also typical of the German working class and was dictated by the difficulties of paying rent and the search for ever cheaper accommodation.

The presence of pockets of Cameroonians in other parts of the city bespeaks the mobilisation of long-standing connections to generate new kinds of community. The relatively comfortable southeastern suburb Karlshorst is perhaps an unexpected place to find the shoemaker Anton Egiomue and his family, but he was the first of three distant relations from Kribi to move there around 1913. He was followed by Jakob Malapa, who together with his German partner moved into Egiomue's old apartment, after the latter found a new flat fewer than 400 metres away. A third man, Josef Boholle, who like Egiomue had been part of the Colonial Exhibition, settled in Karlshorst with his family around 1918, initially staying in the same building as the Egiomues. Although Egiomue himself moved away shortly after, his wife, Alice, remained a close neighbour of the Boholles after the Egiomues divorced. In the mid 1930s Josef Boholle's oldest son, Rudolf, moved out of the family home and into the same nearby building that Alice Egiomue was now living in, taking his own wife, who was born in Karlshorst, and their children with him.[14] They were joined in Karlshorst around this time by two of the Michael siblings, Theodor and Juliana, who were in the care of a German-Moroccan couple.

The Boholles' Karlshorst apartment in the Gundelfinger Straße 38 was in a row of villa-style buildings; the Berlin city directory lists only six other main tenants in the building, whose occupations were suggestive of a largely middle-class existence. Other districts where Cameroonians and other Africans lived in close proximity to one another – Mitte, Kreuzberg and Wedding – were characterised by a more uniformly working-class milieu than Karlshorst or West End. Here they rented rooms or apartments in tenements where their neighbours were skilled and unskilled workers, small tradesmen and war widows and where overcrowding was common. For over three decades Victor Bell rented an apartment in the Driesener Straße 4, Wedding. The 1930 city directory listed forty-one apartments in the building by the names of their main tenants. What the city directories do not record are the numbers of other family members, subtenants, paying transients or lodgers living in a building. After 1918, many war widows eked out a living by letting

[13] StAHam 741-4 K6594 (Paul Messi); BArch R1001 4457/6 and R8023 1077/a and *Berliner Adressbuch* (Manga Akwa).

[14] *Berliner Adressbuch*, 1913–17, 1930, 1934–43; RKA to District President, Potsdam, 6 January 1917, BArch R1001 5570, p. 1.

rooms, and single men typically began their careers in the big city in furnished rooms – sometimes, as we have seen, finding marriage partners there.

It was not uncommon for former colonial subjects to share accommodation as a means of pooling their resources as well as helping newer migrants to find their feet, and the intricacies of migrant housing patterns throw light on evolving mutual aid and friendship networks. Bonifatius Folli, working as a language instructor at the Berlin Seminar for Oriental Languages, hosted Joseph Masso in his apartment, when the latter was unemployed in 1926.[15] Upon his arrival in Hamburg the traveller and sailor Manga Bell found accommodation first with Mathias Ndonge and then with Joseph Muange and his partner Pauline Kallscheuer.[16] Ndonge himself had previously spent time with Muange and Kallscheuer. Christoph Anjo Dick lived for a time with Georg Menzel, while Joseph Bell also temporarily stayed first with Menzel and later with Menzel's parents-in-law. Menzel had lived in the same apartment as Peter Makembe, who in turn had shared accommodation and/or lived in the same building as a handful of other Duala. Indeed, at various times Makembe, Menzel, Ndonge, Rudolf Steinberg, Bulu Malapa and Heinrich Dibonge all lived on or around the Adolphstraße (now Bernstorffstraße) in Altona. Living close by were several other African men. These accommodation arrangements and housing patterns bespeak both a social support network among Africans and a basis for sociability, among men at least.

Social gatherings such as baptisms, marriages and funerals provide further evidence of the extent of friendship ties. Thus Hermann Same Ngange acted as a witness to the marriage of his fellow Duala Jakob Mandenge with Barbara Heinrich in Heidelberg in 1920.[17] In 1923 in Hamburg a large number of well-dressed Cameroonians turned out for the funeral of Joseph Bell; they included Mandenga Diek, who had to make the trip from Danzig to which he had relocated in 1913.[18] A group photograph from around 1928 shows the black community in Hanover, half a dozen African men with their white German partners and five of their German-born children, celebrating

[15] DGfE to Foreign Office, 13 September 1926, BArch R1001 4457/6, p. 242.

[16] For the following, see the registration cards of the named individuals in the Hamburger Meldekartei 1890–1925 and the Altona Meldekartei 1919–43, in StAHam 741-4.

[17] Copy of Certificate of Marriage, Mandenge – Heinrich, 19 November 1926, StAW Würzburg Regierung Unterfranken Einbürgerung 982, p. 8.

[18] 'Paul Malapa Décryptage', p. 5. Although Malapa does not name the member of the Bell family who died, the available information suggests that this must have been Joseph Bell.

the Christening of a new black German child.[19] The presence of a group of white women in this picture is a reminder that sociability and networking must have been a feature of their lives, too, though we know less about how the wives of African men got along than about male sociability. In Berlin in 1933 Elisabeth Makube, daughter of a Cameroonian man, acted as godmother to Ahmed Adam, son of a German East African man.[20] Such expressions of friendship and solidarity also took on other visible forms. In an interview in later life Paul Malapa recalled being visited by his father in the orphanage in Hamburg where he had been placed. Having been previously denied access to his son, Bulu Malapa now returned accompanied by several other Cameroonian men, including Louis Brody (normally based in Berlin), whose German language skills were more advanced. The men successfully persuaded the institution's director to allow Bulu to see his son. Paul's interview also makes clear that the connections between African men extended to their children. He remembered playing with Hanzen Ndonge, son of Mathias, during his childhood as well as knowing Erika Mandenga Diek, who helped him with his German homework, and her son Carl-Heinz.[21] Similarly, in Berlin Theodor Michael grew up knowing the children of Gottfried Egiomue, who were of a similar age, a link that was perhaps solidified when the Michael children moved to Karlshorst.[22] Alongside these informal connections attempts were also made to give an organisational structure to this burgeoning community. The earliest example of this was the creation of the AH.

The African Welfare Association

The AH was formally created on 1 May 1918 in Hamburg, with the Togolese trader Wilhelm Anumu as its chairman and Peter Makembe as its secretary and treasurer.[23] Later Mathias Ndonge replaced Anumu as chairman. The AH was envisaged as being open to anybody of African heritage; the very first paragraph of its statutes declared: 'Every member of our black race and every person of colour can be a member.'[24] This was indeed reflected in the association's makeup, which demonstrated the creation of links that transcended ethnic, tribal, social or linguistic

[19] The image, originally property of the Ngando family, is the cover picture for our book; it is also reproduced in Martin and Alonzo, *Zwischen Charleston und Stechschritt*, pp. 52–3.
[20] Bechhaus-Gerst, *Treu bis in den Tod*, p. 70.
[21] 'Paul Malapa Décryptage', pp. 13, 77, 4, 7, 78.
[22] Correspondence with Theodor Michael, August 2009.
[23] On Anumu, see Hopkins, 'Einbürgerungsakte 1154'.
[24] Statut des Afrikanischen Hilfsvereins, StAHam 331-3, SA 2819.

ties. The only known membership list, dated June 1918, noted thirty-two members, all men, and although over half were from Cameroon, predominantly Duala, men from Togo, the former German East Africa, Liberia and the Virgin Islands were also involved. Anecdotal evidence suggests that later members included men from Sierra Leone and the United States.[25]

The association was conceived of as a mutual aid society, its aim to provide a support network that would replace, as far as possible, ethnic and family ties in Africa and take away 'the feeling of being isolated amidst the white population'. Its documents stressed the importance of 'the unity of all' members. Among other things, it looked to offer practical and financial help as well as support for members in their dealings with the German authorities, in the search for employment and in the case of the death of a family member. Membership fees were 1.25 Marks a week or 5 Marks a month, but those who earned well were expected to contribute more. Moreover, it was to function as a 'communication point' which would enable family members in Africa to keep up to date with news about their relatives in Germany and vice versa. This underscored the continuing importance that family and hometowns in Africa had for these men. The preamble of the AH explicitly stated that it would not involve itself in political affairs.[26]

The AH's membership list illustrated the geographical spread of Africans in Germany as well as the supra-regional reach of their networks. Members are named as being based in Bavaria, East Prussia, Westphalia and Mecklenburg. Over half the members were living in Hamburg and Berlin, however. Makembe was responsible for centralising and updating this list, copies of which were distributed to all involved, thus enabling members to keep in contact with one another.[27] The association's official address and telephone number were those of Makembe's import-export firm at Dammtorwall 113, Neustadt.[28] Meetings were held in his flat in the building next door. A then young Paul Malapa later recalled being taken there by his father. While the adults talked, Paul played with other African-German children. His abiding memory of these visits was the fact that Makembe had a telephone in every room of his flat.[29]

By 1922–3, during part of which time Makembe was in Cameroon, the AH had ceased to function.[30] On the one hand, it was unable to meet the

[25] Evidence suggests that with time new members also joined the association; Martin, 'Anfänge politischer Selbstorganisation', p. 199

[26] Statut des Afrikanischen Hilfsvereins.

[27] Note on interview with Manga Bell and Ngando, 14 October 1919.

[28] *Hamburger Adressbuch* 1921.

[29] 'Paul Malapa Décryptage', p. 7.

[30] Hopkins, 'Einbürgerungsakte 1154', p. 168.

increasing financial and social needs of its members, who in return were unable to pay their fees. On the other hand, a handful of members such as Paul Messi, the East African Abdullah bin Mohamed and Reinhold Ngando had left Germany by this time, while the Liberian Hans Nio had died.[31] Given that several members were employed as sailors it is highly possible that those whose fate remains unknown also left Germany in this period, thus leading to a further reduction in the association's numbers. This was far from the end of African organisational life in Germany, however, and both formal and informal friendship networks remained largely intact. Juliana Michael, born in 1921, remembered her father Theophilus playing a similar role in Berlin to the one that Mandenga Diek had had in Hamburg, as 'protector of all Cameroonians'.[32]

The search for work

One of the AH's stated aims was to help members with their search for work, and throughout the Weimar years finding stable employment remained a major problem for most black Germans. In the aftermath of World War One, ex-colonial subjects, like all Germans, were exposed to the economic hardships of hyperinflation and the uncertainties of the labour market that persisted even after the currency had been stabilised. Cameroonians who had completed their education or apprenticeships with the hope of finding work in the protectorates, be it as metal worker, carpenter, tailor or even within the colonial administration, often found that their opportunities were limited in Germany, where their respective fields of employment were often overpopulated. Although the 1918 AH membership list suggests that a number of its members were earning well, the Cameroonians who sought repatriation in the immediate post-war years were often moved by unemployment and a lack of opportunities. For the majority who remained in Germany finding employment proved to be challenging. Some like the craftsmen Anton Egiomue and Josef Boholle were able to piece together a living in their trades, while others like the engineer Joseph Bilé, himself a war veteran, lost their positions to returning soldiers.[33] A handful of Cameroonians found temporary employment in unskilled positions as porters, doormen, waiters or labourers and it was often the case that they were forced to

[31] See StAHam 741-4 K6594 (Messi), K5765 (Mohamed), K4511 (Nio). On Ngando, see correspondence in ANCY APA 11295.

[32] Reed-Anderson, *Eine Geschichte von mehr als 100 Jahren*, p. 43.

[33] On Bilé, see Kümpel to German Colonial Department, 13 December 1920, BArch R1001 4457/6, pp. 134–5.

change jobs repeatedly in order to stay in work. But, in spite of the impediments that African residents faced in establishing a foothold in Germany, the metropole also offered new opportunities. One potential means of making a living was for them to turn their colonial background, connections and knowledge to their own advantage and to find a way in which to market this.

Language assistants

The thirst for colonial knowledge and the need to prepare civil servants, missionaries and traders for life in the overseas German empire opened up opportunities for Africans to offer their services as language assistants at academic institutions in Hamburg and Berlin, which trained future colonists. In 1908 the Hamburg Colonial Institute was opened and from 1910 onwards African assistants were employed as language instructors. Notable among them was Karl Atangana, the future Ewondo and Bane paramount, who was personally invited to teach Ewondo at the Institute from 1911 to 1913, as was his nephew Paul Messi. Atangana's wife Maria Biloa also spent time with him in Hamburg. Positions were, however, limited: from the time of its opening to the end of World War Two only nine men from the protectorates were employed there as language assistants: four Cameroonians, three East Africans and two Togolese. Nine other African men also found work at the Institute over this period.[34] There were more opportunities at the various incarnations of the Seminar for Oriental Languages in Berlin. As early as 1889 the Seminar had been employing Africans, but here too the numbers involved were small. In total thirty-one men found employment between 1889 and 1945; over half this number was made up of Swahili speakers from East Africa and only six were from Cameroon.[35]

With the loss of the colonies there was a sharp decline in the numbers studying African languages; positions for language instructors dried up and those already in jobs faced unemployment. Among them was Subeiru bin Adamu, nephew of the Sultan of Garoua who had arrived in Germany in February 1914 to teach Haussa and Fula. When the Berlin Seminar suspended its African language courses at the end of the war, he successfully applied to the French authorities to be allowed to return to Cameroon.[36]

[34] Meyer-Bahlburg and Wolff, *Afrikanische Sprachen*.

[35] Stoecker, *Afrikawissenschaften*, p. 318.

[36] Subeiru bin Adamu to Minister of Colonies, 7 September 1920, FR ANOM 2300 COL 31/285.

While the Seminar reinstated its courses in the 1920s no Cameroonians were employed as full-time instructors though other former colonial subjects, like Bonifatius Folli, were able to secure steady work.[37] Cameroonians did continue to play a role in Berlin. As the Seminar strove to develop an archive of language and text recordings the Kribi man Davis Innak Dipongo, whose first language was actually Ngi, found fleeting employment in 1926 providing examples of the varying tonality of the Duala language and of Cameroonian songs and fables.[38] In subsequent years the seaman Georg Menzel and then the performer Richard Dinn were invited to demonstrate their expertise in Cameroonian drum language. Despite the wishes of Martin Heepe, the Seminar's Bantu specialist, Menzel was not retained as a language assistant.[39] The situation was similar in Hamburg.

Colonial businessmen

Faced with unfavourable economic circumstances, around a dozen black migrants attempted to establish themselves as independent traders or entrepreneurs, often selling or trading products from or associated with the former protectorates. The sale of colonial products never made a great impression on the German domestic market. However, the exoticisation of consumer goods in Imperial Germany, as evidenced by the ever-increasing use of colonial images and especially images of Africans in advertising campaigns, along with the growth of both small and larger businesses selling colonial wares provided an opportunity for migrants to exploit their colonial connections.[40] The size of their enterprises varied greatly; Tom Jak Bower made a living from selling coconuts in Munich while Theophilus Michael sold on for profit goods sent to him by relatives in Cameroon.[41] By contrast, Mandenga Diek and Peter Makembe sought to create international import and export ventures. Unsurprisingly most of these businessmen were based in port cities, primarily Hamburg, the principal port for the Africa trade. There, a group of interconnected individuals involved in trade included Lewis Elidio

[37] Stoecker, *Afrikawissenschaften*, pp. 87–94.
[38] The online catalogue of the Humbolt University's sound recording archive lists the various recordings that Dipongo made and also suggests that his first language was Ngi. See www.sammlungen.hu-berlin.de/dokumente/21037/.
[39] Stoecker, *Afrikawissenschaften*, pp. 97–8.
[40] On the use of images of Africans and Africa in advertising campaigns see Ciarlo, *Advertising Empire*.
[41] Interview with Theodor Michael, August 2009. On Bower, see Bavarian State Ministry, Munich to RKA, 19 June 1913, BArch R1001 4457/6, p. 90.

Larcheveaut from the Virgin Islands, the Togolese Wilhelm Anumu and the Cameroonians Makembe, Bulu Malapa, Daniel Ipuabato and Joseph Muange. At least four of the men were linked through the AH. The fortunes of these business ventures were mixed. Muange appears to have been frequently in financial trouble, while Anumu ran a largely successful tooth-powder production company.[42] Makembe in particular provides an example of the ways in which Africans could turn their colonial background to their own benefit. Having arrived in Germany in 1910 to carry out an apprenticeship, he came into contact with the noted specialist in African languages Carl Meinhof. Meinhof took him on as a language assistant in Hamburg and from 1913 until around 1917 he was employed at the Colonial Institute to teach Duala. Their relationship soured when Makembe felt that he was not given enough recognition in Meinhof's book on the Duala language, and Meinhof later suggested to a Hamburg city councillor that Makembe's continued presence in Germany was undesirable.[43] By the end of 1917 Makembe had left the Institute and set up his own trading company. This was originally a fruit-importing business which was then reestablished as Makembe & Co in 1919, when he acquired a licence for the wholesale import of colonial goods. The company's base in Neustadt was less than a mile from Larcheveaut's place of business. For several months Bulu Malapa, who had once lodged with Makembe, was a short-term partner.[44] An advertisement for Makembe & Co in the 1920 Hamburg city directory claimed an office in Douala and advertised the sale of cacao, rubber, cotton, palm oil, ivory, tobacco and wood.[45] Under the conditions of blockade and the economic controls that prevailed during and after World War One, anyone announcing their involvement in international trade, and any traffic in luxury goods, was likely to attract police attention. Makembe, like Anumu, was convicted and fined three times for various offences; first for selling goods without a licence in 1917, and then in 1918 and 1920 for price gouging and illegal trading in tobacco respectively.[46] On

[42] Leroy Hopkins has sketched Anumu's biography and has also made reference to several other African traders: Hopkins, 'Einbürgerungsakte 1154', pp. 161–70.

[43] Note on interview with Manga Bell and Ngando, 14 October 1919. Meinhof's book is very likely the 1912 publication *Die Sprache der Duala in Kamerun*. Together with Meinhof Makembe also published a set of Duala texts, largely written and translated by Makembe: Makembe, 'Duala-Texte'; Meinhof to Zache, 24 July 1925, BArch R8023 1077a, p. 110.

[44] Registration of Makembe and Co. Hamburg, 15 March 1919, StAHam 231-7 Amtsgericht Hamburg, Handels- und Genossenschaftsregister AI, vol. 85 20635, p. 119.

[45] Hopkins, 'Einbürgerungsakte 1154', p. 166.

[46] Extract from the Criminal Registry, 12 August 1926, LAB A.Rep. 58, Acc. 399/No.958, Criminal Proceedings against Makembe and Munumé, vol. 1, p. 14.

the first occasion Makembe was also given a month-long prison sentence; his employers at the Colonial Institute asked that this be delayed until his term-time teaching commitments were fulfilled – a reminder that neither of Makembe's occupations was sufficient to support him.[47]

The actual scale of Makembe's business remains unclear. He appears to have had contacts to exporters in Douala itself, whom he wished to use as representatives for a branch of his firm in Cameroon.[48] These included former AH member Reinhold Ngando; ties forged in Germany were now being exported back to Cameroon. Ngando had run a short-lived independent business similarly dealing in colonial goods in Zoppot around 1917.[49] Now back in Douala he continued to work as a trader and was an obvious choice for Makembe to work with.[50] The Hamburg authorities, however, doubted whether Makembe had his own plantations in Africa and a raid on his business in 1920 found nothing of value that could be seized.[51] Meanwhile the French authorities suspected that Makembe's company was actually a joint venture with one or more German businessmen, and that the purpose of this was to reestablish a German foothold in Douala at a time when German traders were prevented from operating in the French territory. They did what they could to prevent him from travelling to Douala.[52] Nonetheless, in the aftermath of the war Makembe returned to Douala twice, in 1921 and 1922, attempting to expand his business. His first visit was a disappointment. Makembe had sought to purchase land in Douala close to the river Wouri, but local leaders refused his offer, believing him incapable of meeting his financial commitments. In spite of the not inconsiderable 70,000 Marks of capital he was said to possess it was reported by the mandate authorities that Makembe did not enjoy much credit in his own quarter of Deido. Not to be deterred Makembe returned to Cameroon several months later, this time staying for around a year. This second trip was even less successful and Makembe was forced to flee Douala for the British mandate territory after accusations of deception were brought against him in the native court. Oral tradition in Deido tells of Makembe disappearing on the day of his supposed marriage to a Duala princess,

47 Von Joeden-Forgey, 'Nobody's People', p. 482.

48 Commissioner Cameroon to Minister of Colonies, 7 September 1920, FR ANOM 2300 COL 31/284.

49 *Adressbuch Ostseebad Zoppot* 1917/1918.

50 Minister of Colonies, Chief of District (Douala) to Commissioner Cameroon, 30 December 1921, ANCY APA 11295.

51 StAHam 213-11 (Public Prosecutor Landgericht – Criminal Proceedings), L 416/23 – Schlüter, Dr Joe Morton, Indictment, here pp. 40–1.

52 Commissioner Cameroon to Minister of Colonies, 7 September 1920 and 13 February 1921, both FR ANOM 2300 COL 31/284.

Figure 4.2 Colonial trader Mandenga Diek, 1920

just before the colonial authorities could arrest him. From the British mandate Makembe managed to secure passage back to Germany despite the attempts of the French authorities to have him extradited to their territory. Back in Hamburg in summer 1922, Makembe was bankrupt and relying on public assistance by the end of the year.[53]

Mandenga Diek (Figure 4.2) was the most consistently successful in business. His success was a precondition for his role as a community leader in Germany, but it depended in turn not only on his considerable entrepreneurial drive but also on his ability to negotiate relationships and connections in and between Europe and Cameroon, including family ties on both continents. Having arrived in Hamburg in 1891 and taken up and completed an apprenticeship with the shoemaker Fischer, he moved on to working for a Cameroon-based planter and then as a cigar

[53] Commissioner Cameroon to Minister of Colonies, 13 February 1921; Commissioner Cameroon to Minister of Colonies, 15 September 1922, FR ANOM 2300 COL 31/284; Minister of Foreign Affairs to Minister of Colonies, 20 May 1923, FR ANOM 2300 COL 24/208; Moumé Étia, *Histoire de Bona Ebele Deido*, p. 56; Martin, 'Anfänge politischer Selbstorganisation', p. 200.

salesman. It is highly likely that he met Makembe in Hamburg as they lived close to one another at various times in Neustadt and St Pauli.[54] Diek moved with his family to Danzig in 1913; there he likely encountered Reinhold Ngando who was briefly living in the city less than a mile away from where the Dieks were living. After initially working as a clerk Diek set out on his own and established himself as an importer of colonial goods with a telephone listing in the city directory.[55] At the same time he exchanged currency for foreigners arriving in the city.[56] Having sustained financial losses during the war he planned on expanding his business and forming a far larger trading company with the help of two of his brothers in Douala as well as his friends the notable Richard Din Manga Bell and the wealthy trader David Mandessi Bell. The intention was to export European goods such as processed foods, cloth, porcelain and ironware, and to import ivory, cacao, rubber and palm kernels for sale in the United States, Great Britain, Poland and the Orange Free State. To do this he required a licence from the French colonial authorities in Paris and he further requested permission for a short-term visit to Douala in order to oversee the setting up of the business. He asked that his German brother-in-law and two European women assistants, who were to be responsible for accounting matters, be allowed to accompany him. Diek's request was backed by the French consul in Danzig, where he was already a licensed importer. The authorities in Paris, inherently suspicious of any German presence in the mandate territory, refused permission for the three Europeans to travel, just as they had previously deemed it undesirable for Makembe to travel with his German business partners. This appears to have been only a minor setback for Diek, however; entries from the Danzig directories make clear that he was able to continue to operate successfully as a wholesaler of colonial goods and keep his family in comfort throughout the Weimar years.[57]

Economic dependency and the Deutsche Gesellschaft für Eingeborenenkunde

By contrast with Diek, many ex-colonial subjects were forced to seek public assistance. Ineligible for municipal unemployment benefits because they lacked German citizenship, by the mid 1920s an increasing

[54] StAHam 741-4 K4365 (Diek), K6555 (Makembe).
[55] Entries under *Kolonialwaren* in section III of the *Danziger Adressbuch*, 1918–34.
[56] Minister of Foreign Affairs to Minister of Colonies, 8 January 1921, FR ANOM 1 AFFPOL 614/2.
[57] Oguntoye, *Eine Afro-Deutsche Geschichte*, p. 153.

number of Africans in Berlin were approaching various government departments and agencies such as the Welfare Ministry, the Foreign Office and the DKG asking for help. Among them was Wilhelm Munumé. Since his arrival as a servant in 1912, Munumé had been involved in a number of legal as well as more dubious schemes in order to make a living.[58] He came to Berlin in spring 1925 by way of Wiesbaden where he had run a failing clothes shop and where he had also spent thirty days in jail after holding a provocative patriotic pro-German speech in the French-occupied territory. In Berlin he presented himself to both the Prussian Minister for Welfare and Theodor Seitz, former Governor of Cameroon and President of the DKG, asking for aid. Both were initially responsive to Munumé's plight: in April 1925 he received a one-off payment of 130 Marks with the help of the former and between May and December 1925 he received 405 Marks with the help of the latter.[59] Seitz was particularly concerned about the negative effect that abandoning Cameroonians and Togolese remaining in Germany to their fate might have on the prospects for German colonial policy. In May 1925 he had written to the Foreign Office pleading for a fund that would either provide financial support to such individuals or finance their return to Africa. His note suggested that Munumé was not the first African that the DKG had supported.[60]

In order to win Seitz over, Munumé offered his services as a propagandist and proposed that he act as a middleman between the German authorities and Germany's African population. As a sign of his intentions he supplied Seitz with a list of names, addresses and occupations for sixteen ex-colonial subjects living in Germany.[61] Of these he named only one, the Togolese tailor Joseph Garber, as fully employed. While Seitz and the colonial authorities welcomed this information they were unwilling to encourage Munumé; in view of his criminal record, there was even some discussion of deporting him. This did not deter Munumé, who now approached Alfred Mansfeld, a former colonial civil servant who had served under Seitz in Cameroon. In October 1925, on behalf of sixteen contemporaries, most of them in Berlin, he asked that Mansfeld act as representative of their legal, social and economic interests. According to Mansfeld, jobs were found for all but four of the men.[62]

58 État Nominatif des Indigènes du Cameroun Résidant en Allemagne, no date, FR ANOM 2300 COL 31/294. For sources on Munumé's subsequent career, see below.
59 Klausener by order of the Prussian Welfare Minister to DKG, 18 April 1925, BArch R8003 1077/a, p.158; receipt, 13 February 1926, BArch R1001 4457/6, p. 193.
60 Seitz to Foreign Office, 20 May 1925, BArch R1001 4457/6, p. 178.
61 Seitz to Colonial Department, 14 October 1925, BArch R1001 7562, pp. 41–2.
62 Mansfeld to Foreign Office, 24 November 1925, pp. 44–5.

Mansfeld, who maintained correspondence with a number of Cameroonians in Cameroon itself as well as being in contact with Africans in Germany, was involved in the recently created DGfE.[63] Formed in Berlin around February 1925, its purpose was the study and protection of the indigenous populations of the former German protectorates along with their traditions. It was the spiritual successor to the Deutsche Gesellschaft für Eingeborenenschutz (German Society for the Protection of Natives), which had been created in 1913 with similar intentions and in which Mansfeld had also played a central role. In January 1914 this organisation had decided to take responsibility for looking after Berlin's African population, but it had ceased functioning in the aftermath of World War One, when Mansfeld's solicitude for German Africans had expressed itself in trying to assist their repatriation. A number of prominent Africa experts such as Meinhof and Diedrich Westermann were behind the establishment of the DGfE and Mansfeld stood at its head.[64] Like Seitz, Mansfeld was not in favour of allowing Munumé to become a spokesperson for resident Africans. His plight, however, had reinforced both men's conviction that action needed to be taken to confront the issue of poverty-stricken former colonial subjects. Seitz therefore called a meeting with representatives of the Foreign Office and various interested parties on 8 February 1926. Nineteen days later the Foreign Office presented its solution.

In a letter to the DGfE the head of the Colonial Department wrote: 'In principle the Foreign Office is prepared to provide support for natives from the former German protectorates who are residing in Germany, who, through no fault of their own, find themselves in great economic distress and who are not eligible for unemployment support.'[65] Monetary support was to be offered as a short-term measure with the Foreign Office insistent that recipients not become dependent on such handouts. In the longer term it remained committed to repatriating Africans so long as they were not married to white European women and as long as they were unlikely to be subject to persecution upon return. An alternative plan to transport former colonial subjects to Liberia was dropped once it became clear that there were no job opportunities for them there, although the authorities would continue to view Liberia as a possible

[63] Epanya to Mansfeld, 26 October 1926, BArch R1001 4457/6, p. 253; Mansfeld to Steane, 11 June 1926, ANCB Pc/i1928/88.

[64] Deutsche Gesellschaft für Eingeborenenschutz, n.d. (around 1925/1926), and Schreiber, The Tasks of the DGfE, BArch R1001 6379, pp. 30–1, 34–8; Möhle, 'Betreuung, Erfassung, Kontrolle'; 'Deutsche Gesellschaft für Eingeborenenschutz', in Schnee (ed.), *Deutsches Kolonial-Lexikon Band 1*, p. 300.

[65] Foreign Office to DGfE, 27 February 1926, BArch R1001 7562, pp. 57–8.

destination for German Africans.[66] The task of distributing financial aid and seeking employment opportunities was delegated to Mansfeld and the DGfE.[67] This established the DGfE as the central organ responsible for the welfare of former African colonial subjects, a role which it carried out into the 1940s. Drawing on Foreign Office funds, it was to provide limited help usually in the form of 50 Marks a month for rent and 60 Marks for living expenses. This sum, although not generous, was around the same amount of money that the average worker in Prussia earned in a month in 1926.[68]

More than a dozen Africans, all but two of whom were from Cameroon, feature in the archival record as recipients of DGfE aid from its inception through to the early 1930s.[69] There were probably more. Among them were war veterans, former language assistants and qualified tradesmen, men with partners or wives and families to support like Thomas Manga Akwa and Alfred Köhler as well as single men. For some these payments provided temporary financial help in periods of short-term unemployment. In other cases money was granted to help recipients secure jobs. Otto Makube received a loan of 110 Marks, which he was expected to repay, in order to help him take up a position in Allenstein, East Prussia while Dominikus Manga from Yaoundé received funds to undertake an apprenticeship as a chauffeur.[70] For others, it became almost impossible to escape from dependency on DGfE handouts.

Among those who regularly collected payments from the DGfE's office in the Martin-Luther-Straße 97 were Thomas Manga Akwa, Munumé and Makembe. The three men's frequent requests for payments in advance were a source of continuing tension, and a violent confrontation arose between Makembe and Mansfeld in May 1926 when Makembe refused a job at the Health Exhibition in Düsseldorf because the pay was low and no accommodation was provided and Mansfeld responded by threatening to cut his monthly allowance. Mansfeld sought police protection and initiated steps to deport Makembe. The three Cameroonians then engaged a lawyer to represent them, claiming that funds were being withheld from them and that they were being forced to accept jobs which were beneath their levels of training and social standing. The Foreign

[66] German Consulate Monrovia to VfdSW, 16 April 1926, BArch R1001 4457/6, p. 214.

[67] In most cases it was through the VfdSW, which Mansfeld also headed, that he sought employment for Africans.

[68] This figure is based upon a worker earning around an average of 25.87 Marks a week: von Saldern, 'Gesellschaft und Lebensgestaltung', p. 88.

[69] See the BArch files R1001 4457/6, R1001 4457/7 and R8023 1077a.

[70] Mansfeld to Foreign Office, 16 May 1928, pp. 121–2.

Office, in consultation with Mansfeld, replied that economic conditions were such that many German workers were underemployed and that the Foreign Office was under no legal obligation to financially support the men. Even before this response had been delivered, Munumé returned to Mansfeld's office and pleaded that the DGfE once again take up their case. This Mansfeld agreed to do.[71]

Despite this incident Manga Akwa enjoyed a close relationship with both Mansfeld and Seitz, whose acquaintance he had first made in Cameroon. Both men tried to use their influence and connections to find work for him. In particular Seitz, aware of Manga Akwa's social position in Douala, deemed this to be politically important.[72] When their efforts proved unsuccessful, Seitz concluded that in Manga Akwa's case an exception might be made to the Foreign Office's policy against repatriating Africans married to European women. He argued that the whole family should receive paid passage to Cameroon. The Foreign Office warned Seitz against pursuing the plan, whereupon Seitz suggested that government departments be asked to either find or create a position for the Cameroonian. In spite of the positive references Seitz provided for Manga Akwa, the various replies the Foreign Office received to this request were negative.[73] This was the situation in which Manga Akwa appealed for aid in the name of his family, and which contributed to his separation from his wife.

The effects of unemployment were even more devastating in other cases. Richard Dinn, a recipient of DGfE aid and acquaintance of Manga Akwa, was at times reduced to living in a homeless shelter in Bremen and later a Salvation Army home in Berlin.[74] In and around Bremen Dinn had scraped a living finding jobs in a variety of small shops and a shoe factory with the help of German acquaintances, before moving to the capital. There he was temporarily employed as a dancer at the Admiralspalast in 1927 and he occasionally provided assistance at the Seminar for Oriental Languages. He died in Berlin in abject poverty in winter 1929. Much like Joseph Bell's funeral six years previously, Dinn's funeral became a demonstration of solidarity among the African

[71] Correspondence in BArch R1001 4457/6, pp. 204–21.

[72] Seitz to Police Commissioner (Traffic department) Berlin-Charlottenburg, 25 April 1925, BArch R8023 1077a, pp. 152–3.

[73] Mansfeld to Seitz, 16 February 1928, BArch R8023 1077a, pp. 9–10; Seitz to Foreign Office, 8 March 1928; Brückner to DKG, 16 March 1928; Seitz to Foreign Office, 18 June 1929; Foreign Office to DKG, 30 July 1929: BArch R1001 4457/7, pp. 100, 102, 143, 154.

[74] Berlin Police Commissioner to Foreign Office, 9 March 1927, p. 18; Pastor Kramer to the Foreign Office, 31 March 1927, BArch R1001 4457/7, pp. 27–8.

community. Several of those in attendance were in circumstances hardly better than Dinn's, and resorted to pawning their winter coats to pay for the funeral.[75]

In the context of the approaching world economic crisis and the growth of unemployment in Germany in the late 1920s and early 1930s it became increasingly difficult for the DGfE to find positions for its protégés. In 1928 unemployment was around 1.3 million; by the end of 1930 it had jumped to over 4 million and was rising, particularly in the larger cities.[76] This led to a change of tactic by the Foreign Office; from spring 1928 efforts were to concentrate on pressurising recipients of aid into returning to Africa.[77] Now Africans receiving financial support had to put in writing that they were willing to return to Africa before being granted aid. As we have seen, the attitude of the French colonial authorities, as well as the costs involved, made this plan unrealistic in practice.[78]

The DGfE was not the only organisation financially supporting former colonial subjects. A handful of Africans, including Johannes Kohl and Thoy Esomber, both living outside of Berlin, received aid from local agencies. Kohl's various unstable incomes as a boxer, performer and dock worker were supplemented by funds from the Bremen social security office while the Munich-based performer Esomber was assisted by Bavarian state agencies to support his family when municipal welfare support was denied him.[79] The fact that both men's applications for naturalisation – which would have qualified them for municipal welfare – had been rejected partly because they were unable to support themselves underlines the peculiar difficulty of their situation. In Berlin, the carpenter Josef Boholle was at various times forced to seek financial help in order to support his family of four. On his 1926 citizenship application he declared that during a good year he could earn up to 2,000 Marks.[80] Until recently, however, he had only been earning an average of 76 Marks a month and at present he was unemployed. Boholle stated that it was only with the support of municipal unemployment benefit that he was able to provide for himself and his family – evidence either that the local welfare agency was ignorant of his status or that welfare workers

[75] Kurzer Tätigkeitsbericht der Liga zur Verteidigung der Negerrasse, 30 September 1930, RGASPI 495/155/87, pp. 404–8.

[76] Figures from Bracher, Funke and Jacobsen (eds.), *Die Weimarer Republik*, p. 637.

[77] Mansfeld to Foreign Office, 16 May 1928, pp. 121–2.

[78] Mansfeld to Seitz, 16 February 1928, pp. 9–10.

[79] On Kohl, see Welfare Department to Police Department, 27 April 1928, StABremen B.6. no. 374 4,13/5. On Esomber, see Fehn to Eltester, 21 November 1929, p. 182.

[80] Report about the accompanying Citizenship Application, 8 February 1926, LAB A.Pr. Br.Rep. 030-06 no. 6473 Einbürgerungsantrag Josef Boholle, p. 1.

who knew the family chose to overlook it. Two years later Boholle had successfully secured a new job, was earning around 180 Marks a month, and was no longer reliant on assistance.[81]

It was not simply economic factors that hindered Africans' employment opportunities. Their lack of citizenship and identity papers discouraged many employers from taking on African workers. In February 1928 the DGfE complained that employers often asked about the citizenship status of former colonial subjects when in negotiations over employment offers.[82] Once they were informed that those concerned were not German citizens and never had been they frequently lost interest in employing them. More ominously, particularly from the late 1920s onwards, on a day-to-day basis Africans were confronted with racial prejudice which increasingly affected their working lives. In November 1929 the Foreign Office expressed anger at the racially motivated dismissal of Manfred Kotto Priso from his job in a shoe-polish company in Dresden.[83] Priso had been active in the German colonial revisionist movement and had given public presentations in Germany and Austria about the benefits of German colonial rule in Cameroon. The Foreign Office described him as 'educated', 'skilled' and 'someone who both feels and thinks German'. He was dismissed after the nationalist Union of Travelling Salesmen pressurised his employers into letting him go on account of his skin colour, accusing them of a lack of 'racial feeling'.[84] The company tried to defend itself by arguing that Priso, like a 'female coloured' and a '*Neger*' chauffeur, was only employed for publicity purposes to promote their shoe polish and not as a proper salesperson. The DKG provided Priso with financial aid and a temporary position while Seitz made attempts to find him a new job.

What continued to worry the Foreign Office was that news of such incidents could reach the former German protectorates in letters sent by Africans in Germany to family and friends back home. In fact, it is one such letter, sent by Kwassi Bruce to his sister in Togo, that offers the most explicit testimony to the increasingly hostile atmosphere. Bruce wrote of the misery and what he called the 'racial hostility' against Africans that he experienced in Germany: 'At this moment now [1932] here in Germany a hostile atmosphere against the Africans prevails,

[81] Citizenship Application Josefa Boholle, 2 July 1928, LAB A.Pr.Br.Rep. 030-06 no. 6473, p. 28.

[82] Mansfeld to Seitz, 16 February 1928, p. 9.

[83] Eltester to Union of Travelling Salesmen, 9 October 1929, BArch R1001 4457/7, pp. 162–3.

[84] Günther (Welt-Wachs-Werk Dresden) to Union of Travelling Salesmen, 14 August 1929, BArch R1001 4457/7, p. 171.

regardless of whether they come from the former German colonies or not . . . This letter to you is a cry for help out of great distress, because things are absolutely terrible.'[85] Similar sentiments were expressed by Otto Makube in a letter to the French authorities in which he referred to a 'new situation' in Germany in 1930 which made life increasingly difficult for African residents and which impinged upon his ability to provide for his family.[86] This had moved him to request repatriation. As with the documentation regime, it is clear that the economic and political conditions of the Depression years brought the beginning of a qualitative change for the worse that would accelerate after 1933.

The official records foreground unemployment and economic dependency in the lives of Africans, but there were at least some Cameroonians and their children who succeeded in finding long-term employment. Erika Mandenga Diek worked from 1927 onwards as a secretary in Reich Accident Insurance Office in Hamburg, earning 200 Marks a month in 1933.[87] Similarly, Heinrich Dibonge worked almost continuously from 1916 through to the 1930s in the large Theodor Zeise iron works in Altona. Dibonge had entered Germany on at least two separate occasions from Cameroon before accompanying the colonial trader Hugo Daehnel to Hamburg in 1914 as the latter's personal servant and cook.[88] By 1916 he had left Daehnel's service and found employment with Zeise, which had established itself as Germany's largest producer of ship propellers and employed somewhere between 400 and 700 workers at any one time.[89] There, at various times, he worked as a crane operator and in the lathe-operating department. As a skilled worker Dibonge was relatively well paid. In 1927 he was earning 50 Marks a week, which he supplemented through occasional employment with film companies or through teaching Duala at the University of Hamburg for 3 Marks an hour.[90] This allowed him to move from Altona Altstadt into a three-room apartment for himself and his family in suburban Eimsbüttel. Dibonge's relationship with his employers at Zeise appears to have been a positive one. In the first half of 1927 he was granted an extended leave of absence to allow him to participate in a world tour with Circus Krone.

[85] Bruce to Anny Bruce, 28 June 1932, FR ANOM 1 AFFPOL 613/1071.
[86] Makube to Minister of Colonies, 2 March [1930], FR ANOM 1 AFFPOL 613/1073.
[87] Citizenship Application, Erika Diek, 24 May 1933, StAHam 332-7 B IV 1993, no. 138.
[88] Citizenship Application, Heinrich Dibonge, 19 April 1930, StAHam 332-7 B VI 1930, no. 132, pp. 3–4; Passenger List, Hamburg West Africa, 11 October 1903, StAHam 373-7 I, VIII A 1 Band 148, p. 2566.
[89] Figures from McElligott, *Contested City*, p. 3.
[90] Citizenship Application, Heinrich Dibonge, 19 April 1930, pp. 3–4.

His employer also backed his ultimately unsuccessful 1930 citizenship application, by providing him with a positive reference.[91]

Performing blackness

In December 1929 a photograph of Dibonge and nine other Cameroonians described as 'movie actors of the Race who have been given a chance in Berlin' featured in an article in the African-American newspaper the *Chicago Defender*.[92] This was one of two articles written by its editor Robert S. Abbott on the lives of 'Colored People in Berlin' and in Germany. Abbott's articles reflect the strengthening of contacts between German Africans and African Americans between the wars; he was one of several African-American journalists who visited Germany as part of larger tours of Europe and reported back to their readers about the lives of black people in Europe.[93] On the basis of his conversations Abbott reported that it was primarily in employment that they faced discrimination – with the exception of one field: 'It is in the arts that black people who have made their homes in Germany have found the greatest welcome.'[94] For former colonial subjects and their children a central means of making a living was to take to the stage or the screen. Many of the Africans whom Abbott encountered in the German capital, and whose pictures featured in his articles, were performers, and in particular movie actors.

Individual Africans worked as entertainers or in circuses in Germany from the mid nineteenth century onwards. Before World War One the Barbadian circus impresario Charles Burkett and the Togolese J. C. Bruce established their own travelling performance troupes, composed partly of family members.[95] After the war, thanks in part to the emergence of mass popular culture, the rapid growth and development in popularity of the film industry, and popular enthusiasm for North American cultural products such as jazz, black performers were in high demand. As the German economy stabilised increasing numbers of

[91] Theodor Zeise, Reference, 10 May 1930, StAHam 332-7 B VI 1930, no. 132, no number.

[92] Abbott, 'My Trip Abroad. VII', pp. 1, 10.

[93] The reports of J. A. Rogers and Lewis K. McMillan were among those reproduced in several publications. See J. A. Rogers, 'A City of 4,000,000', *New York Amsterdam News*, 21 December 1927, p. 14; 'Seeing Germany by Rail', *New York Amsterdam News*, 4 January 1928, p. 6; McMillan, 'Berlin receives Negro', p. 1.

[94] Abbott, 'My Trip Abroad. VIII', p. 1.

[95] On Burkett, see the interview with his grandson Charley Dünkeloh, in Bauche, '"Im Zirkus gibt es keine Hautfarbe"'. On Bruce, see Brändle, *Nayo Bruce*. See also Martin, *Schwarze Teufel, edle Mohren*, pp. 173–6.

African-American entertainers toured Europe and Germany from the mid 1920s onwards, often as part of revue shows. Josephine Baker, the Sam Wooding orchestra and Paul Robeson enjoyed enormous success. Their popularity was linked to a general German fascination with the United States as a model of economic and cultural modernity as well as popular interest in exoticism, both of which offered escape from the harsh realities of life in post-war Germany.[96] In this context new employment opportunities also opened up for German Blacks. As the cases of Johannes Kohl and Heinrich Dibonge suggest, performing could be a secondary occupation, a way of earning casual money for some. For others, performance became a central survival strategy. More than half of the first-generation Cameroonians who remained in Germany as well as a handful of their children are known to have worked as performers at one time or another during the Weimar years – in all, just over forty individuals are documented, though the actual number is likely to have been higher.

The job title 'Performer' (*Artist*) was used by these men and women to describe a wide range of often overlapping roles, including theatre, cabaret or film actor, musician, dancer and circus entertainer. Among those who abandoned their previous employment entirely was Kala Kinger who reinvented himself in 1920s Germany as the dancer and entertainer King Charles.[97] Similarly Hermann Kessern, who began an apprenticeship as a tailor in Breslau and was later a house servant with the Herzog von Croy, left service in Westphalia and proceeded to carve out a career with various circuses. Together with Adolf Ngange, Jakob Mandenge and briefly also Hermann Ngange, he toured under the name The Bonambelas.[98] The name, a reference to the fact that all the men belonged to the Akwa lineage in Douala, was a demonstration of ethnic and friendship ties being utilised and formalised in working life.

The roles that African entertainers were expected to perform typically reflected continuing stereotypes of the Black as primitive or exotic and tended to reinforce ideas of European superiority and African inferiority. Circus performers like Kessern appeared as fire-eaters, snake handlers or trapeze artists, acting out popular fantasies of savagery and primitive physicality.[99] Meanwhile stage and film actors like Louis Brody

[96] Tower, '"Ultramodern and Ultraprimitive"'; Naumann, 'African American Performers', p. 100.

[97] Berger, '"Sind Sie nicht froh?"'.

[98] G. S., 'In Kamerun geboren und seit 40 Jahren in Crailsheim daheim', in *Hohenloher Tagblatt*, 19 May 1961; Firla, *Der kameruner Artist*, pp. 20, 34, 81–2.

[99] In the short film *Die alte Stadt* from the 1930s Kessern can be seen arriving in Crailsheim as part of the Horaffia-Zirkus and demonstrating his skill as a fire-eater.

performed in servile roles, such as servant, cook, chauffeur or seaman or in roles that tended to 'demonise black manliness' as something sexually threatening and dangerous.[100] The difficulties that black entertainers faced in finding roles that moved beyond existing racial stereotypes mirrored the experiences of their contemporaries in the United Kingdom, who likewise struggled to be perceived as serious actors.[101] Pascal Grosse has argued that Africans were constantly on show as 'representatives of ethnocultural difference'.[102] In the context of stage and film it mattered little whether Africans played African Americans or vice versa; what counted was the performer's skin colour and the authenticity or at least illusion of authenticity of their supposed otherness that this brought.

The choice of a suitable stage name was all part of creating an air of authenticity and a means by which German Africans could take advantage of enthusiasm for African-American performers. Americanised or Europeanised stage names were adopted by several Cameroonian actors including Louis Brody, while Sam Dibonge appeared as Karl Herring and Benedikt Gambe performed as James Dickson. Kala and Bertha Kinger advertised their show as being 'Original American Singing and Dancing'.[103] But it was not just African Americans that former colonial subjects were called on or chose to represent. In effect, they frequently represented a generic figure of the racialised exotic Other, whose nationality and ethnic background were largely irrelevant. Thus, on several occasions Brody appeared in film roles portraying Asian, Arab and Malayan characters. Among the images featured in Abbott's reports was a picture of Brody as a 'Moroccan Prince' as well as a film still of Joseph Bilé in a turban opposite an actress dressed in harem costume.[104] Similarly, the Bonambelas were at various times promoted as a 'sensational Indian' or 'Hindoo' act who wore turbans and whose performances included 'oriental' scenes.[105] The performers knew to use their adaptability to their own advantage; on his calling card, advertised in the journal *Der Film*, Brody described himself as a 'performer of all exotic roles on the stage and in film'.[106] Self-promotion was crucial to increasing a performer's visibility and African entertainers, like their German

Our thanks to Folker Förtsch at Stadtarchiv Crailsheim for providing a copy of the film as well as newspaper clippings about Kessern.

100 T. Nagl, '"Sieh mal den schwarzen Mann da!"', p. 84. See also T. Nagl, *Die unheimliche Maschine*.

101 Bourne, *Black in the British Frame*.

102 Grosse, 'Koloniale Lebenswelten', p. 196.

103 Firla, *Der kameruner Artist*, pp. 70–1.

104 Abbott, 'My Trip Abroad. VII', p. 10; Abbott, 'My Trip Abroad. VIII', p. 8.

105 Firla, *Der kameruner Artist*, pp. 72–80.

106 See T. Nagl, '"... und lass mich filmen"', p. 145

counterparts, used industry magazines or postcards to advertise the roles they could play and increase their employability citing films that they had already appeared in and directors they had already worked with.

Brody and another Duala Anjo Dick were probably among the first migrants from the protectorates to find acting work even before the end of the war.[107] Born in Douala in 1892 and educated at the colonial administration's school in the city, Brody arrived in Germany sometime between 1912 and 1914.[108] As early as 1915 he appeared in the Joe May film *Das Gesetz der Mine*. Such opportunities increased after the war. The hugely popular Viennese director May was responsible for a number of sensational monumental films of early Weimar cinema featuring non-European actors. May's film company constructed a spectacular Film Town dubbed the 'German Los Angeles' on the edge of Berlin by the small town of Woltersdorf, and this provided temporary employment for almost two dozen Africans living in Germany in the immediate post-war period. Indian temples, a Chinatown and an African village were among the lavish scenes recreated there. Here, May shot the epic film series *Herrin der Welt* (1919) and *Das indische Grabmal* (1921) featuring a number of these exotic locations populated by 'authentic' non-European performers. According to the *Illustrierte Filmwoche*, seventy-two Chinese men and women, imported from Scandinavia, Norway and Switzerland, as well as a number of Arab extras were involved in the shooting of *Herrin der Welt*. In addition, around twenty African men, women and children, costumed as 'savages' in little more than loincloths with bows and arrows and headdresses also participated.[109] When asked in a newspaper interview where these African performers came from, the film's assistant director responded: 'Everywhere. Coal trimmers from Hamburg, tap dancers, doormen from panopticons. There are all sorts here.' The reporter himself commented: 'All types of blacks are to be seen here. All dialects whirl in confusion; Swahili, Duala, Pidgin-English, Slang.'[110]

Parts of May's sets would be borrowed by the Africa explorer and film director Hans Schomburgk to build an even bigger African village at Kalksee, near the Teltow canal in Berlin, which featured straw and clay

[107] Diek (alternatively Dick), who was related to Mandenga Diek, was credited with appearing in the 1916 film *Das Skelett*. In 1918 he advertised himself as a dancer performing with a female partner in the industry journal *Artist*. See Schröder, *Tanz- und Unterhaltungsmusik*, p. 287.

[108] Vice-Consul, Hamburg, to the Minister of Foreign Affairs, 24 March 1939, ANCY 10124/B.

[109] Entry on May in Bock (ed.), *Cinegraph*; '*Die Herrin der Welt*', *Illustrierte Filmwoche*, 27 September 1919; Ramm, *Woltersdorf*, pp. 51, 53.

[110] B. E. Lüthge, 'Die May-Stadt in Woltersdorf: *Die Herrin der Welt*', *Film-Kurier*, 13 August 1919.

huts and palm trees. All this was in order to finish his adventure film *Eine Weisse unter Kannibalen*, which had been partly shot in Africa before World War One and which told the story of a German woman captured by an African chief. Filming provided short-term employment for some twenty Africans mainly living in Berlin, including, according to the *Film-Kurier*, a number of 'really good actors'.[111] Identifying the individual African actors who featured in these films is made difficult by the fact that their roles were rarely credited but at least three Cameroonians, Köhler, Munumé and Brody, are known to have performed in segments of *Herrin der Welt*. Brody, who appeared in four of the film's eight segments and three times as a Chinese character, was without doubt the most successful of these performers. While others struggled to find regular engagements, he managed to find fairly constant work throughout the 1920s and 1930s, and was one of the few black actors whose roles were often credited and who was known by the wider public. In a career that lasted over three-and-a-half decades he acted in over fifty films, working together with a number of greats of German cinema, actors and directors such as Fritz Lang, Peter Lorre and Hans Albers.[112]

With the completion of these early monumental films, it appears that the number of cinematic roles for Africans declined, causing some to look for other forms of performance work. Köhler, for example, intermittently found work as a cabaret and circus entertainer, while Munumé, as we shall see, found more ingenious ways to supplement his handouts from the DGfE. But new opportunities emerged in the late 1920s with the development of sound film. Individuals like Bonifatius Folli were employed in dubbing documentary and cultural films set overseas. Typically they lent their voices to the role of the 'natives'. A 1931 newspaper article reported on an unexpected problem one popular black female performer encountered which prevented her from finding voiceover work. She had lived in Germany so long that she could no longer speak her native language, nor could she hide her Berlin dialect. This at any rate was the reporter's version; given what we know about the travel patterns of African women, it is more likely that German was her native language.[113]

[111] H. K., 'Südafrika in Südende', *Film-Kurier*, 25 June 1919. See also B. E. Lüthge, 'Die Wunderstadt Joe Mays', *Film-Kurier*, 17 September 1919; T. Nagl, *Die unheimliche Maschine*, Chapter 3.

[112] T. Nagl, '"... und lass mich filmen"', p. 144.

[113] Franse Schnitzer, 'Neger Gesucht: Als farbige "Gespenster" – Folli und seine Kollegen – An der Börse für "Eingeborene" – Turkos und Riffkabylen die kommende Mode', *Berliner Volkszeitung*, 1 January 1931, p. 11.

Alongside cinema work, Cameroonians and other ex-colonial subjects found employment in the burgeoning Weimar jazz and revue scene as musicians, dancers and waiters at jazz bars and cafés. As early as 1921 the Togolese migrant Joseph (Joe) Sewonu advertised the availability of his 'original Jazz Band' in Wiesbaden.[114] But it was from the mid 1920s, as increasing numbers of African-American entertainers performed in Germany, that the demand for black musicians grew.[115] Especially in Berlin, the cosmopolitan centre of German cultural life, black jazz bands were common. Announcements placed in industry publications like *Der Artist* by music clubs often advertised positions for black musicians.[116] At the same time such publications enabled performers to advertise their own availability either as part of bands or as soloists looking to connect with a group. Dualla Misipo, playing at the Timbuktu Bar in Frankfurt am Main in August 1928, publicised his upcoming availability as a first-class violinist able to play both concert and dance music.[117] He also advertised his own musical repertoire, smoking jacket and elegant appearance. As part condition of employment Misipo expected travel costs to be refunded and payment to be made daily. The downside of the publicity provided by *Artist* was that squabbles with unsatisfied employers could also be aired in this forum, as the East African Eduard bin Minjuma Ramses experienced when he was accused of breaching his contract.[118]

It is unclear whether these musicians were self-taught or trained, but it was rarely their musical talent that was of foremost interest to employers. According to Michael Kater former colonial subjects 'were used in dance formations in the manner of a circus attraction – preferably as noisemakers on the drums'.[119] It was in this role, as drummer and '*Stimmungsmacher*', that Heipold Jansen, at the time working in Dessau, advertised his availability to potential employers in the musical press.[120] It was thus black performers' skin colour that employers and audience paid for, their presence in a jazz troupe being perceived as a marker of the group's authenticity and a promise of 'original' jazz.[121] Accordingly black performers universally referred to themselves as *Neger* in their advertisements.

[114] Advert reproduced in Schröder, *Tanz- und Unterhaltungsmusik*, p. 288.
[115] See Schröder, *Tanz- und Unterhaltungsmusik*; Lotz, *Black Entertainers*.
[116] For examples, see the following issues of *Artist*: 1907 (24 November 1921); 2179 (15 July 1927); 2186 (18 November 1927); 2228 (31 August 1928).
[117] Advert, 1a Neger-Stehgeiger, in *Artist*, 21 August 1928, no. 2227.
[118] Notice, *Artist*, 9 November 1928, no. 2237. [119] Kater, *Different Drummers*, p. 18.
[120] Advert, Heybold (*sic*) Jansen, in *Artist*, 9 November 1928, no. 2237.
[121] Schröder, *Tanz- und Unterhaltungsmusik*, p. 288.

Jansen and Misipo were among only a handful of Cameroonians who tried to make money as musicians, and their careers as 'jazzers' were short lived. Otto Makube enjoyed a longer career, but it was irregular, and by the beginning of the 1930s both he and Jansen were actively seeking to leave Germany. Several Cameroonians and their children also found work in revue shows staged at venues like Berlin's Admiralspalast and the Nelson Revue.[122] Rudolf and Josefa Boholle in particular enjoyed success as dancers. In general, however, much as in the case of Weimar cinema, black performers, whether they were touring African Americans or former colonial subjects, were 'on the periphery of the jazz scene'.[123] In 1927 the Jamaican-American journalist J. A. Rogers commented on the struggle that Africans from the former protectorates had in finding engagements as musicians. The men he encountered in Berlin complained that white musicians were insisting that they be given preferential treatment when competing for jobs.[124] By the end of the 1920s, conservative nationalist forces which had long condemned jazz as a 'primitive' music form were increasingly vocal. In this context a 'Parisian and exotic' 'Negro Bar' which opened on Berlin's Tauentzienstraße in 1932 provoked the ire of the conservative National Federation of German Housewives' Associations. The bar, in which visitors were served by black waitresses, was deemed a 'place of debauchery' and an 'affront to culture' in an open letter sent by the federation to the Berlin Police Commissioner.[125]

Circus shows remained an important form of mass entertainment in the 1920s and several of the large German circuses like Sarrasani, Althoff and Krone featured former colonial subjects and their children. Around a dozen Cameroonians are known to have worked with a variety of German circuses, more than half of them with the Munich-based Circus Krone.[126] These performers rarely spent their entire time with only one company. Kessern, for example, toured most of Europe and parts of

[122] Richard Dinn appeared as a dancer at the Admiralspalast: Berlin Police Commissioner to Foreign Office, 9 March 1927, p. 18. According to his landlady Peter Makembe was involved in a show at the Nelson Revue: Criminal Process against Macembe (*sic*) and Munumé, witness statements, 17 August 1926, LAB A.ReNo.958, vo/No.958, vol. I, pp. 40–1.

[123] Kater, *Different Drummers*, p. 18.

[124] Rogers, 'Negro Colonies Lost', p. 9.

[125] 'In der ersten Neger-Bar von Berlin', *Neue Zeit: Das Illustrierte Morgenblatt*, 4 March 1932, p. 6; Regional Association of Greater Berlin of the National Federation of German Housewives' Associations to Berlin Police Commissioner, 2 May 1932, LAB A.Pr.Br.Rep 030 no. 21307. The letter was reproduced in the *Markische Volkszeitung*, *Deutsche Zeitung* and the *Tägliche Rundschau*.

[126] The lack of archival material has inhibited research on circus life. The archive of Circus Krone, for example, was destroyed in a fire during World War Two: communication from Dr Susanne Matzenau of the press office of Circus Krone, 20 September 2005.

South America with more than six circuses during a career that lasted almost forty years.[127]

The life of a performer demanded a willingness to travel and in general terms African performers enjoyed a great deal of mobility. But this meant that their lack of identity papers or citizenship status could prove an obstacle to earning a living. As part of her successful 1928 citizenship application Josefa Boholle cited the problems she had travelling outside of Germany as her reason for wishing to be naturalised. Her employer Otto Fettin, of Fettino's Hawaiian Revue, had written to the Berlin authorities asking that the process be speeded up otherwise Josefa would not be able to tour with the show.[128]

The fact that Josefa was earning well certainly helped her application. In 1928 she was earning up to 300 Marks a month dancing while her father earned an average monthly wage of 180 Marks as a craftsman.[129] Film work, if it could be had, was especially well paid. The African actors and actresses involved in *Herrin der Welt* were provided with daily meals and were reportedly paid the considerable sum of 1,200 Marks for four weeks' work.[130] This was more than some German workers earned in an entire year. Similarly, Munumé's theatre and film work afforded him a comfortable lifestyle and he reportedly received 500 Marks for ten days' work in a film production in 1926.[131] As Tobias Nagl has suggested, African film performers were aware of their market value; unlike white extras they could not easily be replaced, and this at times could lead to hefty disputes over fees.[132] Artistic engagements, however, provided only fleeting and unreliable income. Work was frequently seasonal and based on short-term contracts which could be easily broken by employer and employee alike. Most performers required a second source of income in order to survive.

Performing also played an important role in helping to foster a sense of community. The film set, theatre and circus functioned as spaces which brought black people into contact with one another. In particular, the unofficial 'Filmbörsen' in the Friedrichstraße in Berlin became popular meeting places for ex-colonial subjects and other black residents. This term was used to characterise the cafés in the heart of the city where the

[127] S. G., 'In Kamerun geboren'; see also Firla, *Der kameruner Artist*.
[128] Citizenship Application, Josefa Boholle, 7 August 1928; Otto Fettin to Berlin Police Commissioner, 14 July 1927, LAB A.Pr.Br.Rep. 030-06 no. 6473, pp. 33, 19.
[129] Figures from Citizenship application, Josefa Boholle, 7 August 1928 and 2 July 1928, pp. 32, 28.
[130] Lüthge, 'Die May-Stadt in Woltersdorf'.
[131] DGfE to Foreign Office, 8 December 1926, BArch R1001 4457/6, p. 255.
[132] T. Nagl, '"... und lass mich filmen"', pp. 142–3.

capital's would-be film extras met in the hope of being discovered and they were often the first port of call for film directors looking for black performers. During the Weimar period one café in particular became established as the place to recruit Blacks, where employers could search through a card file listing performers and their talents and replete with photographs.[133] It is highly likely that this was Café Central, attached to the Central Hotel and next to both the Friedrichstraße station and the world-famous Wintergarten variety theatre. James Michael, son of Theophilus, later recalled that it was here that non-German performers from all over the world met. This was where he himself began his performing career aged twelve when he was brought to the café by his father, a sometime visitor, and introduced to a Moroccan acrobat who was looking for a new member for his troupe.[134] Such points of contact helped to establish and strengthen ties. Similarly, the touring nature of performance life allowed for at least fleeting connections to develop. The circus performer Charley Dünkeloh, grandson of Charles Burkett, recalled that it was only natural for touring African performers to seek contact with other black entertainers in the towns they visited or who were likewise touring.[135] Similarly, the daughters of Mandenga Diek recalled that when African entertainers or individuals came to Danzig their father welcomed them to his home to eat with his family.[136] Touring also enabled friendships to be renewed. When the Bonambelas performed in Vienna in 1928 they met up with Joseph Bilé who was living in the city at the time.[137] Bilé came from the same village as both Kessern and Adolf Ngange and was a fellow former member of the AH. On the wider circuit, it was not only other Africans that former colonial subjects encountered; they also shared the stage with African-American entertainers. Bilé, for example, performed with Josephine Baker in Vienna and in March 1930 he appeared on the stage of the Deutsches Künstlertheater in Berlin for the first German performance (in English) of the Eugene O'Neill play *The Emperor Jones* alongside Paul Robeson. At the same time, more ironically, twelve African actors appeared in a German version of Michael Gold's play about Harlem Blacks, *Hoboken Blues*, staged at the progressive Volksbühne – but in that case all the speaking roles were taken by white Germans.[138]

133 Schnitzer, 'Neger Gesucht'.
134 Reed-Anderson, *Eine Geschichte von mehr als 100 Jahren*, p. 45.
135 Bauche, '"Im Zirkus gibt es keine Hautfarbe"', p. 39.
136 Oguntoye, *Eine Afro-Deutsche Geschichte*, p. 154.
137 Firla, *Der kameruner Artist*, pp. 97–8.
138 Naumann, 'African American Performers', p. 112; 'Robeson in Berlin in "Emperor Jones"', *New York Times*, 1 April 1930, p. 10.

Encounters within the arena of entertainment undoubtedly helped strengthen developing African social and political networks that Cameroonian migrants and their children were at the heart of. Moreover, although in the normal course of things black performers could hardly avoid being 'complicit' in the kinds of representations that reinforced negative stereotypes of black people, it was in the same context that an initiative arose for Africans and other people of colour to reclaim their image by appropriating the power of representation. This was the project for creating a black theatre in Berlin. Although that project can be seen as a form of self-help in straitened times, it was more than implicitly political. Victor Bell made it known to the African-American press in the name of the recently formed League for the Defense of the Negro Race (LzVN) when in January 1930 he announced plans for a 'race theatre', which was to be a cross between a 'dramatic theatre and a revue'.[139] Indeed, the little that is known about this project comes largely from the interested coverage it received in the African-American press. From German sources it is clear that the German authorities were also aware of the plans.[140] The revue itself was to be written by Brody, a member of the LzVN, whom the NAACP journal the *Crisis* described as 'an educated writer and actor'.[141] According to the *Crisis* the revue offered 'a picture of the development of the Negro race', featuring 'thirty colored men, eight colored women, and three whites' as well as a band and a fourteen-piece orchestra. It was to be staged in a restaurant that was popular with Berlin's black community. The National Socialist newspaper the *Völkischer Beobachter* expressed contempt at the prospect of a play centring on African culture and performed in German, French, English and African languages being put on in Berlin.[142] It remains unclear when, where and how often Brody's revue was staged, but in December 1930 the *New York Amsterdam News* was the first of several African-American newspapers to report that *Sunrise in Morning Land*, as the revue was known, featuring Helen Allen and 'Mr. R. Makube' (probably Otto Makube), had already been performed.[143]

139 'Berlin to have a Race House', *Baltimore Afro-American*, 18 January 1930, p. 8. On the League, see Chapter 6.

140 Eltester to Brückner, 8 January 1930, BArch R1001 4457/7, p. 232. On the revue see also T. Nagl, *Die unheimliche Maschine*, pp. 572–4.

141 'Along the Color Line', *Crisis*, 37/3 (March 1930), p. 94.

142 'Ein Negertheater in Berlin?', *Völkischer Beobachter*, 24 January 1931, p. 2.

143 'At Berlin's Negro Theatre', *New York Amsterdam News*, 31 December 1930, p. 9. See also 'The Long and Short of Sunshine in Morning Land', *Baltimore Afro-American*, 3 January 1931, p. 10; 'Playing in Berlin', *Chicago Defender*, 10 January 1931, p. 9.

Crime as a survival strategy

A further form of performance as a survival strategy was the kind associated with complicated criminal schemes. Crimes revolving around forgery and deception were certainly not uncommon during the Weimar period and a handful of African men were involved in them.[144] Most prominent among them were Wilhelm Munumé and Peter Makembe, whose imaginative 'tricksterism' self-consciously exploited stereotypes of the African. As we have seen, both men tried to establish independent businesses just after the war. In neither case did these businesses survive, and by the mid 1920s both were living in Berlin, where it is likely that they met in the offices of the DGfE or on the entertainment scene. They seem to have appeared together in a production of Marcellus Schiffer and Paul Strasser's play *Die fleissige Leserin* at the Renaissance Theatre in June 1926.[145] Munumé's calling card referred to him as 'the well-known Negro actor Wilhelm Munumé' and featured a picture of him in a dinner jacket with monocle, gloves and cane.[146]

Munumé had been involved in criminal scams as early as 1921, when he approached various German banks, calling himself John Black, a representative of the Republic of Liberia, and attempted to exchange forged cheques made out in British pounds. In preparation for his scheme he had placed an advertisement in the *Berliner Börsenkurier*, claiming that the Liberian government was paying out on all its stocks in pounds.[147] The scam failed and he received a three-year custodial sentence. The pair's 1926 forgery plan, like Munumé's early plan, was based on exploiting their visibility as Africans. The two men planned to print British five-pound notes, and this called for the help of professional printers, paper makers and equipment suppliers. In order not to arouse suspicion they created roles for themselves when dealing with German contacts. They introduced themselves as official representatives of the fictitious King Bondongulo from Accra, British West Africa. They claimed that the materials that they required to print the notes were all part of an advertising campaign organised by the king to protest against British rule. To back this up they presented order forms with the king's

144 See for example Draft Criminal Proceedings against Josef Benjamin Coblina Ackon and Joseph Samuel Salomon, 21 November 1924, LAB A.Rep. 58, Acc. 399/No.958, vol. 1, pp. 122–3, and for an earlier case 'Die Verhaftung zweier Dualaneger', *Der Tag*, 20 May 1914, BArch R1001 4432, p. 165.

145 Communication from Information Office of Renaissance Theatre, Berlin.

146 Business card, no date, BArch R8023 1077/a, p. 132.

147 Eltester to Seitz, 7 April 1925, BArch R1001 4457/6, p. 167; 'A Negro's Adventures', *The Times*, 2 November 1921, p. 9.

letterhead on them, playing on the naiveté of their 'audience' and their lack of first-hand contact with 'real' Africans. As a result they were successful in winning the confidence of a number of suppliers and in producing their own banknotes. In spite of the attention they gave to making the notes look authentic, the scam came to grief when Munumé was arrested trying to pass one of them in an exchange office on Berlin's Friedrichstraße. This led to a search of his apartment where incriminating evidence was found.

On 22 January 1927 the men went on trial.[148] The court heard that Munumé was well connected among Berlin Blacks; his landlady testified that he constantly had African visitors and Munumé himself somewhat dramatically declared, 'I was the boss of all Blacks in Berlin and they all came to see me.'[149] In fact friends and associates, including Makembe's German girlfriend, packed into the courtroom to witness the trial. Within minutes, however, the room was cleared and only registered members of the press were allowed to remain. On the witness stand both men protested their innocence before Munumé finally broke down and admitted his guilt. He received a three-year, one-month jail sentence as the mastermind behind the scheme. Makembe was sentenced to one year and six months in prison, despite Munumé's protests that Makembe knew nothing about the scam. Both sentences, to be spent in Plötzensee prison, were, however, far milder than the public prosecutor had hoped for and they were further reduced in consideration of the two men's time in custody. The presiding judge explained his leniency by arguing that the men, as Africans, were unaware of the seriousness of their crimes. Furthermore, he argued that a custodial sentence would bring extra hardships for them because in prison they would no longer come into contact with members of their own 'race'.[150] Ironically, the next morning's newspapers explicitly remarked upon the two men's intelligence.[151]

One of the consequences of Munumé and Makembe's scams was that the DGfE seriously considered cutting its financial support to the African population. Moreover Manga Akwa complained that press coverage of the trial had made it harder for Africans to find work by reinforcing racial prejudice.[152] At the same time he wrote to German President Paul von Hindenburg 'in the name of the German colonies and of the natives

[148] The case against Munumé and Makembe and subsequent trial proceedings are found in LAB A.Rep. 58, Acc. 399/No.958, 2 vols. See also Malzahn, 'Black Captains'.

[149] *Berliner Börsen-Zeitung*, 23 February 1927, clipping in BArch R1001 4457/7, p. 6.

[150] Open sitting of the Court of Lay Assessors (*Schöffengericht*), 22 January 1927, LAB A.Rep. 58, Acc. 399/No.958, vol. 2, p. 69.

[151] See, for example, *Berliner Börsen-Zeitung*, 23 February 1927, p. 6.

[152] DKG to Mansfeld, 5 February 1927, BArch R8023 1077/a, p. 44.

living in Germany' asking that Munumé be pardoned.[153] On completion of his sentence Makembe was held for deportation to Cameroon, and he sailed from Hamburg on 15 February 1928. Less than a week later, however, he jumped ship at Rotterdam and made his way back to Berlin.[154] Similar measures to deport Munumé were dropped, partly as the result of protests from the International League for Human Rights prompted by his fellow Africans.

In winter 1931 when Munumé and Makembe were once more penniless they returned to a familiar survival strategy, posing as representatives of the Emperor of Abyssinia and attempting to exchange forged cheques, this time in Antwerp.[155] Munumé was arrested and sentenced to three years' imprisonment in Antwerp, while Makembe, who fled to Germany, was tried and sentenced in Berlin to two and a half years' imprisonment. Once more the case of the two Cameroonians received coverage from the Berlin media and again many Africans were present to witness Makembe's trial.[156] Munumé never returned to Germany. Instead he was transferred from The Hague to the state psychiatric clinic in Eindhoven in July 1935. As yet it is unknown why he was committed, but he remained there until his death in 1940.[157] Makembe managed to leave Germany after his release in 1935, and made his way to Strasbourg where he set up a small business selling cola.[158]

A similar strategy of deception was employed by Joseph Muange, who in Germany restyled himself as Dr Joseph Morton von Schlüter and whose various guises included a rich African-American doctor looking for a German wife, a plantation owner, a wine trader, an importer-exporter and a film director. The limited source material on Muange provides few clues as to his social and material circumstances and offers no explanation for his criminal activities. Nonetheless, it is clear that he often had no legal source of income and in the files of the Hamburg public prosecutor he is frequently described as being 'without means'.

[153] Manga Akwa to Hindenburg, 13 September 1928, LAB A.Rep. 58, Acc. 399/No.958, vol. 1, no number.

[154] Woermann Shipping Line to Foreign Office, 22 February 1928, BArch R1001 4457/7, p. 95.

[155] Rijksarchief Beveren EA ANTW c 2003 81. While in custody Munumé used at least two aliases: George Johnstone from Sierra Leone and Makonen Waldimarian.

[156] See, for example, 'Munumé und Macembe: Zwei Schwindler aus dem Morgenland', *Berliner Tageblatt: Morgen-Ausgabe*, 21 January 1932, p. 6; 'Abgesandte des Abessinierkönigs', *Berliner Volkszeitung: Morgen-Ausgabe*, 21 January 1932, p. 5.

[157] Information from Regionaal Historisch Centrum Eindhoven. See also, Minister of Colonies to Commissioner Cameroon, 20 March 1940, ANCY APA 11202/F.

[158] Special Police Headquarters, Strasbourg, to Prefect of the Department Bas-Rhin, 1 February 1939, CAC 940469-425-37178.

Like his friends Munumé and Makembe, Muange went to great lengths in creating these different personas. This started with the calculated choice of the name von Schlüter, which was designed to give him an air of nobility, as well as his doctoral title which he claimed came from the (fictional) university of Harlem in the United States. He frequently established contact with, and gained the trust of, those he aimed to defraud through written correspondence or by advertising in regional newspapers. He used advertisements in particular to establish contact to single German women whom he proceeded to relieve of considerable sums of money and jewellery on vague promises of marriage. For those whom Muange actually met the aristocratic name and doctor title likely evoked ideas of a noble African heritage, an image which he cultivated through his appearance and by tales of his descent from wealthy plantation owners. Muange took pains over his fraudulent schemes and he too developed an elaborate array of props and disguises, complementing his various personas with suitable letterheads. His projects ranged from the simplest, such as buying goods with fake cheques or alleging that orders made were never received or even stolen, to an ingenious 1921 film scam. In the course of the latter he not only created his own fictional film distribution company and found two wealthy investors willing to part with large sums of money to finance a sham film project, but he also set up a fraudulent film school where the students, selected for their lack of talent, were failed after having paid their fees. Among the many people Muange successfully managed to deceive was also Anumu, who sued him for stealing his toothpaste recipe. Over four years, after many creative and intricate scams and before Hamburg police managed to connect Muange to his alter-ego von Schlüter, he managed to trick victims out of a remarkable sum of over 375,000 Marks. As a consequence he was sentenced to one year and six months in prison.[159]

As a survival strategy, these criminal scams can be interpreted as a form of 'strategic exoticism'.[160] Exclusion from normal routes to employment and dependency on welfare hand-outs led men like Munumé, Makembe and Muange to take risks and exercise their resourcefulness and ingenuity to the limits of the law. Central to the

[159] Prosecution documents on von Schlüter/Muange in StAHam, 213–11 (Staatsanwaltschaft Landgericht – Strafsachen), L 416/23, pp. 1–4; Rosenhaft and Aitken, '"König der Abenteurer"'.

[160] Graham Huggan describes 'strategic exoticism' as 'the means by which postcolonial writers/thinkers, working from within exoticist codes of representation, either manage to subvert those codes or succeed in redeploying them for the purposes of uncovering differential relations of power': Huggan, *The Postcolonial Exotic*, p. 32.

various scams they employed was a performance of blackness in which the men deliberately played upon and subverted European representations of the Black and their own visible 'otherness' in order to delude and deceive their victims. When, through their skilful use of props and the multiplicity of roles they assumed (especially notable in Muange's case), they took on the personas of noble, aristocratic and wealthy (and foreign) black men, they were mining the persistent ambivalence of European stereotypes of the Black.

By 1918 there were some Cameroonians who had already spent over two and a half decades in Germany, and during the Weimar years the transient population of the pre-war period largely stabilised. The growth that this population experienced was now almost entirely through the second and third generation of children born to migrants and their European wives. The experiences of these men and women were unsettling and their life choices were frequently limited by both open and latent prejudice, which could inhibit their ability to establish roots. These circumstances called for flexibility, resilience and ingenuity, and the men typically responded by deploying the resources inherent in their experience as colonial subjects. This involved them in complicated negotiations with Germans like Seitz and Mansfeld, who sought both to support and to control them. It also saw them negotiating a wider majority culture increasingly saturated with demeaning images of Blacks but still fascinated and ambivalent in its everyday treatment of them, particularly in the kinds of formal and informal performance that became an important source of income as the 1920s drew on. At the same time they built on the forms of individual mutual aid characteristic of new migrants to develop networks of support and sociability that expanded beyond kin and countrymen. In the metropolitan 'contact zone' formal and informal associations emerged in which they were connected to ex-colonial migrants from Togo and East Africa as well as Africans from countries such as Liberia and Sierra Leone, African Americans, and men from the Antilles, with identifiable places of residence and sociability.

The documentation for these developments shows them happening in a largely masculine, homosocial milieu; beyond some anecdotal evidence of families like the Dieks socialising at home, the ways in which Africans' European wives related to these networks in everyday life are still obscure. The performance milieu was one in which there was a place for black women, and the presence of 'negro waitresses' in key meeting places is a reminder that the black community as a whole was more mixed and variable in many respects than the core of Cameroonian families that we have focussed on. With our own subjects in view, we need also to emphasise the ambivalence of the position of Cameroonian men. The performance of blackness had the potential to be subversive, and even in the performance context we have seen Cameroonians take the lead in claiming the power of representation. What we might call the revenge of the *Hosenneger*, however, arose from circumstances that posed severe challenges to African men's sense of self. Gender practices and identities are the subject of the next chapter.

5 Problem men and exemplary women? Gender, class and 'race'

Both men and women found their sense of themselves challenged by the encounter with German metropolitan society, in the protectorate itself and even more intensely once they arrived in Europe. The term *Hosenneger* which we have seen deployed in the 1880s and 1890s at moments of contest between the self-image of the African subjects and the expectations placed upon them bespeaks the ways in which articulations of race and gender were inflected by notions of class and status that had a particular character in colonialism. In the post-colonial situation, a relationship persisted between the ex-colonial subjects and the German authorities which perpetuated many of the terms of this configuration, and the vicissitudes of masculinity under these circumstances are a central theme in this chapter. Dignity and self-respect could not be asserted except in gendered terms. But forms of masculinity shaped in a patriarchal home culture in which African men were members of the majority population, often prosperous and of high social status, and relatively free to manage their affairs in negotiation with the colonisers, came under particular stress under metropolitan conditions.[1] This chapter begins by considering some cases of inappropriate or ill-adapted sexual behaviour as a way of opening up the problematic question of the relationship between acculturation and gender expectations in the first generation as well as illuminating the consequences for real lives of the sexual stereotyping of Africans. It goes on to explore the self-presentation of Cameroonian men, both their verbal accounts of themselves and the markers of gender and status most apparent in their dress – the nexus that produced the term *Hosenneger*.

If we approach the ways in which these men expressed their masculinity in the light of models of emergent black community, we may think of

[1] The literature on masculinities in Africa and among Africans abroad remains sparse, by comparison with work on women. The introduction by Lisa Lindsay and Stephan Miescher to their edited volume is particularly suggestive in pointing not only to the varieties of masculinity/manhood but also to the kinds of transformations and challenges that notions of manhood arising from native tradition undergo in colonial and metropolitan 'contact zones' and in periods when their subjects are absent from home.

them in terms of a developing subculture which implicitly at least answered back to the figure of the *Hosenneger* by insisting on a certain style.[2] Subcultural practices can serve to consolidate community, particularly where they are associated with occupations that underpin its material survival, and dressing stylishly was certainly linked to the performance milieu that most of our male subjects came to depend on. At the same time, off the stage, black masculinity was not open to performance as a positive value in white society, particularly in the wake of the moral panic of the *schwarze Schmach* campaign. In the cases where men got into trouble for acting out their masculinity, we can see one consequence of the threshold character of this black community – large enough to reinforce shared practices but too small to incubate new ones in safety – which often left men poised between the models offered by 'here' and 'there'.

The second part of the chapter steps back in time again to consider the careers of the handful of Cameroonian women who travelled to Germany in the first generation. All of these women returned to Cameroon, though like their male counterparts and kinsmen they provide evidence of links among Africans in Germany and between them and sympathetic Germans, many of which survived separation and war. Their lives in some respects offer a foil both for the 'unsuccessful' male returners of the first generation and for men who remained in Germany. Four elite women in particular succeeded in asserting their status and developing productive lives within their home communities, consciously negotiating the terms of femininity offered respectively by their home and metropolitan cultures. One of them, Maria Mandessi Bell, was more than present at the birth both of a Cameroonian national myth and of post-colonial pan-Africanist culture. Both as a facilitator of diasporic cultural discourse and in her person as a networker and practitioner of 'diasporic home-making' on two continents, she represents a dimension of community that has been largely overlooked in studies of Black Germany.

Problem men? Misreading sex

Anxieties about the presence of African men in Germany were informed by a tradition of popular and scientific discourse that constructed them as oversexed and predatory on white women, and the *schwarze Schmach*

[2] For a foundational work on style as subcultural practice, see Hebdige, *Subculture*. Cheddie, 'Troubling Subcultural Theories', reviews the literature on black style and subculture, emphasising its limiting focus on practices of masculinity. On the ambivalence of style-as-resistance in black cultural practice, see Miller, *Slaves to Fashion*, pp. 14–16, and the literature cited there.

campaign visualised those fears in vivid graphic and cinematic imagery.[3] The complementary apprehension that their very exotic character carried an erotic charge for susceptible German women informed the planning of the 1896 Colonial Exhibition and appeared to be confirmed by the behaviour of some of the spectators. The suitcase full of love letters that scandalised Bernhard Epassi's minder at the turn of the century also showed, if proof were needed, that the men could be responsive to these attentions. With the exception of Dualla Misipo's autobiographical novel, all the documentation we have that reflects on the way in which Cameroonian men perceived themselves as specifically sexual subjects, particularly in their interactions with white people, takes the form of police and prosecution records. Documents in the first instance of white society's apprehensions of transgressive sexuality on the part of black subjects, they nevertheless help us at least to see the occasions when sexuality became an issue.

All of the relationships that feature here were between men and women, but the possibility that some of our subjects may have established homosexual relationships cannot be dismissed. The overlap of black and gay milieus in Hamburg, Berlin and Paris, and in the cosmopolitan nightclub and jazz subculture, meant that they certainly encountered gay black men; during the 1930s the Senegalese dancer Féral Benga, who performed all over Europe, served as both masculine counterpart to Josephine Baker and gay icon. The biographical literature on gay and bisexual African-American and Afro-Caribbean writers who visited Europe, including Alain Locke, Countee Cullen, Langston Hughes, Claude McKay and James Baldwin, is suggestive though entirely inconclusive as to their possible encounters with African partners. Paul Malapa was very sensitive to this question, reporting that one of the Hamburg Duala had a drag act 'but he wasn't homosexual'. In his interview he twice talked about a man from Kribi who performed both in Hamburg and at the Lido and the Empire in Paris and who was homosexual; it is not possible from the interview transcript to reconstruct who this was.[4]

When Heinrich Dibonge applied to the Hamburg authorities for naturalisation in April 1930, citing his German education and twenty-seven years of residence in the city, off and on, as grounds, his application was rejected because of a criminal conviction from 1924.

[3] El-Tayeb, *Schwarze Deutsche*, pp. 148–55; T. Nagl, *Die unheimliche Maschine*, pp. 154–220.

[4] Smalls, 'Féral Benga's Body'; 'Paul Malapa Décryptage', p. 77, 54, 85. For a survey of the limited scholarship on homosexual practices in Africa and among Africans, see Epprecht, *Heterosexual Africa?*

He and his wife of four years had been sentenced to short prison terms for procuring; the indictment was that they had compelled three women living in their apartment in the Adolfstraße to have sex with African men for money. In his letter of appeal, Dibonge acknowledged that he had made an error and broken the law, but his own brief account is more ambiguous than the police statements: 'In 1923, through ignorance of the German laws, I let myself be misled by my countrymen into letting them meet German girls in my apartment.'[5] The trial record has not been preserved, so it is not possible to assess the quality of the original evidence for the nature of the meetings in the Dibonges' apartment. It is quite plausible that in the inflation year 1923 money changed hands around an arrangement that was not exclusively mercenary and had no element of compulsion in it. The apartment was in a street, and indeed in a building, in which Peter Makembe, Bulu Malapa and Georg Menzel all lived at some time, Malapa at least as a lodger with Dibonge. It was a short walk from other streets in which Africans resided; since it was also near the entertainment and red-light district in St Pauli, there was certainly scope for conviviality and prostitution to overlap.

The judgement of the police and the courts in a case like Dibonge's can be read as reflecting a presumption in the majority population that sexual relations between white women and African men were bound to be in some sense deviant. But elsewhere there is evidence of some uncertainty on the part of African men about the dividing line between legitimate and illegitimate forms of interaction between the sexes. The Berlin police reported that Thomas Manga Akwa repeatedly accosted women on the street in Berlin. Following an incident in 1923 he refused to give his name to a policeman and then refused to follow him to the police station: 'He resisted the officer violently, hit him with a walking stick and punched him so hard in the chest that his helmet fell off.' Questioned about the incident by Seitz (to whom the police had turned for advice about whether Manga Akwa should be granted a driving licence), Manga Akwa reportedly declared that the accusation of harassment was based on a misunderstanding. And in a letter of his own to Seitz he described the act for which he had been convicted as 'a trivial business'. Like Heinrich Dibonge he invoked the idea that he was ignorant of the ways of the Germans, noting that in sentencing the court had given him the benefit of the doubt as a 'foreigner'.[6]

[5] Heinrich Dibonge to Interior Minister, 23 June 1930, StAHam 332-7, B VI 1930, no. 132.

[6] Police Chief (Traffic department) Berlin-Charlottenburg to Seitz, 11 April 1925, and reply; Manga Akwa to Seitz, 4 April 1925: BArch R8023 1077/a, pp. 154, 152, 98–9.

Manga Akwa had reason to believe that his appeal might be successful. Like many former colonial officers, Seitz harboured a patronising sympathy for Africans which complemented and reinforced a tendency to blame the white woman for the consequences of any encounter which involved the hint of complicity.[7] The most notorious case of an African who suffered for alleged sexual misbehaviour is that of Douala-born Jonas N'Doki, executed in June 1942 on a charge of attempted rape.[8] Here a series of incidents in which guilt could not easily be apportioned had a genuinely tragic outcome when N'Doki encountered a woman who was unequivocally 'pure'. As noted in Chapter 3, N'Doki had first come to Germany in 1920 and settled to a career as a performer in 1926. He married a German woman in 1932, and they divorced in 1937; the couple had no children. We have no further details on N'Doki's German family, though there is a hint of a wider network in the fact that he was visited in prison by a 'mulatto' with a German name and German identity papers who introduced himself to the prison authorities as N'Doki's nephew. In the summer of 1934 N'Doki had attempted without success to volunteer for the French army.[9] By September 1937 he was performing with the Deutsche Afrika-Schau, an officially sponsored touring colonial exhibition.[10] N'Doki was dogged by reports that he had committed offences against women at the Afrika-Schau's stopping places (although it was notorious that much of the sexual attention originated with women spectators). The grounds for complaint cited in the prosecution files included otherwise unspecified acts of insult and harassment, appearing in public dressed in nothing but a bathrobe and forcing his way into a woman's hotel room. A leitmotif in these cases, none of which came to a successful prosecution, was the offer of money or gifts as a prelude to an act or gesture of intimacy. A prosecution for rape and attempted rape in Munich in late 1940 ended in a 'not guilty' verdict when the court found the accusers, two women of dubious character, to be unreliable witnesses.

N'Doki's awareness of himself as a sexual subject was not in dispute on either side. In this case he stated that he had already had drinking

7 See for example Lindequist to KPA, 20 May 1939, BArch R1001 6383, pp. 324–9. Cf. Bechhaus-Gerst, '"Hinrichtung 6.18 Uhr..."', p. 46; Bechhaus-Gerst, 'Alexander N'Doki'.

8 Except where otherwise indicated, the sources for this account are in the files of the 1941 prosecution: StAHam 213-11 4807-42.

9 Colonial Office (Pierre Laval) to Foreign Ministry (France), 17 July 1934, FR ANOM 2300 COL 30/277.

10 List of wages paid in the Deutsche Afrika-Schau between 1 and 30 September 1937, BArch R1001 6383, p. 21. For a detailed account of the Afrika-Schau, see Chapter 7.

sessions and sexual relations with the two women on previous occasions and had paid them for it. When he was arrested in March 1941 he declared to the police that he 'regularly' had sex with German girls, most recently the day before his arrest; at his trial he repeated the assertion, using the phrase 'am laufenden Band' ('non-stop'). In the two cases for which he was finally convicted he acknowledged that he had wanted sex and denied only the use of force. In the first of the cases, an incident in Friedrichshafen in February 1939, he had walked the woman home and on the doorstep offered her 20 Marks and a ring; according to her own account, when she refused the offer and entered her building he followed her in, embraced her, threw her to the ground and choked her while attempting to initiate intercourse. In the second episode of February 1941, a similar pattern of events allegedly ended with him violently pulling down the underpants of the woman and going so far as to expose his tumescent penis. The fact that the woman was due to be married the next day gave credence to her claim to have been a victim.

The extent to which N'Doki was culpable or cynical in each of these cases is difficult to establish; Marianne Bechhaus-Gerst has used the term 'date rape' to signal the ambiguity of the situations in which N'Doki found himself as long as he continued to seek sexual satisfaction in casual encounters. Any interpretation based on trial records is bound to be skewed equally by the notorious dynamics of rape trials and by the particularly charged circumstances under which these trials were held. Thus the findings in earlier cases in both Munich and Hamburg bespeak the prejudice of the police and courts in favour of the accused in light of presumptions about the accuser's character. By the time of the final trial, with Nazi Germany at war, the political cards were definitively stacked against N'Doki as a black defendant. The decision of the Hamburg prosecutor to add a retrospective charge in respect of the 1939 episode to the 1941 prosecution was in itself evidence of an intention to make an example of N'Doki. Between July and November 1941 the case was passed on from the ordinary criminal court for trial before a special tribunal, and indictments under 1939 decrees against *Volksschädlinge* (people whose actions were parasitic on or endangered the nation) and violent criminals and more recent changes to the criminal code were added to the original charges of attempted rape. Of these, only the charge (under the *Volksschädlinge* decree) that he had used the wartime blackout as cover for his criminal actions was a substantive addition to the case against him, and even the special tribunal rejected it. The other new charges had the functions of moving the case from the ordinary jurisdiction to the special tribunal, enabling a retrospective charge, and mandating the death penalty. The tribunal justified the death penalty for N'Doki in terms of the need for 'just retribution' against a sex criminal (*Sittlichkeitsverbrecher*). The judges based their determination that N'Doki was indeed an incorrigible *Sittlichkeitsverbrecher* on the fact that he had continued in his unacceptable behaviour even after the Munich prosecution, which was deemed to constitute a formal warning, and went on to assert that this was rooted in 'a racially determined domination by physical urges and lack of self-control' which made him 'a permanent threat to German women'.[11]

Against the strong presumption that N'Doki was an innocent victim of a vindictive racist system there is the consistency of testimony to N'Doki's readiness to use verbal violence and physical force when he was rejected. His reactions betray not only irritability but also a considerable degree of acculturation to the prevailing rhetorics of race and sex; when repulsed by a woman in the Rothenbaumchaussee he had reportedly shouted, 'Then go and sleep with some other man, you Jewess!' After the 1941 incident he was heard to remark: 'And that claims to be a German woman, and she expects to get married ...'. In the Friedrichshafen incident, the woman claimed that N'Doki had choked her; evidence of this was found in marks on her neck the next day, and according to the indictment she was sufficiently frightened by the incident to refuse to identify N'Doki face to face.

A more sympathetic court might have asked what circumstances might have led him to feel 'justified' in an expectation of satisfaction that then proved to be mistaken. Even in the hearing before the special tribunal the Friedrichshafen 'victim' described the incident in terms that suggested that she had not been averse to N'Doki's company. He and a fellow Afrika-Schau performer had been guests in the café where she worked and approached her in the street after the café closed. She described his behaviour as 'downright refined' as he walked her home, steered her out of the way of a passing drunk, and chatted about his life in Africa and on the stage. For his part, N'Doki reported that in refusing to take the money and the ring he offered, she had said 'if she was going to do it she'd do it for free' – which he interpreted as acquiescence. In the Hamburg case, the accounts of N'Doki and his accuser coincided up to the point where he claimed that she had willingly followed his invitation to have a look at his penis in the light of a torch which she was carrying and she claimed that he had torn her pants off (she denied showing interest and he maintained that she had taken her own pants down); they agreed that beyond this there had been no use of force.

[11] The July prosecution was under the provisions of the Reich Criminal Code. Text of the additional legislation invoked in November is in *RGBl* (1939), 1: 1679, 2378, and (1941), 1:549–50.

The possibility that what violence there had been in these incidents was the result of intercultural misunderstanding was raised in N'Doki's defence. The copy of the first indictment which has been preserved in the Hamburg archives carries a set of notes in his handwriting: '4 points: 1. Women and girls make a fuss: Oh let me go etc. 2. There just isn't any woman who would say to any strange man come on and kiss me or hold me. 3. Europeans sensitive skin. 4. Curiosity of the white woman and girl.' It is not clear whether these represent his own propositions or notes on the arguments of his defence lawyer. Following the judgement of the special tribunal N'Doki applied for a retrial on the grounds of new evidence, to include the results of a psychological examination. One object of the examination would have been to determine whether he really could be characterised as a *Sittlichkeitsverbrecher* in the light of his character and sexual history. Another was to determine whether or not his 'race' and 'frame of mind' put him in a position to recognise whether a woman was genuinely resisting his advances. The hypothesis that the incidents might have arisen from cultural misunderstanding was explicitly rejected by the tribunal, on the grounds that N'Doki had spent twenty years in Germany and was perfectly familiar with German life and culture; he had boasted about his experience with German women and had been in trouble on account of it often enough to recognise rejection. Paradoxically, then, N'Doki was convicted not as a foreigner or even as a Black but as a good German, though it was almost certainly because he was black that he had to die. By this time being both black and German constituted a perilous double-bind.

Positive self-images: dandy, soldier, prince, *paterfamilias*

N'Doki was not of the Duala elite, but he was a man of parts. In Cameroon he had been educated in German schools, and he worked for the postal service of the colonial army during the first year of the war. The British occupation of Cameroon prompted him to learn French and English. His habitus was acknowledged to be that of a 'gentleman', and the list of personal effects he left behind at execution tells us something about his self-image. His belongings included a full set of men's clothing – coat, jacket, trousers, scarf, gloves, shoes, socks, hat, necktie, braces/suspenders, a collar – and a pipe, tobacco pouch, wallet, pocket-knife, a pair of cufflinks and two gold rings.[12] The debts which he asked

[12] N'Doki's note on settlement of his debt, Report on execution of Jonas N'Doki, 11 June 1942, and Notes on post-mortem disposition of effects, StAHam 213-11 4807-42, pp. 53 and 49.

to be discharged from his prison earnings were three: one to his lawyer in Munich, one to his landlady and the third, in the amount of 7.75 Marks, to the Douglas perfume shop in the Große Burstah. There is no way to be certain what N'Doki's purchases might have been. Given his work as a performer, which often required that he appear stripped to the waist, they may have included skin cream. Soap is also a plausible candidate, given the extent to which the values of cleanliness and its achievement through the consumption of soap were promoted in the colonies.[13] Scents of various kinds and mouthwash are also possibilities. The Douglas line in the 1920s included all of these items.[14] Whatever he was spending on, his debt for the purchase of toiletries was the equivalent of over one-fifth of the weekly wages of a skilled worker, and of what he had taken home each week as a performer in the Afrika-Schau.

N'Doki's care for his appearance, and in particular his determination to dress at the height of European fashion, seems typical of African men in Germany, as attested by textual evidence and by contemporary images produced in both domestic and public situations (Figure 5.1). When twenty-two-year-old Wilhelm Munumé composed a circular to leading figures in Cameroon appealing for money for the cause of the freedom of the protectorate, he headed it up with a portrait of himself in a suit, bow-tie and monocle.[15] A photograph of the courtroom taken during the 1927 fraud trial of Munumé and Peter Makembe shows three African men, spectators or witnesses, clothed in stylish dress coats and wearing spats, one of them holding a walking stick and an eye-catching light-coloured fedora – in contrast to the more workaday suits of the white men on either side of them. Makembe himself appeared stylishly and carefully dressed, making the most of an inexpensive ensemble.[16]

Most of these men worked as performers at one time or another, and in view of the Americanisation of black performance in Europe it is tempting to situate their self-styling in the phenomenon of the black

[13] On the consumption and cultural valences of soap in colonial and post-colonial Africa, see Burke, *Lifebuoy Men, Lux Women*. For evidence of a high level of soap consumption in West Africa before World War One, see Fieldhouse, *Unilever Overseas*, p. 341. Paradoxically, and we may surmise particularly infuriatingly, among the racist comments that Africans heard on German streets were mothers telling their children that they were black because they had not washed; see, for example, Kwassi Bruce to AAKA, Autumn 1934, BArch R1001 7562, pp. 91–100, reprinted in Martin and Alonzo, *Zwischen Charleston und Stechschritt*, pp. 411–17.

[14] J. S. Douglas Söhne Price List 1927, courtesy of Till Schröder.

[15] Munumé to 'Dear friends and chiefs' (including Sultan Njoya of Bamun), Munich, 7 April 1920, FR ANOM 2300 COL 30/294.

[16] Photographs reproduced in Rosenhaft and Aitken, 'Edimo Wilhelm Munumé und Peter Mukuri Makembe', pp. 153, 159.

Figure 5.1 'In colonial days they used to run around in figleaves; now they're better dressed than we are!', *Der Wahre Jakob*, 14 September 1929

dandy. Contemporaries observed the intimate relationship between stage or screen presence, public approval and sartorial style in the case of black performers in Germany; a critic of 1920 remarked sardonically that the '*Neger*' received '100 Marks per day in a suit, 150 Marks in tails, according to the latest pay scales'.[17] The authorised photographs of the actor Louis Brody show him in fashionable suits and tail-coats.[18] A publicity photograph of Gregor Kotto taken while he was working

[17] Erwin Bryl, 'Ich werde Neger', *Film-Kurier*, 13 May 1920, cited by T. Nagl, *Die unheimliche Maschine*, p. 542.

[18] T. Nagl, *Die unheimliche Maschine*, photos on pp. 541, 560, 565.

Figure 5.2 Gregor Kotto, publicity postcard, around 1929

or seeking work as a performer in 1929, and inscribed to 'my dear Miss Emma', shows him carefully and fashionably dressed (Figure 5.2).

But while the origins of the figure of the dandy have conventionally been located in American minstrelsy, recent studies have shown us the same figure as one that was subject to exchange and critical refashioning between continents and between intellectuals and travellers of distinct races and cultural formations in the lifetime of Brody and Kotto. W. E. B. Du Bois created a revolutionary dandy in *The Dark Princess*, whose action is set in Berlin and the United States; he reported that his visit to Europe in the 1890s had taught him 'to open his soul to elegance'.[19] It is worth considering, too, that the kind of performance in which most Africans were involved called on them to wear not white tie and tails, but various forms of exotic, oriental or 'native' dress; from this point of view the appropriation of European style was both a relief and a statement.

There is a second context for the sartorial self-expression of Cameroonian men, and that is the use of European dress in the protectorate itself. Images of travelling Cameroonians as children and young men confirm that the wearing of fashionable Western clothing was part of

[19] Miller, *Slaves to Fashion*, p. 171.

the training that they received even before they left; it was entirely characteristic for the fourteen-year-old Richard Mbene to turn up at the Bethel Mission in Berlin in a sailor suit and with a walking stick. For adults in colonial Cameroon, the purchase and wearing of European clothing was an extension of the practices by which the members of elite households used costume to express their intimacy with power. Karl Atangana was the son of a Beti headman who began his career as a clerk-interpreter and went on to become a district judge. In March 1914 the German administration designated him *Oberhäuptling* or paramount chief of the Ewondo and Bane, an invented title that confirmed the position he had established as an influence broker and effective representative of native interests in relations between his compatriots and the Germans.[20] Atangana's claim to politico-moral authority among his kinsmen was based partly on his ability to boast that he had 'captured' his wife from a European lover.[21] But Atangana consistently wore European dress even when he was not in military uniform. The extent to which his sense of self was implicated in his visible affinity with the coloniser is reflected in his account of how he came to be selected to travel to Germany as a language instructor with the colonial administrator Kirchhoff. This was in 1911, a year after the death of Atangana's friend and mentor Major Hans Dominik with whom he had worked in the context both of civil administrative and of military pacification.

> When we had gone inside and I was lying on a couch, one of ... Kirchhoff's servants came into my house and found me thinking about Dominik and looking at his photograph and mine. The lad took a picture of me and showed it to his master.[22]

This is echoed by a scene in Dualla Misipo's autobiographical novel *Der Junge aus Duala*; the narrator's father, a farmer, is pictured wearing khaki and high boots in imitation of the portrait of Chancellor Otto von Bismarck hanging over his desk. The narrator's mother, too, is visualised in terms of her clothing: a made-to-measure dress ordered from Hamburg and matching accessories.[23] But other evidence indicates that investment in Western clothing was particularly a feature of Duala men. A 1930 survey showed both that the Duala spent (or claimed to spend) significantly more than other social groups on clothing – often purchased by mail order from Europe – and that Duala men spent nearly three times as much as women.[24]

[20] Quinn, 'Charles Atangana of Yaounde'. [21] Laburthe-Tolra, *Vers la Lumière?*, p. 197.
[22] Atangana and Messi, *Jaunde-Texte*, p. 107. [23] Misipo, *Der Junge aus Duala*, p. 50.
[24] Schler, 'Bridewealth, Guns and Other Status Symbols', 223. For observations about the adoption of European fashions in other parts of colonial Africa, see Martin, *Leisure and*

Exiled in Madrid after defeat and internment as a German sympathiser in World War One, and entirely dependent on the goodwill of the French, Karl Atangana laid aside his uniform and presented himself as a man of fashion.[25] This is a reminder that in the metropolitan context these men's self-styling bespeaks a determination to maintain and assert a particular – indeed exceptional – kind of dignity under circumstances of insecurity and dependency that conspired to deny it. J. A. Rogers observed in 1927: 'Every Negro I saw in Berlin was fairly well dressed ... though several of them said they hadn't been able to get a job in months. Please do not ask me how this is done, as I will be forced to choose between being truthful and being polite.'[26] For many Cameroonians, this tension was inscribed in their original status as colonial subjects; a relatively high status among their peers in Africa qualified them for education abroad, but only for manual and subordinate positions. At the same time, their labour was rarely celebrated. A composite souvenir photograph of Heinrich Ndine is among the very few that show Africans in working clothes. Here the cook's apron is draped incongruously over his tailored school uniform, the tools of his trade props in a display of suggestive physicality rather than skill. It is entirely possible that Ndine chose to pose as he did. Nevertheless, the visible revaluing of his labour illustrates a double-bind in the gendering of African subjects in the colonial eye: the same ideology that imagined their hypermasculinity as a threat tended to feminise them once they were safely in positions of service or subjection (Figure 5.3).[27]

For men of the first generation, their extended sojourn in Germany enforced this dual challenge to their sense of themselves as men. Mandenga Diek was exceptional in managing to establish himself in business twice, and in Danzig he maintained a five-room flat and sent his daughters to a private school even when the business was failing.[28] Alexander Douala Manga Bell never relinquished the lifestyle of a prince. His kinsman, minder and sometime interpreter Reinhold

Society in Colonial Brazzaville, pp. 157–63, citing women from Cameroon as fashion pioneers at the beginning of the century, and the literature on the (male) *sapeurs* of Brazzaville and Paris in the 1950s, cited in Auslander, 'Accommodation, Resistance and *Eigensinn*'. On the cultural valences of the wearing of uniforms, see Geary, 'Political Dress'. On contests over dress in colonial settings, Comaroff and Comaroff, *Of Revelation and Revolution*, vol. II, pp. 218–73; Hay, 'Changes in Clothing and Struggles over Identity'.

25 See photograph in Laburthe-Tolra, *Vers la Lumière?*, n. p.

26 Rogers, 'Negro Colonies Lost', p. 9. See also Rogers, 'Berlin – A City of 4,000,000', p. 14.

27 Maß, *Weiße Helden – schwarze Krieger*, pp. 177–84.

28 [Reiprich and Ngambi ul Kuo,] 'Unser Vater war Kameruner', p. 69.

Figure 5.3 A souvenir montage for Heinrich Eugen Ndine, 1890, Photo Ernst Raessler, Stadtarchiv Langenau, with permission

Ngando, according to his abandoned wife, 'has offered up furs and expensive gifts to strange women [and] spent a lot of money himself, never wore anything but silk'.[29] The Malapas testify to the continuation of sartorial and consumer self-awareness in the second generation. Paul Malapa vividly remembered the interwar funerals at which the African men all appeared in top hats, and he insisted on dressing stylishly himself even when he was short of money to support his family after World War Two, his 'super-chic' outfits an expression of a self-image belied by the circumstances.[30]

The walking stick with which Manga Akwa defended himself when his sexual integrity was roughly impugned by the police declared his status as a more than respectable party; it had dual symbolic valence for him, since walking sticks not only signalled membership in the European leisured classes but were also attributes of chiefdom in Douala.[31] But Manga Akwa's tussle with the policeman shows him acting out the challenges of a class position critically complicated not simply by 'race' but by the fact of being African, and this was equally true of other men whose interactions with metropolitan authority are documented. In terms of their employment and living conditions most of them became assimilated to the urban working class, though when they worked as performers they moved in a world that was outwith the class structure of industrial society and provided some access to transnational networks. As a group, they retained a privileged relationship with the state apparatus (via the DGfE and their 'friends' in the Colonial Department), but one in which the stereotypes and expectations generated in the colonial period were constantly reinscribed. The ghost of the *Hosenneger* haunts Eltester's remark in the course of the dispute over Peter Makembe's refusal to go to Düsseldorf in 1926: 'It can't be left to these ... *Neger* to decide what kind of work is appropriate to their station.'[32]

When Manga Akwa justified his deployment of his walking stick in his letter to Seitz, he did so in terms that displayed a well-developed capacity to articulate his personality in metropolitan terms. His words reveal a knowingness about what it meant to be a man in Germany, entwining claims to consideration as a political actor with his moral claim as a husband and father: he began by citing his credentials as son of a Duala prince and a loyal supporter of the German cause during the War (as a munitions worker) and after it (as a suspected German spy

29 Lisbet Elong Ngando to French consul, Douala, 30 June 1925.
30 'Paul Malapa Décryptage', p. 6; interview with Benny Malapa.
31 Gouaffo, 'Prince Dido', p. 29.
32 Mansfeld to Foreign Office, 14 May 1926, BArch R1001 4457/6, p. 215.

during his sojourn in French-controlled Cameroon), and ended by pleading for support in his application for a driving licence in order that he might begin to earn a decent living and support his wife and child; he signed himself 'Manga Akwa of Bonambela'.[33] A striving not only to be a good husband and father but for a particular kind of gendered respectability in marriage is also apparent in the life of Dualla Misipo; although the circumstances in which they married and his own employment history do not suggest that the family was economically secure, his wife gave up working as soon as they married.[34] All these markers of masculinity are anticipated in Martin Dibobe's representations to the German and French authorities. In seeking permission to marry, and then in arguing for licence to return to Cameroon, he presented himself as the son of a prince who had signed the treaty with the Germans in 1884, faithful servant of Germany in peace and war, activist in the cause of social progress, solicitous brother, uncle, husband and father, and not least reliable and striving employee: 'Diligence and impeccable behaviour allowed me to gain a position of trust in the city railways, and I have been working as first-class conductor without being dismissed since 1902.'[35]

While the only uniform in Martin Dibobe's life was that of the Berlin Transport Company, he wore it with pride. The appeal to a record of military service or willingness to sacrifice, as a claim to respect or a statement of allegiance, is a further theme in the self-presentation of Cameroonian men. Seeking the help of the DKG to find employment in 1929, Manga Akwa asserted 'I almost gave my life for Germany' when he was victimised by the French in Cameroon.[36] Others could cite actual military service, their own (Wilhelm Sambo, Heipold Jansen, Mathias Ndonge, Max Same Bell, Alexander Douala Manga Bell, Joseph Bilé) or that of their fathers (Jonas N'Doki's father had died serving in the colonial army during World War One, and in the Afrika-Schau he 'performed' the Askari). A note in Josef Boholle's citizenship application file observed that he was rejected when he 'reported for service with the other Cameroon-*Neger* in 1914'.[37] Celebrating the loyalty of Africans to the German colonisers in the person of the 'faithful Askari', or colonial native soldier, as evidence of the legitimacy of Germany's claim to be a colonial power, became a stock feature of colonialist propaganda,

33 Manga Akwa to Seitz, 4 April 1925, pp. 98–9.
34 Decision in the compensation claim of Luise Misipo née Dutine, 13 October 1960, HHStAW 518/2469/22, pp. 18–21.
35 Dibobe to Noske, 15 November 1919, BArch R1001 3930, p. 269.
36 Manga Akwa to [Seitz] [transcript copy], 15 June 1929, pp. 144–5.
37 LAB A Pr.Br.Rep. 030-06, no. 6473, p. 21.

particularly after 1918.[38] And Africans in their turn were well aware of the sentimental power of declaring a willingness to fight and die. When N'Doki volunteered for service in the French army in 1934, the French authorities refused to act on his offer, fearing a wave of applications from Africans seeking a ticket out of Germany.[39] Certainly, military service in this case presented itself as a possible emigration route. But Cameroonians in Paris would also make the gesture as the crisis of the 1930s deepened and it became apparent that Germany would be the enemy in the next war – a characteristically masculine way of asserting allegiance.[40]

Exemplary women?

African women's lives under colonialism were characterised by a tension between parameters of femininity set respectively by their families and the Europeans who sought authority over their education (notably the missions), each with their own prescriptions of duty and domesticity, and the expectations of a more distant metropolitan culture for which African women embodied the quintessence of exoticism and the lure of illegitimate sexuality. Lynn Schler speaks of 'multiple sites at which two systems of patriarchy converged'.[41] The lives of our women subjects exemplify these tensions, and in some cases show us their successful negotiation. This is particularly true of four elite women, who successfully asserted and retained their elite status and developed careers within their home communities, using skills acquired in Germany, while adhering to the terms of an explicitly 'domesticated' femininity. Because they were dutiful daughters, two of them – Katharina Atangana and Maria Mandessi Bell – were placed at the centre of the epochal events that shaped relations between the Cameroonian population and Germany in the run-up to the end of empire. They also played active roles in maintaining the continuing communication between Cameroonians in Africa and Germany and between Africans and their European friends which remained a feature of immigrant life even after 1914. And Maria Mandessi Bell, while accounting for her own actions in entirely familial terms, became a key figure in the transnational and transcontinental networks through which diasporic black consciousness came to be articulated.

38 See Michels, 'Askari – treu bis in den Tod?'; Maß, *Weiße Helden*; Michels, *Schwarze deutsche Kolonialsoldaten*.

39 Colonial Office (Pierre Laval) to Foreign Ministry (France), 17 July 1934. On attempts by Africans to leave Germany after 1933, see Chapter 7.

40 See Chapter 8.

41 Schler, 'Writing African Women's History', p. 332.

Relatively few women travelled from the protectorate to Germany, but their routes to the metropole were largely similar: they came (or were sent) to be educated, in connection with ethnological or entertainment shows, or as servants. By contrast with men, there are no records of women arriving independently before 1914. Conversely, it is likely that some German men brought African wives back when they returned from the colonies; few in number and disguised in the records by the fact that the wife would have a German name and nationality, none of these couples appears in our sample.[42] Of the women in our records, two arrived in 1886 as part of the visit of Samson Dido's troop organised by Hagenbeck and were recorded as being his wives; Bebe Etama and Singi returned to Cameroon after the tour.[43] Anna (or Emma) Ndungo and Elisabeth Esangi travelled to Berlin to take part in the Colonial Exhibition, along with their husbands. Like their husbands, they were among the Africans whom Felix von Luschan subjected to anthropometric examinations on that occasion, but while von Luschan made observations about the personalities of the men he recorded only physical descriptions of the women. They both returned to Cameroon with Esangi's husband, while Ndungo's husband, August Ewane, stayed behind to seek his fortune in Germany.[44]

There are two cases on record of girls being adopted into German families. Maria Ngambe was born in Douala in 1908, the illegitimate daughter of the German traveller Arthur Kaltenbach. He adopted her and she returned with him to Germany, where she grew up as a German citizen.[45] Titia is the only name given by key sources to a Cameroonian girl who lived for some years on the Plehn family estate in Lubochin, West Prussia. Probably born in 1891, she – according to her hosts – lost her parents in a local war or police action, and Albert Plehn, a physician in the colonial service who was stationed in Cameroon between 1894 and 1903, brought her to Lubochin at some point after 1895. The Plehns were an enlightened and educated family. Alfred's sister Marianne was a leading academic biologist. Their sister Rose was a painter, as was her partner Mimi von Geyso who lived with her on the Lubochin estate and who helped her to

[42] El-Tayeb, *Schwarze Deutsche*, pp. 142–3.

[43] 'Aus Berlin', *Norddeutsche Allgemeine Zeitung*, 20 July 1886, clipping in BArch R1001 4297, p. 26.

[44] Von Luschan, *Beiträge zur Völkerkunde der deutschen Schutzgebiete*, p. 19; Meinecke and Hellgrewe (eds.), *Deutschland und seine Kolonien*, p. 25.

[45] Registration card Arthur Kaltenbach, Stadtarchiv Darmstadt; French Consulate Frankfurt to Minister of Colonies, 4 November 1938, FR ANOM 1 AFFPOL 614/2; registration cards Maria Kaltenbach, ITS 2.2.2.1 Kriegszeitkartei; and see Chapter 7.

manage it and entertain a wide circle of artists and intellectuals. Titia's education was accordingly observed and remembered by more than one member of the intelligentsia, on some of whom she exercised a real fascination; von Geyso painted her portrait. The pioneering social worker Marie Baum recalled that Titia was treated as a 'spoiled plaything' who 'did light housework and amused everyone with her naively clever questions and opinions'. Titia returned to Cameroon in 1900 with Plehn and his wife, but was back at Lubochin in 1901 when Rose Plehn invited friends to see this 'lovely wild creature completely outside our everyday world'. According to Marie Baum, Titia was sent back to the protectorate, to an arranged marriage with a mission-educated native, at the point when she had reached marriageable age. Since Baum was able to report more than forty years later that Titia had died young, it appears that she remained in touch with her friends in Germany.[46]

In Titia's case, the wider sources suggest that the gossip of romantic intellectuals disguised a more complex and possibly more prosaic story. A Titia Koni was among the young Africans who were in attendance when August Manga Bell and his delegation visited Eduard Scheve in Berlin in 1902 (Figure 1.2), and she returned to Douala on 7 December 1907, this time without the Plehns and registered as a sixteen-year-old 'servant'.[47] This gives us some insight into overlapping African and colonial-missionary networks; at the very least Titia's hosts seem to have ensured that even in the metropole she was inserted into a wider set of educational, support and disciplinary mechanisms than the Lubochin household could supply.

The Bilé women

Marriage arrangements also featured in the concerns of the missionaries who sponsored Esther Sike Bilé and Bertha Ebumbu Mbenge, the daughter and niece respectively of James Bilé a M'bule. Both arrived in Germany from Douala in 1899 to be educated at the Berlin Bethel Mission. They did not live with Pastor Scheve's household, but in the Bethel complex in Moabit; this included a hospital and a residence

46 Baum, *Rückblick auf mein Leben*, pp. 65–72 (also cited by Wildenthal, *German Women for Empire*, pp. 49–50); Schröder, *Ludwig Klages*, vol. I, p. 346; obituary for Alfred Plehn, *Klinische Wochenschrift*, 14/25 (22 June 1935), 911; passenger lists StAHam 373-7 I, VIII A 1, vol. 108, pp. 402–3; Plehn, *Die Malaria der afrikanischen Negerbevölkerung*.

47 See Figure 1.2. Passenger list StAHam 373-7 I, VIII A 1, vol. 197, p. 3178. Two colonial military officers were among the passengers on Titia's return journey, and she was probably travelling in the 'service' of one of them.

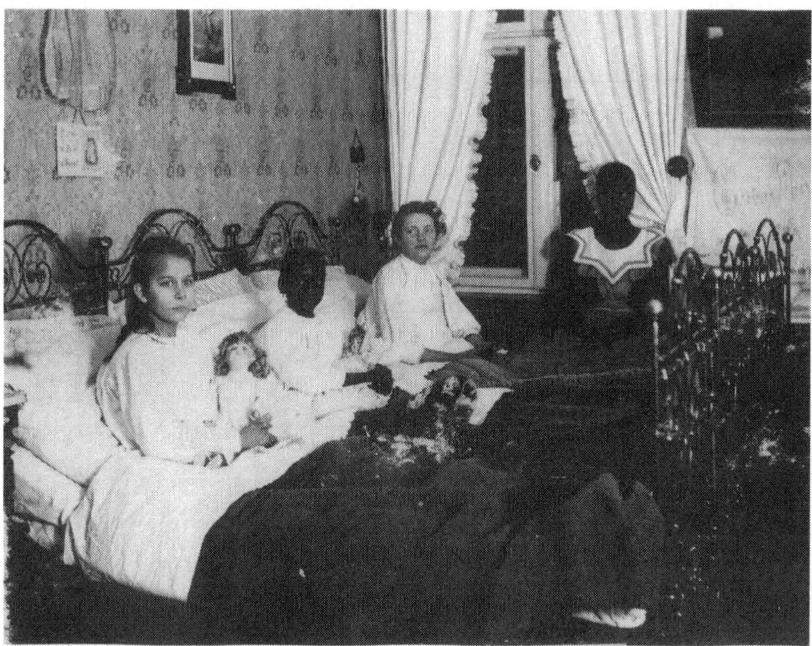

Figure 5.4 Bertha Ebumbu Mbenge and Esther Sike Bilé, Berlin 1901

for deaconesses, who took responsibility for the girls' education (Figure 5.4). Ebumbu, christened Bertha in Berlin at her own request, was only six years old when she arrived, and she stayed for thirteen years before she declared before the mission assembly that she was ready to follow the call of the Lord and go back to teach in the mission's girls' school in Bonamuti. In the eyes of the mission, at least, she made a success of her time in Berlin. Scheve reported that the local school which she attended (there was a primary school next door to the Bethel complex) always marked her work 'good' or 'very good'.[48] When Bertha left Berlin she was engaged to a fellow Cameroonian who had spent four years in Germany himself. Before she embarked in February 1912 the Chief Deaconess asked that the Colonial Office instruct the administration in Cameroon to look after her, particularly 'in case whoever has rights of control or guardianship over her according to Duala law should make demands on her about marriage

[48] Scheve, *Die Mission der deutschen Baptisten*, pp. 103–4; *Unsere Heidenmission*, 3 (March 1912), 20. Bertha also appears in Figure 1.2.

or the like which do not accord with the girl's European upbringing'.[49] Once back in Cameroon Bertha did marry her fiancé; the marriage remained childless and she made a career as a teacher.[50]

Bertha Mbenge proved an ideal pupil, giving every impression of having internalised the values of piety and service exemplified by the Baptist deaconesses. In spite of the anxieties of the Chief Deaconess, her education seems to have eased rather than prevented her reintegration into Duala society. Esther Bilé seems to have been more problematic, possibly evincing some of the resistance to missionary values around sexuality and wedlock hinted at in this report of 1903 from the Bonamuti girls' school:

> If I could already report lessons learnt, awakenings or other such successes I would gladly do so, but my first experience was that among these girls sin has already gained the upper hand, and that Satan seems to have them firmly in his grip. Some of the girls have already had to be expelled as a result of scandalous episodes.[51]

At the time when this report was written, Esther was already back in Cameroon and working in the Bonamuti school herself; she supervised pupils at handiwork and in the garden while others were in the classroom.[52] She had been considerably older than Bertha when she arrived in Berlin; a contemporary photograph shows her as a smartly dressed slender teenager, sitting stiffly and without expression among the Bethel pupils. She only spent two years in Berlin. Scheve commented laconically that she 'was educated for the Mission and we have no evidence that our efforts were unsuccessful'.[53] Once back in Cameroon, however, she displayed a distinct resistance to the moral authority of the missionaries. By November 1912 she had married one of the elders of the Basel Mission congregation and the marriage had ended in divorce. The report back to mission headquarters in Basel observed, 'she has been guilty of all sorts of transgressions against her husband' which created 'a great scandal' for her and her father. In fact, the burden of the report was a complaint about Bilé père, who was nagging the mission about his son Robert's education and who so far from doing anything to keep his daughter in line had supported and promoted her separation.[54] Esther did not remarry, and she remained

[49] Handwritten note by Solf, February 1912, BArch R1001 4457/6, pp. 79–80.
[50] Interview with Dr Thomas Barla Moukoko, Douala, March 2006.
[51] Report of Marie Bechler, quoted in 'Unsere Mädchenschule und ihre Bewohner', *Unsere Heidenmission*, 3 (March 1903), 20–2, here 22.
[52] Ibid., 21–2.
[53] Scheve, *Die Mission der deutschen Baptisten*, p. 103, photo between pages 104 and 105.
[54] J. Vöhringer, Douala, to Basel Mission, 8 November 1912, Mission 21, E-2.36 1912, p. 116.

childless. She earned a living using and transmitting the domestic skills she had acquired in her work with the mission; working from an atelier on her father's estate, she was much sought after as a couturière and teacher of dressmaking.[55]

In the memory of their nieces and nephews, Esther Bilé and Bertha Mbenge remained unaffected by the political storms of the twentieth century: 'In this country women didn't do politics.'[56] This is not strictly true. In 1931 Duala women protested openly against the French authorities' imposition of a head tax from which they had previously been exempt, and the demonstrations in which three women were wounded by police gunfire were led by women of elite families.[57] There is no evidence of the involvement of any of the Bells or Bilés, though. There was, of course, a politics implicit in Esther's scandalising of the missionaries; her assertion of a degree of sexual independence was facilitated by her father's insistence on dealing with the colonisers as a free and equal agent on what was after all his own territory. In this sense, the Bilé women were better placed to realise the logic of their inherited social position than men of their generation who remained in Germany. Two other women of the Cameroonian elite, Katharina Atangana and Maria Mandessi Bell, were more directly affected by and implicated in political developments. Indeed in their persons they represent direct links between the experience of Africans in Europe and the two political events that had significant impact in Cameroon itself between 1913 and 1920, the 'revolt' of the Duala notables under Rudolf Duala Manga Bell and World War One. They are also unusual in having left evidence of their personalities and experiences in their own words.

Katharina Atangana

Katharina Nnomo (Atangana) was born in 1902, the daughter of Karl Atangana and his wife Maria Biloa. Like her parents and brother, Katharina was baptised a Catholic by the Pallottine missionaries. She entered the Government School in Yaoundé at the age of eight, and after a year moved on to study with the nuns at the Pallottine Mission. The principal object of educating girls in the mission was to train up Christian brides

55 Interview with Dr Thomas Barla Moukoko; interview with Guillaume Dina Ekwe and Grace Eyango Ekwe Bilé, Douala, March 2006; information from Victor Dicka, Douala, February 2010. According to Victor Dicka Esther died before 1950.

56 Interview with Grace Eyango Ekwe Bilé.

57 Reports and correspondence in ANCY APA 11217/B. See also Moumé Étia, 'La Révolte des femmes'; Austen and Derrick, *Middlemen*, pp. 150–1.

for the young male converts, and over four years Katharina perfected the knitting, sewing and embroidery skills that her mother had begun to teach her.[58] It appears that she was then sent to Germany to attend a Catholic school in Boppard, a small town on the Rhine; she described this in later life as a housewifery school.[59] She also learned German at school; an account of her life which she wrote for the missionaries when she was fifteen suggests that she was not a natural linguist herself, although her father was fluent in German and spent time as a translator-interpreter at the Colonial Institute in Hamburg during 1912–13.[60] By 1917 when she wrote that account she had returned to Cameroon from Boppard, but was already back in Germany. It seems likely that the plan had been for her to continue her education there, but she must have been called back to Cameroon at the outbreak of the war. At the end of 1915 Atangana was forced to flee Yaoundé in the face of the advancing British troops, together with the Germans and several thousand Africans. As Katharina put it: 'In the great forest were English Blacks, they wanted to kill German Europeans.' While Maria remained behind, Katharina and her brother Johann Ndenge accompanied her father. Their trek across country to Bata on the coast of Spanish Guinea covered 150 miles and lasted several weeks, plagued less by hostile military action than by hunger and disease. Atangana and the Germans surrendered to the neutral Spanish in Bata, and the majority of the refugees, something over 15,000, were transported to the island of Fernando Po, where the Africans were employed in road-building.[61] Karl Atangana remained on Fernando Po until he left for Spain in September 1919. Anxious about his pro-German sympathies, the French authorities debated for another nine months whether to allow him to return to Cameroon. In June 1920 he and other Beti chiefs were given permission to return, but on their arrival they were effectively exiled to Dschang in the north of the territory.[62]

[58] On mission schooling, see Laburthe-Tolra, *Vers la Lumière?*, pp. 156, 167; Messina and van Slageren, *Histoire du christianisme au Cameroun*, p. 162; Orosz, 'The *Affaire des Sixas*'. The need for Christian brides was reinforced by the programme of challenging polygyny among the Beti.

[59] 'Fortbildungskurse für Ausländer im Goethe-Institut. Kameruner Prinzessin als Stipendiatin in München', *Bulletin des Informations- und Presseamtes der Bundesregierung*, 157 (1961), 1519–20. So far no other record of her presence in Germany before World War One has been found.

[60] Katharina Nnomo, 'Mein Lebenslauf', *Stern von Afrika* (1917), 139–41.

[61] Report of the Commissioner Cameroon to Minister of Colonies, 18 May 1918, CADN 222PO/1/1.

[62] The correspondence about Atangana from 1919 and 1920 is in FR ANOM 2300 COL 31/279. Much of it is reproduced verbatim in Laburthe-Tolra, *Vers la Lumière?*, pp. 258–77.

Katharina's own perception of the events of 1916 was that she had been fetched to Fernando Po by Pallottine nuns who were already interned there, with a view to sending her on to Europe. She clearly travelled in privileged circumstances, compared with the roughly 6,000 other women and children who made the journey to Fernando Po. She was escorted by the Deputy Governor August Full, although she did not figure on the passenger lists for this journey, either through oversight or because she travelled secretly or as a servant. After spending some weeks with the nuns on the island, she was among 837 German military staff and civilians who sailed for Cadiz, arriving at the beginning of May. With the Pallottine nuns who had accompanied her, she proceeded to Aranjuez, where she was sheltered in a convent until mid-August, when the Pallottine group set out for Germany at their own initiative.[63] They were issued with passports ('a big letter with four photographs') in Madrid. Sailing from Vigo on a Dutch ship under threat of attack from German U-boats, they made their way to Amsterdam via an unnamed British port, where they were held and their papers checked. Katharina noted the British official's question – 'Should we let a black girl go to Germany?' – and obliquely recorded a search of her belongings by two female officers. Permitted to sail on to Holland, they continued their journey by rail to the Pallottine convent Marienborn at Limburg an der Lahn. One of the things she did there was to contact her cousin Paul Messi. By her presence she provided him with a psychological lifeline, separated as he was from his wife and kin back in Cameroon and suffering acute loneliness as well as the physical deprivations of wartime Germany. He visited her in Limburg and received the first news he had had from home since the outbreak of the war.[64] She was still in Germany in August 1919, when Atangana – anticipating early repatriation to Cameroon – began to request permission to visit France so he could meet her and they could return home together. As his own sense of urgency grew, he went so far as to claim that Katharina was being held hostage in Limburg.[65] By June 1920 she and Paul Messi had joined him in Madrid, and they sailed together for Fernando Po, arriving

[63] C. Fuller, Captain of HMS *Astrea*, to Foreign Office, 19 May 1916, NAK, FO 383/213; Ebermaier to German Embassy, Madrid, 14 and 27 August 1916, PAAA Madrid 160-3. See also report of the Commissioner, Douala to Colonial Office, 18 May 1918. On numbers of women and children, see Governor General of Fernando Po to French Consul, 12 August 1919, CADN 222PO/1/1.

[64] Atangana and Messi, *Jaunde-Texte*, pp. 286–7.

[65] French Consul, Fernando Po, to Foreign Office, 15 August 1919; Charles Atangana, Madrid, to French Government in Cameroon, 22 November 1919; French Chargé d'Affaires, Madrid, to Foreign Ministry, 20 November 1919, all FR ANOM 2300 COL 31/279.

on 8 August.[66] There Atangana spent some months negotiating with the German authorities for payment of compensation for his and his people's losses during the war. Atangana finally disembarked at Douala on 28 November 1920.[67] It is not clear whether Katharina returned with her father to Douala. By her own later account she spent time at a convent in Amsterdam before finally going back to Cameroon in 1921.[68]

Once back in Cameroon, the Atanganas lived in reduced circumstances which one observer described as 'a kind of detention', in which Karl, now charged with developing the road network in the north, was 'treated like a labourer'.[69] Still barred from claiming his patrimony in Yaoundé until he was finally recalled and restored to his status as chief of the Ewondo and Bane in early 1922, Atangana was determined to convince the French authorities that he would be as trustworthy a collaborator with them as he had been with the Germans. In the hope of re-establishing some influence with the new rulers, he arranged for Katharina to be married to the man whom the French had appointed as their agent in Yaoundé, Joseph Atemengue. The marriage was unhappy, and Katharina returned to live in her father's home, where she remained until his death in 1943.[70] Her attachment to German language and culture remained, and she fostered it through contact with Swiss missionaries in Cameroon. In the 1960s she worked with the German-language teaching staff at the Goethe-Institut in Yaoundé, supporting Ewondo speakers who were learning the language. By this time she had established a reputation as a leading Germanophile and promoter of nostalgia for German culture. In the best tradition of native petitions, she wrote directly to the German Chancellor Adenauer to request a subvention for a trip to Germany to visit former schoolmates; in her letter she declared, 'Cameroon cannot and will not forget Germany.'[71]

Katharina Atangana remained childless, as did Esther Siké Bilé and Bertha Mbenge. In traditional Cameroonian society this would have been regarded as a significant failure in a woman.[72] While it is particularly difficult to do more than speculate on psychological, cultural and

66 Memo Dettinger, 'Betrifft Atangana', 12 February 1920, and German Consul, Fernando Po, to Chancellor, Foreign Office, Berlin, 22 October 1920, BArch R1001 4104, pp. 70–2 and 251.
67 Commissioner Cameroon to Minister of Colonies, 30 November 1920, FR ANOM 2300 COL 31/279.
68 'Fortbildungskurse für Ausländer', p. 1519.
69 Blaise Diagne to Minister of Colonies, 27 December 1921, FR ANOM 2300 COL 31/279.
70 Quinn, *In Search of Salt*, p. 81. The source appears to be a male contemporary.
71 'Fortbildungskurse für Ausländer', p. 1520; Kerker, 'Ende einer Koloniallegende'; Kerker, 'Du liebes Deutschland'.
72 Schler, 'Writing African Women's History,' p. 331.

familial dynamics at work in their lives, it is worth noting that in sum each of them continued to enjoy the protection of their fathers or other male relatives while establishing a degree of economic independence through the exercise of skills learned in the metropolitan context and marked in European terms as conventionally feminine.[73] The career of our fourth elite woman, Maria Mandessi Bell, offers a further variation on women's management in the field of tension between African and European culture, since (in her own perception and that of her contemporaries) she made a mark beyond the borders of family and country by fulfilling all the expectations placed on her by a nexus of African and European patriarchies.

Maria Mandessi Bell

Maria Mandessi Bell was exceptional among the travelling women of her generation in many respects. Significantly, she was destined for an academic education comparable to that of her male kin. She was born in Douala in November 1895 to David Mandessi Bell, the adopted son of King Bell and owner of a substantial cocoa plantation. Her education may well have benefited from the fact that she had no brothers near her own age. She was the eldest of seven sisters, and her brother Sam was only born in 1911. One of her granddaughters reports that there was an element of competition involved: it was the news that Alexander Douala Manga was on his way to Germany that precipitated the decision.[74] In any case, David Mandessi Bell was well travelled and ambitious for his daughter; he was also an active member of the Basel Mission congregation in Douala – though it was under the aegis of the Baptists that Maria travelled to Germany. Interviewed in her nineties, she remembered an extended stay in Berlin during which she received private lessons in academic subjects such as German, geography and mathematics as well as developing her domestic skills. She also recalled being in a choir, and her most vivid memories were associated with a variety of songs which she could still sing in word-perfect German.[75] In fact, the record shows that she spent very little time in Berlin. On arriving in Germany she briefly stayed with a pastor's family in Hamburg, and then moved on to Wolfsdorf in East Prussia,

[73] Esther Bilé's career might be compared with those of women in small garment businesses in post-colonial Nairobi, whose success as entrepreneurs builds on their middle-class background and family connections: McCormick, 'Women in Business'.

[74] Interview with Suzanne Kala Lobe, Douala, March 2006; interview with Emilien Joseph Manga Douala Bell, Douala, March 2006.

[75] Sadji, 'Höhere Tochter'.

Figure 5.5 Maria Mandessi Bell at the inauguration of Pastor Wißtoff in Eberswalde, 1912

where she was baptised in February 1912 and taken into the household of the pastor, Ernst Wißtoff. The following November she followed the Wißtoffs to Eberswalde, north of Berlin, where Ernst took up the office of pastor (Figure 5.5). Her time with the Wißtoffs was clearly a happy one; her memories of outings with the choir must date from this period, and once she had returned to Douala she tried to keep up her contact with her 'dear uncle and dear aunt', in letters that expressed warm thoughts and greetings to them and to other members of the Eberswalde congregation.[76]

That her later memories of those months were imprecise may be a result of the traumatic nature of what followed. On 1 April 1914 Maria left Eberswalde and joined the young Baptist congregation in the Schönhauser Allee in the north of Berlin. There she lodged with Ernestine Weber, a well-to-do member of the congregation; for the children of the Weist family, who lived in the same house, the memory of walking

[76] Parish Register of the Bethel-Gemeinde Eberswalde (courtesy of Pastor Martin Grawert, Eberswalde); Maria Mandessi Bell to Ernst and Maria Wißtoff 1 August 1916, Mission 21, E-4.4. Contemporaries of Maria in Eberswalde suggest that she may have returned to Berlin for schooling after 1918: communication from Pastor Martin Grawert, Eberswalde, 25 February 2010.

the 'heathen princess' to school became part of the family lore.[77] In old age Maria did remember Fräulein Weber, and the thing she remembered most clearly about her was that it had been Fräulein Weber who told Maria that her fiancé, Adolf Ngoso Din, had arrived in Berlin. His presence there marked the climax of events which acquired the status of a national myth in post-colonial Cameroon, namely the resistance of the Duala to German plans to expropriate their property in preparation for rebuilding Douala as a new and purely European town. Rudolf Duala Manga, Maria's uncle, had since 1911 been spokesman for the Duala notables in a campaign of representations and petitions against the plan. In late 1913 events started to accelerate, as the expropriations began and the German authorities removed Duala Manga from his official positions in retaliation for his continued opposition. Ngoso Din was Duala Manga's secretary, and when he travelled to Germany at the beginning of 1914 it was to bring the complaints of the Duala directly to the attention of the Reichstag. In this he had the support of German citizens, notably the journalist Helmut von Gerlach and the campaigning lawyer David Halpert. Discussion of their petition in committee in the Reichstag in March coincided with the arrival of information from Cameroon that Duala Manga was actively fomenting rebellion in the back country. Ngoso Din was arrested and jailed in Berlin before being forcibly returned to Cameroon. As the outbreak of war in Europe raised metropolitan anxieties about the control of empire, he and Duala Manga, among others, were executed on a charge of high treason on 8 August 1914.[78]

It seems very likely that Maria's move to Berlin was prompted by these events. By the beginning of April 1914 the missions in Cameroon had adopted a position that went beyond a humanitarian critique of government policy to positive support for the Duala cause, and they were paying close attention to events in Berlin as well as in the protectorate. There is evidence to suggest that plans were already in place to bring Maria home, either at her own request or for prudential reasons.[79] But the detour via Berlin seems calculated to put her in a position where she could at least gather information to bring back to Douala. By her own account she met Ngoso Din in Ernestine Weber's apartment more

[77] Parish Register Eberswalde; *Der Gemeinde-Bote. Monatliche Mitteilungen der Ersten Baptisten-Gemeinde Berlin SO., Schmidstraße 17*, 6, 7–8 (May and July 1914) and poem written on the sixtieth birthday of Herbert Weist, Berlin, 1962, both courtesy of Pastor Reinhard Assmann, Berlin.

[78] For the history of the Duala 'rebellion' and its consequences, see Austen and Derrick, *Middlemen*, pp. 128–37.

[79] Vöhringer to Inspector, 21 May 1914, Mission 21, E-2 1914 41 I, no. 92.

than once before he was arrested, and then in jail before he was deported to Cameroon; police reports suggest that she and her fiancé may have had more private meetings.[80] It is very likely that she also met Alexander, Duala Manga's son, in Berlin.[81] And before she began her own journey back to the protectorate in June, she spoke to Halpert and brought back with her the report that he was hoping to go there himself to defend Duala Manga. On the return journey ('I always travelled first class, it was a wonderful trip'), she found herself in the company of Rudolf Dix, Assistant Judge in the protectorate, and his wife, and as a result of their contact she was able to visit Ngoso Din in prison in Douala. On the day of his execution she was locked in her room in her father's house. 'I came back from Germany, almost a German myself, and the Germans killed members of my own family like that. At that time I told the others that the people back in Germany aren't so cruel as they are in the colonies. But this event shocked me to the core and changed my relationship to Germany.'[82]

In fact the following years show the focus of her life shifting from the Germanophone past to the Francophone future, but two features of her later activities echoed her 1914 role: she continued to play an important role in maintaining communication among Africans across borders, and she continued to do this in and from the context of family – to the extent that her later public vision of herself was almost entirely as the maternal facilitator of men's cultural and political action.

In Douala Maria rejoined the household of her father, whence under the difficult conditions of wartime she strove to maintain contact by letter not only with the Wißtoffs but with her cousin Dualla Misipo back in Germany. (Now that Douala was enemy territory, Germans were asked to send their letters to Dualla Misipo for forwarding via the Basel Mission, while answers from Douala travelled either via Basel or

[80] Notes on observations of Ngoso Din's movements, May 1914, LAB A.Pr.Br.Rep 030, no. 16118, p. 6.

[81] [David] Mandessi Bell to A. Bell, 5 August 1916, Mission 21, E-4.4. David had provided a stipend for Alexander during his stay in Germany before the war and was a member of the 'regency council' which advised Alexander after his father's execution: note signed Louis Fourneau, Paris, 17 June 1919, FR ANOM 2300 COL 31/289.

[82] Sadji, 'Höhere Tochter', p. 147; cf. StAHam 373-7 I, VIII A 1 vol. 279, p. 1498 (passenger list of *Lucie Woermann*, sailing from Hamburg 9 June 1914). Dix (1884–1952) became President of the German Association of Lawyers, whose nazification he attempted to forestall; under the Nazi regime he defended opponents of the system, and he defended Hjalmar Schacht at the Nuremberg trials: www.anwaltsgeschichte.de/fotogalerie/dav_biographie.html [accessed 21 February 2009]. David/Dodo Halpert (1863–1938), too, was still practising when the Nazis came to power; he committed suicide shortly after the pogrom of 1938: Arndt, 'Vor 70 Jahren'. On Helmut von Gerlach, see Chapter 8.

through American contacts.)[83] Once the war was over David Mandessi Bell's wealth and influence among a native elite with enduring ties to Germany made him an object of French interest and surveillance. A 1927 police report, drawing on information from two of their tenants, painted a picture of the Mandessi Bells that would have fitted any educated German household: they entertained the officers of German ships to dinner, with repeated toasts and German songs including 'Deutschland, Deutschland über alles'. David's study contained documents sorted into files headed 'correspondence received' and 'correspondence sent', and one ominously headed 'Woermann Line'. 'Finally, almost everywhere in the house it isn't unusual to see books, newspapers and journals in German lying around, apparently of recent date (though I don't know the language myself).' And more touchingly: 'I had occasion to speak German . . . with two young men who work as clerks for Mandessi Bell. I was struck by their attentiveness and the obvious pleasure they took in speaking to me in that language.' Both David and Maria were making regular trips to Victoria, in the British-occupied part of Cameroon.[84]

By this time Maria was married to Mamadou Diop Yandé, a Senegalese railway technician in government employment in Douala, and had two daughters by Diop and at least one child born during her marriage to Ndumbè Kala Lobe who had died in 1918. The French authorities hinted that her marriage to Diop was a political one.[85] Certainly, the union had material advantages for the family; it also made Maria once again a key figure in the networks through which information and influence of many kinds were transmitted. As a native of Dakar, one of the privileged *Quatre Communes* of French Africa, Diop enjoyed the status of a French citizen, as did his wife and children. He and each of them could travel freely within the French *imperium* and beyond. He was also in contact with compatriots in France. Diop's friendship with Blaise Diagne, Senegalese Deputy in the National Assembly, helped to bring the grievances of the Cameroonian native population to metropolitan attention. When the French authorities

[83] Maria Mandessi Bell to Dualla Misipo, 1 August 1916, Mission 21, E-4.4. The 1916 correspondence indicates the real or anticipated difficulty of corresponding directly between Douala (now enemy territory) and Germany.

[84] Police Headquarters, Douala, records of interviews with Alexandre Pinchon, 10 December 1927, and Jean Simard, 22 December 1927, FR ANOM 2300 COL 31/294. Among the suspicions of the French was that the Mandessi Bells were conspiring with German planters in the British Zone. Victoria was also the headquarters of the Basel Mission.

[85] Commissioner Cameroon to Minister of Colonies, 21 May 1928, FR ANOM 2300 COL 31/294, copy in ANCY APA W572/N.

resurrected the German plan to expropriate native holdings in Douala David Mandessi Bell helped to finance the local opposition and was able to mobilise Diagne to write to the Colonial Office in support of the Duala claims.[86]

Among Diop's kin in France were Lamine Senghor, journalist and anti-colonial activist, and Léopold Sédar Senghor, theorist of Negritude and later first president of the independent Republic of Senegal.[87] There may be more than coincidence in the fact that the Diops' visit to France during a period of leave in 1927 coincided with Lamine Senghor's imprisonment and the illness which ended in his death in November of that year. The Diops spent some weeks in Bordeaux and in September they moved on to Paris. There they stayed at 32 rue des Écoles, in a flat that Lamine Senghor had found for them and a few doors away from Senghor's fellow activist and rival Tiemoko Garan Kouyaté. Police spies reported that Diop was involved in the winding-up of Senghor's effects, including the question of custody of his young daughter, and that he was close enough to radical circles to be asked to take subversive material with him to Senegal on the way back to Douala – a suggestion which he allegedly turned down.[88]

While they were in France, on 11 July 1927, Maria's second son was born. This was David Léon Mandessi Diop, who would become a significant voice in black African poetry between 1948 and his death in an air crash in 1960. Maria Diop's own story has tended to be overshadowed by his. Among the Diop women it is her daughter, Christiane, who has been celebrated as a significant public and cultural figure. Christiane was the director of the bookshop and publishing house Présence Africaine, founded by her own husband Alioune Diop in 1947. The journal *Présence Africaine* was the first outlet for David's poetry and provided a platform for two generations of African and diasporic literary and political expression.[89] The only account of Maria's travels between the 1920s and 1960 that she published before her death in 1990 was a homage to her son.[90]

In Maria's account, she presents herself as a loving mother and grandmother and dutiful daughter-in-law, hardly more than the vessel through

[86] Commissioner Cameroon to Ministry of Colonies, Political Directorate, 1 July 1927, and Head of Political Directorate to Blaise Diagne, 1 September 1927, FR ANOM 2300 COL 31/294.

[87] On Senghor and Negritude, see among others Miller, *Nationalists and Nomads*, pp. 9–54; Wilder, *French Imperial Nation-State*.

[88] Reports of Agent Désiré, 5 November 1927 and 3 January 1928, FR ANOM 4002 COL 5. For more on these networks, see Chapters 6 and 8.

[89] See Mudimbe (ed.), *The Surreptitious Speech*.

[90] Diop, *Biographie*.

which the qualities and efforts of others came together to make her son the poet of black liberation. Those who encountered her in later life attested to her independence of mind and intellectual acuity. She is reported as saying in 1975 that the fact that she and her husband had gone through a civil marriage (as well as both Christian and Muslim ceremonies) had protected her from the claims of Diop's family after his death, ensuring her right to maintain control of her children.[91] And there are hints even in her memoir of the extent to which she was able to use and to extend her networks as well as the personal effort that it cost her to keep her family together and educate them as an African widow in a time of crisis. Her husband died in 1935, her father in 1936, and in 1938 she was persuaded by friends to leave Dakar, where she had been living for seven years, and go to France. An Association of Protestant Ladies helped to find her a flat in Nîmes. She recalls the horror of the customs officers when she arrived at Marseilles with five children in September 1938: 'My good woman! Where are you going with those little ones? There's going to be a war soon.'[92]

David's introduction to African intellectual circles in the metropole was the work of his mother, who by her own account tracked down Léopold Senghor and moved her family to Joinville-le-Pont in 1943 so David could attend the *lycée* at which Senghor was teaching. And it was Maria who took the family back to 32 rue des Écoles in 1945, to the centre of metropolitan intellectual life.[93] Her flat in the 'mini-Tower of Babel' in the Latin Quarter became a meeting place for Africans of two generations – intellectuals, *artistes* and refugees who had survived the war alongside the first post-war flowering of black student life – and the incubator for *Présence Africaine*. Maria's own guests included priests and pastors; overtly pious and sceptical of articulate radical politics, she continued to delight in group singing and (after all) in opportunities to speak German with people of her own generation.[94]

In the network around Maria Diop we might speak of a transmission of black politics through the female line. Notably, this was a line that largely bypassed Germany, although the Germanophilia of Léopold Sédar Senghor and others of his circle is well attested and the way in which the roots of Negritude were entangled in the reception in the

[91] Coquery-Vidrovitch, *African Woman*, p. 156. [92] Diop, *Biographie*, p. 16.

[93] Ibid., pp. 21–4. See also Senghor's funeral oration for David Diop, reprinted in Badji, 'Itinéraire d'un homme sacrifié', pp. 36–8; Grah Mel, *Alioune Diop*, pp. 67–8.

[94] The phrase 'mini Tower of Babel' comes from Maria's elder son Iwiyè Kala Lobé, who had a distinguished career as a journalist and critic in Cameroon and died in 1991: Kala Lobé, '"Ensemble" avec David Diop', pp. 78–82. Maria returned to Dakar after David Diop's death and died there on 20 May 1990.

Francophone world of the work of Frankfurt professor Leo Frobenius was certainly a subject of conversation among the visitors to 32 rue des Écoles.[95] The men whom Maria Mandessi Bell and the other Cameroonian women 'left behind' in Germany found their own way to forms of solidarity that became explicitly politicised and 'diasporic' in the sense of a growing awareness of a global black community. This is the subject of the next chapter.

[95] A. Sadji, 'L'Héritage germanophile de la négritude en Afrique francophone', 242–53; U. Sadji, 'Les racines de la germanophilie de Senghor'; Städtler, 'Léopold Sédar Senghor'; Edwards, *Practice of Diaspora*, p. 74. After World War Two, Dualla Misipo claimed to have worked as an assistant for Frobenius; there is no evidence to confirm this.

6 Practising diaspora – politics 1918–1933

We proposed in the introduction that one defining feature of the growth of black communities has been the development of a diasporic consciousness: the articulation of a sense of connectedness with other black people that reaches out from local relations to envision black interest and identity as something shared across the globe. This is a political vision, but in the lives of our subjects and their contemporaries it was typically something that arose out of everyday experience and was worked out in concrete encounters that called for practices of negotiation and translation. This chapter traces the institutions through which political action developed among Africans in Germany and the terms in which collective interest was articulated. Politics here means both prosecuting collective interests through interaction with external actors (including the state) and articulating those interests in terms of shared qualities and needs (or identities). Cameroonians were well practised in negotiations with German state power. Under colonialism they had developed practices and rhetorics to defend their local and family interests (material and moral) in the protectorate and taken them direct to Germany's rulers and the German public. Once settled in Germany, Cameroonians continued to display considerable confidence in their dealings with authority. While drawing on familiar languages and means of self-representation, they increasingly deployed them in the service of interests that were specific to the circumstances of the metropole.

When Wilhelm Munumé approached the German authorities for financial support for himself and others in 1925, thereby initiating the welfare activities of the DGfE, he was engaging in a new politics in the style of the old. In traditional mode he offered a service that appealed to the ex-colonisers' interest in maintaining contact and control, while he now spoke for (or in the name of) a population of Africans defined no longer by originary kinship but by shared presence in Germany. A key feature of this kind of démarche was that it presumed a community of interest between the Africans and the metropolitan authorities. Over the interwar period, we can see some of the same individuals moving towards the articulation of a new community of interests which was international in scope but defined by blackness, and which was expressly oppositional. Carried forward in new forms of organisation and through formal and informal contacts with people of colour that reached beyond Germany and Africa to the rest of Europe and the United States, this was a politics of diaspora – though one in which African Germans were condemned by their numbers and embattled position to a minor and contested role. From the late 1920s onwards, the international Communist movement was an important enabler of black political activism. The career of Joseph Bilé within that movement, though exceptional, illustrates one trajectory for political engagement in his generation. At the same time, the specific character of his situation as a German African, poised unwillingly between Africa and Europe, shows up with particular force the uncertainties and fissures inherent in practising diaspora in a genuinely global context.[1] And the possibilities for 'closing the circle', by exporting back to Africa anti-colonial politics learned in Europe, proved particularly problematic in view of the way in which Cameroon itself was poised between French and German ambitions.

A politics of petition

Before World War One the native Cameroonian elites, and in particular the Duala, saw themselves not as subjects but as partners of the German imperial power.[2] The Treaty of 1884 in which they had accepted German 'protection' was in keeping with a long history of arrangements through which the Duala had entered into strategic alliances with foreigners arriving on their shores – most recently the British. Up to a point the German administration appeared to accede in this partnership, particularly in the first decade and a half of German rule. And when the German administration gave cause for complaint, the expectation of the Duala was that formal representations or petitions would be met with a reasoned and respectful response. The way in which protests to Bismarck and the Reichstag about Governor Soden's treatment of Ndumbe Lobe were channelled through Alfred Bell in 1888 is an example of the presumption of relatively open communication among equals.[3] As the Germans began to intervene more directly in social and property relations after the turn of the century, following a scheme for modernising

[1] Edwards, *Practice of Diaspora*, p. 11, refers to 'constitutive differences'.
[2] For what follows, see Austen and Derrick, *Middlemen*, pp. 93–7; Eckert, *Die Duala und die Kolonialmächte*.
[3] See Chapter 1.

the urban and transport infrastructure of the protectorate, the Duala continued to respond with formal protests. This began with the 1902 visit of the Akwa and Bell chiefs to Germany followed by a further petition in 1905. Entirely unreceptive to the Africans' collegial vision of their relationship, the German authorities now viewed any protest as illegitimate political activity. The signatories to the 1905 petition were put on trial and punished. Ludwig Mpundu Akwa, who had stayed on in Germany in 1902, encouraged people back home to see him as leader of a liberation struggle, inviting financial contributions to his Altona address and sponsoring the publication of a short-lived newspaper in the Duala language. When he returned home in 1911 he was arrested and exiled up-country to Ngaoundéré; he died under obscure circumstances during World War One.[4]

The Germans looked for conspiracies between colonial subjects and Social Democrats where there was little more than a series of casual contacts, and imposed successive restrictions on travel and communication, and the consequence was to provoke distrust and make conspiracy unavoidable. This came to a head as a result of the German plan, promulgated in 1910, to develop the city of Douala by establishing separate European and African zones, expropriating native property in the new European zone for redevelopment. The Duala, represented by Bell paramount Rudolf Duala Manga, responded with formal protests and direct petitions to the Reichstag. But when the result of the Reichstag debate on the expropriation proved unfavourable to the Duala cause, and with the expropriations already underway native opposition was increasingly construed as treasonous activity. The consequence was the 'martyrdom' of Bell and Ngoso Din, the personal effects of which we have seen in the lives of Maria Mandessi Bell and Duala Manga's son Alexander, and which became the basis of a national myth.

World War One brought a break in the continuity of protest activity, and when political agitation resumed after the war it was shaped by a reconfiguration of the relationships between Cameroonians in Europe and those in Cameroon itself. The change in the terms and personnel of colonial rule meant that the Duala elite ceased to be privileged spokesmen for the interests of 'Cameroon', as it became more difficult for them to represent their particular interests as those of the native population. At the same time, Cameroonians in Germany had less and less reason to identify in political terms with a regional or ethnic interest defined by their place of birth (though, as we have seen, they continued to articulate

[4] See von Joeden-Forgey (ed.), *Mpundu Akwa*; annual report, Bonaku 1907, no date, Mission 21, Basel, E-2.25 1907, no. 10.

their personal identity in terms of both ethnicity and status). Educated Cameroonians in France, sustained by vital links between the old territory and the new mandate power, continued and developed native traditions of protest during the 1920s and 1930s. In their public activities, they engaged as much with questions of French policy in the mandate territory as with the interests of their compatriots in France, while at the same time developing alliances with non-Cameroonian Blacks.[5] Those in Germany, physically separated not only from Cameroon but from the men who held power there and increasingly rooted willy-nilly in metropolitan society, necessarily developed new concerns, new languages and new partnerships.

This process can be traced in the petitions that Cameroonians addressed to various authorities between 1919 and the 1930s around issues of colonial governance. The Duala notables identified early on where power lay. In the first months after the armistice they resisted French requests for their support and directly approached the British about the possibility of being placed under British protection.[6] Their next démarche was directed at the politicians deliberating on the peace settlement at Versailles. On 18 August 1919 twelve named Duala, including Lobe Bell and Eboa Deido the respective Bell and Deido paramounts, petitioned the Allied powers to request a say over the future of the former German protectorate.[7] In their address, which was written in German, the men expressed their satisfaction at the Allies' military victory and the beginning of a perceived new world order. They appealed to the principles of self-determination preached by the American President Woodrow Wilson and they asked that Cameroon be allowed to become a neutral territory free of outside influence. If this request was not to be granted the signatories were willing to consider being placed under the protection of an Allied power of their own choosing.

Their petition comprised seven further points. These included calls for the guarantee of civil rights for 'natives of Cameroon (Duala)', freedom for natives to engage in commercial and cultural activities and freedom of movement in pursuit of them, the creation of a system of local self-government, the introduction of the rule of law based on due process and a guarantee that under any European administration the native

[5] See Chapter 8.

[6] Commissioner of the Occupied Territory of Cameroon, Fourneau to Governor General of French Equatorial Africa, 20 January 1919, FR ANOM 2300 COL 30/268; Austen and Derrick, *Middlemen*, pp. 145, 147–8.

[7] Petition of Duala leaders to Peace Conference, 18 August 1919, FR ANOM 1 AFFPOL 615/2.

population rather than the governing authority should determine appointments of native chiefs to act as local rulers. Further demands were linked to the contentious issues highlighted by the 1913–14 expropriations: the notables called for the reversal of the Germans' expropriation policy both in respect of the urban plan for Douala and in association with the construction of rail facilities in the town, which had affected several of the signatories, and a guarantee of the security of native property in future. They also asked that the native population be compensated for material losses incurred by the war. In an extensive coda, they asked for investigations to be carried out into the banishment of Mpundu Akwa and the executions of Rudolf Duala Manga and Ngoso Din.

While speaking in the name of the 'natives of Cameroon and their chiefs', the August 1919 petitioners clearly identified the needs and grievances of those 'natives' with those of the Duala. The 1919 petition was ignored, and their claim to speak for the wider population progressively lost plausibility in subsequent years. This became clear in the responses to a further seven petitions originating in Douala or presented in the name of the Duala notables by their agent in Paris between 1924 and 1931. All addressed to the League of Nations, those petitions had as their common objects compensation for the expropriations of 1913–14 and/or protest against the revival of the urban plan for Douala and renewal of expropriations by the French, as well as challenges to the terms of the French mandate. All were dismissed by the League's Permanent Mandate Commission. The French had not, after all, signed a treaty with any chiefs (unlike the Germans), and could dissociate themselves from the negative aspects of German rule while benefiting from its consequences. Moreover they were able to capitalise on (or mobilise) the resentment of non-Duala natives at the Duala claims to leadership.[8]

The Duala were emboldened in their post-war claims by the momentum that had developed around the expropriation issue in the pre-war protectorate and the German metropole, events that had already conferred mythic status on Rudolf Duala Manga, Ngoso Din and Mpundu Akwa in their eyes. But things had changed in Germany as well as in the colony. Defeat in war led to the abdication of the Kaiser in November 1918 and a provisional government led by Social Democrats set about constructing a republic. Against this background, Cameroonians in Germany drew up their own petitions, and in doing so they took the history

[8] See Austen and Derrick, *Middlemen*, pp. 144–52, which presents an analysis of the Duala petitions in tabular form.

of anti-colonial protest in a different direction.[9] Three successive submissions made by Martin Dibobe during 1919 reflect the way in which life in Germany was reconstructing Africans' sense of themselves and their needs. They are in many ways puzzling and contradictory documents. On 22 May 1919 Dibobe wrote to the Reich Colonial Minister to protest in the name of 'the natives of Cameroon and East Africa resident here' against 'the theft of the colonies' and their subjection to the British and French. He expressed the firm desire of the natives to 'remain German', in view of the fact that the Social Democrats ('*die Sozialen*'), now in power, had always supported the interests of the natives against the Imperial government. He invoked the binding power of the Treaty of 1884, which the natives would acknowledge subject only to the new Germany's fulfilling its part by granting autonomy and acting humanely. This letter was followed a month later by a submission to the National Assembly in Weimar, which was deliberating on a constitution for the new republic. The message of the main text was similar to that of the May letter; it made no reference to East Africa, but among the eighteen other signatories were two East Africans, as well as Cameroonians who were not Duala but natives of Kribi (Anton Egiomue) and Victoria (Theophilus Michael). Finally, on 27 June 1919 Dibobe and Thomas Manga Akwa personally visited the Reich Colonial Ministry to present a 32-point set of 'conditions' for the Africans' continued allegiance to Germany.[10]

The letters of May and June, and a subsequent letter of July, deployed much of the familiar language of Duala petitions. Dibobe introduced himself as a member of the Duala elite, son of one of the signatories of the 1884 Treaty, which figures in the letters as the token and cement of common interest between colonisers and colonised. He added a revolutionary 'twist' to the rhetoric of shared interest by claiming that he had cooperated with the Social Democrats before 1914, and offering to go back to Cameroon and argue the case for Germany among the natives there.[11] But in other ways these texts represent a new departure. The reference to Africans and Africa beyond Cameroon remains elusive

[9] The petitions headed by Martin Dibobe pre-date that of the Duala notables, and Austen and Derrick treat them as the first in a continuous series. We propose that they mark the beginning of a broadly independent development.

[10] Dibobe to Reich Colonial Minister Bell, 22 May 1919; Dibobe *et al.* to National Assembly, 19 June 1919; both BArch R1001 7220, pp. 130–1 and 231, reprinted in Rüger, 'Imperialismus', 1301–8.

[11] Dibobe to Reich Colonial Office, 11 July 1919, BArch R1001 7220, p. 231. Dibobe again asserted his authority as mediator between the German government and the Cameroonian chiefs in September 1919: Dibobe to Reich Government, 13 September 1919, BArch R1001 3930, pp. 226–7.

(and had almost entirely disappeared by 27 June), but its presence is significant. Moreover, the range of concerns covered by the thirty-two points reflects the wide spectrum of metropolitan as well as colonial experiences that Cameroonians shared with other Africans; this is unmistakeably a diasporic document in its origins if not yet in its conclusions.[12] The distance of its authors from the standpoint of their kin back home is apparent in its handling of the expropriation theme; they demand the cancellation of the 'decree of 1914 which ordered the expropriation of D[o]uala', but make no reference to the national martyrs. It includes broadly constitutional demands which echo those of the Duala notables: autonomy and equality of treatment for natives in the colony, the rule of law and due process (though here on an explicitly German model), freedom of the person and of commerce, guarantees of native property, checks on the power of administrators and the involvement of natives in their selection. A novel proposition is that there be a 'permanent representative of our race' in the Reichstag (in the first instance Dibobe himself). Then there are a number of points of detail that reflect very specific colonial experiences. These include the call for all public notices to be issued in at least five native languages, for the maintenance of native customs, for any police formations to be made up of natives (even if under white command), for the obligation on natives to salute senior administrators to be lifted, for an increase in wages and for a native-managed tax fund. Noteworthy too are calls for specific reforms drawing on one of two models. The first is metropolitan Germany, which provides the model for compulsory schooling, reform of the police and workers' right to co-determination; more generally, administrative and constitutional reforms are justified by reference to 'how things are now in Germany'. The second is Britain's African colonies, notably the Nigerian coastal cities of Lagos, Bonny and Old Calabar – models for the civil equality of natives with whites, the deployment of natives in senior administrative posts, and a society characterised by 'few civil servants and many merchants'.

The things that mark the document as a product of its time and place are those points that allude to the problems faced by the signatories as travellers between colony and metropole; all of these invoke issues of private life and personal dignity. Point 17 reads simply and poignantly: 'Marriages between natives and whites are legitimate. We are determined to take our wives and children back home.' The next point deals at length with the situation of the children of white men and native women

[12] [Dibobe *et al.*] to Reich Colonial Ministry, 27 June 1919, BArch R1001 7220, pp. 224–9.

abandoned in the colony, calling for the father to be required to marry the mother or pay for the support of the child, and for the state to maintain the child if the father could not be traced. Given the administrative obstacles placed in the way of 'natives' who married white women, there is a touch of irony in the proposal that any white man leaving the colony be required to keep the governor informed of his address in Germany so that child-support payments can be monitored. Conversely, the petitioners call for a guaranteed right of natives to emigrate from the colony. They also 'demand, since we are Germans, equality with [Germans], because in public we are always described as foreigners. The new government must issue a public statement to eliminate this misapprehension.' This looks like a reference to life in the metropole, although the external point of reference remains colonial: 'Equal rights have already been introduced in the English colonies.' Finally, they demand that white people cease to 'separate themselves' from the Blacks in shops and places of entertainment, 'as has hitherto been the case in Cameroon' – possibly a reflection on the relative *liberality* of life in the metropole, though one that invokes the abiding hurt of everyday racism.

The radicalism of the 1919 petitioners' ambitions – a renegotiation of the relationship between Cameroon and Germany that would liberate Cameroon from the hold of colonialism and aid the country's development – should not be underestimated. And it is not surprising that they were disappointed. Even before the terms of the Versailles settlement became clear in mid-1919, there was little realistic prospect of Germany recovering the protectorates. While the German colonial authorities harboured irredentist hopes in the face of the peace settlement, proposals for a new order in the colonies held little appeal. The petitioners received nothing more than a simple acknowledgement that the Colonial Ministry had taken note of their demands and their request that the petition be published in the German press was ignored; rather, an 'expurgated' version was published in a volume of documents supporting the German claims in the colonial question.[13]

The quality of the political engagement that informed Dibobe's claim to a leadership role in 1919 remains unclear. The first historians to write about the events of 1918–19 were concerned to identify a continuous anti-colonial movement among Germanophone Africans and to link it with labour radicalism.[14] They tended to fix on Dibobe as

[13] Hans Poeschel, *Die Kolonialfrage im Frieden von Versailles* (Berlin: Mittler, 1920), pp. 87, 94, cited by Austen and Derrick, *Middlemen*, p. 148.

[14] Rüger, 'Imperialismus'; Martin, 'Anfänge politischer Selbstorganisation', pp. 193–206.

a pioneering figure, in part because in his correspondence with the German authorities he stated that he had been radicalised by contact with Social Democrats in Berlin and had attempted to spread the socialist message to railway workers on a visit to Cameroon in 1907; he also claimed to have played a key role as intermediary in the 1914 expropriation protests.[15] But there is nothing to corroborate this. Similarly, there is no evidence for Dibobe's claims to be in contact with native leaders in Cameroon apart from a letter of October 1919 from his brother. The French authorities read this as conveying political messages in code, but while it suggests that Dibobe had used the language of 'liberation' in an earlier letter, it does no more than report on the persistence of Germanophile sentiment in the former protectorate.[16] The contrast between Dibobe's petition and that of the Duala notables reinforces the impression that he and the other Africans in Germany were acting on their own.

Indeed, we cannot even be sure that the thirty-two points had the endorsement of all of the men who signed the 19 June submission. The uncertainties of formal and informal association apparent in the fragmentary evidence are characteristic of the circumstances of 1919, which constituted an existential crisis equally for Germany, for its former protectorates and for Africans in Germany. One feature of this crisis was a degree of opportunism on all sides. Dibobe followed up his petitions with more personal requests that the German authorities fund his return to Cameroon, in which his willingness to act as an agent for German interests was more explicitly a bargaining point in the pursuit of family concerns. These, too, were rejected.[17] More inclined than the Germans to take Dibobe at his word, French agents observed his movements closely during the first ten days of December 1919 and found evidence of conversations going on in the background. They reported that he met with officers of the War Ministry on various occasions and in various locations, sometimes in company with one or two other (unnamed) Africans.[18] This confirmed them in their view that he was an actual or potential spy for the Germans, but once he had succeeded in taking his family back to Africa, Dibobe never again caught the eye of the authorities in either country.

15 Dibobe to Reich Colonial Minister Bell, 22 May 1919.

16 Minister of Colonies to Commissioner Cameroon, 5 November 1920, Annex 5, ANCY APA 10222.

17 Dibobe to Noske, 25 November 1919, Dibobe to Müller, 18 December 1919, BArch R1001 3930, pp. 269–70, 300–1 and marginalia. Dibobe's return to Africa in 1921 is described in Chapter 3.

18 Minister of Colonies to Commissioner Cameroon, 5 November 1920.

Organising in the metropole

Opportunism – exploiting the political conjuncture to achieve personal ends – is one way in which private life and politics 'mix', particularly in the lives of those whom political power holds at arm's length. The thirty-two points illustrate a different kind of development: the way in which an explicit politics emerges from the exigencies of daily life. This is also apparent in the shifting role of the AH. The principal purpose of the AH was 'to replace a bit of home' for Africans. The signatures of six of its members on the June 1919 letter to the Weimar National Assembly breached the commitment in its regulations to avoiding political involvement. But by its very existence the AH contained the germ of a new kind of metropolitan politics in being open explicitly to all people of colour. And during its few years of existence it also showed signs of developing into a self-conscious interest group – or at any rate its existence gave its members a collective persona through which to intervene publicly in defence of a common interest. Here, too, challenges to personal and family integrity in daily life prompted Africans to take a stand on public events: it was in the name of the AH that Louis Brody published his letter of protest of May 1921 against the *schwarze Schmach* campaign, and there he made a point of drawing attention to the political context for the African presence in Germany: 'The Germans appear completely oblivious to the fact that they once had colonies too and that up to now there has been no decision about the fate of the natives in the former German colonies.'[19]

Once the AH had ceased to function a number of its members moved into the ambit of new, more self-consciously political movements. We can observe in their activities the same ambiguities, combining personal opportunism, the existential anchoring of self-help efforts in wider networks and protest based on political conviction and directed at whole structures of oppression. At the same time we can see them abandoning the languages of petition and loyalty and adopting new voices. These enabled new alliances and identities, but they also generated new tensions as it proved difficult to articulate the specific needs of Germanophone Africans in Europe and Africa within increasingly 'global' movements.

From the mid 1920s, the context for African involvement in political organisations was provided by the anti-imperialist and anti-colonial projects that developed in the ambit of the Communist International. The

[19] Louis Brody, 'Die deutschen Neger und die "schwarze Schmach"', *BZ am Mittag*, 24 May 1921, cited in T. Nagl, '"Sieh mal den schwarzen Mann da!"', p. 85. See also Chapter 3.

League against Imperialism (LAI) was founded in February 1927, as a broad-based front organisation. It stood under the informal (and from 1928 formal) leadership of the prolific German Communist organiser and propagandist Willi Münzenberg, and had its headquarters in Berlin.[20] Part of Münzenberg's mission in this context was to mobilise colonial subjects and to make them visible as agents of their own liberation even in the European metropoles. By 1926 he had established contact with Berlin Africans, by means or through encounters that remain unclear. Wilhelm Munumé and Peter Makembe attended the founding meeting of the LAI's predecessor organisation, the League against Colonial Oppression, in Berlin in February of that year.[21] Munumé was characterised in the minutes of the meeting as a West African delegate among the 'colonial representatives', Makembe as a spokesman for an 'Association of Cameroonians' (Verein der Kameruner).[22] This sounds very like the Verein der Gemeinschaft der Duala-Leute, for whose help Richard Ekamby expressed his gratitude a few months later.[23] This may be an example of Africans' own efforts at mutual aid embedding themselves organically in a more explicitly political frame, or the association may itself have been formed in order to justify Makembe's role as its 'representative'. The kinds of informal mutual aid in which members of this circle engaged often found them speaking in the name of organisations whose existence was at best ephemeral. In July 1928 Manga Akwa wrote in a letter to President Hindenburg in support of Makembe (now in prison); he wrote under the typed letterhead of 'Deutsch-Eingeborene', or German Natives, and employed the familiar rhetoric of invoking the service of African soldiers and the continued loyalty of Africans in Germany to the colonial empire. After Makembe was released from prison, he presented the social worker managing his case with a testimonial from a 'German League of Negroes for Mutual Understanding and Advancement of the National Sense of Community and Advocacy of the Rights of German Negroes' (Deutsche Negerliga zur Verständigung und Förderung des Reichsgemeinschaftsgefühls und Anwaltschaft für deutsche Negerrechte).[24]

20 On Münzenberg, see McMeekin, *The Red Millionaire*.

21 Peter Martin, 'Die "Liga gegen koloniale Unterdrückung"', pp. 261–9.

22 Conference of members of the German Organisations and Colonial Representatives held in the Berlin Rathauskeller on 10 February, RGASPI 542/1/4, pp. 2–6; Weiss, 'Glimpses of African Political Engagement'.

23 Richard Ekamby to Verein der Gemeinschaft der Duala-Leute (Kamerun), 31 July 1926, LAB A.Rep. 58, Acc. 399/No.958, vol. 2, pp. 56–7.

24 Manga Akwa to Hindenburg, 13 July 1928, and Jaksch to Tiergarten District Welfare and Youth Bureau, 29 December 1930, LAB A.Rep. 58, Acc. 399/No.958, vol. 1, n.p. and vol. 2, p. 139.

There is reason to suspect at least a degree of opportunism on the part of these two men, and particularly Munumé. Makembe had a history of associational engagement, as Secretary and Treasurer of the AH and signatory to the Weimar petition. He had been in active contact with Martin Dibobe in the first post-war years, travelling to Berlin to meet him on several occasions.[25] Munumé had a history of deploying political rhetoric to his personal advantage. In April 1920 he sent a circular letter in Duala to the Cameroonian leaders calling on them to unite in anticipation of their liberation (but also to make sure their children learned French), declaring himself the spokesman for their interests in Europe, and asking them to raise several thousand Francs for his use.[26] In 1923, he got himself arrested in Wiesbaden by making inflammatory speeches against the French occupiers, and then proceeded to appeal to the public for financial aid, presenting himself as a black German patriot.[27] Two months after the meeting in Berlin Munumé and Makembe wrote to Moscow invoking their connection to Münzenberg and asking to be allowed to enrol in the Communist University of the Toilers of the East (KUTV), where colonial activists were trained.[28] And by the following summer they were embroiled in the forgery scheme that would end in their arrest and imprisonment in early 1927.

But if Munumé and Makembe were opportunists, the Comintern organisers were more than a match for them – men whom Münzenberg and his colleagues characterised as 'the available political material'.[29] The next evidence of organisational activity is from 1929, when Makembe was back in circulation. He was among seven Duala men who founded the German section of the League for the Defence of the Negro Race (LzVN) in Berlin in September 1929.[30] The formation of the LzVN was one outcome of the Comintern's move towards a positive and explicit commitment to representing the collective interests of black people following its Sixth Congress (July–September 1928). The

25 Commissioner Cameroon to Minister of Colonies, 13 February 1921; French Ambassador in Berlin to Minister of Foreign Affairs, 24 May 1921: both FR ANOM 2300 COL 31/284. Dibobe was not among the recorded members of the AH.

26 Munumé to 'Dear friends and chiefs', Munich, 7 April 1920, FR ANOM 2300 COL 31/294.

27 Circular of the Prussian Minister of the Interior, 17 April 1926; Munumé to Seitz, 26 June 1925: BArch R8023 1077/a, pp. 91–3, 58; postcard 'Opfer des deutschen Vaterlandes!', BArch R1001 4457/6, p. 163.

28 Wilhelm Munumé and Makuri Makembe to Administration of KUTV, 1 April 1926, RGASPI 532/205/9340, p. 1.

29 Münzenberg, Smeral, Chatto and Ferdi to Comintern, 3 November 1930, RGASP542/1/40, pp. 69–72, here p. 69.

30 LAB Rep. 42, Acc. 1743, no. 9054 (Akten des Amtsgerichts Charlottenburg betr. Auflösung der Liga).

Comintern analysis of those interests was notoriously problematic. It encompassed the vision of African Americans as a national minority with a claim to an independent state and the promotion of black activism and militant anti-racism alongside a persistent refusal to acknowledge racial oppression as something distinct from and as real as class exploitation. The fusion of race and class struggle was embodied in the creation of an International Trade Union Committee of Negro Workers (ITUCNW).[31] LAI officers, too, sought new partners, and in October 1928 invited the Paris League for the Defence of the Negro Race (LDRN) to work with them.[32] The Paris League had been formed in 1927 under the leadership of Lamine Senghor. It was the most active and long-lived of a number of initiatives on the part of black and colonial subjects in France dating back to the early 1920s, most of which had some association with French communism. Senghor was a Communist, as was Tiemoko Garan Kouyaté, who was Secretary and leader of the LDRN at the time of the LAI's approach. While Kouyaté's rootedness in and primary allegiance to the cause of Blacks meant that he retained considerable intellectual independence of the Comintern line, the LDRN was substantially funded by the French Communist Party and firmly incorporated into Comintern structures by the beginning of 1929.[33] As early as March of that year Kouyaté was envisaging Berlin and Moscow as hubs for the circulation of the LDRN's own material, firmly seeking to insert the 'Negro' interest into the activities of the LAI.[34] He visited Berlin after having attended an LAI conference in Frankfurt at the end of July 1929, and he organised the meeting out of which the LzVN emerged. It seems likely that his contact with Münzenberg enabled him to gain access to Africans in Berlin, and the principal LAI officers there, Bohumir Smeral and Virendranath Chattopadhyaya (better known as Chatto), assisted in the drafting of the constitution of the new organisation.[35] The LzVN, officially registered on 27 September 1929, was formally the 'Berlin section' of the LDRN, and it had its offices at the same address as the LAI, Friedrichstraße 24.

The LzVN's constitution marks it as a hybrid product of the intersection (or collision) of the workerist vision of the Comintern/LAI,

[31] Resolution of the Sixth Comintern Congress on the Negro Question, partial reprint in Degras (ed.), *The Communist International*, pp. 552–6.

[32] Note on revolutionary propaganda relevant to overseas territories, 31 October 1928, ANCY APA 11705.

[33] On the LDRN and its predecessor organisations: Derrick, *Africa's 'Agitators'*, pp. 216–26; on Kouyaté: Dewitte, *Mouvements nègres*, pp. 179–216, and Edwards, *Practice of Diaspora*, pp. 240–305.

[34] Note on revolutionary propaganda relevant to overseas territories, 31 March 1929, ANCY APA 10367.

[35] Smeral and Chatto to 'Dear Friends', November 1929, RGASPI 542/1/A 30, pp. 110–11.

Kouyaté's pan-Africanism and the concerns of its Berlin members. The practice of organised mutual aid in cases of sickness, unemployment and accident, begun in the AH, was inscribed here as one of the duties of the European 'sections' of the LDRN, whose guiding role was acknowledged. Membership was open to 'any person descended from *Neger*' and also their white wives.[36] In fact the LzVN reported five women among its thirty Berlin members in September 1930, though they were not named and it is not clear whether they were white wives or (as the wording implies) themselves black. It also reported on good prospects for setting up a branch in Hamburg, which had been frustrated by lack of funds. While the founding group – Joseph Bilé, Louis Brody, Richard Dinn, Thomas Ngambi ul Kuo, Victor Bell, Thomas Manga Akwa and Manfred Kotto Priso – were all Duala, there were also members from other parts of Africa and further afield.[37]

The political aspects of the constitution focussed on the international dimensions of the global struggle against colonialism and white oppression. The LzVN's overarching aim in 'international' terms was declared to be 'the emancipation of the Negro race in every respect and by all means in active solidarity with the intellectual and manual workers of the whole world'. Under the 'national standpoint', the LzVN committed itself to 'seize the national independence of the Negro people of Africa and to establish a large modern state [by organising] the peasants, workers, officials, merchants, soldiers and sailors, students and black schoolchildren on the basis of their particular demands'. In association with this, the independence of the African islands was to be fought for. The independence of the Antilles was also an objective, though subordinate to that of black Africa. The demands of the American Negroes were to be supported, and all moves to consolidate white colonial rule opposed. The independence of Abyssinia and Liberia were to be defended, and the abuses of colonial rule exposed. The earlier provisions contain a strong echo of Kouyaté's own characterisation of the objectives of the LDRN, namely

> the political, economic and intellectual emancipation of the negro race in its entirety. What we need to do is seize back, by all reasonable means, the national

[36] Satzungen der LzVN, LAB Rep. 42, no. 1743, pp. 4–5.

[37] Kurzer Tätigkeitsbericht, pp. 404–8. In March 1930 the French police received a report that the LzVN had 200 members and branches in Hamburg and Frankfurt as well as Berlin: Central Commissioner Bordeaux to Directeur of the Sûreté, 19 March 1930, FR ANOM 4003 COL 111. It is not clear how the 1930 information might have reached the Bordeaux police, who were at that time engaged in monitoring Kouyaté's agitation among black seamen in the city, or how much credence to give it. In the light of the LzVN's own report of September it seems exaggerated.

independence of the negro people of the ... colonies and to establish a great negro state in black Africa. The negro peoples of the Antilles will be entitled to form a confederation or to return to a recovered Africa.[38]

By contrast, the closing exhortation that in Europe sections must 'as far as possible organise their members in the white trade unions in their own trade' and work together with the unions to find work for unemployed Blacks betrays the hand of the Comintern officers, pushing hard against the tactics of organising everybody in sight that could just about be tolerated in the African context.

Practising diaspora: Joseph Bilé and the dilemmas of black internationalism

The career of Joseph Bilé, the secretary and most consistently active member of the LzVN, provides the best insight into the way in which Africans of this generation negotiated these programmatic tensions, and into the contours of their political engagement more generally.[39] Bilé was born in Douala on 13 September 1892. From 1912 until 1914 he attended the technical school in Hildburghausen, qualifying as an engineer.[40] As we have seen, his brother Robert, sister Esther and cousin Bertha all sojourned in Germany, but he was the only one still there at the outbreak of war. While his brother was able to return and made a career in the French colonial administration, Joseph was cut off from his family in Cameroon once war began. Reduced to a state of poverty he was entirely dependent on the support of his former mathematics teacher, Kümpel, in order to survive. On Kümpel's advice Bilé entered the army as a volunteer, but a foot injury led to his release without compensation within months. Once again Kümpel took it upon himself to look after Bilé, until he found work with a municipal construction bureau in East Prussia.[41] In 1921 he was dismissed from this position in favour of returning veterans; Kümpel's renewed efforts to find him a job or help him to return to Cameroon failed, and he embarked on

[38] Kouyaté to W. E. B. Du Bois, 29 April 1929, cited by Dewitte, *Mouvements nègres*, p. 191.

[39] The French authorities, interested in him not least because of his brother's position back in Douala, identified Bilé early on as the dominant figure in the LzVN: note on revolutionary propaganda relevant to overseas territories, 31 December 1929, ANCY APA 10367.

[40] Bilé's academic performance declined with each year of study: Kreis- u. Stadtarchiv Hildburghausen, Stadt Hildburghausen, no. 281c/7060; Thüringisches Staatsarchiv Meiningen, Staatliche Ingenieurschule Hildburghausen, no. 202, 203, 204.

[41] Kümpel to Reich Colonial Office, 13 December 1920, BArch R1001 4457/6, pp. 134–5.

performance work.[42] He took up a job with a film company in Berlin, but moved on to Vienna in 1923 to work with a circus. He was based there for most of the period between October 1923 and April 1929, registered as a performer and working in circuses and the film industry.[43] By the middle of 1929 he had returned permanently to Berlin, and in August of that year he was receiving financial aid from the DGfE.[44]

Bilé was well established in the networks of Africans in Germany and a presence in successive associational projects. He had been a member of the AH and a signatory to the 1919 letter to the Weimar Assembly. And he was clearly ready to put some effort into this new political initiative. The main task of LzVN members was to attend and participate at political gatherings organised by the LAI and associated organisations in the ambit of the KPD. This called for schooling both in what to say and in how to say it. At their own request, Smeral delivered a series of political training sessions for the LzVN members in spring 1930, and in the following autumn Bilé, the LzVN's chairman Victor Bell and Hermann Ngange were selected for further training. Bilé and Ngange attended sessions on agrarian policy taught by the sociologist Karl Wittfogel at the German Academy for Politics. Together with Bell they were also signed up to attend a series of evening lectures given by the German Communist Party (KPD) functionary Hermann Duncker at the Marxist Workers' School (MASCH).[45] Through these sessions, and by their presence in the LAI offices, Bilé and the others came into contact with intellectuals, activists and would-be revolutionaries from all over the globe; their fellow students included East Asians and Indian and Arab nationalists, and most of the members of Berlin's progressive intelligentsia lectured at MASCH at one time or another.[46]

Bilé rapidly became a featured speaker at public meetings. In December 1929 he appeared at an anti-colonial demonstration organised by the Communist school-pupils' organisation, Sozialistischer Schülerbund, in Berlin.[47] He was arrested at a Communist trade union meeting in

42 Kümpel to Minister for Reconstruction, 22 July 1921, BArch R1001 4457/6, p. 154.

43 Registration details in Stadt- und Landesarchiv Vienna; report on 'Morris', 23 September 1933, RGASPI 495/279/67, p. 5; interview with Guillaume Dina Ekwe Bilé. In December 1929 the *Chicago Defender* pictured Bilé along with nine other Africans as one of the 'movie stars of the Race' in Germany: 'Germany also Turns Cold Shoulder on Race Prejudice', *Chicago Defender*, 21 December 1929, p. 10.

44 DGfE to Foreign Office, 5 August 1929, BArch R1001 4457/7, p. 150.

45 Kurzer Tätigkeitsbericht, p. 407; courses for colonial students, 5 November 1930, RGASPI, 542/1/40, pp. 119–23.

46 Gerhard-Sonnenberg, *Marxistische Arbeiterbildung*.

47 '"Politik" mit der Zigarette im Munde', *Lokal-Anzeiger*, 15 December 1929, clipping in BArch R1001 4457/7, p. 228.

Siemensstadt, Berlin, the following March, and again after the Anti-Imperialist Youth Conference in Berlin on 30 May 1931, at which he had appeared alongside British and Indonesian speakers and the Indian Saklatvala.[48] He formally joined the KPD around the end of 1930, and the KPD executive in Berlin reported back to Moscow some time later that

> [he] was active in various large factory cells and street cells. Everywhere he performed his role (agit-prop leader among other things) to the complete satisfaction of the comrades. In the 1½ years of his agitation in the KPD he has developed well and gained experience in the Party and its organisations.[49]

The best evidence we have for the character of Bilé's political commitment is his own report of September 1930 on the activity of the LzVN and the documentation generated by two visits he made to the Soviet Union, one in summer 1930 and one between October 1932 and February 1934, when he attended the KUTV in Moscow. They indicate that for him engagement with the LAI did represent a way of realising his personal ambitions. In 1929 he was seeking the means to return to Cameroon, and his desire to get home for family reasons is a leitmotif in the documentation. In 1933 one of his tutors in Moscow, who had known him since he was first involved with the Communists, pointed out that he had not seen his mother for twenty years.[50] He was also expecting to be given a salaried post as organiser in the LAI offices. Alongside this he had expectations in the name of his fellow LzVN members that the LAI would assist in meeting the commitment to their material welfare that was written into its constitution. His 1930 report included a list of complaints against the LAI officers. The report accused Chatto of having failed to reimburse the costs of registering the LzVN as well as breaking a promise to Bilé that he would be paid for his political work. He blamed the LAI for the fact that LzVN member Richard Dinn's fellow Africans had had to pawn their coats to pay his funeral expenses in winter 1929, and reported that the episode had provoked resentment against the LAI. This was further compounded when Chatto and the LAI failed to support the campaign to prevent Munumé's deportation after his release from jail in February 1930. It was only thanks to the efforts of the

[48] Kurzer Tätigkeitsbericht, p. 405; minutes of the Berlin Anti-Imperialist Youth Conference, 30 April–1 May 1931, RGASPI 542/1/51, pp. 81–2, here p. 81.

[49] Quoted in letter from the German Representative, Executive Committee of the Comintern, to Secretariat for the Romance Countries, 8 March 1934, RGASPI 495/205/1802, p. 3.

[50] Comments of Alexander Zusmanovich, Conference of Comrade Morris with Teachers, 25 December 1932, RGASPI 532/1/439, pp. 21–6, here p. 22.

German branch of the International League for Human Rights and, in particular, Bilé that Munumé was able to stay in Germany.[51]

At the same time there is evidence of an early readiness on Bilé's part to hitch his personal aims to a political engagement that drew him deeply into the international network of Communist, anti-colonial and black liberation movements and provided him with the opportunity to demonstrate a potential for leadership. In this context the fragmentary evidence indicates that he was aligning himself within those networks in ways that might have led to his becoming a German counterpart to Kouyaté had the National Socialist takeover not cut off both his own personal career and the development of the first Afro-German community. His report of September 1930 came at the end of his first sojourn in Moscow. That visit had been precipitated by his attendance at the first International Congress of Negro Workers in Hamburg in July. Organised under the auspices of the Red Trade Union International, or Profintern, the congress was attended by seventeen delegates. They included some of the most prominent black activists in the anti-colonial movement, notably the Trinidadian George Padmore and the African American James Ford. The main political demands formulated by delegates were equality for Africans and the realisation of the right of self-determination, or the creation of independent states in Africa. Central to the achievement of these demands was the promotion of closer ties between trade unions in Europe and those developing in the colonies as well as the development of the anti-colonial movement in Africa. The organisational result was the election of a new executive for the ITUCNW, now spearheading the Comintern effort to organise African colonial subjects in Europe. From 1931 it was led by Padmore and based in Hamburg, which was envisaged as a strategic link between centres of European revolutionary activity and the colonies.[52] Bilé's involvement suggested that the Comintern activists attached some importance to Cameroonian and African-German affairs, or at any rate took him and his compatriots seriously as a political cadre. At the same time, from his own perspective the Congress was a disappointment; having been called upon to attend at the last minute with the promise of a chance to confer with Kouyaté, he arrived to find himself the sole representative of the Ligue/Liga.[53] At its

[51] Kurzer Tätigkeitsbericht, pp. 404–8; the authorship is clear from internal evidence.

[52] On the Congress, see Schmidt, '"Die kolonialen Sklaven sind erwacht..."'; Rüger, 'Erste Internationale Konferenz'; Pennybacker, *From Scottsboro to Munich*, pp. 69–72; Derrick, *Africa's 'Agitators'*.

[53] Kouyaté had apparently not been invited because he was in dispute with French Communists and trade unionists about his efforts to organise black seamen: Dewitte, *Mouvements nègres*, p. 203.

conclusion, however, he was one of the delegates who were encouraged to travel on to Moscow to attend the Fifth Congress of the Profintern. He agreed to do this at his own expense in the expectation that the money he had saved to pay his passage to Cameroon would be reimbursed from Comintern funds.[54]

It seems likely that Bilé's disappointment at missing Kouyaté in Hamburg was compensated by the chance to meet George Padmore. Once arrived at the Profintern Congress he immediately became embroiled in debates around the future balance in the Comintern's 'Negro work', and the outcome seems to have been a self-conscious alignment with those sections of the movement which prioritised the interests of black people in the widest sense. When he and two other Africans – the Gambian E. F. Small and Nigerian Frank Macaulay – were 'de-briefed' by LAI officers on their return to Berlin in October, they reported two linked impressions: that the comrades associated with the ITUCNW did not take anti-imperialist work seriously, and that the African-American delegates were guilty of a degree of 'chauvinism' or arrogance in their relations with other black delegates. Small was particularly dismissive of the insistence on class consciousness alone and called for an acknowledgement of the power of 'race consciousness'; in this he was supported by Macaulay and Bilé. By the end of 1930 at the latest the ITUCNW was fully and explicitly prioritising action in the colonies, and particularly in Africa. This confirmed the position of the Comintern Executive, which had intervened directly in the discussions at the Profintern Congress to reinforce the importance of anti-imperialist work, and according to Small this was the outcome of a 'serious conflict between Bilé and the Comintern bureaucrats'.

This conflict seems to have had both personal and programmatic dimensions: in Moscow Bilé went straight to Comintern officers to ask again that he be sent back to Cameroon to agitate and recruit new trainees for the struggle. His report of September 1930 was written in Moscow for their attention. In it, he took a creative approach to the breakdown of trust between the LAI and the LzVN, and looked for ways of anchoring the particular interests of Africans and Blacks while bypassing the LAI. He asked that Africans be taken on in the Colonial Secretariat of the KPD to maintain a direct link between the LzVN and the party. He also proposed direct liaison with International Red Aid, the mass organisation responsible for raising funds and

[54] Note on Bilé, Joseph Ekwe, May 1934, FR ANOM 4002 COL 3; McClellan, 'Black *Hajj*', p. 68; Wilson, *Russia and Black Africa*, pp. 175–85; Kurzer Tätigkeitsbericht, p. 407.

agitating around human rights issues which was already heavily committed to campaigns against racism in the United States, and he added the request for training for LzVN members and other Africans in Berlin and Moscow. The response of the 'Comintern bureaucrats' to Bilé personally was to insist that he postpone any return to Cameroon until he had joined the KPD and taken the opportunity for further training. At the same time they showed some sympathy for his expectation of material support from the LAI and the party in Berlin. It is noteworthy, too, that they envisaged Bilé working in Hamburg – presumably in the ITUCNW offices.

The LAI officers remained sceptical of the usefulness of the Berlin Africans; Chatto in particular was unconvinced of Bilé's abilities and dismissed the Africans in Berlin as not 'sufficiently revolutionary' in their outlook.[55] The October de-briefing meeting in Berlin was one of five held over three days; they were intended in part to resolve local conflicts as well as to begin drafting a plan of action for agitation in Africa, and were attended by Kouyaté as well as Bilé, Macaulay and Small and the LAI officers.[56] In programmatic terms, the outcome of the meetings represents an interim compromise. The four Africans themselves were divided over a number of issues. While Kouyaté favoured a single 'negrican republic' for the whole of Africa, Small, Macaulay and Bilé argued that the individual territories had to achieve their own independence. Expropriation and the revolutionary potential of African 'peasants' were other issues of contention.[57] The result of the meetings was a provisional programme to be applied to the whole of West Africa which echoed the sentiments of the Negro Congress in condemning imperialism, demanding independence for West African countries and emphasising the need to organise the masses.[58] A list of concrete political, economic and cultural demands followed, though without a plan of action for achieving those aims. The minutes of the meetings demonstrate that the LAI was looking to set up cells in West Africa and to recruit African agitators for training in Moscow. Both Macaulay and Small were being considered as potential recruiters and Kouyaté was already involved in this process. Bilé's role, however, remained unclear.[59]

55 Kouyaté to unknown, 27 October 1930, RGASPI 542/1/44, pp. 75–6.
56 Münzenberg, Smeral, Chatto and Ferdi to Comintern, 3 November 1930, pp. 69–72. Minutes and the resolutions of the meetings can be found in RGASPI 542/1/40, pp. 77–103.
57 Minutes of meetings on 16 and 17 October 1930, RGASPI 542/1/40, pp. 88–9.
58 The Anti-Imperial Struggle of the West African People, no date, RGASPI 542/1/40, pp. 90–3.
59 The usefulness of Macaulay and Small as agitators is also questioned in the letter: Münzenberg, Smeral, Chatto and Ferdi to Comintern, 3 November 1930, pp. 69–72.

The question of the relationship between the LAI and the LzVN remained unresolved. The LzVN placed very firmly before Comintern activists the challenge that agitation around issues of race posed to a Marxist organisation. Among the few recorded public activities of the LzVN was the black theatre project described in Chapter 4. The plan and the revue *Sunrise in Morning Land* that grew out of it were conceived by members of the League and announced in its name by Victor Bell in January 1930.[60] Always dependent on Kouyaté's group in Paris, the LzVN requested its support for this purpose as early as February 1930. The request was turned down on the grounds that all the central funds of the League must be reserved for 'propaganda'.[61] It is by no means clear that the League in Paris could have afforded to subsidise any of the LzVN's activities. But the dismissal of a black theatre initiative as something less than propaganda was a gesture of extreme obtuseness in view of the League's aims. It is a reminder of the differences between the conditions for Communist agitation among Africans in Germany and France respectively. In early 1930 Kouyaté was engaged in organising black seamen's trade unions in Bordeaux and Marseilles, with a view simultaneously to reinforcing black solidarity and extending the revolutionary workers' movement to Africa via diasporic activists. The Comintern executive judged this a dangerously divisive deviation from the principle of organising black workers in white trade unions, but at least there was something like a black proletariat to propagandise in France, and even one that was strategically placed at the nodal points of the national economy.[62] There was no disguising the fact that the conditions for this kind of revolutionary propaganda did not exist in Germany. The absence of a critical mass of black seamen and harbour-workers in Hamburg allowed racial divisions between potential recruits and the political caution of visiting seamen to undermine the ITUCNW's efforts at organisation there.[63] And the problem was not simply one of numbers. Bilé's September 1930 account of the LzVN bravely declared that all its members were 'proletarian' – and then proceeded to list 'chauffeurs, performers, artisans, porters,

60 'Berlin to have a Race House', *Baltimore Afro-American*, 18 January 1930, p. 8.

61 Note on revolutionary propaganda relevant to overseas territories, 28 February 1930, ANCY APA 10367.

62 Bilé noted in his 1930 report that efforts to organise black seamen in Hamburg had failed because all LDRN funds had been spent on the Marseilles and Bordeaux operations: Kurzer Tätigkeitsbericht, p. 405.

63 Ford to Padmore, April 1930 and Ford to Secretariat RILU and Padmore, 6 August 1931, RGASPI 534/3/668, pp. 72–3, pp. 102–9. The teenage Paul Malapa's brief involvement with Hamburg Communist politics came to grief on routine racist comments: 'Paul Malapa Décryptage', pp. 56–7.

barmen etc'.[64] A revolutionary politics that could not articulate the interests of these people within a wider movement was likely to lose them, or (like Chatto) to find itself dismissing them as marginal: 'not sufficiently revolutionary', or nobody's people in political terms.

In the event, faced with Chatto's outright dismissal of the potential of the Afro-German comrades, Kouyaté came to their defence. After the return of the delegation from Moscow in October 1930 and their deliberations in Berlin, Kouyaté stayed on to discuss plans for work in the French colonies, only to find that discussion was stalled by the dispute between the LzVN and Chatto. He reported back to a sympathetic colleague in Moscow on his observations.[65] Kouyaté's perspective is particularly interesting in that it is the only view we have of our subjects and their situation through African eyes. He was able to report some 'real obstruction' on the part of the LAI officers; Chatto had told Bilé to his face that he would rather fund the recruitment of students in India than in Cameroon and that if the LzVN were to disappear it would not do the LAI any harm. But Kouyaté also wrote more generally of 'an intolerable state of mind'. Alongside the direct statements of the LAI officers, Bilé's account of their actions in evading and postponing action on verbal commitments of material support, failing to carry through an agreed training programme, communicating key information late or not at all, leaves the distinct impression that their attitude to the Africans who had placed themselves in a position of dependence on them was very like that of the German authorities: politically, the Africans had nothing to offer except their misery. It is telling that Chatto's interest was most successfully sparked by the potential of the Munumé deportation case. While Bilé and his comrades hoped it could be used to open up the urgent question of making citizenship available to ex-colonials, Chatto saw support for Munumé primarily as a way of 'exposing' the hollowness of Germany's moral claims to recover its colonies.[66] Otherwise, the LAI officers seem to have experienced the Blacks as querulous, materialistic, primitive and suffering from inflated expectations.

Kouyaté (who had commented on the large hotel bill that the West African delegates ran up in Berlin only to have his own expenses claims queried by the LAI officers)[67] looked at the same men and the same

[64] Kurzer Tätigkeitsbericht, p. 404. [65] Kouyaté to unknown, 27 October 1930, p. 75.

[66] Kurzer Tätigkeitsbericht, p. 406.

[67] The LAI officers commented on this themselves the following week, remarking that the LAI could not afford to support the LDRN as Kouyaté expected (let alone all the 'Negro friends'), and observing that Bilé not only expected to be paid for his political work but was hoping the party would pay for him to return to Cameroon for family reasons: Münzenberg, Smeral, Chatto and Ferdi to Comintern, 3 November 1930, pp. 69–72.

expectations and commented, 'I don't want to support the negro comrades here in all their exaggerated claims. I can see now that they have been very malcontent and that [Bilé] has made himself the echo of their feelings in Moscow.' But he also insisted that the movement must not neglect 'any elements, whatever their strength'. He characterised the perception that the Africans were politically underdeveloped and (implicitly) economically marginal as a 'new ideology. For I think that the revolutionary spirit is reinforced, developed or acquired through education and militant action – essentially supported by the individual's economic situation.'[68] The Berlin meetings between the Africans and the LAI officers had thrown into relief the real tensions between black activists' interest in mobilising around race and the continuing insistence of the Comintern on class-based agitation, as well as the difficulty of applying European visions of exploitation and expropriation to the complexity and variety of African societies. As much in his language as in his arguments, Kouyaté's comments on the Berlin situation reflect the way in which his own formation allowed him to mediate between the two positions.

Kouyaté's dismissal of the black theatre project contrasts sharply with the enthusiasm displayed by the African-American press, and this is a reminder of the transnational discursive field in which Africans in Germany increasingly operated, with points of reference both cultural and political in both Europe and America. In relations between American and German Blacks the traffic went both ways. Where it was mediated by the Comintern, the encounter exposed the real differences of experience and expectation, as the Africans' grumbles about the 'chauvinism' of the Americans at the Profintern Congress show. The sense of difference within a yet-to-be-explored diasporic community was also expressed in other contexts. In May 1930 Victor Bell wrote on behalf of the LzVN to congratulate the black publisher Robert S. Abbott on the silver jubilee of his paper the *Chicago Defender*. The voice Bell adopted was one of race solidarity but from a distinct geographical perspective: Abbott's work, he remarked, 'cannot have been an easy task, in a country where our Race is exposed to the brutalities of the white man'.[69]

The high point of public solidarity between Africans at home and in the diaspora and African Americans during these years was the Scottsboro campaign, which also provided a new theatre for Joseph Bilé's

Nevertheless, Münzenberg now formally supported Bilé's KPD membership: Münzenberg to KPD Central Committee, 28 October 1930, BArch RY1/12/5/33 Bd a, p. 121.

68 Kouyaté to unknown, 27 October 1930, p. 76.

69 Victor Bell, Letter, *Chicago Defender*, 24 May 1930, p. 4.

political activity. Beginning in April 1931, the Comintern – working primarily through International Red Aid – set out to mobilise international opinion behind a legal and media campaign to 'rescue' eight young black men who had been falsely charged and convicted of rape in Scottsboro, Alabama. The campaign reached its peak in Europe in summer 1932, when the mother of one of the 'Scottsboro boys' toured Europe. Germany was a focus for the campaign on the Continent, both in that it was organised from the Hamburg headquarters of the ITUCNW and in terms of the number and size of meetings held and the extent of other expressions of public sympathy there.[70] With Bilé's party credentials and experience established, by autumn 1931 he was actively cooperating with the LAI in supporting African students and others arriving in Berlin.[71] He was also well known to Padmore now, and this helped to establish him as a key speaker who featured at a number of organised demonstrations, frequently speaking to audiences of up to 2,000 people. A letter from Padmore to the International Red Aid organisers explained Bilé's suitability as a speaker: 'As a Negro-Comrade he can best represent the Scottsboro case to the assembly and especially also because he speaks fluent German. Here, in Hamburg, where there are many seamen it is important to have such a speaker who can effectively emphasize the international side of the campaign.'[72]

Bilé was not the only Cameroonian who featured in the Scottsboro campaign, and conflicts among Africans in Germany were among the outcomes of the heated activity of 1931 and 1932. The upshot was a crisis of the LzVN which throws the particular quality of Bilé's politicisation into relief. Munumé toured Saxony as a speaker in summer 1931, addressing audiences in the depressed manufacturing towns on the horrors of lynch justice.[73] On the basis of this, he hoped to gain KPD membership, but Bilé, mindful of Munumé's history of opportunism and criminal record, advised against it. This precipitated a letter from Munumé to the party in which he claimed in the name of himself and six other LzVN members that Bilé was an enemy of the working class and the son of a slave trader.[74] The other members named were Thomas

[70] Miller, Pennybacker and Rosenhaft, 'Mother Ada Wright', 387–403.

[71] LAI to Padmore, 9 and 11 November 1931, and Padmore to Secretariat (Moscow), 16 November 1931, RGASPI 534/3/668, pp. 114–15, 117, 118.

[72] RGASPI, Padmore to International Red Aid, 21 March 1932, RGASPI 534/3/754, p. 179.

[73] *Zwickauer Neueste Nachrichten*, 21 August 1931, p. 7; *Der Kämpfer* [Chemnitz], 22 Aug 1931, p. 6; Report of the Saxon Ministry of the Interior, 22 September 1931, StABremen 4,65 – IV.23.4.

[74] Munumé to KPD, 22 November 1931, BArch RY 1/I 2/5/33, p. 122.

Ngambi ul Kuo, Peter Makembe, Victor Bell, Louis Brody, Thomas Manga Akwa and Gregor Kotto. The list was probably fabricated, but it is a reminder not to exaggerate the political solidarity of this generation under stress; Manga Akwa had already distanced himself from the LzVN in a report to Seitz, expressing discomfort with the Communist link, and Comintern agents reported on associations of Africans from the former colonies in both Bremen and Hamburg whose members actively participated in events celebrating Germany's colonial heritage.[75] Padmore dismissed the charges against Bilé, and offered an analysis of the Berlin Africans – a black though not an African perspective – which bears comparison with Kouyaté's.[76] He began by pointing out that there were not, after all, many Africans in Berlin, and continued:

> Because of the social character of its members, many of whom are only living by racketeering, such as [Munumé], the League has ceased to really exist as an auxiliary organisation of our movement ... Like most emigrant organisations it has degenerated into warrying [*sic*] fractions ... Much of the attitude to Bilé is personal ... [H]e was a delegate to Moscow and they have the distorted idea that the Soviet government is so passionately out to help the Negroes that they gave Bilé a pocket full of money and that Bilé is using it for himself. It is the same sort of situation that we fight in every emigrant group. Furthermore, Bilé has entered the party and is working while most of them are not working.

Padmore went on to report that by Bilé's own account he had confronted Munumé about his counterfeiting activities and told him that it would be one thing if he were prepared to use his earnings for revolutionary activity, but it was completely disreputable to engage in criminal activity for his own gain. Padmore was careful to characterise Bilé as 'politically closest to us' and 'although ... a young party member ... a tremendous asset to the party'. But he concluded by proposing that the LzVN be liquidated, 'as it serves no useful purpose'. He proposed rescuing Bilé from 'this continuous mess and waste of time' by sending him to Moscow for training and then back to Cameroon: 'It is a disgrace to be [sic] the only African comrade we have in the party shining shoes in Berlin when we want to build up a movement in Africa.'

Even as he was throwing himself into the Scottsboro campaign, Bilé continued to hope that Moscow would fulfil its promise to send him back to Cameroon. The issue remained alive in correspondence between the KPD and the Comintern Executive, with the KPD urging Bilé's case and

[75] Seitz to Colonial Department, 17 December 1930, BArch R1001 4457/7, p. 228; 'Deutsche Kolonialpropaganda', 22 October 1930, RGASPI 542/1/40, pp. 56–61, here p. 58.

[76] Padmore to Comrade B, 17 December 1931, RGASPI 534/3/668, pp. 136–7.

the Comintern temporising. By mid-1932 he had declared himself ready to raise the necessary funds from his family back in Cameroon, but he was discouraged from returning.[77] In September 1932 he was sent to attend the KUTV, in the firm expectation that at the end of his training he would be able to return to Africa. At the University Bilé, under the party name Charles Morris, was enrolled in Section 9, an English-speaking section reserved for black activists.[78] His eighteen-month stay brought him into contact with a number of future black leaders, including the Kenyan Jomo Kenyatta and the South African Edwin Thabo Mofutsanyana. Bilé followed courses in political and economic theory focussing on themes such as the Soviet economy, Leninism and dialectical materialism as well as a course on party and trade-union organising tailored to the backgrounds of the individual students. He also studied Russian and French.

Bilé's progress was closely monitored by his tutors. They identified some weaknesses, like his preference for rote learning. His reticence in discussion raised suspicions of un-bolshevik lack of intellectual courage, though it more likely reflected what he had learned about negotiating the circuitry of Comintern discourse; he described it to his tutor as 'tactical'. At forty possibly the oldest student in the Section, Bilé approached his sometimes fractious classmates not as a political leader but as 'a father towards his children'. On his politics, his tutors were divided over whether he was a 'fiery nationalist' or avoided nationalist entanglements. Overall, however, they were agreed that he was a model student and entirely reliable politically.[79] Most interesting are the observations of the Africanist Alexander Zusmanovich, which resonate with Padmore's characterisation of the Berlin Africans as 'emigrants'. While acknowledging Bilé's continuing sentimental ties to Cameroon, Zusmanovich (who knew Bilé from his own work with the ITUCNW in Germany in 1929 and 1930) saw these as politically worse than irrelevant. He described Bilé as a 'Communist educated in the European mould' who has 'become so German that colonial problems seem rather abstract, at times even somewhat mythical'. Detached from the realities of Africa and disinclined to conspiratorial work, Bilé would need to be pressed hard to formulate a realistic vision for future activity in Cameroon.[80]

[77] Florin to [Comintern Executive], 21 June 1932, RGASPI 495/205/1802, p. 5. The whole correspondence fills pp. 3–18 of the file.

[78] On the education of Africans in Moscow, see McClellan, 'Africans and Black Americans', 371–90.

[79] Reports on Bilé, RGASPI 495/279/67, pp. 1–10; Conference of Comrade Morris with Teachers, 25 December 1932.

[80] Conference of Comrade Morris with Teachers, 25 December 1932, p. 21.

Much as German civil servants had reflexively used racial terminology in their draft correspondence and then struck it out, the Head of Section 9 now wrote 'German discipline!' and crossed it out. Bilé's rootedness in European conditions became apparent when the students were moved to complain openly about aspects of their situation, in January 1933. The food was neither tasty nor warming (three of the students were chefs so had a professional eye for this point) and the clothing they were given was not appropriate to the Russian winter. These issues had been raised by black students before, and had prompted the creation of a separate section for them.[81] The focus of this complaint however was a new one: the racism they had witnessed and encountered. They were offended by the stereotypical representations of Africans in a play they had attended, and this brought a simmering discontent to a head. In a letter 'to the Comintern' signed by all members of the Section they set out in measured terms that and why – for example – the portrayal of Africans as degraded and without language (even when it was meant to be sympathetic) and the persistent use of the terms 'nigger' and 'darkey' to translate the Russian 'negr' in officially sanctioned dictionaries were intolerable: 'It will be incorrect to translate the word "Jedovka" as meaning Jew, the former is vulgar and dictionary explains this ... Shiny, Kike does not mean jew, and Jim Crow does not mean Negro.'[82] Their protest precipitated a meeting with the Comintern leader Dmitri Manuilsky, at which they rehearsed in detail the kinds of images and experiences that troubled them, several recounting incidents of being spat on or pointed at, or overhearing comments about their colour. They also showed a noteworthy interest in the plan for a film about race relations in the United States which had brought a number of African-American writers and actors to Moscow but been frustrated by the objections of the American engineer leading a major dam-construction project. Manuilsky responded by reminding them that at least racism was a punishable offence in the Soviet Union and that the building of Soviet socialism was the only guarantor of social justice in the long run.[83]

Bilé's contribution to the discussion was broadly conciliatory, but his sensibility reflected his experience – possibly unique among the students – of having lived for an extended period in a majority white

[81] McClellan, 'Black *Hajj*', pp. 66–8.
[82] Joken [Jomo Kenyatta] *et al.* to Comintern, *c.* 21 January 1933, RGASPI 532/1/441, pp. 22–7.
[83] [Meeting of Section 9 Students with Manuilsky, February 1933?], RGASPI 532/1/441, pp. 1–14. On the film, see Mukherji, '"Like Another Planet"'.

society without (like the African Americans) being acculturated to endemic racism. He acknowledged that 'there have been occasions when children have called me a "nigger" in front of their parents', but also gave the Comintern credit for its anti-racist campaigns. Here his own positive reception as a speaker for International Red Aid in the Soviet Union reinforced the positive impression that the Scottsboro campaign had made on him. To underline his assent to the general thrust of the protest, with its emphasis on the politics of representation, he referred specifically to the impact that the *schwarze Schmach* campaign, with its images of 'Negro soldiers terrorising the white population' had had on German public opinion.[84]

The short history of African political organisation in Germany shows black Germans building on their European experience to develop quite new and distinct forms of engagement, but the idea that Bilé had become a 'European' detached from a 'native' understanding of Africa is best understood as evidence of the way in which even experienced black activists like Padmore (never mind the white specialists in the Comintern) were still working through what it meant to organise around questions of race in a global context. Bilé's role in the German movement had been to mediate between 'Europe' and 'Africa', rhetorically at least. But his speeches were predicated on an assumption that this was coterminous with mediating between white and black. On Scottsboro platforms he 'performed blackness'. The blackness he presented here was a more positive image of the Negro than was permitted by most circus, cabaret or film performances. But it was one whose political force lay in the portrayal of Africans as victims. In his speeches Bilé always began with reference to the most scandalous episodes of physical brutality on the part of the German colonisers – those which he might have experienced in his own youth in Cameroon.[85] And particularly in the context of the Scottsboro campaign his task was to emphasise the systematic connection between the suffering of Africans under colonialism and that of African Americans under 'lynch justice'. Bringing the authenticity of visible blackness to the stage even when there was not a 'real' African

[84] [Meeting of Section 9 Students with Manuilsky, February 1933?], pp. 3–4. 'Nigger' here is a translation of the *negr* in the original Russian document. Like *Neger* in German, *negr* has both descriptive and pejorative force (though Russian has another, explicitly negative term for Blacks: *hernomazyj*); the translation seems appropriate to the context, namely Bilé's perception of the term as hurtful. We are grateful to Brian Murphy for pointing this out.

[85] For Bilé's speeches, see '"Politik" mit der Zigarette im Mund'; reports of Berlin Police 21 January, 4 April and 13 May 1932, GStA Rep. 219, Landeskriminalpolizeiamt Berlin, no. 19, pp. 45–8, 92, 107–8.

American there to speak of the scandal of Scottsboro, he was presumed to speak with equal authority on the situation of any and all Blacks.[86]

Even in these terms Communist anti-colonialism created a space in which Bilé and others could reposition themselves discursively. Bilé's attacks on the German record in the protectorate were some way from the republican empire loyalty that he had endorsed in adding his signature to the letter to Weimar in 1919. And in the same speeches he verbally took a stand against aspects of his own family history. He criticised the Christian missions for their failure to act against police brutality. Reflecting on the situation in Cameroon since 1919 he said that while the French were less violent than the Germans they were more devious in their policy of integrating complaisant natives into the local administration. Here he must have been conscious of the position of his brother, Robert, who was by then a member of the Administrative Council of French Cameroon. In Hamburg and Moscow Joseph Bilé was prompted and enabled to articulate a shared interest with a global black population – exceeding in his explicit commitment to 'race consciousness' the terms of the Comintern script. What the Communist movement did not offer was the opportunity to speak as a black European.

In another sense, the uncertainties about Bilé's position are characteristic of a diasporic condition. He was negotiating being neither European nor African but (after all) both and above all black, and this is apparent in the ways in which he was positioned and positioned himself. The teaching programme and the system of self-management imposed by the KUTV involved more or less constant discussion and collective reflection on the students' experiences in section meetings. Even more than the cultural programme and the visits to farms and factories, the intense conversations among men of very different backgrounds from the United States, Liberia and Britain's African colonies will have provided the beginnings of an education for Bilé, though there are hints in the documents that he was as much frustrated as elevated both by the Soviet offerings and by the wrangles among his fellow students.[87] Away from Moscow, he actively sought affiliation with Kouyaté and Padmore when the opportunity arose. Paradoxically, what these

[86] On authenticity, see Miller, Pennybacker and Rosenhaft, 'Mother Ada Wright', and E. Johnson, *Appropriating Blackness.*

[87] The handwritten minutes of a meeting of the Section's Cultural Commission, of which Bilé was a member, offer an example of discussion among the students: RGASPI 532/1/442, pp. 65–79. Cf. Bilé's observations about an 'unhealthy atmosphere' created by party manipulation in the School: [Meeting of Section 9 Students with Manuilsky, February 1933?], p. 10.

affiliations offered – indeed demanded – was a way to close the diasporic 'circle' by taking lessons learned in Europe 'back' to Africa.

Back to Africa?

In fact, it is clear that Bilé, like many others of his generation in Germany, was never completely out of touch with Cameroon. The kinship links of Duala in Germany could in principle keep them aware of the rhythms of protest 'back home'. Among the members of the native intelligentsia who flirted with the black nationalist politics of Marcus Garvey in the early 1920s was the Native Baptist pastor Lotin a Samé, who ten years later undertook a large-scale mobilisation against the power of the European missions that crossed ethnic boundaries. Samé was a kinsman of the Bilés, and Robert Bilé joined the Native Baptist Church in the early 1930s.[88] Moreover, while Paris became the focus for political activity around Cameroonian interests in Europe after 1919, there were points of intersection between the French and German networks in the metropole. Richard Din Manga Bell, educated in Germany but back in Cameroon by 1914, was the brother of the martyred Rudolf Duala Manga and became Bell paramount chief himself. After the war he played a key role in the mobilisation of Duala efforts against French plans to renew the redevelopment and Europeanisation of Douala (building on but modifying the German plan), which came to a head in 1926. In 1927 he resigned as chief and moved to Paris to prosecute the campaign.[89] He and other Paris-based activists were in correspondence with Manga Akwa, and during 1931 he visited Berlin on an information-gathering mission and in the hope of gaining some support for the Duala from the German administration. When he fell ill in June and was taken into hospital with tuberculosis, it was LzVN officers who cabled his family in Douala to alert them and ask that money be sent to pay his medical bill. The fact that their appeal was in vain may be an indicator that the Berliners had miscalculated Richard's status and the reality of relations between the Duala in Cameroon and in Paris.[90]

[88] On Lotin a Samé, see Austen and Derrick, *Middlemen*, pp. 159–64. On Robert Ebolo Bilé and the Native Baptist Church, see interview with Guillaume Dina Ekwe Bilé; Report of Minister of Colonies, Political Section, 3 February 1934, ANCY 1 AC 107/2; Rev. Charles Maître to Society of Protestant Missions, 8 May 1923, reprinted in Hill (ed.), *Marcus Garvey*, pp. 48–9.

[89] See the summary of these events in Austen and Derrick, *Middlemen*, pp. 152–9, and Chapter 8 below.

[90] Head of Douala District to Commissioner Cameroon, 12 July 1929, ANCY APA 10222; Head of the Douala District to Commissioner Cameroon, 3 June 1931, FR ANOM 2300 COL 31/288.

The premise of anti-imperialist work in the ambit of the LAI and the LDRN was that it *was* possible for them actively to intervene in developments in Africa. When it comes to the activities of these organisations in Cameroon itself, however, there is more evidence of effort than of impact. Bilé's 1930 report emphasised how LzVN members were acting to use personal contacts in Cameroon as channels for political communication. He claimed that members were smuggling propaganda material and copies of the LzVN's statutes in private letters being sent to friends and relatives, and receiving an enthusiastic response.[91] The colonial authorities for their part reported that not only the LDRN's newspaper *La Race Nègre* (now carrying articles that focussed on the situation in Cameroon) but also the KPD newspaper *Die Rote Fahne* was reaching Cameroon and being distributed in Douala and beyond.[92] As Duala protests against expropriation mounted again in 1929, the French authorities were particularly alert to the danger of a new alliance between local malcontents and pan-African radicals. Vincent Ganty, a Guyanese living in Kribi, briefly established a branch of the LDRN there.[93] When women protesting against the imposition of a poll tax on them were fired on by the police in Douala in July 1931, the LDRN's was among the protests that reached the League of Nations.[94]

Official nervousness was reflected in the suppression of openly anti-colonial activity when it showed itself in Cameroon.[95] But both the terms in which opposition to French rule was articulated and the ways in which the French authorities perceived discontent were shaped in peculiar ways by European politics. The unstable status of the French mandate authority and the fact of German colonial irredentism, and the close attention paid by the French to the question of the loyalty of former subjects of the German empire, add an additional dimension to the meanings of 'politics' for this generation. Throughout the entire interwar period the mandate administration was concerned that French control over Cameroon

[91] Kurzer Tätigkeitsbericht, pp. 404–5.

[92] Chief Administrator for the Colonies to District Head, Yaoundé, 28 August 1931, ANCY APA 10226 Agissements Allemands; note on revolutionary propaganda involving the overseas territories, 30 November 1930, ANCY APA 10367; Derrick, *Africa's 'Agitators'*, p. 232.

[93] Owona, 'A l'aube du nationalisme camerounais', 204; Derrick, *Africa's 'Agitators'*, p. 232; Commissioner Cameroon to Minister of Colonies, 20 February 1930, FR ANOM 4008 COL 7.

[94] Telegram of Douala women to Ganty, 3 August 1931, FR ANOM 4003 COL 34; Derrick, *Africa's 'Agitators'*, p. 233. On the women's protest: Austen and Derrick, *Middlemen*, p. 151; Moumé Étia, 'La Révolte des femmes', 12–16; reports of police and administrators, ANCY APA 11217/B.

[95] Commissioner Cameroon to District Head, Dschang, 22 November 1933, ANCY APA 11223/B.

was being undermined by German efforts to regain the territory as well as by indigenous protests against their rule, and in official French minds fears about Germanophilia pre-dated and often overshadowed sensitivity to anti-colonialism. The threat of a renewal of German influence was heightened in the mid 1920s by a series of developments. These included the legal return of German citizens as traders and planters to Cameroon, Germany's entry into the League of Nations and the German government's purchase of plantations in British Cameroon for return to German ownership and control.[96] And while the hopes of German colonial revisionists were rapidly receding by the end of the 1920s, it was in Cameroon that the German Foreign Office still saw a small chance of being granted a mandate.[97] French paranoia peaked after 1936, as the possibility that Germany might reconsider its European expansionist policy in return for overseas possessions came onto the diplomatic agenda.[98] Increasingly, any signs of indigenous dissatisfaction with the French regime were interpreted as examples of pro-German agitation, and any signs of attachment to the pre-war order as politically subversive.[99]

The consequence of these anxieties was a regime of surveillance of individuals both in Germany and in Cameroon, generating a mass of documentation on 'pro-German' activity. When we read this documentation for evidence of 'politics' – Germanophile or anti-colonial – what we find is a range of individual and associational activities that echo patterns of African activity in Europe in their fluidity and ambiguity. The question of their significance for politically relevant identities, or their place in the history of African nationalism, has been canvassed in the historical literature.[100] In the Cameroonian case, the evidence for any continuous links between Germanophone activism as such and the growth of a native anti-colonial or nationalist movement is not strong.[101] They are thus easily dismissed as fantasies of the colonisers or as opportunistic episodes. They invite attention, though, as evidence of the ways in which the time that Cameroonian actors spent in Germany *might have* fed back into developments in Cameroon had the precarious balance of power and interest in Europe not collapsed into world war. They also tell us something about the afterlife of that experience in individuals' lives.

In the 1930s one former German colonial subject in particular was singled out by the French authorities as a significant threat to public

[96] Austen and Derrick, *Middlemen*, p. 172; Joseph, 'The German Question', 75, n. 36.
[97] Eberhardt, *Zwischen Nationalsozialismus und Apartheid*, pp. 135–6.
[98] Callahan, *A Sacred Trust*, pp. 118–48. [99] Joseph, 'The German Question'.
[100] See Austen, '"Ich bin schwarzer Mann"'.
[101] This contrasts with the situation in Togo. See Lawrance, *Locality, Mobility and 'Nation'*, pp. 121–47.

order in Douala. This was Thomas Manga Akwa, who returned to Cameroon for good in 1932.[102] By this time, Manga Akwa was someone to be watched on the grounds equally of his kinship, his involvement with anti-colonial groups in Germany and his links to key figures within the German colonial revisionist movement. The French authorities knew that he had been sponsored by the DGfE, whose director Alfred Mansfeld they suspected of actively organising the return of African 'agents' to Cameroon.[103] They also knew of his association with the LzVN. Moreover, Manga Akwa was the cousin of the pretenders to the title of Akwa paramount, Dibussi, Din and Betote Akwa as well as of the late Ludwig Mpundu.[104] Each of his cousins in turn had been recognised and then deposed as Akwa leader by the French, and Betote Akwa was a known associate of Lotin a Samé. Manga Akwa himself had been under the eyes of the mandate authorities since his 1921 visit to Douala and in 1930 he had been denied re-entry on the familiar combination of grounds: previous troublemaking, having a white wife and the suspicion that he was a German agent.[105] It is not clear why he was nevertheless allowed to return two years later. Perhaps the French Foreign Office felt that it was easier to keep him under control in Cameroon, or perhaps they were worried that he would join anti-colonial activists in France, as he himself had suggested he might.[106]

In Manga Akwa's subsequent activities it is difficult to disentangle the political activist from the disillusioned returnee. His return reportedly provoked counter-suspicions on the part of his kin that the French authorities intended to install him as paramount. The result was that his own relatives denounced him as a German agent and his papers were seized by the police. As late as January 1934 he was still understood to be in correspondence with activists in Paris, but it was his Germanophile tendencies that were of more interest to the French police.[107] Suspicions that he was in the pay of the German authorities, which persisted into the

[102] The date is in the German sources: Brückner to Josef Freeborn, n.d., BArch R1001 4037, p. 65; Brückner to the Chairman of Small Criminal Division 7, 9 January 1933, BArch R1001 5149, p. 156. For Manga Akwa's previous return and run-ins with the mandate authorities in Cameroon, see Chapter 2.

[103] French Consulate, Berlin to Minister of Foreign Affairs, 16 May 1929, ANCY APA 10226; Minister of Colonies to French Commissioner in Cameroon, 22 June 1929, ANCY APA 10226.

[104] Manga Akwa's father, known as Manga Mpondo Akwa, was the brother of King Dika Mpondo Akwa.

[105] District Head, Douala to Commissioner Cameroon, 17 September 1930.

[106] Manga Akwa to Minister of Colonies, 4 February 1931.

[107] Report on the Committee Members of the Association France-Cameroun, 22 January 1934, FR ANOM 4003 COL 36.

late 1930s, may have been justified given the readiness he had shown to denounce fellow activists to the German Foreign Office in 1929.[108] Manga Akwa left for the British mandate territory and by 1938 at latest he had settled in Tiko, where he worked for the Hamburg-based African Fruit Company. Tiko was known as a base for fugitive Duala malcontents, as well as being home to a large number of German planters and colonists. While Manga Akwa had every reason to turn his back on Douala, the fact that he chose to go to Tiko heightened the authorities' suspicions; they characterised him as a 'political refugee'.[109] He reportedly sent several communications to the French administration accusing them of violence and cruelty and citing the case of their mistreatment of the Sultan of Bamoun N'Joya, who died during deportation up-country in 1933.[110] Otherwise, no concrete examples of political activity on his part are documented. Nevertheless, by November 1938 the office of the Minister of the Colonies had identified Manga Akwa as being responsible for spreading the most dangerous anti-French propaganda among the coastal Duala, Bassa, Bakoko and Batanga populations. A 1938 police report described him as being of 'pure German formation' and went so far as to suggest that a renewed impulse in anti-French activities within the mandate had coincided with his arrival.[111]

What is certainly true is that the Cameroon he had arrived in was a place in which the anxieties of the French authorities hampered productive relations with the population and fuelled discontent, so that his own protests however motivated became part of a wider movement.[112] Not long after Manga Akwa re-entered Douala, the administration discovered a genuine pro-German organisation whose members included at least one Duala who had spent time in Germany. Peter Mukuri Dikongue de Mbongo, also from the quarter of Akwa, established the Association of German-Spirited Cameroon Natives (KEDGV), also known as the Society of Friends of Education and the Association of Cameroon Coloureds for German Spirit, sometime before summer 1933. When the French authorities became aware of it, houses in the Akwa quarter of Douala were searched, correspondence was confiscated,

[108] Note on Manga Akwa, Sûreté, 24 November 1938, CAC 19949462-71-6971.

[109] Deputy Commissioner to Commissioner Cameroon, 4 February 1939, ANCY APA 11201/K. Here he is referred to as Manga Manga.

[110] Author unknown, note 12327VI, 16 November 1938, FR ANOM 2300 COL 30/277; note on the state of mind of the natives of Cameroon, 16 November 1938, CAC 1994464-28-2432. Manga Akwa's communications have not survived.

[111] Minister of Colonies, Information on German Propaganda in Cameroon in the French and British Mandates, 17 November 1938, ANCY APA 10124/B; note on Manga Akwa, Sûreté, 24 November 1938.

[112] Joseph, *Radical Nationalism*, p. 39; Austen and Derrick, *Middlemen*, pp. 163–4.

and half a dozen arrests resulted. Among the information seized was material describing the group's aims, written by Dikongue. According to his own account Dikongue had been educated by Catholic Pallottine missionaries; he described the origin of his own project in terms of a mission. During World War One he had been captured by the British and escaped from a prisoner of war camp in Lagos. Horrified at the establishment of French and British mandate control over Cameroon, he had sought out others who shared his views, and in secret meetings they had formed the KEDGV. The group included some twenty members, the majority of whom were Duala and all of whom were educated during the German period. One of the other named members, Paul Muduru Dibongo Nsahme, was described as living or having lived in Germany. Another was Ferdinand Edingele Meetom; he brought to the association the credentials of an active anti-colonialist who had clashed with both the German and the French occupiers. Several of the men, including Dikongue, were employees of the Woermann shipping company, while two were auxiliaries of the French administration.[113]

KEDGV members had to sign a written oath of allegiance to Germany, and they made a point of establishing direct communication with Germans whom they knew or thought to be influential. In particular they were in correspondence with the former colonial civil servants Hermann Hertig and Mansfeld as well as with the DKG. They sent Mansfeld a long report entitled 'The voice of the Duala People, Cameroon' written in German, which they asked him to pass on to the League of Nations. According to Dikongue, Mansfeld arranged for the publication of this report in German newspapers. To the DKG they wrote a letter in June 1933 proclaiming their continued support for Germany and requesting rosettes with the German eagle and the swastika, which they wanted to wear as a public demonstration of their sentiments, in anticipation of a return to German rule.[114]

There is no evidence that KEDGV members had any realistic sense of what the swastika stood for. Their message was as much anti-French as it was pro-German; the report to Mansfeld exposed what they saw as the brutality and injustice of French rule, and this aspect of their agitation struck a chord. In the wake of their activities, the French authorities

[113] For the following account: Translation of Documents seized from Mukuri Dikongue from Akwa, sent with letter of Commissioner Cameroon to Minister of Colonies, 2 November 1934, FR ANOM 2300 COL 31/294; French Commissioner Repiquet to Public Prosecutor, 11 August 1934, ANCY APA 10190. See also Joseph, 'German Question'; Austen, '"Ich bin schwarzer Mann"', p. 31.

[114] KEDGV to DKG, 24 June 1933. A copy of the letter is reproduced in Jacob, *Kolonialpolitisches Quellenheft*, pp. 178–9.

reported that rumours were spreading throughout Douala and beyond about the imminent return of the Germans. As far away as Edea, some sixty kilometres southeast of Douala, a local leader was arrested for possessing a signed note of allegiance to Germany, similar to those undertaken by KEDGV members.[115] He was sentenced to ten years' banishment to Mokolo in the far north of the mandate. KEDGV members in Douala who were arrested during the administration's raid in 1933 received similarly lengthy deportation sentences ranging from five to ten years.

The severity of these measures reflected the extent to which the French authorities saw the KEDGV as part of a wider groundswell of opposition, identifying links between its members and other protest movements, including the Native Baptist Church. The tenacity of the organisation seems to confirm the persistence of dynamic networks. A small number of its members, including Dikongue and Meetom, successfully escaped. They had formed a new KEDGV base at Tiko by 1936, and were suspected of smuggling copies of the DKG-sponsored journal *Der koloniale Kampf* on banana ships bound for Douala.[116] Flyers also appeared on French territory advertising a 'Cameroon Association of Germanophile Natives' based 'for the present' in Tiko, and the KEDGV reportedly sent observers to the founding meetings of a new pro-French youth group, the Jeunesse Camerounaise Française in 1939.[117] Meanwhile, French officials stepped up their efforts to silence pro-German Dualas, imprisoning suspects or exiling them to the north of the territory. Meetom (and probably also Dikongue) was apparently captured by the British and handed over to the French. The men, along with dozens of Cameroonians including other members of the KEDGV and the Native Baptist Church, were tried in 1941. While the majority were acquitted, Dikongue, Meetom and Muduru Dibongo were among those who were convicted of spreading anti-French propaganda and disturbing the peace, for which they received long prison sentences.[118]

[115] French Commissioner Repiquet to Public Prosecutor, 11 August 1934.

[116] Information bulletin on German propaganda (4th trimester 1936), 15 February 1937, ANCY APA 11225/C. In the document the second man mentioned is referred to Edinguele Mouangue, but other documents suggest that this was actually Edingele Meetom.

[117] Lawless, Chief of Political and Administrative Affairs to CAI, 7 December 1936, ANCY APA 11225/C; Chief of the Sûreté to Commissioner Cameroon, 25 February 1939, ANCY APA 10124/B. On the Jeunesse Camerounaise Française, see Joseph, *Radical Nationalism*, pp. 41–4.

[118] Derrick, 'Free French and Africans'. Dikongue Meetom was later executed for anti-French activities: Austen and Derrick, *Middlemen*, p. 173.

Although no explicit connection is drawn in the sources between Manga Akwa's activities and the agitation of the KEDGV and its associates, it is not impossible that there were points of contact. Both developed out of the quarter of Akwa and they followed a similar trajectory and time-scale. Moreover both can be seen as part of a wider if still inchoate pattern of discontent and proto-nationalism evolving in Douala and informed by some communication with Cameroonian anti-colonialists in Europe. And in the case of the KEDGV activists at least a degree of real commitment is evidenced by their tenacity in the face of the threat of prison and worse. The significance of the 'German' experience here is worth reflecting on. In the case of Germanophone Cameroonians who had not left the territory, nostalgia provided a language in which to express real opposition to present circumstances. The kinds of personal and kinship relationships that seem to have propelled Manga Akwa into opposition could be particularly powerful in the case of men who had been away from home for long periods. If his personal discontent was articulated in politically dangerous terms this could reflect new contacts, or the persistence – equally dangerous in the eyes of the authorities – of old ones. The French authorities reported that Manga Akwa remained in contact with Joseph Bilé once Bilé succeeded in returning to Cameroon, though nothing came of the connection.[119]

In the short term, both of these episodes proved relatively inconsequential. The activities of the KEDGV were ended by French repression; Manga Akwa disappears from the archival sources in 1939 and his fate remains unknown.[120] If it is easier to see incoherence, opportunism or nostalgia than any productive continuity in these traces of political action, this may be because the rise of National Socialism in Germany and its challenge to the European and world order changed the terms of engagement for radical politics in Africa and Europe. This culminated in war on both continents, but it began with the destruction of the conditions for the development of black politics in Germany.

119 French Commissioner Repiquet to Public Prosecutor, 11 August 1934, and see Chapter 8.

120 Anecdotal evidence suggests that he died on Fernando Po in the 1940s: Communication from Victor Dicka Akwa, November 2009.

7 Under the shadow of National Socialism

At the beginning of 1933 Victor Bell was 'invited' to discuss the future of the LzVN at the Horst-Wessel-Haus in Berlin; formerly KPD headquarters, the building now housed both police offices and an unofficial detention centre for political opponents, and it is likely that Bell was at least threatened and possibly beaten there.[1] With Hitler's appointment as Chancellor on 30 January 1933 black political activists and their supporters in Germany had come under immediate pressure. The ITUCNW was forced from Germany, its leader Padmore arrested and eventually deported, while the LAI was permanently shut down.[2] The result of Bell's interview was that the LzVN was declared dissolved, but Bell continued to be harassed for at least another year. In September 1934 he was again summoned to give information about the Liga; he reported that membership had fallen below three, and he had no knowledge of the whereabouts of his fellow officers Joseph Bilé and Thomas Ngambi ul Kuo.[3] The LzVN was formally dissolved in October 1935. Within months of the Nazi takeover of power not only black political activism but also the associational framework that had developed over fifteen years was brought to an end.

In the National Socialist regime that Hitler led, the suppression of political dissent served the vision of a new kind of national community, or *Volksgemeinschaft*. The future of this new order depended on excluding individuals and groups who were deemed undesirable or unfit. Insofar as their unsuitability for life in the *Volksgemeinschaft* was regarded as inherent in their genetic makeup, policy also required that they be prevented from having children. Central to this vision was the notion of purity of the blood. The inherent unity of 'racial and eugenic policy' towards those of 'alien blood' (*Fremdblütige*, like

[1] Bell to Amtsgericht Charlottenburg, 24 August 1934, LAB Rep. 42, Acc. 1743, no. 9054, p. 22. Bell survived the war: ITS 2.3.3.4, Berliner Kartei.

[2] Peter Martin, 'Schwarze Sowjets', p. 187; Pennybacker, *From Scottsboro to Munich*, p. 77.

[3] Statement Bell, 4 September 1934, LAB Rep. 42, Acc. 1743, no. 9054.

Jews, Blacks and Gypsies) on the one hand and those who were of 'German blood' but genetically damaged, incurably ill or incorrigibly deviant (*gemeinschaftsfremd*) on the other, was axiomatic for Hitler.[4] Among the other leading Nazis who shared this view was Wilhelm Frick, now Reich Interior Minister. His key project was the creation of a legislative framework that would realise this unity by preventing the birth of undesirables (through a radical reform of the institutions and principles of the public health system that promoted both positive and negative eugenic measures) and enabling the exclusion of those already present (through changes to the laws governing citizenship, civil rights and civic status).[5]

It is in this sense that Nazi Germany has been characterised as a 'racial state'.[6] But the experience of Blacks is a reminder that the 'racial state' remained a work in progress, as uneven in its operations as it was fantastical in conception. The single most consistent element in the thinking of the Nazi leadership was the determination to remove the Jews from German society, and the first outcome of Frick's legislative efforts was the 1935 Nuremberg Laws, directed in the first instance exclusively at Jews. The only groups to be expressly and systematically targeted for mass murder were Jews and the incurably disabled, while Sinti and Roma, or 'Gypsies', were interned, sterilised and finally consigned to slow death in Auschwitz. Each group that the Nazis subjected to their peculiar 'racial' gaze had its own history of social negotiations around 'otherness' and of cultural racialisation, and those histories informed the way that they were treated in practice.[7]

The experience of Blacks in Nazi Germany accordingly displays some paradoxes. The early deliberations of Nazi policymakers – like Frick's own pre-1933 legislative interventions – reveal the extent to which questions of relationships between black and white people and fears of the growth of a 'mulatto' population in Germany prompted and shaped the debates that led to the Nuremberg Laws. These were informed both by Germany's post-World War One experience and by awareness of American models of racial segregation. In practice, though, for ex-colonial subjects, the paternalism and ambivalence of white Germans manifested (for example) in the work of the DGfE, and attitudes to difference (or forms of racism) that were so ordinary that they were

[4] On the *Gemeinschaftsfremde*, see Peukert, *Inside Nazi Germany*; Gellately and Stoltzfus (eds.), *Social Outsiders*.

[5] Neliba, *Frick*, pp. 161–83. [6] Burleigh and Wippermann, *The Racial State*.

[7] On the links between 'euthanasia' and genocide, see Friedlander, *The Origins of Nazi Genocide*. On 'Gypsies': Lewy, *The Nazi Persecution of the Gypsies*.

perceived as being outwith the terms of the Nazi 'revolution', made for tensions in official policy and even some safe spaces for individuals and families in peacetime.

Accordingly, where men, women and children of African heritage ended up between 1933 and 1945 depended to some extent on where they had started from. At the beginning of 1933 the number of first-generation Cameroonians living in Germany had declined to thirty-four, largely as a result of emigration. The number of second- and third-generation German-born children was around fifty and around a dozen more children were born before the end of World War Two. The black community also included nearly forty former colonial subjects from Togo and the former German East Africa, some settled African Americans and West Indians, and a possibly substantial number of Africans, primarily men, from other sub-Saharan African countries such as Liberia and South Africa; many of them, too, had established families in Germany.[8] Their experiences varied and most of our subjects who were in Germany in 1933 survived the war. Over the course of the Nazi regime, however, Germany's black population was subject to increasingly deliberate practices of exclusion which contained at least the germs of a progressively 'racial' annihilationism. Social, economic and political marginalisation was accelerated when Frick extended aspects of the Nuremberg Laws to explicitly cover *Neger* and their children. This challenged their citizenship status and exposed them to scrutiny and harassment under anti-miscegenation policies, rendering them open to compulsory sterilisation and the breakup of families. The trajectory of policy, later taken up by Heinrich Himmler as SS Leader and Chief of German Police, shows Blacks being assimilated to the spiralling radicalisation of policy, particularly during wartime. As Europe's Jews and 'Gypsies' were targeted for annihilation, the protection that Africans had enjoyed from local police and from old colonial hands in the ministries was drastically eroded.

As they developed over time, then, the official policies and practices outlined below represent an accelerating process of racialisation that tended towards defining our subjects entirely in terms of undesirable physical (genetic) characteristics; they became no more than *Neger*, with nothing to distinguish them from other people of African descent. The practice of forced sterilisation, which began with the Rhineland children fathered by French occupation troops, targeted Blacks as dangerous

[8] An African-American reporter estimated the size of the Liberian population in Germany to be around 300 in 1933: William N. Jones, 'Liberia May Drive All Germans from Republic', *Baltimore Afro-American*, 9 December 1933, p. 11.

bodies. More particularly, it targeted those of mixed heritage (*Mischlinge*). In the colonial situation, *Mischlinge* posed a danger as evidence the colour line really could be crossed and a threat to political order; in the context of *Volksgemeinschaft* they signalled the combined danger of progressive pollution and invisibility of its source. From this point of view, the measures taken against mixed couples and their children were a response to and an assault on the fact of settledness and the families and communities that those mixed couples had formed, and they brought the growing black community to a breaking point. But in peacetime and beyond there were also aspects of daily life that fostered new connections and provided opportunities for resistance, while the evidence of persecution and flight also contains evidence for sustained networks of communication and mutual support.[9] In this sense Clarence Lusane's perceptive observation that under Nazism the 'construction … of blackness from above struggled with the reality of an uninformed blackness from below' calls for some modification: by the 1930s, and to a very significant extent, black Germans recognised themselves and each other as members of a community under threat.

Troubled times

Even before the takeover of power some Nazi officials were expressing an unhealthy interest in Germany's black population. By 1930 Frick was already Interior Minister in Thuringia, and his attacks specifically on Blacks began early. In April 1930 he issued a decree banning *Negerkultur* – the public performance of black music like jazz or by black performers in Thuringia. Similarly, in September 1932 in Oldenburg, where the Nazis achieved their first absolute majority in a state parliament, they sought to prevent a visiting Togolese pastor, Robert Kwami, from addressing a local church. Nazi Minister President Röver described Kwami's visit to Oldenburg as an 'affront to culture' and he entered into a hostile debate with church officials, who successfully defended Kwami's right to preach. The public's response was overwhelmingly in Kwami's favour and the Lambertikirche was packed out to hear him speak.[10] But within months of the Nazi takeover of power verbal and physical abuse of black people by party activists had increased. In Düsseldorf members of the SS were responsible for the murder of

[9] Lusane, *Hitler's Black Victims*, p. 3.

[10] Scholder, *Churches and the Third Reich*, vol. I, pp. 181–4; Wiegräbe, *Pastor Robert Kwami*, pp. 26–9. For evidence that the African-American press was watching, see J. A. Rogers, 'Germans Eject Negro Preacher from Pulpit', *Philadelphia Tribune*, 13 October 1932, p. 7.

Hilarius Gilges.[11] Gilges, the son of an unknown African man and a German woman, was a well-known agitprop actor and activist in the city who had already come into conflict with the Nazis.

Meanwhile the difficult living conditions that ex-colonial subjects, their children and their wives had faced since the late 1920s became increasingly acute, as verbal and physical abuse became a part of day-to-day life. They remembered the establishment of the dictatorship as a watershed moment in their personal histories. In July 1945 the Berlin-based performer Josie Allen, from a large Somali-German family, told an African-American reporter: 'Berlin was fine until Hitler came ... After Hitler came colored people began dropping out of sight.'[12] The comments of Luise Misipo from 1958 provide a more detailed insight into her family's experiences in Frankfurt.

> It was impossible to be seen with my husband, whether on the street, in a pub, or in the theatre without being subjected to verbal abuse. When I went out for walks with our child members of the SA spat on the poor boy and I, as a mother, had to look on without being able to do anything about it.[13]

Dorothea Diek concluded: 'The "Adolph time" was the worst that anyone can imagine.'[14]

Against this background, in May 1933 the Foreign Office reported that increasing numbers of Cameroonians and Togolese were requesting financial help to return to Africa.[15] A detailed picture of their deteriorating situation was revealed in a 1934 letter sent to the AAKA by Kwassi Bruce. Writing in the name of Africans in Germany, he displayed a thorough knowledge about their circumstances and an understanding of the priorities of the regime. He described himself as a 'pure-blooded [*reinrassiger*] Togolese' who had received a respectable education from pure Aryan foster parents, and went on to give an account of his personal experiences of everyday racial abuse and discrimination, including losing his job as the leader of an orchestra in March 1933. Bruce wrote: 'Directors are always rejecting [me] on account of my skin colour. And the same is happening to my fellow countrymen. What is to become of us?' According to Bruce what lay at the heart of all problems they encountered was their liminal civil status.[16]

[11] Sparing, 'Hilarius Gilges'.

[12] Josie Allen quoted in Edward B. Toles, 'Where is Hitler? German-born Negroes Free in Berlin', *Chicago Defender*, 14 July 1945, p. 1.

[13] Luise Misipo, Account of Persecution, 17 March 1958, HHStAW 518/2649/22, pp. 4–5.

[14] [Reiprich and Ngambi ul Kuo,] 'Unser Vater war Kameruner', p. 71.

[15] Brückner to Reich Finance Minister, 31 May 1933, BArch R1001 7562, p. 85.

[16] Kwassi Bruce to AAKA, Autumn 1934; BArch R1001 7562, pp. 91–100, reprinted in Martin and Alonzo, *Zwischen Charleston und Stechschritt*, pp. 411–17.

Policies of exclusion: challenges to civil status

By 1933 only a handful of Africans and their German-born children had acquired German citizenship. For most, the German identity papers that were their primary form of identification required renewal on a regular basis with the local police. These were now withdrawn and replaced by a new form of identification – the *Fremdenpaß* (alien's passport). As early as June 1933 Mohamed Husen, a Sudanese from the former German East Africa, complained to the Foreign Office about receiving this new form of passport.[17] Although the *Fremdenpaß* was introduced in law before Hitler took power, the fact that its issue coincided with a rise in hostility to black residents and that it was in most cases implemented only from 1933 onwards meant that it has been remembered by black Germans as a critical moment, the beginning of the end of relative freedom. In practice the new policy was not always rigorously enforced. It was not until 1938 that Hermann Kessern was forced to relinquish his German identity papers, while Dualla Misipo claimed that he and his family were still in possession of German papers at the beginning of 1937.[18]

Nonetheless, anyone found to be without a valid and up-to-date form of identification faced prosecution, as the case of Josef Garber illustrates. Between 1934 and 1938 he was arrested and prosecuted four times, on three counts of 'unauthorised residence within Reich territory' and on one similar count of lacking valid identity papers.[19] Twice his sentences were rescinded thanks to an amnesty. On the two other occasions he faced a fine or short prison sentence. Following these convictions Garber not only had a criminal record, but was a repeat offender. This was a dangerous status to have under a regime in which habitual criminals were regarded as candidates for 're-education' and sterilisation and even in conventional prisons conditions grew progressively more brutal.[20]

Africans who had successfully applied for naturalisation were initially able to retain citizenship, although their status as Germans was rendered unstable by the shifting legal situation. This was the case even before

17 Gunzert to Hussein (*sic*), 30 June 1933, BArch R1001 5148, p. 95.
18 Firla, *Der kameruner Artist*, p. 159; Reparations Claim, Dualla Misipo, 5 January 1954, HHStAW 518/40437, p. 88.
19 Extract from the Criminal Registry, 26 April 1944, LAB A.Rep. 341-02 no. 11649 Josef Garber, p. 4. See also the case of the Liberian Joe Barre Mowan who was also convicted of lacking valid papers, Holocaust Memorial Museum Archives, Washington, RG-14 011/01.
20 Wachsmann, *Hitler's Prisons*.

December 1935, when Frick publicly named Blacks and 'Gypsies' as 'of alien blood', disqualifying them from citizenship along with Jews under the terms of the second Nuremberg Law, the Reich Citizenship Law.[21] But it is characteristic that even after Frick's statement was published there was no consistency of practice; local authorities showed varying attitudes to the question and used varying rationales when they chose to challenge people's citizenship. In spring 1935 the Boholles were among those subjected to a stringent review of their citizenship by the Berlin police, probably at the behest of the Interior Ministry, on the basis of the Law for the Revocation of Naturalisation and the Withdrawal of German Citizenship. Introduced on 14 July 1933 and aimed primarily at political émigrés and later the thousands of Jewish migrants who had entered Germany from Eastern Europe following World War One, this dictated that any undesirable person who had gained citizenship between 9 November 1918 and 30 January 1933 could be denaturalised.[22] Police investigators focussed primarily on the father Josef, his two adult sons Rudolf and Paul, and his grown-up daughter Josefa, because, unlike Josef's wife (born a Russian national in Poland) and the white partners of the children, they were deemed to be *fremdblütig*. Josefa's situation was further complicated by her 1934 marriage to the German Julius Schülte, which made her a German citizen irrespective of her status before the wedding. This made it more difficult to find any legal justification for refusing her claims to citizenship.

Among the reports that followed were statements in their favour from the local police precinct in Karlshorst. The family was long established there and the local police had backed their original naturalisation application. They referred (once again) to the positive reputation that family members enjoyed and they vouched for the financial situation of Josef and Josefa. The position of the two sons, however, was more precarious. Neither was able to find regular work as a performer. Rudolf, a father of two, had only recently found a low-paid job as a labourer after a long period of unemployment. He and his family relied on payments from the Nazi Winter Welfare Fund. This in itself is noteworthy, given that Jews were actively disqualified from this form of assistance from its very introduction, while other *Gemeinschaftsfremde* were excluded soon after.[23] Paul, who was living

[21] Wilhelm Frick, 'Das Reichsbürgergesetz und das Gesetz zum Schutz des deutschen Blutes und der deutschen Ehre vom 15. September 1935', *Deutsche Juristen-Zeitung*, 23/40 (1935), 1390–4, here p. 1391.

[22] For the following account: LAB A.Pr.Br.Rep. 030-06 no. 6473. On the 1933 law, see Gosewinkel, *Einbürgern und Ausschließen*, pp. 370–3.

[23] Burleigh and Wippermann, *The Racial State*, pp. 69–72.

in Essen with his white wife, was dependent on unemployment support, for which his citizenship qualified him. He had also been sentenced to three months' imprisonment for stealing in 1933. This misdemeanour alone, coupled with the sons' history of unemployment, would very likely have provided grounds for reversing the family's naturalisation even before their racial status was considered. Nonetheless Frick received a letter from the office of the Berlin Police Commissioner in June 1935 asking that in the Boholles' case an exception be made. Although the racial arguments behind the initiative to exclude the family were acknowledged, the request was legitimated with reference to Josef being a former colonial subject. It appears that this request was successful.[24]

Like the Boholles, the Diek family in Danzig was initially affected by legislation that primarily targeted others. In the aftermath of World War One Danzig was declared an autonomous city state under the protection of the League of Nations and the residents were issued with Free City of Danzig passports. In the Dieks' case these new passports replaced their Hamburg ones. Crucially, the new documentation did not automatically bestow German citizenship upon the holder. This became significant once the Germans annexed the city in October 1939, bringing an end to its Free City status and rendering thousands of its residents, principally Poles, effectively stateless.[25] Those adjudged to be non-German lost their existing citizenship and many, including the Dieks, were refused Reich citizenship.[26] Their Free City passports were revoked and instead they were each eventually issued with a *Fremdenpaß*. For Dorothea Diek the consequences were almost catastrophic. In December 1944 she was stopped on the street by SS men and asked to show her identity papers. When she produced her 'alien's passport' she was promptly taken to a forced labour camp for foreign workers at the Danzig dockyard. Weeks later following an Allied air raid she managed to escape.[27]

Dorothea's half-sister, Erika Mandenga Diek, is one of those whom we know to have fallen foul explicitly of Frick's reading of the Reich

[24] In a list of Africans resident in Germany drawn up two months later Josef was still referred to as a Prussian citizen while on a 1941 police report Paul was categorised as a German citizen. See Gunzert to Interior Ministry, 18 September 1935, BArch R1001 7562, pp. 114–16, here p. 115; Draft, Criminal Case, 24 October 1941, LAB A.Rep. 369, no. 954, pp. 7–9. He does not feature in lists of Berliners denaturalised during the Nazi period: Personal communication from Gisela Erler, 18 December 2008.

[25] Majer, *Non-Germans under the Third Reich*, pp. 236–8.

[26] [Reiprich and Ngambi ul Kuo,] 'Unser Vater war Kameruner', p. 72.

[27] Oguntoye, *Eine Afro-Deutsche Geschichte*, pp. 139–40.

Citizenship Law – thanks to her extraordinary tenacity in defending her right to be an ordinary German. In 1933 her claim to be re-naturalised following her divorce had been acknowledged, along with the fact that her Hamburg-born illegitimate son had never lost his German nationality.[28] Two years later she came to the attention of Frick's Interior Ministry again when she was dismissed from her post in the Hamburg office of the Reich Accident Insurance Agency. When she protested and was reinstated, the Hamburg Election Bureau assumed that this meant that her citizenship rights must be unchallenged. The Bureau was acting on the assumption that while as a non-Aryan she fell under the provisions of the Reich Citizenship Law, as a *Mischling* she must enjoy the 'temporary citizenship' granted to half-Jewish Germans in a supplementary decree.[29] In July 1936, however, the Interior Ministry advised that this was not the case; as a non-Jewish *Mischling* Erika was a Reich national (*Reichsangehörige*), but not a citizen. This time her petition to recover her rights was unsuccessful.[30]

The records in other cases bespeak at least a growing awareness on the part of local authorities that the terms of reference for the civil status of Africans had shifted. It is entirely possible that the Frankfurt police were acting on Frick's interpretation of the Nuremberg Laws when they withdrew Dualla Misipo's German identity papers in 1937, and also in the case of Maria Ngambe.[31] On the basis of her adoption by her natural father Maria held a German passport. Just one month after her father's death in November 1938, the Frankfurt Police Commissioner chose to review her legal status and concluded that adoption had not conferred citizenship and that she had inherited the status of her Cameroonian mother. As a result her passport was confiscated. For Maria, a choreographer, who regularly travelled outside of Germany to Holland and Belgium, this had serious consequences. Unable now to leave the country, she ended the war doing clerical work in a BMW plant in Munich. It says much about the vagaries of terminology and practice at different levels of administration that her 1944 police registration card shows her as the holder of a *Fremdenpaß*, as stateless, as a former German national and as a *Reichsdeutsche* – the last a term normally used for German residents of the Reich, but in this case selected as the only available

[28] See Chapter 3 for detail on Erika Mandenga Diek's citizenship situation.

[29] See *RGBl* (1935), 1:1333.

[30] Reich Accident Insurance Agency (Hamburg) to Police Authorities Hamburg, 27 February 1935; Richter to Ministry of the Interior, 20 September 1936, both StAHam 332-7 B IV 1993, no. 138. The circumstances of her dismissal and reinstatement in 1935 are discussed below.

[31] See Chapter 5.

alternative to 'Jew' on the form.[32] In Hanover, the endorsements 'Prussian' and 'German' on the police registrations of the Ngando family were struck out some time after November 1936 and replaced with 'Subject of the German Reich' (*Untertan des deutschen Reiches* or *Reichsuntertan* – and in one case 'not *Reichsangehöriger*') – a term inherited from the colonial past which the new regime precipitated back into circulation.[33]

The above cases provide a sense of the increasing social and political exclusion that people of African heritage faced as well as illustrating how unpredictable their individual fates were. Ngambe and Erika Mandenga Diek suffered because they were black, whereas the Boholles and Dieks were affected by wider policies aimed at foreigners in general. The cases also demonstrate how crucial individuals' and families' relationships to local officials could be in modulating the effect of discrimination. There was, however, a limit to the help that local officials could offer. While support of the local police precinct worked in favour of the Boholles, Luise Misipo reported that her local police lieutenant in Frankfurt expressed regret at having to cancel the family's German identity papers, but felt he had no alternative.[34] Decisions made by officials at all levels could be entirely arbitrary and often depended on an individual officer's vested interest in or commitment to the regime's overarching ideology. Ultimately, what came to the aid of the Boholles was the Berlin Police Commissioner's sentimentality about the colonial connection, as well as the backing that this received from senior officials at a national level. Similarly, Kwassi Bruce was able to hold on to his citizenship, most likely on account of his colonial background which underpinned the support he enjoyed from Foreign Office officials. Ironically, it was precisely because of his status as a German citizen that he was arrested and held by French officials after

[32] French Consulate, Frankfurt a.M. to Minister of Colonies, 4 November 1938; Police Commissioner, Frankfurt a.M. to French Consul, Frankfurt a.M., 26 January 1939: both FR ANOM 1 AFFPOL 614/2; ITS 2.2.2.1 Kriegszeitkartei 72858687, 72858688; Kaltenbach's Darmstadt Registration card, Hessisches Staatsarchiv Darmstadt.

[33] Registration cards, Stadtarchiv Hannover. In each case reference is made to an authoritative document dated 16 November 1936; it has not been possible to identify the document or its source. The same phrase occurs on Johannes Kohl's Bremen registration: StABremen Meldekartei 4,82/1-3/175. The status of 'subject' had applied to natives of the protectorates in the colonial period; it seems to have been in unofficial use in various contexts under National Socialism and was formally revived during the war in the context of the annexation of territories in Poland and discussions about future colonial legislation.

[34] Luise Misipo, Account of Persecution, 7 March 1958, p. 4.

the outbreak of World War Two while on board a ship heading for Lagos. There he was expecting to work in the German consulate; instead the French sent him to Lomé.[35]

The cases of Dorothea Diek and Josef Garber underline the real dangers that went with losing citizenship and being identified as an 'alien'. Particularly in the wartime context the holder of a *Fremdenpaß* was exposed to the risk of criminalisation and incarceration; Dorothea was not the only second-generation Cameroonian who was interned in a labour camp as a foreigner. Bruce articulated his own awareness of the logic of the new form of identification and the effect it was having on his contemporaries, remarking in 1934: 'At this time the stateless passport is like neurasthenia; it will not kill you, but it also will not let you live.'[36] Declared foreigners and subject to increasing stress in everyday life, more and more former colonial subjects sought to leave Germany or turned to France, as the mandate power in most of Cameroon, for protection. Yet one of the immediate results of the introduction of the *Fremdenpaß* was that the ability of stateless individuals to leave the country was sharply reduced.

The reluctant guardian: Cameroonians and the French mandate authorities

In response to her loss of citizenship Maria Ngambe unsuccessfully appealed to the French consulate in Frankfurt to provide her with a French passport.[37] Maria was one of over a dozen Cameroonians and their children, as well as several Togolese, including Bruce, who are known to have requested a French passport during a new wave of applications that followed the Nazi takeover of power (Figure 7.1). For some applicants this was the first step in a request for repatriation to Africa or another form of emigration. For others, emigration was either not realistic or desirable or not seen as immediately necessary. Having valid papers to replace the *Fremdenpaß* offered a degree of protection against police harassment. It also enabled travel abroad even for those who anticipated returning to Germany, like the many who still made

[35] Minister of Foreign Affairs to Minister of Colonies, 4 June 1940, FR ANOM 1 AFFPOL 610/3.
[36] Bruce to Foreign Office (Pol. X), *c.* 1934, p. 98.
[37] Her request was denied by the French Minister of Colonies on the basis that she had spent too long in Germany: French Consulate, Frankfurt a.M. to Minister of Colonies, 4 November 1938; Minister of Colonies to Minister of Foreign Affairs, 24 March 1939: both FR ANOM 1 AFFPOL 614/2.

Figure 7.1 Pauline and Heinrich Muange, French Consular Registration, 1934

their living touring around Europe. Indeed, in correspondence with Cameroonians in Paris in 1937 Kala Kinger insisted, 'The only problem we have here [Germany] is that we need passports in order to return to Cameroon or to go to France ... it is the same thing for our Togolese colleagues' – but the French consulates were refusing or delaying the issue of passports.[38]

The French colonial authorities were no less reluctant to fulfil their obligations towards these people in the 1930s than they had been in 1919, and between 1933 and 1945 there is no evidence that any of them was able to reach Cameroon directly from Germany. Requests received by the French authorities were either turned down or remained unanswered. Applications were dealt with on a case-by-case basis, but rejections were typically justified with reference to the potential impact returning migrants would have on local society and politics. Mandenga Diek, who had received permission to return to Douala in 1921, was refused passage seventeen years later to travel with his white wife and an unmarried daughter.[39] Hermann Ngange's 1935 repatriation request was also turned down. Ngange, who was suffering from a heart condition and urgently wanted to return home, had been a member of the LzVN.[40] In rejecting his appeal the French Commissioner stressed that the greatest source of unrest and subversion among the indigenous population continued to be either Cameroonians who had returned from Germany or groups and individuals in Cameroon who maintained contact with German citizens. In the same year the request of Victor Bell was likewise rejected.[41] Similarly, in 1935 the French Commissioner in Togo asked that any response to Bonifatius Folli's passport request be delayed; Folli, he argued, was the key liaison figure among the Togolese based in Germany.[42]

Although denied the possibility of returning to Africa the majority of German-based Cameroonians who applied for passports were eventually successful. Of the seventeen documented cases twelve applicants received French passports for themselves and their family, four were turned down, and the outcome of one case remains unknown. At least eight other Cameroonians or children of Cameroonians had already received passports by the beginning of the 1930s. Applicants whose passport application expressed the desire to be repatriated were likely to be turned down, and travel restrictions could be imposed upon successful applicants in order to prevent them from returning to Cameroon. In 1938 Anton Egiomue asked for French papers to enable him and his family to embark on a six-month tour of Sweden with a group of

[38] Kinger to CNDIC, 29 March 1937, FR ANOM 110COL 1003/3560, our emphasis.
[39] Mandel to Director of Political Affairs in the Foreign Office, 29 April 1938, FR ANOM 1 AFFPOL 614/2.
[40] Repiquet to French Consulate, Berlin, 23 February 1935, ANCY APA 110190.
[41] Dossier Victor Bell, 1928–35, FR ANOM 1 AFFPOL 614/2.
[42] Commissioner Togo to Minister of Colonies, 6 July 1936, FR ANOM 1 AFFPOL 614/2.

performers, because the German police had refused the family permission to travel outside of German territory. His request was granted by the French authorities, but only on the condition that he and his family return to Germany once the tour was over.[43] Having a French passport thus brought some advantages in terms of mobility, including the possibility of moving to France. But before 1945 the advantages were limited. In theory mandate subjects could seek consular support when victimised by the German authorities, but this was actually the case even if they were not in possession of a French passport. At the same time, simply holding a French passport did not confer French citizenship. Moreover, the passports had to be regularly renewed at the nearest consulate, and their holders still had to check in regularly with the local police to register themselves as foreigners living in Germany. The passport in itself did not prevent them from being subjected to institutional and popular racism and once war broke out their French status offered little protection against Nazi terror.

Employment

During the first years of the dictatorship Africans living in Berlin met informally in a city-centre bar to help one another with the job search and to offer mutual support, much as they had done in the Weimar period.[44] With varying degrees of success most persisted with trying to find performance work. A handful of others found employment in factories or in other low-paid jobs such as waiter or doorman. Josef Boholle and Anton Egiomue, like some of the other older men, struggled on in their learned trades. Boholle, who was in his mid-fifties when the Nazis came to power, was increasingly unable to meet the physical demands of his work, and he asked the authorities to help him find a less demanding job.[45] Later he and Egiomue worked as performers. Richard Ekamby and Manfred Priso sought to make a living as petty traders selling 'colonial' goods. Priso had a banana stall, while Ekamby sold peanuts and cola from his small car.[46] Such pursuits were only seasonal, but they could keep people going. Nonetheless, unemployment was a growing reality for former colonial subjects and their children as they found themselves shut out of normal and legal routes of employment.

[43] Minister of Foreign Affairs to Minister of Colonies, 20 April 1939, FR ANOM 1 AFFPOL 614/2.
[44] Personal communication from Theodor Michael, June 2009.
[45] 'List of unemployed Africans in Berlin', appendix to Brückner to KPA, 29 March 1935, BArch R1001 7562, pp. 104–6, here p. 106.
[46] Gunzert to Interior Ministry, 18 September 1935, pp. 115–16.

Here again individual Cameroonians and their families were specifically targeted by local Nazi Party groups. In Danzig in 1933 Mandenga Diek's successful colonial wholesale firm was the object of a coordinated boycott by party activists, which resulted in his orders dropping significantly. Soon afterwards he was pressurised into surrendering his business, and to compound matters the family was expelled from its accommodation without warning. Diek eventually found work in a formerly Jewish-owned firm now being run by an SS officer.[47] Dualla Misipo reported after the war that he and his family had been subjected to a sustained campaign of persecution in 1930s Frankfurt led by the local party newspaper the *Frankfurter Volksblatt*. Misipo argued that this made it impossible for him to find work. In one verifiable incident he lost earnings after a local party functionary complained about the public lectures he had been giving on African culture. The Reich Ministry of Education issued an edict in January 1936 legally prohibiting *Neger* from speaking in schools, with specific reference to Misipo. The discrimination also impacted upon the job prospects of his wife Luise. On at least two occasions she was dismissed within days once her employers found out that her husband was black and despite the efforts of the local job centre it proved impossible to find her work.[48] The Misipos fled to France in 1937.

At a national level the Nazis' forcible coordination of German economic life and their attempts to purge it of non-Aryans also directly harmed Africans and their children. The Law for the Restoration of the Professional Civil Service of 7 April 1933 and its various amendments primarily sought to remove political opponents and Jews from employment in the public sector. At least two Cameroonians appear to have fallen victim to paragraph 3, which allowed for the dismissal of non-Aryans. One of these was Erika Mandenga Diek, whose 1935 dismissal from the Reich Accident Insurance Agency was justified in terms of the Law. The other was Misipo. In a letter to the French authorities he claimed to have lost his position as a bacteriologist at the Frankfurt Institute for Experimental Therapy as part of the purge of the University of Frankfurt's non-Aryan staff.[49] Evidence also suggests that people of

47 Personal history, undated (around October 1954), LABO 6/691 Emilie Diek, pp. 18–19, here p. 18; [Reiprich and Ngambi ul Kuo,] 'Unser Vater war Kameruner', p. 69; Oguntoye, *Eine Afro-Deutsche Geschichte*, p. 155.

48 Dualla Misipo, Account of Persecution, 5 January 1954, HHStAW 518/40437, pp. 4–6; 'Abhaltung von Vorträgen durch Neger', 22 January 1935, reprinted in Buchheim, *Arbeitsmaterial zur Gegenwartskunde*, p. 135; Luise Misipo, Account of Persecution, 7 March 1958.

49 Misipo to Minister of Colonies, 24 March 1937, FR ANOM 1 AFFPOL 614/2. This claim remains unsubstantiated and Misipo makes no mention of it in his later reparations application.

African heritage were typically (though not always) shut out of the German Labour Front (DAF), the successor organisation to the outlawed independent trade unions. Membership in the DAF was a precondition for legal employment. Theodor Michael lost his job as a bell-boy in Berlin in the early 1940s after the hotel in which he was working and its staff joined the DAF. Michael was refused membership after being adjudged to be too 'alien' (*artfremd*).[50]

Nazi coordination of the German cultural sphere had a more significant impact on the lives of black people. Attacks on jazz music continued once the Nazis were in power. Nazi publications and radio broadcasts condemned it as '*Niggermusik*'. Jazz was already officially banned in three German cities in 1933. In the same year the broadcasting company Funk-Stunde Berlin was prohibited from playing jazz during its broadcasts and a nationwide radio ban followed two years later. From 1938 onwards several local and regional bans were introduced, although there was never a national ban, and swing and jazz became part of a growing youth counter-culture.[51] The campaign against jazz created an atmosphere in which employers were increasingly unable or unwilling to take on black entertainers. Newly Nazified non-state bodies such as the Reich Association of German Performers actively protested against public appearances by African performers and musicians; several Cameroonians working in an amusement area of Berlin's Potsdamer Straße had to close down their activities at the behest of the Association.[52]

The Reich Cultural Chamber was created in September 1933 to enforce conformity in German cultural life. Anyone who hoped to work in any area of culture or entertainment had to be a member of the relevant subsection, or Chamber. Only one African is known to have gained membership, Kwassi Bruce. According to his own account he was admitted to the Reich Music Chamber sometime around 1933/34, thanks to a letter of reference from the Foreign Office and to his status as a German citizen. As he testified, his skin colour continued to act as a barrier to finding employment.[53] Exclusion from the Cultural Chamber effectively prohibited people from working or forced them to find employers willing to offer them illegal engagements. In 1933 Rudolf Boholle was informed that he was no longer allowed to perform in public.

[50] Michael in 'Die erste Erfahrung' (radio broadcast).

[51] Schröder, *Tanz- und Unterhaltungsmusik*, p. 11; Kater, *Different Drummers*, pp. 101–10; Peukert, *Inside Nazi Germany*, pp. 166–8. See also Wulf, *Musik im Dritten Reich*.

[52] Note, 12 November 1935, BArch R1001 6382, p. 5; Brückner to Head of the Allocation Office of the Reich Association of German Performers, 3 August 1934, BArch R1001 7562, p. 87.

[53] Bruce to Foreign Office (Pol. X), *c*. 1934, p. 94.

Like other unemployed Germans, he now had to carry out compulsory labour in order to receive benefit. The weekly 26 Marks he received in 1935 was around the minimum daily fee he had previously commanded as a step-dancer.[54] Boholle's situation was not unusual. Of a Foreign Office list of ten unemployed Cameroonians and Togolese based in Berlin in March 1935 seven were musicians or performers.[55]

Exclusion from German cultural life was not total, however, and for some individuals it was still possible to find work as entertainers either in Germany or abroad. After considerable effort, Boholle persuaded the authorities to allow him to work again, and he did so from the end of 1936 until the outbreak of World War Two. Together with his partner Gerhard Kromm he appeared on stage as the duo 'Tommy and Gerrard'. For every engagement the pair successfully secured they had to apply for a 'special permit' to allow Boholle to perform. This enabled him to enjoy a relatively comfortable lifestyle, earning around 750 to 1,000 Marks a month.[56] By contrast, his brother Paul scraped a living as a casual labourer and through staging a weekly puppet theatre.[57] It is unlikely that Rudolf was the only black entertainer granted an exception to the blanket performance ban. Louis Brody's successful film career remained largely unhampered by the change of regime. Similarly, many of the large circuses still featured Africans, and the Bonambelas continued to tour both in Germany and abroad.[58] Some Cameroonian and Togolese performers were able to gain visas for travel abroad in spite of the terms of their *Fremdenpaß*, though always on the proviso that they and their employers agreed to them returning to Germany once their tour was over.[59]

Colonial paternalism

While Rudolf Boholle's continuing citizenship entitled him to public assistance, this kind of help was not available for non-naturalised individuals who were unemployed. Their welfare continued to come under the remit of the DGfE, the Colonial Department, and by extension the

[54] Rudolf Boholle, Account of my Career, undated (between 1954 and 1957) and Damage in Professional Life, 3 March 1955, LABO 200/780, pp. E1 and E3; Report, Police Station 259, Berlin Karlshorst, 31 May 1935, LAB A.Pr.Br.Rep. 030-06 no. 6473, p. 51.

[55] Appendix to Brückner to KPA, 29 March 1935, p. 106.

[56] Kromm to lawyer Cholewa, 27 August 1957, LABO 200/780, p. E4.

[57] Draft, Criminal Case, 24 October 1941, pp. 7–9.

[58] Firla, *Der kameruner Artist*, pp. 148–55, 165–72; T. Nagl, *Die unheimliche Maschine*, pp. 581–90.

[59] French Consulate, Berlin to Minister of Foreign Affairs, 4 April 1938, FR ANOM 1 AFFPOL 614/2.

Foreign Office. The number of individuals receiving financial support, both short and long term, increased substantially after 1933. A DGfE list of former colonial subjects, primarily Cameroonians, and their children from September 1935 named thirty men and three women who had all received some form of support by this time. Not all were totally dependent on aid; another document suggests that only eight to ten Africans and their families were regularly receiving support.[60]

The difficulties they experienced in finding employment worried leading figures in the Foreign Office. In 1933 and again in 1934 Edmund Brückner, once Governor of Togo and now head of the Colonial Department, expressed concern at their situation. Like Friedrich von Lindequist, another former governor and now DGfE head, he was moved by his personal links to the former protectorates to intercede on behalf of these Africans and their children. Continuing colonial fantasies as well as real expectations of a future redistribution of the existing mandates or the chance to acquire new overseas possessions guided the policies of the Colonial Department, the Foreign Office and the DGfE towards former colonial subjects.[61] Until 1938 these agencies were relatively consistent in their efforts to protect Africans and their families. This brought them into conflict with other state and party organisations that were intent on excluding Blacks from German society.

Bruce's 1934 letter sparked a debate among state and party officials as to how former colonial subjects should be treated. Brückner forwarded copies of the letter to several state and party departments along with his own report, arguing that there was a need to create a space in which ex-colonials could forge a living, even if this was at odds with the Nazis' overall racial ideology. He and Lindequist adduced the propaganda usefulness of treating them well.[62] As early as 1933 the increasingly open racism and antisemitism in Nazi Germany were being cited in the French and British press as grounds why the Reich should not be allowed to regain its overseas protectorates.[63] Although these reports made no reference to the fate of former colonial subjects, the African-American press was vigilant from a very early stage in monitoring and drawing attention to the deteriorating situation of black Germans.[64]

60 Note, Brückner, n. d. (1935), BArch R1001 7562, p. 113.

61 On colonial irredentism, see Linne, *Deutschland jenseits des Äquators?*.

62 Lindequist to KPA, 20 May 1939, BArch R1001 6383, pp. 324–9. See also Grosse, 'Zwischen Privatheit und Öffentlichkeit', p. 102.

63 Lewerenz, *Deutsche Afrika-Schau*, p. 59.

64 For examples, see '300 Families affected by Hitler ban', *Baltimore Afro-American*, 30 December 1933, p. 1; 'Africans feel lash of Adolph Hitler', *Philadelphia Tribune*,

Foreign Office support should also be seen in the context of a general anxiety within the department in the early 1930s that the regime's policies towards 'coloured' people could damage Germany's relations with potential allies in Asia, South America and Africa. In reaction to the 1933 publication of a draft penal code which would have criminalised not only sexual relations between members of different 'races' but also 'shamelessly consort[ing] in public with members of the coloured races', Liberia reportedly threatened sanctions against Germans resident there. Boycotts of German goods around the world were narrowly averted.[65] In late 1934 Foreign Office representatives met with officers from other key state and party departments, including Frick's Interior Ministry, the party's Office of Racial Policy and the Office of the Führer's Deputy to outline their concerns.[66] The result of the discussion was an acknowledgement that while the party's basic worldview was not to be compromised, in practice this should not damage foreign-policy interests unnecessarily. In future, cases involving the application of Nazi policy to non-Jewish *Fremdblütige* were to be referred directly to the relevant ministry. This applied equally to foreigners, stateless persons and German nationals, though it was nationals of foreign powers who posed the real challenge to a consistent implementation of 'racial' policy. Africans continued to have the 'privileged' attention of the authorities; their situation was repeatedly brought to the personal attention of some of the most powerful men in the Reich – Frick, Goebbels, Himmler, Hitler's Deputy Rudolph Hess and his secretary Martin Bormann. Moreover, their interventions, like those of the Colonial Department, often seem unexpectedly favourable. When Erika Mandenga Diek protested against her 1935 dismissal, it was in consultation with the Foreign Office, the Ministry of Propaganda and the Office of Racial Policy that the Interior Ministry decided to reinstate her – explicitly on the grounds of colonial policy aspirations.[67]

In fact, the Foreign Office's call for former German colonial subjects as a group to be provided with the means to earn a living found approval

18 October 1934, p. 4; 'Africans in Germany living in terror, French Report', *Norfolk Journal and Guide*, 20 October 1934, p. 5.

65 Jones, 'Liberia May Drive All Germans from Republic'; Gruchmann, '"Blutschutzgesetz" und Justiz', 419. The draft in question was Kerrl, *Nationalsozialistisches Strafrecht*, p. 48. See also 'Latest Hitler Edict Seeks to Keep German Blood "Pure"', *Chicago Defender*, 14 October 1933, p. 4.

66 Ministry of the Interior to District President, 18 April 1935, Haupstaatsarchiv Düsseldorf, Regierung Düsseldorf 54465, Part 1, reproduced in Pommerin, *Sterilisierung der Rheinlandbastarde*, pp. 102–4.

67 Hauptmann, Gauleiter Hamburg to Wiedemann Adjutant to the Führer, 2 May 1938, BArch NS 10-374, p. 111.

from within the very top echelons of the Nazi hierarchy. In October 1935 Bormann wrote to the Foreign Office informing them that Hitler did not want 'deserving' former German colonial Africans (*Kolonialneger*) to experience unnecessary difficulties in their search for work and in their everyday lives. This was justified with a reference to the fact that many had fought for Germany in the war.[68] Bormann sent a confidential note in March 1936 to all Nazi Gauleiter telling them that former colonial subjects deemed deserving of support would receive a written certificate produced by the Foreign Office. This would state that there were no reservations against these individuals finding employment. A later document suggests that these certificates were introduced. The circular, however, was to remain secret lest it be 'misunderstood' by rank-and-file party members.[69]

Further efforts were made by the Colonial Department and the DGfE in cooperation with the Nazi Party's Office of Colonial Policy (KPA) and the VfdSW to find employment opportunities for colonial migrants and their children. Typically the jobs they sourced were limited to things like working at pro-colonial events or at zoological gardens as animal keepers or feeders, and where individuals were found jobs, they were compelled to accept them or face losing financial support.[70] Longer-term solutions were being considered, but a suggestion that former colonial subjects be repatriated was rejected by the Foreign Office as unrealisable, given the costs and the attitude of the French authorities to mixed couples. Discussions in 1935 and 1938 to deport Germany's African population to Liberia also came to nothing.[71] A kind of solution, however, appeared to present itself when the Colonial Department was approached for support by the organisers of an 'African show'.

The Deutsche Afrika-Schau, colonial films and a ban on black performers

In November 1935 two organisers of a 'Negro Village' (*Negerdorf*) approached Brückner to ask for his support for their enterprise. The

[68] Bormann to Foreign Office, 31 October 1935, BArch R1001 6383, p. 330.

[69] Bormann to all Gauleiter, 30 March 1936, BArch NS 6/222, p. 102; DGfE to Foreign Office (Pol. X), 7 February 1938, BArch R1001 7562, p. 127 (referring to similar documentation being ready for distribution to six individuals). The certificates were probably based on employment identity cards drafted by the Colonial Department in 1935 for ex-colonial subjects to carry: Draft Identity Card, BArch R1001 7562, p. 105.

[70] See example in Strohm to DGfE, 8 September 1937, BArch R1001 6382, p. 236.

[71] Notice, Brückner, n. d. (1935), p. 113; French Chief of Affairs (Liberia) to Minister of the Foreign Office, 19 August 1938, CADN 442PO/A/5.

'village', a private venture under the proprietorship of Heinrich Goslau, was run by Kwassi Bruce and the German Adolf Hillerkus, whose wife Juliette Tipner was the Vienna-born daughter of a Liberian mother and Austrian father. Bruce and Hillerkus explained that they needed permission to stage what was essentially a travelling show featuring African performers, since local authorities were reluctant to approve performances without higher authority.[72] It is unclear when exactly the show was created, but as early as February 1934 Cameroonians in Paris were talking about a 'German circus' called 'Our Colonies', featuring over a dozen of their compatriots, that was touring Germany.[73] It is highly possible that this was Bruce and Hillerkus' enterprise.

Bruce and Hillerkus promoted their show to Brückner as a means by which some thirty Africans, based primarily in Berlin and Hamburg, could make a living through performing their 'customs and traditions'. They thus consciously presented Brückner with a solution to the problem of finding work for Blacks. He responded positively and set about trying to win support for the show from other key state and party organs. His argumentation was no longer based upon colonial revisionism, but was instead couched in terms of the racial policy advantages to be gained.[74] Not only would the state be relieved of the need to support these people, but having them in the show would allow the authorities greater control over their movements and contact with the German public. In particular, socially and physically isolating them would prevent unspecified 'racial offences' – sexual relationships between Blacks and white Germans.[75] The Office of Racial Policy even suggested that to prevent this happening male participants could be paired up with teenage girls from among the Rhineland children.[76]

Support for the show, which came to be known as the Deutsche Afrika-Schau, was secured from the KPA and the Propaganda Ministry. Until around autumn 1936 it continued to exist as a private enterprise touring Germany and appearing at local festivals and markets. Following a serious road accident, which led to increasing financial difficulties, the DGfE asked the DAF Section for Itinerant Trades to become involved and the participants joined the DAF. The increasing state oversight of the enterprise was underlined when Hillerkus and Bruce were replaced by

72 Minutes Brückner, 18 November 1935, BArch R1001 6382, pp. 3–4.

73 Report of Agent Moise, 6 February 1934, FR ANOM 4002 COL 3.

74 See also Lewerenz, *Deutsche Afrika-Schau*, pp. 90–1.

75 See similar and linked concerns about a planned show featuring Samoans: Office of Racial Policy to Foreign Office, 27 February 1935, BArch R1001 7562, p. 107.

76 Minutes of meeting on the future of the Afrika-Schau, 10 October 1936, BArch R1001 6382, p. 38.

'Captain' Alfred Schneider, a loyal SA man with experience in running travelling shows. Schneider was a racial purist and expressed his determination to keep the performers in a closed community under constant observation.[77] Under his directorship, however, the show was so poorly run that performers received little pay and huge debts were incurred.[78] The show's final director Georg Stock took over in summer 1937, but he too had difficulties keeping it financially afloat.

Throughout much of its life the Afrika-Schau mixed elements of the *Völkerschau* tradition and the variety show.[79] Against the backdrop of a recreated African village performers typically sang songs, danced and performed acrobatics and exotic acts such as breathing fire, spear throwing and walking on a bed of nails, all in 'traditional' costumes. Later increased emphasis was placed upon representing customs from the former protectorates.[80] The audience could also visit a small exhibition featuring 'colonial' objects as well as a number of stands where 'colonial' products such as coffee, roasted peanuts and seashells could be purchased.[81] Active colonial propaganda became a regular feature from spring 1937. Audiences were shown a slide-show presentation about the former colonies and were encouraged to join the Reich Colonial League, the Nazi successor to the various independent colonial associations.[82] Between acts individual performers told the audience of their services to Germany. Much was made of the war veterans within the group. They recounted their personal stories and were presented as loyal Askaris, who had fought for the German cause in the protectorates and could speak for the benevolence of German colonial rule. In later years the show was also promoted under the title 'Ein Askari bei uns zu Gast' (an Askari comes to visit).[83]

There was little authentic about the show, since most of the performers had either grown up in Germany or been born there. At any one time it comprised a maximum of around thirty performers and there appears to have been a degree of turnover. In all the names of around forty of the show's performers are known, of whom at least twelve were

77 Schneider to Regional Office of the Propaganda Ministry (Berlin), 11 December 1936, BArch R1001 6382, p. 92.

78 Strohm (Foreign Office, Pol. X) to Reich Minister of Finance, 18 June 1937; Lindequist to Foreign Office, 24 June 1937: BArch R1001 6382, pp. 157, 166.

79 Lewerenz, *Deutsche Afrika-Schau.*

80 Stock to Office of the Führer, 17 November 1940, BArch R1001 6383, pp. 440–2.

81 Current Programme, around autumn 1936, BArch R1001 6382, pp. 22–3.

82 Lindequist to KPA, 20 May 1939, pp. 324–9, here p. 325; Soller to DGfE, 25 June 1940, BArch R1001 6383, pp. 369–70.

83 Bechhaus-Gerst, *Treu bis in den Tod*, pp. 105–9. On the concept of the loyal Askari, see Michels, *Schwarze deutsche Kolonialsoldaten*, pp. 18–25.

Cameroonian or children of Cameroonians. Among the Cameroonian participants were Josef Boholle and his three children, Mathias and Hanzen Ndonge, and Benedikt Gambe, whose non-Cameroonian wife Charlotte Rettig also performed in the show. Jonas N'Doki and Heipold Jansen, who worked as a chauffeur for the show, were among six who featured as Askari at various times. In fact, Jansen had fought in Europe as part of the Prussian army, while N'Doki had been part of the colonial military postal service. The show also boasted a 'South Seas' group, which included Rudolf Boholle and Juliette Tipner. Alongside former colonial subjects and their German-born children several participants, like the Ethiopian Wolde Tadek and the African American Clarence Walton, had no connection to the former protectorates.[84] It is likely that they and others identified themselves as colonials as a conscious survival strategy.[85] It is also the case that a significant number of former colonial subjects were never associated with the show and several others only participated on a short-term basis. Involvement in the show brought two important advantages. At the cost of submitting to a degree of control and surveillance, participants gained a measure of safety from the extremes of official and popular racism, as long as the show continued to enjoy support from state and party. Moreover, they were able to earn their own living. Extra income could also be gained from tips or a share of the money made from the stalls. Performers' wages, however, did not always cover their outgoings, and during the show's winter break they still depended on the DGfE to find them temporary work.[86]

Although participation was not compulsory, pressure could be exerted to persuade individuals to join. After turning down a job at a Munich zoo that the DGfE had arranged for him, Thoy Esomber was told that he would no longer receive financial support and that instead he should apply to join the show.[87] A report from the French consulate in Berlin similarly casts doubt on performers' willingness to remain part of the line-up and demonstrates the difficulties that some experienced in trying to leave. In spring 1938 the four Garber siblings, children of Josef Garber and his German wife Johanna found a long-term engagement in Sweden.

[84] Walton returned to the United States on 8 June 1942, after six months' internment triggered by the entry of the United States into the war. His European wife and child were not allowed to travel with him: see Julius J. Adams, 'Negro Living 35 Years in Germany Tells of Life Under the Nazis', and 'Man Who Lived Under Hitler Predicts Early Collapse of Home Front', *New York Amsterdam Star-News*, 18 July 1942, p. 5, and 25 July 1942, p. 22.

[85] Lewerenz, *Deutsche Afrika-Schau*, pp. 101–2.

[86] For examples see Hillerkus to Seeger, 17 October and 13 November 1936, BArch R1001 6383, pp. 63 and 67.

[87] Strohm to DGfE, 8 September 1937.

Figure 7.2 The Five Bosambos, *c.* 1938

The Garbers, together with the second-generation Cameroonian Sam Dibonge, had performed in the Afrika-Schau as the trapeze act The Five Bosambos almost from its inception (Figure 7.2). In contrast to Dibonge, who had successfully gained a French passport in 1933, the Garbers were considered to be stateless. They successfully obtained valid visas to travel to Sweden, but before they could depart their *Fremdenpäße* were confiscated by the German police and returned endorsed as valid for travel only in Germany. The Garbers were unable to leave Germany and were effectively obliged to continue performing in the show. Their response was to apply for French passports, which they were granted.[88]

The timing was significant and helps to explain why the German authorities were against the Garbers leaving the country. Increasingly the control aspect of the show was used to legitimate its existence, and in October 1938 representatives of state and party met to discuss plans to extend the show's remit and to force all ex-colonial subjects and their

88 French Consulate, Berlin to Minister of Foreign Affairs, 4 April 1938; Commissioner Togo to Minister of Colonies, 23 June 1938, FR ANOM 1 AFFPOL 614/2.

children into joining it. The meeting was organised by Carltheo Zeitschel, former head of the KPA, a consultant in the Foreign Office and soon to be a member of the SS. Among the participants were Ehrhard Wetzel and Gerhard Hecht, key theorists in the Office of Racial Policy who shaped policy towards the Slavic populations of occupied Eastern Europe from 1939 onwards, as well as representatives of the DGfE and the DAF. Also present was SS-Untersturmführer Hans-Walter Ulrich from Reinhard Heydrich's Reich Security Main Office (RSHA). It is unclear whether Ulrich's involvement signals a more sinister project than the physical and social isolation of Africans and their children. The meeting certainly provides evidence of increasing SS interest in the fate of Blacks in Germany. Central to the discussion was once again the spectre of illegitimate sexual liaisons. The concentration of all former colonial subjects in the show was seen as a means of preventing such relationships, but the discussants thought that this would require a special police ordinance.[89]

Following the meeting the authorities sought to determine who was to be categorised as a 'Colonial African' with the probable aim of removing from the show all those who were not from the former protectorates. The Office of Racial Policy had already constructed a database containing the names of sixty-six 'Negroes and Mulattoes' living in Germany.[90] The DGfE combined this information with its own records to produce a larger register containing names and data for eighty-one individuals, including thirty-five from Cameroon or children of Cameroonians, fourteen Togolese or children of Togolese and three men from East Africa.[91] Of those remaining the DGfE believed there were grounds in at least eighteen cases to question whether the individual was a former German colonial subject. The very existence of these lists is evidence of the regime's will to control, monitor and categorise. At the same time they demonstrate the limits to the regime's ability to keep tabs on those within its borders. Not only were the data on a number of individuals incomplete, imprecise or false, but the lists themselves had gaps. Several Cameroonians and Togolese still present in Germany had clearly managed to avoid being registered.

[89] List of participants, 14 October 1938; invitation from Zeitschel to Frercks (Office of Racial Policy), Friedrich (SS Security Service), Neugebauer (DGfE), Wildt (Itinerant Trades), Klapper (DAF), 7 October 1938; notes from the meeting, 14 October 1938: BArch R1001 6383, pp. 262–4.

[90] List of *Neger*, appendix to Office of Racial Policy to Foreign Office, 18 October 1938, BArch R1001 6383, pp. 267–72.

[91] 'List of Natives', appendix to DGfE to Foreign Office (Pol. X), 13 February 1939, BArch R1001 6383, pp. 293–300.

By May 1939 the initiative to expand the show had still not been realised, and by November 1939 the KPA, the Propaganda Ministry and Bormann's Office all declared themselves against the show's continuation, effectively sealing its fate.[92] They argued that the performers, particularly those who had fought for Germany, should be found other forms of employment. On no account should they be allowed to speak openly in public again. The show was officially stopped in June 1940 on the orders of the party's Reich Propaganda Office, following consultation with the Office of Racial Policy.[93]

The reasons for the demise of the Afrika-Schau were manifold. It became clear that the show was unable to provide sufficient supervision of the performers, who were free to move around as they wished outside of performances. This led to accusations of precisely the kinds of sexual misbehaviour that the show was designed to prevent. Lindequist's response was to assert that the male performers were mainly too old and true German women (ought to be) too decent to engage in 'those types of acquaintanceships'.[94] But his optimism was belied by the incidents that led to show member N'Doki being investigated on charges of attempted rape.[95]

In ideological terms, too, the Afrika-Schau was proving counterproductive. Stock reported that the show was being secretly followed while on tour in southern Germany and that anonymous complaints were frequently being made against it to local magistrates.[96] In March 1939 the DGfE was forced to respond to formal complaints from the DAF in Konstanz that the show called into question notions of racial exclusionism. According to a local official the audience was presented with a confused image of Africans as apparent equals within the *Volksgemeinschaft*. He criticised the fact that performers had referred to audience members as 'compatriots' and 'fellow Germans' and that they had compared the dances they performed to traditional Bavarian dances. One performer had allegedly told the audience that Gustav Nachtigall, the German explorer who had helped bring Cameroon under German control, was his godfather and a slide had been shown depicting a young German child and an African child together as an illustration of the positive relationship between Africans and Europeans in German

[92] Reich Propaganda Office, Reich Ring for National Socialist Propaganda and Education to KPA, 8 November 1939, appendix to DGfE to Foreign Office, 1 June 1940, BArch R1001 6383, p. 375.
[93] Soller to DGfE, 25 June 1940, pp. 369–70.
[94] Lindequist to KPA, 20 May 1939, p. 328. [95] On N'Doki, see Chapter 5.
[96] DGfE to Foreign Office, 16 September 1938, BArch R1001 6383, p. 260.

East Africa.[97] Similarly, a local official in the Office of Racial Policy in Niederdonau remarked that the audience was amazed when the performers declared, 'We believe in Germany, Heil Hitler', and he expressed concern that the performers openly talked about being married to German women and having children.[98]

In part, these tensions reflected the fact that the celebration of colonial traditions really could not be reconciled with a consistently racialised vision of the social and world order. That contradiction was reinforced when a new world war followed Germany's invasion of Poland in September 1939. The mobilisation of some 100,000 Africans to serve in the French army in Europe provoked a renewal of vehement racist propaganda against France's use of black soldiers which reprised the imagery and rhetoric employed during the French occupation of the Rhineland. With negative depictions of Africans pervading the media, a continuation of the show was no longer tenable.[99] The DGfE's last action on behalf of its protégés was an unsuccessful request made in October 1940, probably in response to the racist propaganda about the French colonial soldiers, that a nationwide radio statement be broadcast rehabilitating them.[100] For the performers the order to stop was a blow.

The implosion of the Afrika-Schau must also be attributed to the attitudes and agency of the performers themselves. Wilhelm Soller, who helped Stock to run the show, commented on their mood at its closure: 'They have already said that they should be given a rope to hang themselves, and when the colonies are German once more, those who call them an affront to culture [*Kulturschande*], can build their own farms and plantations over there without [the help of] these affronts.'[101]

The note of irony here, even under circumstances that were certainly threatening, is in keeping with the self-awareness that members of the Afrika-Schau manifested in evading controls on their movement and incorporating transgressive elements into their performance. By the same token, the show briefly provided a space which was not only relatively safe, but which allowed for sociable and solidary interchange among black people. In some senses it extended the life of that performance

[97] Lindequist to KPA, 20 May 1939, pp. 324–9.
[98] Office of Racial Policy, Niederdonau to Gauleiter, Niederdonau, 13 May 1940, NS 18/519, p. 5.
[99] Rheinisches JournalistInnenbüro, *'Unsere Opfer zählen nicht'*, p. 94; Scheck, *Hitler's African Victims*, pp. 101–12; Soller to DGfE, 25 June 1940, p. 370.
[100] Notice, Foreign Office, 21 October 1940, BArch R1001 6383, p. 417.
[101] Soller to DGfE, 25 June 1940, p. 370.

milieu which had developed in the urban spaces of Weimar, and it also drew new individuals into it, both men and women.[102]

Performance continued to provide a context for networking and communication. The end of the Afrika-Schau coincided with the introduction of a general ban prohibiting Blacks from performing in public. The exact timing of the ban remains unknown, but those affected were being informed of the new policy as early as autumn 1939.[103] Nonetheless black men and women continued to find employment on stage and screen partly because film companies, theatre directors and local authorities were not always aware of the new restrictions. Fourteen black performers appeared in a production of the opera *Die oder keine* in Berlin in summer 1940 in front of full houses, and Propaganda Minister Goebbels, whose ministry had played a central role in initiating the ban, attended a special performance of the opera staged for wounded soldiers. Two of the performers, Kotto and Bell, were later called to the manager's office where they were told to communicate Goebbels' praise for their performances to the other black actors.[104] Film, too, continued to offer employment opportunities for Cameroonians and their children. In wartime, both colonial propaganda films including *Carl Peters* (1941), *Ohm Krüger* (1941) and *Germanin* (1942–3) and escapist films like *Münchhausen* (1943) called for black actors. In 1941 the President of the Reich Theatre Chamber renewed the prohibition on African performers, but allowances were made for situations in which their involvement was deemed necessary, including film shoots. Some performers were granted an exemption from the general ban; as of 27 May 1942 Rudolf Boholle had permanent permission to perform.[105]

Like the Afrika-Schau, the film set provided a temporary safe haven and occasions for solidarity. Dorothea Diek (who was nineteen when the war began) remembered:

> It was cosy on the film set. In the breaks the Africans would often get out their drums and we'd sing in front of the studios. People from all the other productions would come running . . . We earned good money, had fun, and didn't think twice

[102] See Lewerenz, *Deutsche Afrika-Schau*; Lewerenz points out that women were increasingly sidelined in performances because of the erotic potential of their presence.

[103] Kromm to lawyer Cholewa, 27 August 1957; Curriculum Vitae Dorothea Reiprich (Diek), 9 September 1953, LABO 27/849, pp. M8–10, here p. M8; Dustert to DGfE, 23 October 1940, BArch R1001 6383, pp. 423–6, here p. 423.

[104] Dustert to DGfE, 23 October 1940, p. 424. It is unclear whether the reference is to Victor Bell or Max Same Bell.

[105] On film shoots, see T. Nagl, *Die unheimliche Maschine*, pp. 582–9. On Boholle: Police Commissioner Berlin to Reparations Department Berlin, 18 March 1955, LABO 200/780, p. M11.

about it . . . It was cheerful and cosy: no politics, no Nazis, just happy people. We were all together – young and old Africans.[106]

Here, too, new 'Africans' came on the scene. During the filming of *Ohm Krüger* Max Same Bell and Victor Bell encountered seven Cameroonian prisoners of war who were also from Douala.[107] On the set of *Carl Peters* German Africans briefly worked alongside Togolese prisoners of war, who brought them news of developments in Africa. They collected goods such as shirts, sheets, cigarettes, tobacco and pipes to the value of 108 Marks for the PoWs, who were dressed in little more than rags.[108] For most, though, this idyllic life on the film sets contrasted dramatically with life on the outside. As Werner Egiomue later remarked: 'In the studio you were safe . . . outside of the door you could be arrested but inside you were as safe as in a bank.'[109]

Growing up in the 'Third Reich'

Werner Egiomue was a child and a teenager during the Nazi period, one of a number who grew up in those years and have relatively recently provided accounts of their experiences in recorded interviews and published memoirs. Theodor Michael, born in 1925, effectively had to fend for himself from the age of twelve; his father died in 1934 and his older brother and two sisters had left Germany by 1937. In a 1995 radio interview he spoke of the traumatic nature of growing up in Nazi Germany: 'I had absolutely no adolescence, I also had no childhood. From the age of eight I had no childhood.'[110] On the streets of Berlin Michael was a curiosity for passers-by who felt that they had the right to stop him and ask whether he was one of the Rhineland children. The question itself suggests that they were unable to conceive that Michael could have been born out of a stable, loving relationship; it reflects an assumption that an African-German child must be the product of sexual violence. Others like Hans Massaquoi (whose father was Liberian) and Marie Nejar in Hamburg were equally exposed to public abuse, while Erika Diek recalled that in Berlin she and her sister Dorothea were 'spat upon, jostled and called "mongrel" [*Bastard*] and "half-breed" [*Mischling*] on the street. It was bad.'[111]

106 [Reiprich and Ngambi ul Kuo,] 'Unser Vater war Kameruner', pp. 77–8. See also Nejar, *Mach nicht so traurige Augen*, p. 116.
107 Notice, Foreign Office, 21 October 1940, p. 417.
108 Dustert to the DGfE, 23 October 1940, p. 425.
109 Egiomue in Okuefuna's *Hitler's Forgotten Victims*.
110 Michael in 'Die erste Erfahrung'.
111 [Reiprich and Ngambi ul Kuo,] 'Unser Vater war Kameruner', p. 69.

School could be a particularly hostile environment. Here children were at the mercy of their teachers and fellow pupils. In their published autobiographies both Nejar and Massaquoi tell of teachers who went out of their way to smooth their integration into primary education and who sought to protect them from victimisation.[112] In Massaquoi's case his position worsened as the nazification of the education system took hold over 1933–4 and his familiar teachers were replaced by Nazi sympathisers. The latter made frequent 'snide remarks about my race' and one teacher said, 'When we are finished with the Jews, you and those like you will be next.'[113] The introduction of obligatory lessons in 'racial science' from September 1933 onwards could lead to especially uncomfortable situations.[114] Nejar's teachers largely refrained from discussing ideas of race in her presence and instead waited for occasions when she was absent from school.[115] In contrast Massaquoi and Dorothea Diek were subjected to the humiliation of being presented to their classmates as living examples of racial inferiority. Diek recalled having to listen to slogans like 'God made all Whites and Blacks, but *Mischlinge* come from the devil' and '*Mischlinge* can only inherit the bad characteristics of both races.'[116] Against the wishes of her parents she was also forced to take part in a school visit to an exhibition on 'Race and People'.[117]

Friendships were tested as a result of the Nazis' policy of racial indoctrination of German children, coupled with the general atmosphere of prejudice. It was not uncommon for German parents to warn their children against being seen playing with black children who, as a consequence, were sometimes abandoned by close friends. In other cases, however, white German and African-German children continued playing together out of the sight of the adults. The experiences of Michael, Massaquoi and Nejar testify to the fact that many of their schoolmates failed to see the logic of the regime's racial ideology when it was applied to their own friends. After a class in which they were taught about racial difference, Nejar's friends comforted her by telling her that for them she was an Aryan, while one of Massaquoi's schoolmates

[112] Nejar, *Mach nicht so traurige Augen*, pp. 46–8; Massaquoi, *'Neger, Neger, Schornsteinfeger'*, pp. 47–54, 82–4.
[113] Massaquoi quoted in Terkel, *The Good War*, p. 497; see Massaquoi, *'Neger, Neger, Schornsteinfeger'*, pp. 76–81.
[114] Burleigh and Wippermann, *The Racial State*, p. 202.
[115] Nejar, *Mach nicht so traurige Augen*, p. 87.
[116] [Reiprich and Ngambi ul Kuo,] 'Unser Vater war Kameruner', p. 70.
[117] Sworn Statement, Dorothea Reiprich (Diek), 13 September 1960, LABO 27/849, pp. B8–9.

angered a teacher with his question as to why Africans were supposedly inferior when Hans excelled at both studies and sport.[118]

Until the late 1930s school attendance remained compulsory for all children in Germany, including *Fremdblütige*. In the aftermath of the nationwide attacks on Jewish institutions in late November 1938 Jewish children were prohibited from attending 'German' schools and were now only to be educated in exclusively Jewish schools. A formal ban on the admission of African-German children to public schools did not follow until June 1939, when the Reich Education Minister issued an unpublished edict excluding 'Gypsy' children from schools in Austria and added *Negermischlinge* to the 'Gypsies' who were the original object of local discriminatory measures. The edict was extended to the whole of the Reich on 22 March 1941. The prohibition was absolute for children who were not German nationals, and this now included most African-German children; where the 'Gypsy' or black child was also German, they could be excluded from school insofar as they represented a moral or other threat to their fellow pupils, at the discretion of the local authorities.[119] There is a whiff of the old colonial paternalism in the comment by Herbert Müller of Department D. III of the Foreign Office, that it was just as well that the children of colonial subjects not be exposed to the racism of white schoolmates, and in his suggestion (never implemented) that all such children be isolated and taught together at the Reich Colonial Training School for women in Rendsburg.[120]

In practice some African-German children were already being excluded from school long before any formal nationwide ban was introduced. Zoya Aqua-Kaufmann (daughter of Thomas Manga Akwa) testified that in 1936 she and a Jewish classmate were told their presence was no longer desired at a secondary school in Berlin.[121] Dorothea Diek was forced to leave her secondary school in Danzig three years earlier.[122] Like many of their parents who had first arrived in Germany for educational purposes, these young people had little chance of going on to higher education even if they finished school. But finding either employment or an apprenticeship after leaving school was not easy, as

118 Nejar, *Mach nicht so traurige Augen*, p. 87; Massaquoi, *'Neger, Neger, Schornsteinfeger'*, p. 115.

119 The terms of the decree were published by the Reichskriminalpolizeiamt in November 1942: Luchterhandt, *Der Weg nach Birkenau*, p. 191; Lewy, *The Nazi Persecution of the Gypsies*, pp. 59–62, 89–90; Campt, *Other Germans*, pp. 140–1 (each with a partial version of the story).

120 Müller to Foreign Office (Pol. X), 17 February 1942, PAAA, Inland I-Partei R99166.

121 Zoya Aqua-Kaufmann to Reparations Office, Berlin, 16 March 1952, LABO 1/652, pp. C30–2.

122 Sworn Statement, Dorothea Reiprich (Diek), 13 September 1960, pp. B8–9.

Dorothea's sister Erika discovered: 'When I started looking for an apprenticeship I heard everywhere: "You want to work for us? We only take on Aryans".'[123] In Wiesbaden Arthur Sewonu, whose father was Togolese, encountered similar problems: 'But then after I left school they started getting at me. No one wanted me. I spent two years looking for an apprenticeship.'[124] Popular prejudice, but also pressure from party fanatics, made it difficult for German employers to take on young black Germans. In a post-war reparations claim the German mother of a part-Cameroonian woman in Munich revealed that her daughter's employer had regretfully informed the family that it had been impressed upon him by local Nazis that he should terminate her training.[125] With their career options limited, some, like Dorothea and Zoya, were left with little option but to become performers.[126]

Other forms of social exclusion similarly marked African Germans' childhood. Like Jews and 'Gypsies' they were liable to be denied access to places like parks, playgrounds and swimming baths. More important, they were almost entirely shut out of the various Nazi youth organisations which, by the end of 1933, had subsumed almost all other youth groups and which played a key role in the organisation of young people's leisure time as well as in propagating Nazi ideals. German children were expected to join the Jungvolk for boys aged ten to fourteen or the Jungmädelbund for girls of the same age, followed by the Hitlerjugend (Hitler Youth) and Bund Deutscher Mädel (BDM) for boys and girls respectively. From 1939 onwards membership was compulsory. While there was no law specifically prohibiting Blacks from joining they were almost routinely rejected. Josie Allen later recounted that when party members came to recruit her son for the Hitler Youth, they left almost immediately, stating that they only wanted 'pure Aryans'.[127]

In their recollections several African Germans have told of how like their white German friends they were caught up in the popular enthusiasm for Hitler and his vision of German renewal in the early 1930s, without understanding the consequences that Nazi rule could have for their lives. Massaquoi strongly identified with Germany and as a child sported a swastika on his pullover until his mother removed it. Nejar

[123] [Reiprich and Ngambi ul Kuo,] 'Unser Vater war Kameruner', p. 69.
[124] 'Lydias Geheimis', p. 7.
[125] Frau M to State Reparations Office, Munich, 25 April 1965, BHStAM LEA 10597 BEG 50194, p. 30.
[126] Declaration, Dorothea Reiprich (Diek), 19 November 1963, LABO 27/849, pp. B25–6; Aqua-Kaufmann to Reparations Office, Berlin, 16 March 1952.
[127] Toles, 'Where is Hitler?', p. 1.

wanted to join the BDM.[128] Like Theodor Michael, however, neither was allowed into the Nazi youth organisations. An initial incomprehension was followed by the realisation that they were not to be part of the new Germany that the Nazis were seeking to forge and that they were among the aliens deemed to pose a threat to the 'German' population. As Michael later recalled of being turned away from the Jungvolk: 'And I was rather sad about it all. Because I realised then what it means to be excluded, shut out. And for a child that is a huge, an improbably big experience – and a very negative one: then, where do I belong?'[129]

The short life of Fritz Kohl, whose father Johannes had fought so tenaciously to give him a good home in the 1920s, illustrates how everyday processes of racism and proletarianisation that bore on black families made their children particularly vulnerable when the emphasis in social policy shifted decisively from care to control and selection after 1933. Johannes' wife Veronika, Fritz's adoptive mother, died in February 1933; in August Johannes moved in with Hermine Schläfereit, who was already pregnant with their first child. Eleven-year-old Fritz had been being monitored by the Bremen Youth Bureau since the year before because of 'educational difficulties', and in 1936 Johannes requested that he be placed in the Ellener Hof boys' home in the Bremen suburbs. Fritz was found work on ships leaving the port for a time, and was then sent to work on a farm. This precipitated protests from local Nazis which reached Bormann's office, prompting the observation that a boy working on a farm was bound to be living with the household, and that this was completely unacceptable in the case of a *Negermischling*. The letter from Bormann's office to Frick, copied to the Foreign Office, the Minister for Agriculture and the Security Service, drew for its arguments on the principle represented by the Nuremberg Law which prohibited young Aryan women from working as domestics in Jewish households. After a history of 'indifference and resistance' to work, Fritz seemed finally to be settling down in the country, but the Bremen authorities fetched him back to the city. An attempt to resettle him with his father and find him work in industry failed, and he went back to live in the Ellerner Hof, going out to work for a farmer during the day. In March 1939 the Bremen Mayor's Office began proceedings to annul Fritz's adoption. On 1 June 1939 he was found with a gunshot wound in the forehead, fired from his employer's revolver; the authorities were unable to say for certain whether the wound was deliberately self-inflicted or accidental.

[128] Massaquoi, '*Neger, Neger, Schornsteinfeger*', p. 57; Nejar, *Mach nicht so traurige Augen*, pp. 65–7, 82–4.
[129] Michael in 'Die erste Erfahrung'.

His father visited him in hospital before he died the next day. Fritz Kohl had just turned seventeen.[130]

The assault on families: sterilisation and *Rassenschande*

Visibly marginal, African-German children were also open to scrutiny and harassment under 'racial hygiene' regulations, including compulsory sterilisation. There was a consensus among the experts whose views informed Nazi policy that when it came to non-Jewish *Fremdblütige*, people of mixed heritage – *Mischlinge* – represented a particular danger to the health of the nation. Even before the Nazi takeover, there had been correspondence between the Prussian Ministry of the Interior and the authorities in the Prussian Rhineland territories about the Rhineland children, many of whom were already approaching sexual maturity. In March 1934 the Ministry – now headed by leading Nazi Hermann Goering – wrote to the Foreign Office reporting the results of a survey on the numbers and parentage of those Rhineland children under Prussian jurisdiction.[131] A year later, a committee of anthropologists, medical experts and party functionaries convened by Frick's Interior Ministry met to decide their fate. The result of the deliberations was to organise a targeted programme of sterilisation. It is clear from the notes of the meeting that participants understood that this plan of action was not covered under the 'normal' Nazi legislative framework for compulsory sterilisation. They noted that previous legislation allowing for the sterilisation of the mentally and physically disabled, the 14 July 1933 Law for the Prevention of Genetically Diseased Offspring, had brought Germany considerable criticism from the international community. Thus, instead of introducing a new law that would attract further criticism it was decided to carry out the action without legal sanction and in secret.[132] This took place during the summer of 1937.

From the policymakers' point of view in the mid 1930s the Rhineland children represented a special and priority case because they were concentrated in a politically sensitive border region and were a living reminder of Germany's humiliation and continuing vulnerability. Their numbers, though not absolutely large, were significant in relation to other 'problem' groups. During the 1935 discussions, the issue of what

130 Correspondence in StABremen B.6 no. 374, 4,13/5, pp. 66–72; PAAA Inland I-Partei R99166, pp. 186–7.

131 Prussian Minister of the Interior to Foreign Office, 28 March 1934, PAAA, Inland I-Partei 84/4, reproduced in Pommerin, *Sterilisierung der Rheinlandbastarde*, pp. 96–100.

132 Minutes of the Meeting of the Working Group II, 11 March 1935, PAAA Inland I-Partei, p. 85.

to do with the far smaller number of other children of mixed heritage was raised by a representative of the Interior Ministry. While the idea of extending the sterilisation policy to cover the children of former colonial subjects was not conclusively ruled out, it was dismissed at this stage.[133] Concerns about the impact of Nazi racial policies on diplomatic relations meant that Foreign Office officials were already nervous about the Rhineland children.[134] A domestic-policy obstacle was also raised in the March 1934 letter of the Prussian Interior Ministry: unlike the Rhineland children, most African-German children were the legitimate children of German women, so that a blanket sterilisation policy might have an impact on public opinion at home.

In practice, though, the spectre of sterilisation was a very real one for the children of Germany's former colonial subjects. In his 1995 interview Michael spoke of the continual 'threat of sterilisation'. He referred to the illegal action taken against the Rhineland children and stated that a few of his compatriots also fell victim to this. Erika Diek and Dorothea Diek also spoke by name of members of their generation who were affected. One adult second-generation Cameroonian German was sterilised as early as April 1936, months before the Nazis' move against the Rhineland children. The married father of two who was in his mid-twenties was sterilised under the July 1933 Law on the grounds of suffering from congenital dementia. Several months earlier the man had received a second conviction for theft and he had become a father for the second time.[135] The case is characteristic in the way in which sterilisation was deployed as a 'solution' to 'antisocial' behaviour attributed to an inherited medical condition; it is also likely that the decision of the Hereditary Health Court which was responsible for approving sterilisation cases was prompted by the desire to prevent the birth of more *Mischlingskinder*.

For those who were not otherwise obvious targets for intervention, sterilisation appears as the unofficial last resort of the authorities determined to prevent the growth of the black population. The wider context for the discussion of the Rhineland children was an initiative headed by both the Interior Ministry and Justice Ministry to fix in law the principle and developing practice of excluding *Fremdblütige* from life in the *Volksgemeinschaft*, and from the beginning it was black people that many of the

[133] Ibid., p. 75.

[134] Here, too, the African-American press was paying attention: 'Germany's 600', *Pittsburgh Courier*, 17 February 1934, p. 10; 'Scores Hitler's Proposal of Sterilising Youths', *Pittsburgh Courier*, 24 March 1934, p. 2.

[135] Draft Criminal Case, 24 October 1941, pp. 7–9.

policymakers had in mind. The draft penal code of 1933 not only specified the 'coloured races' as undesirable partners for Germans, but made direct reference to practices in the American South, and it was similarly with reference to the United States (rather than Germany's own colonial history) that the Prussian Interior Ministry spokesman suggested a marriage ban in his March 1934 letter.[136] It was the direct intervention of Hitler, who was eager to accelerate a 'solution' to the 'Jewish question', that dictated that the first legislative outcome of this process, the Nuremberg Laws of September 1935, explicitly targeted only Jews.[137]

On 15 September 1935 the Law for the Protection of German Blood and Honour forbade marriages between Jews and Germans 'of German or related blood' while at the same time making sexual relations between Jews and Germans 'of German or related blood' outside of wedlock a criminal offence. This was supplemented by a decree of 14 November regulating the position of Jewish *Mischlinge* in respect of the marriage law. Although positive qualities of character, Germanness and economic status could be taken into account to permit a marriage between a half-Jew and a non-Jew (it implied), there was a blanket ban on marriages 'in which it can be expected that [the union will produce] progeny who endanger the purity of German blood'. Twelve days later Frick issued an order extending the scope of the earlier decree to 'other alien races', and specified marriages to 'Gypsies, *Neger* and their mongrels' as those which could be expected to produce undesirable progeny.[138]

The logic of these decrees was to prohibit any marriage between people of different 'races' which was capable of producing children. The November order left it to the discretion of the registrar whether a marriage was to be deemed undesirable in these terms. A registrar faced with a problematic couple was expected to demand that they present certificates of qualification for marriage (*Ehetauglichkeitszeugnisse*) produced by the local health bureau.[139] The certificates were issued following a series

[136] Prussian Minister of the Interior to Foreign Office, 28 March 1934, PAAA, reproduced in Pommerin, *Sterilisierung der Rheinlandbastarde*, pp. 96–100.

[137] Neliba, *Frick*, pp. 198–221; Gruchmann, '"Blutschutzgesetz" und Justiz'; Przyrembel, *'Rassenschande'*, p. 142.

[138] Text of Nuremberg Laws in *RGBl* (1935), 1:1146–7; November Decree in *RGBl* (1935), 1:1334–6; Frick's order in *Ministerial-Blatt für die Preussische innere Verwaltung*, 96 (1935), 1426–34.

[139] This extended to 'racially' problematic marriages a requirement that had been in force since 1933 for couples who had applied for marriage loans, and had been implicitly extended to the whole population in the Marital Health Law of 18 October 1935. It was a way of screening out people suffering from hereditary or infectious disease or mental illness, who were henceforth forbidden to marry: *RGBl* (1935), 1:1246. See Czarnowski, *Das kontrollierte Paar*.

of interviews and physical examinations, some of them highly invasive, one of whose purposes was to establish the presence and proportion of 'alien blood' in the veins of the applicants, tracking their ancestry back for up to eight generations.[140]

Although the documentation on African-German couples who applied for marriage certificates is scant, it highlights the danger they risked in drawing attention to their relationships.[141] In Berlin the Cameroonian performer 'Gregor Ratto' (probably Gregor Kotto) and his German partner were denied a marriage certificate, but nonetheless decided to live together. He reported in 1945 that they had been arrested by the Gestapo and imprisoned in a concentration camp. He was eventually released when he agreed to live alone.[142] In Augsburg the local authorities and party officials became interested in the daughter of a Cameroonian performer and a German woman, after she and her white partner applied for a certificate of qualification for marriage at the beginning of 1940.[143] The local health bureau rejected her application, but suggested that she could appeal to the Interior Ministry. Again the application was rejected, specifically on the basis of the November 1935 decree. While the woman and her partner decided to wait until the end of the war before again seeking to marry, she, her mother and her brother were summoned to the Anthropological Institute in Munich. There they were photographed and subjected to degrading physical examinations.[144] In summer 1942 she was taken to the police hospital in Berlin by two policemen. According to her own testimony, she was sterilised alongside two other women, one of whom was also an African German. When she asked what would happen should she not acquiesce to the sterilisation she was told she would be sent to a concentration camp.[145] She was also informed that despite being sterilised she would still not be allowed to marry. In Danzig in 1944 Dorothea Diek was

[140] Przyrembel, *'Rassenschande'*, pp. 111–16. See also Czarnowski, *Das kontrollierte Paar*, pp. 191–210.

[141] See also Martin and Alonzo, *Im Netz der Moderne*, pp. 269–76.

[142] Edward B. Toles, 'Berlin Inter-Marriage Awaits Red O.K.', *Chicago Defender*, 28 July 1945, p. 11.

[143] Römer, *Die grauen Busse*, pp. 12–18 (with no indication of the provenance of the documentary sources).

[144] In their post-war reparations claim a Cameroonian-German family based in Munich reported that they had also been photographed by racial scientists in Bavaria. See claims in folders LEA 10597 BEG 50194; LEA 10598 BEG 50195; LEA 10599 BEG 50505, all in BHStAM.

[145] See also the comments of Gupha Voss, daughter of a German woman and Liberian man, whose parents were refused a marriage licence. They were subsequently harassed by the authorities and Voss' mother was eventually incarcerated following the outbreak of war: Okuefuna, *Hitler's Forgotten Victims* (documentary film).

similarly pursued by the authorities for sterilisation after receiving a marriage ban. After hiding for several weeks she only managed to escape when one of the men bringing her to the gynaecological hospital allowed her to run off.[146]

In the first two of these instances a negative decision from the local registrar or health bureau brought the case to the attention of the Gestapo or Criminal Police who then took decisive measures to end the relationships. Throughout the Reich it was the responsibility of the Criminal Police to investigate couples accused of breaking the Nuremberg Laws. Yet in the above cases the legality of the police actions was dubious. Under the terms of Nuremberg Laws all sexual relationships between Jews and non-Jews, commonly referred to as *Rassenschande*, including non-marital relations, were prohibited. Frick's commentary on the Laws, however, did not explicitly extend coverage to the non-marital relations of other *Fremdblütige*; sexual relationships between 'Aryans' and men and women of African heritage then were not expressly criminalised. Nor were existing marriages between Blacks and white Germans nullified.

Nonetheless there is persuasive evidence that the police in a number of localities acted in the spirit of the existing legislation to put pressure on both married and unmarried mixed couples to separate. In the case of married couples, the German partners were bullied and pressurised through threatening appeals made to their racial consciousness. In Berlin the German husband of Josie Allen was told by SS men that his family was 'tainted'.[147] From 1935 onwards Luise Misipo was visited on several occasions by members of the Nazi Party branch in Frankfurt who made increasingly menacing demands that she separate from her husband.[148] Manga Ngando reported that in Hanover his parents were given no choice but to separate and at least one further Cameroonian-German couple divorced only months after the implementation of the Nuremberg Laws.[149] These years left their mark on other wives.[150] Beginning in 1937, Emilie Diek was regularly ordered to the Party Office of Racial Policy in Danzig and urged to leave her husband. She later stated that the stress and harassment that she and her family were subjected to led to her

146 [Reiprich and Ngambi ul Kuo,] 'Unser Vater war Kameruner', p. 75; Curriculum Vitae Dorothea Reiprich (Diek), 9 September 1953, pp. M8–10; Dorothea Diek to Reparations Department, Berlin, 20 September 1959, LABO 27/849, p. E5.

147 Toles, 'Where is Hitler?', p. 1.

148 Dualla Misipo, Account of Persecution, 5 January 1954.

149 Martin and Alonzo, *Im Netz der Moderne*, p. 266.

150 'Paul Malapa Décryptage', p. 38; Frau M to State Reparations Office, Munich, 5 June 1957, BHStAM LEA 10599 BEG 50505, no number.

suffering a heart attack in 1939.[151] Heinrich Dibonge's wife Wally endured similar hardships and died in a sanatorium aged forty-three.[152] The fact that many other marriages survived the 'Third Reich' is a testimony to their strength and the determination of the individuals concerned.

Unmarried couples appear to have been placed under still greater pressure and were forced to sustain their relationships in secret. When Johannes Kohl requested that Fritz be placed in a home, it may have been because of the pressure he and his new partner were under.[153] By March 1936 their relationship had come to the attention of the Bremen Welfare Bureau, whose officer noted:

> Kohl and Schläfereit both have an exceptionally high sex drive. Frau Schläfereit frequently describes herself as 'man-crazy'; it is therefore to be feared that Kohl will have more children with Schläfereit. That must be stopped at all costs, quite aside from the fact that in any case the cohabitation of the *Neger* with the German ought to be brought to an end.[154]

The Welfare Bureau argued that Kohl should be deported to Togo, but this was rejected by Foreign Office officials. They suggested instead that Schläfereit be persuaded to leave him. The Bremen welfare authorities impressed upon the couple that if Kohl did not move out and if they had any more children they were liable to be prosecuted. Six months later the couple was still living together. They insisted that this was because Kohl had been unable to find new accommodation on account of racial prejudice, but that they had ended their sexual partnership. In May 1937 Schläfereit was called to see the police officer who had taken over the case. She was threatened with being interned in a concentration camp if she did not break off all contact with Kohl and was given a week to do so. Just under three weeks later, before any criminal proceedings were initiated, the couple separated.

The Yemeni entertainer Mohamed Nagel and his German partner Frieda Schack, living together in Berlin, were presented with a similar choice when they were denounced by Schack's landlord to the local police in June 1940. The court that heard their case confirmed that the couple's actions were not subject to a charge of *Rassenschande* under the existing legislation, but the police were not prepared to tolerate Nagel's relationship with a 'woman of German blood' and ordered him

[151] Curriculum Vitae Emilie Diek, 6 October 1954, LABO 6/691, pp. 18–19.
[152] StAHam 355-11 Wiedergutmachungsakte 20514 Wally Dibonge.
[153] Correspondence on this case is in StABremen B.6. no. 374 4,13/5.
[154] Report of the Welfare Office, 26 March 1936, StABremen B.6. no. 374 4,13/5, p. 55.

to move out, which he agreed to do.[155] In Wiesbaden in late 1944 Lydia Dirlenbach, the German partner of Arthur Sewonu, was called to report to the Gestapo after having been denounced for appearing with Sewonu in public. She and her family denied claims that Lydia and Arthur were together and managed to dissuade the authorities from taking further action.[156]

In many respects Sewonu and Nagel were fortunate. Increasingly draconian measures were being applied to other couples. Like her parents, Erika Ngando in Hanover was forced to separate from her German partner. This did not prevent her from being one of several adult children of former colonial subjects to be sterilised.[157] Zoya Aqua-Kaufmann went into hiding in January 1941 just before giving birth to a son for fear of reprisals that might follow the discovery of her relationship with a white German man. Mother and son fled Germany but were eventually denounced in Prague and imprisoned in Pankratz prison where Zoya was sterilised.[158] And just over a year after Nagel had been investigated by the Berlin police, the city's Gestapo arrested Mohamed Husen after he was denounced for having an extra-marital affair with a German woman. As with Nagel, the charge of *Rassenschande* was ruled out, but Husen was nonetheless held in custody before being transferred to the Sachsenhausen concentration camp near Berlin. He died there three and a half years later.[159] Husen's internment took place after the KPA had drafted its 'law for the protection of German blood in the colonies' in September 1940. The draft offers a glimpse into the possible future that awaited mixed couples had the Nazi regime prevailed and had it been successful in recreating the overseas empire. It would have outlawed both marriages and non-marital sexual relations between Germans and those of African or mixed heritage. Germans breaking the law were to face prison followed by expulsion while African men were to be sentenced to death or under certain circumstances to imprisonment.[160] In the light of this it is unlikely that such marriages would have been tolerated in Germany itself.

[155] Ermittlungssache gegen Nagel, Mühamed wegen Rassenschande, LAB A.Rep. 358-02, no. 3706. Cf. the use of the term '*rassenschändische Beziehungen*' to characterise the kinds of relationship which the management of the Afrika-Schau was designed to avoid: Notes of a meeting on the Afrika-Schau, 14 October 1938, p. 264.

[156] 'Lydias Geheimis', p. 7.

[157] Martin and Alonzo, *Im Netz der Moderne*, p. 267.

[158] Information from NN, son of Zoya Aqua-Kaufmann, Berlin April 2011. See also documents in LABO 1/652.

[159] Bechhaus-Gerst, *Treu bis in den Tod*, p. 142.

[160] Kundrus, 'Von Windhoek nach Nürnberg?', pp. 122–5; Linne, *Deutschland jenseits des Äquators?*, p. 127; Gründer, '"Neger, Kanaken und Chinesen"', pp. 265–6.

The punishment meted out to Husen, a well-known member of the black community, no doubt shocked the small group of former colonial subjects in Germany. Worse still was to follow, in the form of Jonas N'Doki's trial and execution for rape. While the terms of the negotiation over his guilt or innocence betrayed a continuing lack of consensus about the criteria for judging the behaviour of Africans in Germany, there is no doubt that he was being made an example of. The language used by the prosecutor before the Special Tribunal that sentenced him in December 1941 foregrounded the explicitly racial threat that N'Doki posed to German women as a black man unable to control his 'natural' instincts.[161] Equally significant in this case is the fact that it was known and talked about by other Blacks. Of the impact of such events on the collective memory of the African-German community Paul Malapa said later: 'I can't give you many details, because even the mulatto women like Erika Diek didn't want to talk about it.'[162]

Wartime and radicalisation

The punishments handed down to N'Doki and Husen as well as the drafting of the colonial law can be seen as part of a radicalisation of Nazi policies towards men and women of African heritage which followed the outbreak of World War Two and was also signalled by the closure of the Afrika-Schau. By the end of 1939 two of the foremost supporters of the interests of Cameroonians and other German Blacks, Mansfeld and Brückner, were long dead. Their fellow colonial paternalists in the DGfE and the Colonial Department were no longer willing or able to fend off the encroachment of party agencies and officials, notably Frick and later the SS, on policy relating to Blacks. By this time too members of the Foreign Office had developed their own racist agenda and were firmly committed to anti-Jewish policy.[163] For Cameroonians, their children and other former colonial subjects who ran afoul of the authorities this meant that recourse to colonial irredentism was no longer likely to protect them from Nazi terror. While in 1936 the intervention of the Foreign Office could save Kohl from deportation or worse on account of

[161] On the N'Doki trial, see Chapter 5 and the sources cited there.

[162] 'Paul Malapa Décryptage', p. 11. Malapa refers here to a relative of his, the Kribi-born Daniel Ipuabato/Epabato, as having been executed by the Nazis in Hamburg on account of an affair with a German woman. There is no independent evidence to substantiate this and it is possible that Malapa was confusing Ipuabato with N'Doki. A Daniel Ipuabato from Kribi was listed as living in Hamburg in the 1920s and 1930s.

[163] Döscher, *Das Auswärtige Amt im Dritten Reich*.

his relationship with Schläfereit, by 1941 there was no one to invoke colonial interests to save Husen or N'Doki. This was despite the fact that both men had been presented in the Afrika-Schau as war veterans and Husen, in particular, had come to embody the figure of the loyal Askari in party-sponsored events and publications.[164] A further ominous harbinger of the changing atmosphere was the stepping up of anti-Black propaganda in the wake of the invasion of France and the direct engagement with French colonial troops. The Hungarian-born Austrian writer Hans Habe reported to American readers in March 1941 on the beginning of 'an anti-Negro campaign which may surpass in violence even the Nazi persecution of the Jews'.[165]

German Blacks who incurred the ire of local party officials or who came into conflict with the law were now more likely to face draconian punishments and internment. The archival record on Blacks in concentration camps, forced labour camps and prisons remains fragmentary. It is therefore impossible to establish with any certainty how many ex-colonial subjects in particular, and men, women and children of African heritage in general, were incarcerated throughout the Reich. Dorothea Diek spoke of often hearing about African Germans being sent to concentration camps, while Charley Dünkeloh testified that many of the Blacks that he knew were either 'interned or abducted'.[166] There is evidence that increasing numbers were interned following the outbreak of war. As early as September 1937 the East African Charlie Mano became the first ex-colonial to be sent to a concentration camp; he was one of at least five black men, including Husen, imprisoned in Sachsenhausen.[167] Just under a year later the Duala Johann Harrison was sent to a forced labour camp attached to the firm Lenz and Co. in Munich.[168] From 1940 onwards at least another fourteen Cameroonians and their children or grandchildren were imprisoned, including five women, while a further five men connected with the former colonies were also robbed of their liberty as were a handful of other sub-Saharan Africans and their children. Dozens of African Americans based or

164 See, for example, 'Der Askari und sein Kompanieführer', *Afrika Nachrichten*, 17 (September 1936), 229; Hermann Valett, 'Schausch Waziri', *Afrika Nachrichten*, 20 (October 1939), 270–3; Bechhaus-Gerst, *Treu bis in den Tod*, pp. 88–93.

165 Hans Habe, 'The Nazi plan for Negroes', *Nation*, 1 March 1941, pp. 232–5. See Chapter 8 for further discussion of the treatment of French colonial soldiers.

166 [Reiprich and Ngambi ul Kuo,] 'Unser Vater war Kameruner', pp. 75–6; Bauche, '"Im Zirkus gibt es keine Hautfarbe"', p. 46.

167 Information from Gedenkstätte Sachsenhausen provided by Monika Liebscher, October 2005.

168 List of Internees Munich, 12 August 1946, ITS 2.1.1.1 US Zone Stadtkreis Munich, Folder 1.1.5.3, p. 95.

stranded in Germany were also held in camps and as the Reich expanded other Blacks fell into the hands of the Nazis.[169]

The lack of archival information makes it difficult to reconstruct victims' experiences and their fates. Of the twenty former colonial subjects and their children who were interned four died and the fates of five others remain unknown. Similarly, the reason for their arrest is provided in only a few cases. Thus, Josefa Boholle and her Dutch husband Cornelius van der Want were both interned in the concentration camp Stutthof in January 1945 after having been accused of listening to enemy radio broadcasts.[170] Comments made later by the couple as well as witnesses, including members of the Diek family, imply that their mixed relationship played an important role in their internment.[171] Dorothea Diek, Theodor Michael and Johannes Kohl appear to have been held in camps for foreign forced labourers in Berlin and Bremen respectively.[172] Four of the men in Sachsenhausen as well as Paul Boholle and Arthur Sewonu were simply listed as being in protective custody (*Schutzhaft*), an umbrella term which the Nazi state used as an instrument of terror in order to incarcerate people without any opportunity for judicial review.[173]

Erika Ngando and Martha Ndumbe, the German-born daughters of Cameroonian participants in the 1896 colonial exhibition, were held at different times in the women's concentration camp Ravensbrück, outside of Berlin. Ngando was eventually freed, while Ndumbe died there in March 1945.[174] The women, who were among at least four Blacks in the camp, were both interned as 'asocials'.[175] This was a term applied

[169] The African-American press brought attention to American citizens being held in camps: Fritz von Schmidt, 'American Negroes Held in Nazi Camp', *New York Amsterdam News*, 13 September 1941, p. 1; 'Reggie Siki, 5 Others in Nazi Camp', *Chicago Defender*, 12 December 1942, p. 8; 'Musician, Refugee from Nazi Camp, Tells of Prison Life', *Atlanta Daily World*, 26 August 1944, p. 1. See also Lusane, *Hitler's Black Victims*, pp. 147–76; Martin and Alonzo, *Zwischen Charleston und Stechschritt*, pp. 624–73.

[170] Internee's Personal Card, Josefa van der Want, 21 January 1945; Report of the Commandant of the Security Police, Bromberg, 12 January 1945: both ITS, Concentration Camp Stutthof, Individual Records.

[171] Correspondence in StaHam 355-11 Wiedergutmachungsakte 42010, Cornelius van der Want; [Reiprich and Ngambi ul Kuo,] 'Unser Vater war Kameruner', p. 75.

[172] For Diek, see Declaration, Dorothea Reiprich (Diek), 19 November 1963, pp. B25–6; for Michael, 'Die erste Erfahrung'; for Kohl, StABremen Meldekartei 4,82/1-3/175.

[173] Data on Mohamed Husen, Charlie Manu/Mano, Abdulla Ben Moosa, Guillermito: Sachsenhausen Database; Gestapo Record for Artur (*sic*) Sewonu, 1944, ITS 1.2.3.1 Index Gestapo Frankfurt.

[174] See the unsuccessful reparations application made by Ndumbe's mother in 1954. StaHam 355-11 Wiedergutmachungsakte 6883, Martha Borck, geb. Ndumbe.

[175] Zugangslisten zum Frauenkonzentrationslager, courtesy of Cordula Hundertmark, Mahn- und Gedenkstätte Ravensbrück; ITS TD 367734.

flexibly to people who in various ways failed to qualify as responsible citizens. Notorious troublemakers, prostitutes, the 'workshy' and others with a marginal or irregular style of life were subject to detention as 'asocial' without having committed a specific crime. Social incompetence, sexual nonconformity or economic marginality could also be associated with a diagnosis of mental incapacity, which could in turn mean sterilisation or detention.[176] Both Ferdinand Allen, brother of Josie, and former Afrika-Schau performer Benedikt Gambe died in psychiatric institutions.[177] In both cases the cause of death is unknown. Gambe died in summer 1940 just before his thirty-sixth birthday; he was a patient at the private sanatorium in Ilten, whose high death rate has led historians to suspect that it was one of the institutions in which the systematic killing of 'incurables' was carried out.[178]

Although Jews and 'Gypsies' could be interned and deported specifically because of their 'race', the nominal grounds on which Blacks were held make it difficult to assess whether and under what circumstances someone could be arrested for simply being black. That 'race' might be a determining factor is hinted at in the surviving camp-registration records of two victims. On Erika Ngando's record '*Negermischling*' is cited as a 'supplementary reason' for arrest, while on that of Gert Schramm, the son of a German woman and an African-American engineer, who was sent to Buchenwald in July 1944, it is the primary reason cited. By Schramm's own account he was told by the Gestapo that his internment was on the grounds of the 'race laws'.[179] The dual notation on Erika Ngando's record may thus reflect a 'reclassification' following her initial arrest. Evidence that people of African heritage could be interned on the grounds of blackness alone is in keeping with the trajectory of policy outlined above. It suggests that in official thinking and practice there was a progressive assimilation of Blacks to a global category of 'racial aliens' subject to removal without any separate rationale and without regard to historical, sentimental or foreign-policy considerations.

Similarly, there is evidence that planning for the future of Germany's Blacks was being informed by the intensification of the dynamic of mass murder, precipitated by the war, and signalled first and most

176 Ayaß, *'Asoziale'*; Burleigh and Wippermann, *The Racial State*, pp. 136–97.

177 For Ferdinand Allen, see Toles, 'Where is Hitler?'; for Gambe, see death record, ITS no. 22948641#1.

178 Reiter, *Psychiatry in the 'Third Reich'*.

179 For Schramm, see Internee's Personal Card, Gert Schramm, 20 July 1944, ITS, Concentration Camp Buchenwald, Individual Records 1.1.5.3; also Schramm, *Wer hat Angst*; von Kempis and das Gupta, 'Gert Schramm'.

momentously by the decision to annihilate Europe's Jews.[180] On 10 October 1942 Heinrich Himmler as SS Leader and Chief of the German Police issued an order for the registration of all Blacks. Local police authorities throughout Germany and the occupied territories were ordered to locate and report back to the Reich Criminal Police Bureau (RKPA) by 1 November on all *Neger* and *Negermischlinge* currently living in their areas of responsibility. The information to be provided included name, date and place of birth, citizenship status (current and previous), employment, address and similar basic details about spouses and children.[181] The motivation behind this measure remains unknown, but its existence is suggestive in the light of other evidence of a radicalisation in policy towards the whole range of 'racial aliens'. The RKPA was the key policing organ of the regime. Its head, Arthur Nebe, envisaged the agency as an instrument not only to end crime, but also to 'preserve the purity of the German race'.[182] In this capacity, it had since 1936 been the principal executive agency involved in the surveillance of 'Gypsies'. Himmler's order for the registration of Blacks was issued in the months when he was giving close attention to the question of how Germany's 'Gypsy' population might be managed. The upshot of his discussions with the RKPA and the Reich Chancellery was his order to deport most 'Gypsies' to Auschwitz, following the selection for rescue of those who were 'pure-blooded' – an order which the RKPA and the local and regional police applied in such a way as to compass the death of the vast majority.[183] From the RKPA's point of view this was part of a wider campaign to normalise the internment of social outsiders (*Gemeinschaftsfremde*) in concentration camps with no expectation of survival or return.[184]

In the end the impact of the RKPA's plan of action appears to have been limited and most former colonial subjects and their children survived the 'Third Reich'. It is possible that the range of responses that the RKPA received convinced it that taking action was not justifiable or necessary. Employers, concentration-camp commandants and local authorities were sometimes simply bemused as to the logic of the request for information on Blacks and their children. The IG Farben plant at Auschwitz reported that no Blacks were present, but it sent a list of

[180] See Gerlach, 'The Wannsee Conference'.
[181] Text of the order in Ministerialblatt des Reichs- und Preussischen Ministeriums des Innern, 103 (1942), 1977–8.
[182] Nebe in Wildt, *Generation des Unbedingten*, p. 321.
[183] Zimmermann, 'Die Entscheidung für ein Zigeunerlager'.
[184] Wagner, 'Kriminalprävention qua Massenmord', p. 383; Peukert, *Inside Nazi Germany*, pp. 220–2.

names of forty-five North Africans who were carrying out slave labour there in the hope that this would be seen as a satisfactory response.[185] A similar negative response was sent from the Lodz Ghetto.[186] In contrast police officials in Bremen, who must have been aware of the presence of Kohl, took note of the decree, but never sent a reply.[187] This suggests that as a policy it was not widely understood as central to regime concerns (as the attack on the Jews certainly was) and/or found less resonance beyond the Nazi hard core than a crackdown on notorious 'problem' groups (like the attack on the 'Gypsies'). It is also possible that local police officials were continuing to protect Cameroonians, their children and other long-standing and integrated members of the local community, or that they were unable to locate those Blacks still resident in their areas. By the outbreak of war the number of men and women considered to be *Neger* still living in Germany was small. Some were actively in hiding.

Nonetheless, the targeting of some individuals may have been prompted by police awareness of Himmler's order and black men and women continued to be incarcerated up to 1945. Equally, unsubstantiated anecdotal evidence exists that hints at more systematic persecution connected to the order. In her post-war reparations application Zoya Aqua-Kaufmann referred to a six-page questionnaire sent to African Germans she knew by an unnamed party department. The questionnaire, which was to be returned to the relevant department, was sent sometime in 1941 or 1942 (she was unsure of the exact timing) and requested basic information as well as two photos of the recipient, one from the front and one from the side. While it is possible that Aqua-Kaufmann was actually describing the certificate of qualification for marriage, which bears a strong resemblance to the questionnaire, it is equally possible that this represents a national or local initiative resulting from RKPA plans. According to Aqua-Kaufmann four people she knew of were sterilised as a direct result of returning the requested personal information.[188]

The inconsistencies and contradictions inherent in Nazi policies and practices towards former colonial subjects at both local and national level continued to be evident even during the final years of the regime. While some were forced into hiding or incarcerated, other Cameroonians and

185 IG Farben to Police Commander Auschwitz, 19 October 1942, State Archives Katowice/Oswiecim, No. 1, p. 59, courtesy of Piotr Setkiewicz. See Setkiewicz, 'Ausgewählte Probleme', 37.

186 Feuchert, Leibfried and Riecke (eds.), *Die Chronik des Ghettos*, p. 512.

187 Communication from Monika Marschalck, StABremen, December 2010.

188 Aqua-Kaufmann to Reparations Office, Berlin, 16 March 1952.

Africans were able to continue with their daily lives in wartime Germany, with less punitive interference from the state. A handful were obliged to contribute to the war effort and recruited to work in factories as the German population was mobilised for total war on the domestic front. At least four second-generation Cameroonians served in the German army alongside several other men of African heritage. Erika Mandenga Diek's son was called up in 1936 and showed himself to be his mother's child by protesting against his assignment to the Second rather than the First Training Division; he suspected it was because of his skin colour.[189] The ambiguities of Nazi policy even played themselves out within individual families. Helmut Egiomue, Anton's grandson, was obliged to work for an aluminium company as part of the war effort, while his older brother Werner was called up for military duty. Like other Germans they found their lives disrupted by the Allied bombing of German cities. Both the Dieks in Danzig and the Egiomues in Berlin survived the destruction of their homes. Others were not so lucky.[190]

When the Reich finally collapsed in May 1945 the small Black population was much depleted. Of the thirty-five first-generation Cameroonians alive at the beginning of 1933 only eleven remained in Germany to experience the Nazis' defeat. At least five had fled to France before 1939, and the fate of six remains unknown. Thirteen Cameroonian men had died, but of those only the death of N'Doki can be directly linked to Nazi persecution. At the same time it is highly likely that the health problems that several of these men suffered as well as the suspicious circumstances under which two died were connected to the conditions that they had to endure under the Nazis. Information on the more than sixty second- and third-generation German-born children is more limited, but there is clear evidence that more than half were still in Germany at the end of the war, while fewer than a dozen had left for France. The deaths of at least three individuals resulted from Nazi maltreatment.

These figures tell us little about the impact that Nazi rule had on the fabric of the community. In the form of families settled and rooted in German society, community was what Nazi racial policy, once set in motion, aimed to destroy. Sterilisation aimed to achieve this by breaking bodies, with lasting effects on its victims. Households and relationships were forcibly broken up. Neighbourhood suffered as men and women went underground or into exile. Both Charley Dünkeloh, who knew

189 Richter to Ministry of the Interior, 20 September 1936.

190 Heinz Bodo Husen, son of Mohamed Husen, died during Allied bombing of Berlin in March 1945: Bechhaus-Gerst, *Treu bis in den Tod*, p. 152. Tina Campt has some telling observations about African Germans in uniform in *Image Matters*.

many of the former colonial subjects and their children remaining in Germany, and Theodor Michael, who was well connected in Berlin, stated that as of the end of 1942 or beginning of 1943 they no longer encountered others of African heritage.[191] At the same time, it is clear that the conditions under which they lived and worked also brought black people together, in peacetime at least, generating new connections and affinities. And even in the worst times information circulated and there were opportunities for solidarity and mutual aid. Anyone in hiding depended on others for food and news; for Zoya Aqua-Kaufmann it was her mother who supplied these – and she also never lost the support of her child's white father. In Dorothea Diek's account of being on the run from the threat of sterilisation, there is a comic moment where she describes her hiding place in her mother's home as rather overcrowded: she had to share it with two people in striped uniforms. These were Cornelius van der Want and a fellow escapee from Stutthof, whom her mother was sheltering as a matter of course; Cornelius was after all Josefa Boholle's husband, and the Boholles were cousins. From this point of view those who were left in Germany at the end of the war had something to build on. Those who had taken refuge in France faced a different set of challenges.

[191] Bauche, '"Im Zirkus gibt es keine Hautfarbe"', p. 46; Theodor Michael, personal communication, June 2009.

8 Refuge France?

Since the end of World War One, France had presented itself as a place of resort for German-based Cameroonians, if only as a staging post on the road back to Africa. The Nazi takeover of power and the challenges of the years leading up to it led some of them to seek refuge in France, even those who were in most respects settled in Germany. Between 1929 and 1939 some two dozen individuals from among our subjects are known to have made the move. They include Thomas Ngambi ul Kuo; Otto Makube and his wife and two children; three of the children of Theophilus Michael; Dualla Misipo and his wife and son; Paul Malapa; Bruno Malapa; Harry Thomson Mandenge; Peter Makembe and his wife; Kassan Ndanke and his son; Dominikus Manga; Ngoto Ebalé; and Andrea Manga Bell and her two children (accompanied by Joseph Roth). In addition, Joseph Bilé spent some months in France, and as noted in Chapter 5 Maria Diop (Maria Mandessi Bell) settled in France in 1938 with five of her six children, arriving from Senegal. It is probable that the actual number of African emigrants from Germany was somewhat higher. Most of them settled in Paris, where they encountered something even more like a black community than they had left behind: a growing black population, concentrated in certain areas of the city, in which people of different regional and ethnic backgrounds were developing a common associational and political culture. The community was stratified and fissiparous, though, and the Cameroonians and Togolese were in many senses its junior members – even though they already included a generation of young adults whose entire education had been under French administration. For many of the new arrivals, the first stage of their sojourn in France was a recapitulation of the experience of arriving in Germany. They often relied on reconstituting networks among Germanophone refugees and rediscovering or rebuilding links with kin who had come direct to France from Cameroon, while at the same time they made new contacts among Cameroonians and interacted with black people from other parts of the French empire and the world. Accordingly Cameroonians who started out relying on practices of everyday mutual aid among themselves grew into more complex structures of solidarity, getting help and advice from more savvy Antillean and Senegalese neighbours. The sources of social and political solidarity in France were significantly wider, too. In Paris, Africans were strangers among others in a large immigrant population that included North Africans, Asians and white Europeans.[1] A strong and still vital radical democratic and human rights tradition, now mobilising against the threat of fascism at home as well as abroad, dynamised anti-colonial and anti-racist politics and made for the kinds of alliance between black and white activists and politicians that were as unthinkable in the German context as they would have been irrelevant. Where the ex-colonial status of our subjects had placed them in a dubiously 'privileged' relation to the German state, in France the fact that they were both colonial subjects (though of a problematic kind) and refugees from fascism meant that for a brief period they had the ear of government and their situation became a point of reference for wider questions of domestic and foreign policy. But the crisis that created new conditions for community ended again in their frustration. As Hitler consolidated his power and steered a course towards war, Germany's renewed claims on its former protectorates added urgency to the question at the centre of conversations between Cameroonians and the French government, of where the allegiance of the Africans lay. The need to take sides in what seemed ever more likely to be a war between Germany and France contributed to dissipating the energy of the anti-colonial movements, while Germanophone Cameroonians remained suspect. And war, once it came, put stresses on the black population that reinforced difference and militated against cooperation. Our subjects continued to rely on old and new friends in wartime, but families which were not only black but also German faced new forms of isolation and threat from both the occupying Germans and suspicious Frenchmen.

Reconstituting networks

Nearly all Germanophone Cameroonians who moved to France settled in Paris where they encountered a small but vibrant sub-Saharan African population, numbering around 2,000 in the mid 1920s and growing.[2] This population was composed primarily of men from the French

[1] See Rosenberg, *Policing Paris*, pp. 111–28 on the fluidity of 'racial' categories in interwar discourses around immigration.

[2] Blanchard, Deroo and Manceran, *Le Paris Noir*, p. 68. See also Dewitte, *Mouvements nègres*, pp. 24–7.

colonial possessions, although a number of women were also present. In particular they came from parts of French West Africa (Senegal, French Sudan, Mauretania, Côte d'Ivoire, Dahomey, French Guinea or Upper Volta) and Madagascar. Many of them had arrived in Europe to fight in World War One and had never returned to Africa. Others had come to France before 1914 as students, servants and sailors, following routes to Europe similar to those taken by Germany's African population.[3] A significant number of people from the French Antilles as well as several hundred African Americans, often performers or writers, were also living in the city. Interwar Paris, as Brent Hayes Edwards has put it, functioned as a unique 'transnational meeting ground' which allowed for exchange and transfer between black intellectuals, artists and workers from very different geographical, socio-cultural and economic backgrounds.[4]

Among the sub-Saharan Africans living in the French capital after World War One were several dozen Cameroonians. In interwar France Africans were a suspect population subject to monitoring, control and police harassment. From 1923 onwards the Office of Control and Assistance for the Indigenous People in the Colonies (CAI), nominally charged with looking after the welfare of colonial migrants in France, deployed considerable resources tracking their movements and political activities.[5] Both the CAI and the Economic Agency in the Ministry of Colonies, which took responsibility for the welfare of colonial and mandate natives, compiled lists of Africans in France between 1937 and 1940. The lists are full of errors and inconsistencies, but they provide a kind of snapshot. The Cameroonians who feature there, almost exclusively men, were from all parts of the French mandate territory, but primarily from Douala. Typically, those who had begun their careers in France were a generation younger than their compatriots who had travelled to Germany and had experienced little or nothing at all of the German period of rule over Cameroon. Several arrived in Paris as students. Among these was Henri Duala Manga Bell, youngest son of Rudolf Duala Manga and brother of Alexander. Another member of the Duala elite settled in Paris was Jean Mandessi Bell, Maria Diop's brother by adoption. He had arrived in Paris in 1924; a decade later, with a French wife and qualifications as an accountant, he was sufficiently confident of his position in metropolitan society to refuse to return to Cameroon even when he lost his job and had to call on the Economic

[3] Dewitte, *Mouvements nègres*, pp. 33–40. [4] Edwards, *Practice of Diaspora*, p. 25.

[5] Wilder, *French Imperial Nation-State*, pp. 157–8.

Agency for help.[6] A list of 1939 names sixty Cameroonians living all over France; those based outside of Paris lived mainly in the port cities Bordeaux and Marseilles and included seamen, dockers, students and a restaurateur. Thirty-two Cameroonians living in Paris feature in a second list, probably from 1940. They include four students, three skilled tradesmen, two labourers, four factory workers, a bus conductor, a typist, four dancers, a gymnastics teacher, a driver, three hospital employees, a laboratory assistant/bacteriologist, two waiters, a shop-boy, a street pedlar, two *valets de chambre* and an unemployed accountant.[7]

Most of these job descriptions echo the ones that attached to colonial subjects in Germany, with a preponderance of manual and casual labour, low-paid work in the service sector and performing. In fact, Africans enjoyed some access to employment in white-collar work and in the professions, since the French had been more consistent than the Germans in training up cadres of native administrators in their colonies and seeking – rhetorically at least – to educate natives to a level at which they could be 'assimilated' to European culture.[8] The distinction in law and practice between *indigènes* (colonials in their 'primitive' state) and the assimilable *évolués* was key to determining the life chances of black Africans, and *évolués* had privileged access both to civic rights and to employment qualifications. Eligible in principle for naturalisation, they stood second in the hierarchy of France's black subjects, after the natives of Guadeloupe, Martinique and the 'four communes' of Senegal who enjoyed French nationality and elected deputies to the National Assembly. But the benefits of this approach rarely extended to mandate subjects. This was the case even for those who had had a French education, and it was a consequence of their indeterminate civil status.

The League of Nations had defined the status of mandate subjects in negative terms only: they were not nationals of the mandate powers, and in the case of the sub-Saharan African territories they could not be nationals of their homelands either. Once in France, they could not be foreigners, because that would have implied they had some nationality – though not French. In fact, they were more like stateless persons than anything else, except that France had accepted full responsibility for their welfare and in practice treated Cameroon and its resident

6 Truitard to Commissioner Cameroon, 2 May 1935; Jean Mandessi Bell to Truitard, 4 September 1936: both FR ANOM 110COL 1003/3518.

7 List of Natives resident in France: Cameroon, May 1939, FR ANOM 110COL 1003/3520; handwritten list of black Africans in Paris, FR ANOM 4003 COL 50. There are further lists in the latter file and in 4006 COL 9.

8 Boittin, 'Black in France', 25.

population very much as part of its colonial empire. As from 1928 any native leaving the colonial territory of French West Africa who was not a French national had to have express permission and an identity document issued by the colonial authorities. Those already residing in France or in French territories outside their homelands were given six months to acquire the necessary identity documents from the local authority.[9] The same restrictions applied to natives of Togo and Cameroon. Many of them, however, entered France without ever having gained permission to leave Cameroon and consequently without the necessary identity papers. And even those who had been in France legally since before 1928 could only regularise their situation by sending back to Cameroon for an official identity card.[10] There were few alternatives to living with the uncertainty. Although it was made possible as early as 1930 for a native of Cameroon or Togo to apply for naturalisation on the same basis and on the same conditions as a native of one of France's own colonies, the authorities discouraged applications and in practice the option for naturalisation was closed to mandate subjects resident outside the territory.[11]

Accordingly, Cameroonians in France were sometimes viewed as colonials, sometimes as foreigners, and sometimes as individuals with a claim on the French state approximating that of a French national; much depended on the agency involved and the circumstances. Pressed on the question of status by Jean Mandessi Bell, Director of the Economic Agency Léon Truitard repeated the ministerial view that Cameroonians were regarded as neither stateless nor foreign ('*ni comme heimatlos ni comme étranger*').[12] Well-meaning though the statement was, it left the question of what they *were* open to the interpretation of the powerful. Having no papers at all made every aspect of daily life problematic. Being of uncertain nationality made it difficult to marry or

[9] *Journal Officiel de la République Française*, 28 April 1928, pp. 4834–5.

[10] Director of Office of Political Affairs, Ministry of Colonies, to Moumé Étia [March 1937], CAC 19940437-185-17000.

[11] Decree of 7 November 1930, in *La Nationalité française: textes et documents*, pp. 283–4. Note, Office of Political Affairs, Ministry of Colonies, 29 May 1934, FR ANOM 2300 COL 25/218; Unknown (Director of Economic Agency?) to Inspectorate of Health Services in the Ministry of Colonies, 12 April 1939, FR ANOM 110COL 1003/3516; Marius Moutet to Henri Piermé [?], 19 September 1938, FR ANOM 1 AFFPOL 1452. For confirmed naturalisations of Cameroonians, including Alexander Douala Manga Bell and his brother Eitel, see Ministère de la santé publique et de la population, *Liste alphabétique*, vol. XI (1931–40), p. 284, vol. XV (1931–40), p. 632, vol. XIX (1941–50), p. 649. See also Bruschi, 'Nationalité dans le droit colonial' for the evolution of policy.

[12] Truitard to Jean Mandessi Bell, 26 May 1936, FR ANOM 110COL 1003/3518. The German term '*heimatlos*' was the standard term for stateless persons used in European policy circles.

to find work.[13] And being assumed to be a foreigner made someone subject to police scrutiny and harassment. Gottfried Chan, born in Douala, settled with his French wife and two children in St-Ouen, and working in the Renault factory, put it this way:

> From 1914 until today the French government hasn't been able to tell us what nationality we are. The police, the Paris district councils ask us to present our papers as 'foreigners' – but of what nationality? Why are our colonial papers not valid in France? What's the difference between Morocco, Tunisia and Cameroon? What are our legal rights? Do we have a consul here in France? Which consulate can we use? . . . If we really are foreigners in France we'll have to appeal to our fathers in Cameroon and ask them to set up a Cameroonian consulate in France, and then we'd be prepared to pay for the alien's identity card that the Paris police are always asking us for. For the moment we're citizens outside the law.[14]

Chan was writing in February 1934, at a point when a swing to the right in French politics coincided with the first wave of refugees from Nazi Germany to toughen police and public attitudes to aliens of all kinds.[15] Africans arriving from Germany knew all about indeterminate status, but there was a particular absurdity in finding on arrival that the French passport which proved they were 'French' to the German authorities was of very little use in France itself. They still had to go through the process of getting proof of identity from Cameroon – all the more difficult when they had been out of touch with the territory for years or even decades.[16]

If most Africans experienced difficulties in finding employment under the best of circumstances, then Cameroonians faced particular challenges, and this was especially true during the 1930s. Nationally, unemployment quadrupled between 1929 and 1936, and in 1932 Truitard reported that increasing numbers of Cameroonians were visiting his offices to seek the proof of status that would qualify them for unemployment benefits.[17] His Agency could provide some help, with cash subsidies or by finding Africans work (for example at the 1937 International Exposition, a position which also made it easy to keep an eye on troublemakers).[18]

[13] Truitard to Office of Political Affairs, Ministry of Colonies, 13 March 1934, FR ANOM 2300 COL 30/277.

[14] Gottfried Chan to Ministry of the Interior, 28 February 1934, FR ANOM 2300 COL 30/277.

[15] Noiriel, *Immigration*, pp. 407–22.

[16] See Peter Makembe's one-sided correspondence with the Ministry of the Interior in 1937–8 for an example of continuing frustration on this score: CAC 19949462-48-6462.

[17] Truitard to Commissioner Cameroon, 5 February 1932, FR ANOM 110COL 1003/3526. On the impact of the Great Depression in France, see Weber, *The Hollow Years*, pp. 30–4.

[18] Correspondence of June 1937 in FR ANOM 110COL 1003/3560.

But unlike migrants from the Maghreb, sub-Saharan Africans were regarded by the municipal authorities as little more than a nuisance and no local resources were devoted to their welfare. In February 1936 the Senegalese deputy to the National Assembly Galandou Diouf expressed his dismay at the sight of black Africans dumped on the pavements of Bordeaux and Paris by unscrupulous traffickers 'in a miserable condition, sleeping rough, living from what they can beg here and there, only to end up in hospital dying of tuberculosis'. Proposing that a hostel be established for unemployed workers from French West Africa such as had been created for North Africans in Paris after the war, he argued, '[w]e will show our humanity and will cease to offer France the spectacle of the debasement of my race'.[19]

For those Cameroonians and their children who had left Germany for economic reasons, there was thus little relief to be found in Paris. When Otto Makube made up his mind to take his family to France at the end of 1933, he was assured by the French Consul in Berlin that he would receive aid in Paris. On arrival, he registered at the town hall as unemployed and received support for eight months; it was one of the many anomalies about their status that for the purposes of unemployment benefit Cameroonians were treated on the same basis as French citizens as long as they had the right papers.[20] When this was stopped, the Makubes found themselves penniless and due to be evicted from their lodgings. Makube wrote to Truitard asking for his intercession to have his unemployment benefit restored if no work could be found for him. The Agency opened a file on Makube and in subsequent years he was reported still living at the same address though still unemployed.[21]

By contrast, Dualla Misipo was able for a time to assert in the new context the elite status to which he had laid claim in Germany. When he arrived with his family on 13 March 1937, they depended on the support of the Parisian Protestant Mission, and Misipo took on a temporary position as a kitchen porter in the Café Rougier. At the same time he wrote to his brother in Douala for money and set about seeking patrons. He represented himself to the authorities as a qualified physician and

[19] Galandou Diouf to Governor General, Dakar, 29 February 1936, FR ANOM 4003 COL 71. The scheme got as far as a proposal to house up to ten Africans for up to ten days at a time each in a separate section of one of the hostels already operating for North Africans; it is not clear whether any action was taken on this. On North Africans, see Rosenberg, *Policing Paris*.

[20] Unknown (Director of Economic Agency?) to Inspectorate of Health Services in the Ministry of Colonies, 12 April 1939, FR ANOM 110COL 1003/3516.

[21] Makube to Director of the Economic Agency, 1 October 1934, FR ANOM 110COL 1003/3532.

claimed that he was hoping to sit his equivalency exams in France so that he could practise in Cameroon. His request to return to Douala was supported by the prominent scientists Édouard de Pomaine and Michel Weinberg at the Institut Pasteur in Paris, whose help Misipo had actively solicited.[22] Despite this endorsement the French Government's Commissioner in Cameroon had already declared Misipo's return undesirable; he had spent too long in Germany and had a white wife.[23] At the same time the authorities recognised that it was impossible for the family to return to Germany and that in order to prevent them from becoming a public charge some form of employment would need to be found for Misipo. In November 1937, a position was arranged for him with the Laboratory Crinex-Uvé, which was within walking distance of the family's apartment in the Avenue Ernest Reyer.

The Misipos were unusual in living in south-central Paris (Map 8.1). Most Cameroonians lived around Montmartre in the city's nineteenth, seventeenth and eighteenth *arrondissements* where rents were lower, immigrants of many origins were concentrated and established networks already existed. As a CAI agent's survey of 1939 put it, the streets around Place Pigalle, Place Blanche and rue Fontaine were the territory of the '*maqueraux*', black performers and others who worked in the jazz-bars and cabarets and met and mingled in cafés like Chez Boudon.[24] Dark-skinned newcomers landed in Montmartre, and most stayed there or did not move far away. In the late 1920s the LDRN had its offices on the north side of Montmartre, though Lamine Senghor and Kouyaté had established an early bridgehead for black radicalism on the Left Bank, living in the rue des Écoles and organising meetings in the Marais.[25]

Here, as in German cities, housing patterns provide some of the evidence of the continuation of old networks among new arrivals and the formation of new ones. At the end of 1933, Otto Makube and his family moved straight into the Hôtel de Laval, a lodging house in the rue Victor Massé (Montmartre) that later accommodated other Africans, including the Cameroonian dancers Victor M'Billo and Vincent Eyoum Moudio. The Misipos' first apartment in Paris, on the Left Bank, was provided by the Protestant Mission, but one of the addresses they later

22 Pomiane to Minister (of the Colonies?), 25 October 1937, FR ANOM 110COL 1003/3554.

23 Commissioner Cameroon to Minister of Colonies and CAI, 12 August 1937, FR ANOM 2300 COL 31/294.

24 J. S. [Agent Joe], On the Nègres of the Paris Region, 4 April 1939, FR ANOM 4003 COL 50. See also Shack, *Harlem in Montmartre*, pp. 76–100; Rosenberg, *Policing Paris*, pp. 32–3. See Map 8.1.

25 See reports of Agent Désiré, 25 February and 1 May 1928, FR ANOM 4002 COL 5.

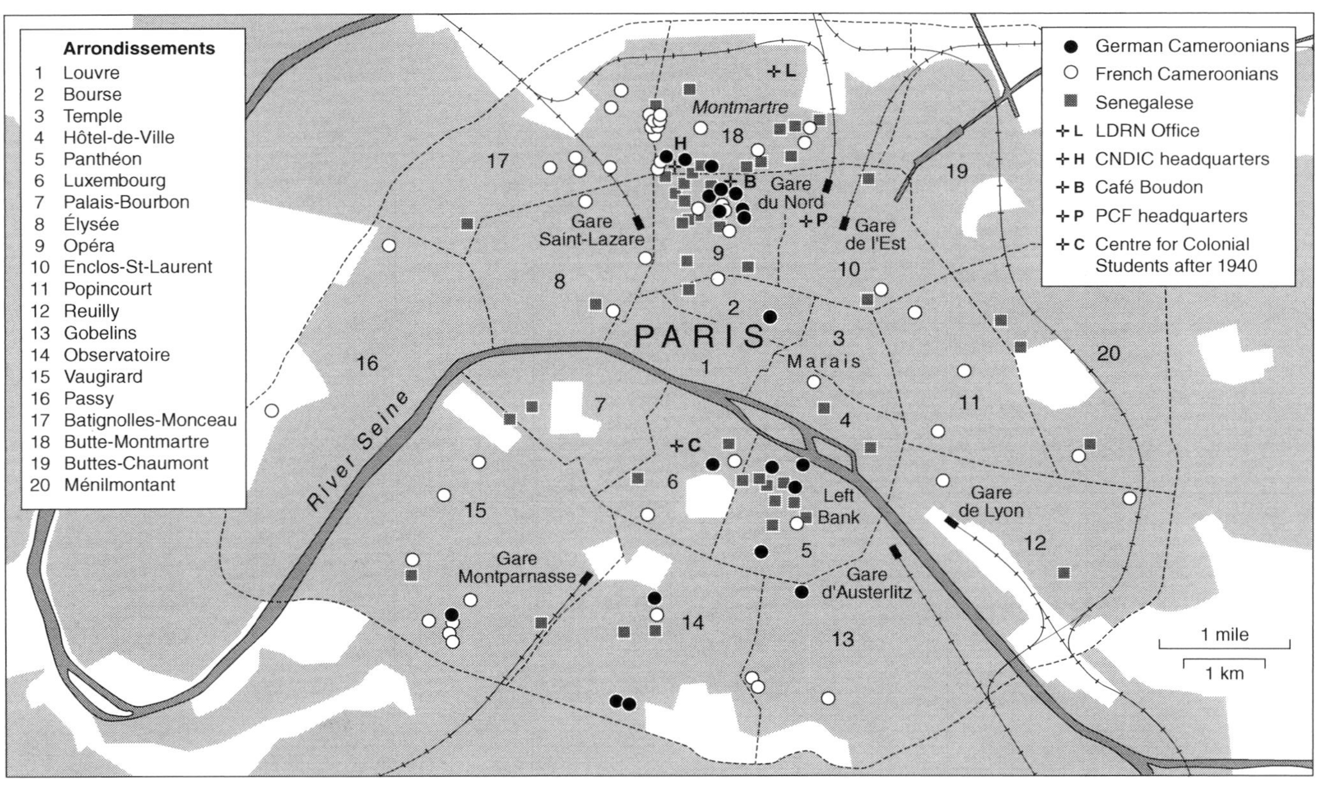

8.1 Africans in Paris in the 1930s

moved to, in the rue Olivier de Serres, was one they shared with kinsmen from the extended Bell family, including Henri Duala Manga Bell.[26] And when Kassan Ndanke arrived in Paris with his fourteen-year-old son in 1939, coming from Frankfurt like the Misipos, it was the Misipos' turn to offer hospitality.[27] Interviewed in later life, Paul Malapa remembered kinship and friendship networks in terms of who had lived with whom. The eighteen-year-old Malapa immediately went down to the Place Blanche when he arrived in Paris in 1932, knowing he would be likely to meet Cameroonians there; he had a 'sort of cousin' (probably one of the Egiomues) living in the rue Fontaine. It was not long before he bumped into Harry Thomson Mandenge, who had come from Berlin and was working as a singer. 'Thomson' introduced him to the boxing scene in Paris, finding him a place to stay and casual work in a gym. His next meeting, at Chez Boudon, was with a 'kid named Jean' who got him a room above the café and sent him to the *arrondissement* town hall to apply for unemployment support.[28] There is evidence, too, of other kinds of practical solidarity: Anna Dick, the widow of a Cameroonian who had settled in Vienna, made her way to Paris with her thirteen-year-old son in 1937. Local Cameroonians raised 900 Francs to supplement the allowance of 200 Francs that she received from the Ministry for the first four months.[29]

That said, it is difficult to identify precisely how the networks ran, and African heritage was not in itself sufficient grounds for membership. As noted in Chapter 5, at some point after her arrival in France Maria Diop made contact with her cousin Dualla Misipo. Her son David was taught by Léopold Sédar Senghor and her own post-1945 Paris circle included Vincent Moudio, operating as a key cultural broker between the Diops and the wider world of Left Bank intellectuals.[30] However, she does not feature in any of the correspondence or reports of Cameroonians in France during the 1930s and 1940s. Paul Malapa, our best source for Paris black networks, makes no mention of the Diops or Senghors, though he was well aware of the Bell presence in Paris and visited the Misipos in the new council flat they moved into during the thirties.[31]

26 Misipo, *Métissages contemporains*, p. 22 on help from the Protestant Mission.

27 List of Natives resident in France: Cameroon, May 1939.

28 'Paul Malapa Décryptage', pp. 41–2, 52–3.

29 [Director of Economic Agency] to Commissioner Cameroon, 12 March 1938, FR ANOM 110COL 1003/3529. She appears to have been living with a Cameroonian in-law at the time.

30 Kala Lobé, '"Ensemble" avec David Diop', p. 80; Grah Mel, *Alioune Diop*, pp. 73–5 on Moudio.

31 'Paul Malapa Décryptage', p. 5. Compare Christopher Miller's account of the difficulties of establishing clear points of overlap between the respective networks of

The household in the rue de Tournon that Andrea Manga Bell shared with Joseph Roth seems to have been embedded in the German-Jewish intellectual emigration and to have had little or no contact with the African community. That Cameroonians in Paris were aware of their presence is evidenced by a bizarre communication in which Gottfried Chan accused Moudio of having 'taken' Andrea Manga Bell's daughter (then fourteen) with the intention of taking her abroad and 'debauching' her.[32]

As these examples suggest, the Cameroonian community in Paris was small enough not to be self-sufficient but large enough to develop an associational life of its own, though those associations could lead to tensions and infighting. As latecomers on the scene, Cameroonians played a marginal role in the ferment of black anti-colonial and cultural politics that characterised interwar Paris. The question of the forcible redevelopment of Douala continued to be a focus of their interests and efforts, and as we noted in Chapter 6 protests around this issue provided a point of contact with the LDRN before 1930. Vincent Ganty, who had formed a branch of the LDRN in Kribi, contacted the non-Communists in the LDRN after his deportation to France in 1930. He also conducted a noisy, independent and fruitless campaign of letters and petitions to the League of Nations, styling himself the 'Delegate in Europe of the Cameroon Negro Citizens'.[33]

The one organisational initiative to arise in these years was prompted by the presence of Richard Bell in Paris. Moving between Cameroon, Paris and Berlin, Bell was well networked: in addition to his contacts in the LzVN and the LDRN, he was a member of the International League for Human Rights, which took an interest in the situation of colonial subjects and victims of racism. In at least one case he represented a German Cameroonian seeking repatriation.[34] He worked with Henri Jean-Louis, a radical lawyer from Guadeloupe, who acted as legal adviser on the expropriation case, and back in Cameroon his name was linked with that of Lotin a Samé.[35] However the Association France-Cameroun which he helped to create in Paris at the end of 1928 was essentially a

black political activists and the Negritude intellectuals in these years: *Nationalists and Nomads*, pp. 37–8.

[32] Chan to Minister of the Interior, 22 December 1937, CAC 19949443-90-8644. The main point of the letter was to object to the issue of passports to Moudio and Harry Thomson Mandenge, whom Chan characterised as Germanophiles.

[33] Derrick, *Africa's 'Agitators'*, pp. 230–4; Dewitte, *Mouvements nègres*, pp. 322–6.

[34] See the endorsement on Otto Makube to Minister of Colonies, 3 March 1930, FR ANOM 1 AFFPOL 613/1073.

[35] Jean-Louis to Duala Chiefs, 1 December 1929, FR ANOM 2300 COL 31/288; Note on Communist propaganda in Cameroon, FR ANOM 2300 COL 31/294.

Figure 8.1 Officers of the Association France-Cameroun, *Mbalé*, January 1929

fraternal rather than a political organisation, a Cameroonian counterpart to similar organisations founded by migrants from France's various colonial territories (Figure 8.1).[36] The other officers included Jean Mandessi Bell and Joseph Ebelé, who became editor of the Association's newspaper *Mbalé* (Truth), published in both French and Duala; apart from Richard Bell no Germanophone Cameroonians were obviously involved. The Association adopted a conciliatory stance on France's relation to Cameroon, and otherwise it presented itself as a motor for personal and cultural development and a clearing-house for questions and complaints. The operation depended on monetary contributions

[36] For example the Société Amicale des Originaires de l'AEF, Report Désiré, 15 January 1928, FR ANOM 4002 COL 5.

from a handful of Cameroonians (it had substantial membership fees and charged for its advice service), and problems and disputes over this as much as political naiveté and a ban on the distribution of *Mbalé* ensured that it was short-lived.[37] Joseph Ebelé remained active on the black political scene, though he seems never to have abandoned his conciliationist views. He was clearly in contact with the LDRN by early 1934 at the latest, and contributed articles on Cameroonian affairs to *Le Cri des Nègres*, the journal of the Union of Negro Workers (UTN) which Kouyaté had founded in 1932; in January 1935 he was elected UTN General Secretary.[38]

Ni heimatlos ni étranger – the politics of refuge

Ebelé was instrumental in introducing Joseph Bilé into black political circles when Bilé arrived in Paris at the beginning of March 1934. Against his expectations, the Comintern had not provided Bilé with the means to return to Cameroon. He left Moscow with no more than a ticket to Paris and the recommendation that he be taken into the French Communist Party (PCF) immediately.[39] It is not clear how he spent his first month in Paris, but he seems to have gone to the PCF offices and been advised there that he needed to have his papers in order before anything could be done for him. He accordingly visited Léon Truitard at the Economic Agency; suppressing his political history, Bilé claimed to have come direct from Germany and asked for the issue of temporary papers to replace his German passport. With these in hand, he once again made contact with the party and then with the UTN; in each case his point of contact was Ebelé. It is not clear how the two met; Bilé's first lodgings were not far from Ebelé's apartment in the ninth *arrondissement*, and in politics as in everyday life black networks developed through chance encounters and moments of mutual recognition as well as through meetings and manifestos. Not long before Bilé arrived the CAI had received a complicated account – probably from Ebelé himself – of conversations involving Harry Thomson Mandenge, Henri Jean-Louis, Kouyaté and Jean Mandessi Bell. The report focussed on Jean-Louis' claim to have contacted Hitler and Mussolini in support of the Duala land claims, but more interesting and plausible than its

[37] Founding documents of Association France-Cameroun, 10 December 1928, FR ANOM 4003 COL 36; Anonymous report, 24 January 1934, CAC 1940443-1-47; copies of *Mbalé* in FR ANOM 4005 COL 44.

[38] Dewitte, *Mouvements nègres*, p. 316; Derrick, *Africa's 'Agitators'*, pp. 323–4.

[39] Heckert to Romanisches Ländersekretariat, 8 March 1934; Note to 'Dear friends', 10 March 1934, RGASPI 495/205/1802, pp. 1 and 3.

political content is the image of the lawyer passing on the news to any Cameroonian he could find, including Jean Mandessi Bell whom he bumped into 'in front of Printemps' (a department store).[40]

As for Bilé, when he arrived in Paris he was asking only for funds to help him recover his belongings from Germany, though he admitted that if the money were forthcoming he would undertake an agitational trip to Cameroon. In any case, in May 1934 he had still not received any formal offer of help from French comrades, though at some point a collection was taken up.[41] He did manage to return to Cameroon in April 1935.[42] In the late thirties the authorities in Paris began to speculate on the possibility of deploying him as a government agent there. They received intelligence that he had turned his back on Communism and remained bitter at the way he had been treated in Germany, and that he had shown 'sincere sympathy for France, land of liberty and enlightened protector of her colonial natives'. In fact he never responded to invitations to assist the police in Cameroon, nor did he engage in any other kind of political activity after his return.[43]

During his year in Paris, though, Bilé was drawn into new kinds of politics and new networks, not least by the international sense of emergency provoked by a newly aggressive fascism. The political configuration that had drawn Bilé into the Communist movement was gone. The Nazi takeover of power in 1933 meant that the Hamburg-Berlin axis ceased to function as a centre of black anti-colonial activism. The focus shifted to Paris, where George Padmore took up residence among the growing German émigré community and Willi Münzenberg, too, found refuge. At the same time, relations between the Comintern leadership and anti-colonial activists had begun to break down. In 1932 the LDRN had split over the question of the group's relationship to Communism. Kouyaté, still aiming to combine struggles around class and race in a modified Comintern spirit, formed the UTN. But by the middle of 1933 Kouyaté had moved to a position which was both more emphatically focussed on the common interests of black people and more open to alliances with anti-racist and progressive forces outside the

40 Report of Agent Moise, 6 February 1934, FR ANOM 4002 COL 3. A comparison of the reports of Agent Joe and Agent Moise suggests that Ebelé was Agent Moise.

41 Bilé to Truitard, 14 April 1934, FR ANOM 110COL 1003/3541; Report of J. S. [Agent Joe], 8 May 1934, FR ANOM 4002 COL 16; Reports of Agent Moise, 9 and 14 May 1934, FR ANOM 4002 COL 3. Paul Malapa remembered donating 100 centimes to help Bilé get home: 'Paul Malapa Décryptage', p. 8.

42 Minister of Colonies to Commissioner Cameroon, 27 March 1935, FR ANOM 2300 COL 30/277.

43 Notes, Ministry for Colonies, 30 November and 5 December 1938; Deputy Commissioner to Commissioner Cameroon, 4 February 1939.

Communist movement. In July 1933 he was removed from the UTN leadership and expelled from the Communist Party on the authority of the Comintern.[44] Padmore stepped into Kouyaté's role as leader of the UTN and editor of *Le Cri des Nègres*. Within a few months, however, he too had broken with the Comintern, and in February 1934 he was actively supporting Kouyaté's initiative for a Negro World Unity conference.[45]

There is no evidence that Bilé attended any political meetings during 1934 and 1935, while he was having conversations with French activists about his personal situation. At the same time, he clearly renewed contact with Kouyaté and Padmore. In February 1935 a Comintern officer accused Bilé of being an 'agent of Padmore' and proposed that UTN activists be warned to avoid contact with him.[46] Both of Bilé's mentors were now preoccupied with what Padmore called the 'fascist danger which threatens our racial extermination'.[47] The Italian invasion of Ethiopia in February 1935 gave this danger a human face, and the defence of Ethiopia became a cause around which organisations of Blacks and other colonial peoples in France began to find their way towards cooperation. At the same time they looked to alliances with white Socialists, democrats, Communists and human-rights activists from many countries who were coalescing around the programme of an antifascist Popular Front. Among the old friends who had reappeared in Paris refugee circles was the liberal journalist Helmut von Gerlach, an early supporter of the Duala cause, member of the International League for Human Rights, and latterly editor of the progressive *Weltbühne*. As recently as 1932 he had written in support of Afro-Germans seeking repatriation, and in Paris he took up a position in the French League for Human Rights.[48] Kouyaté engaged directly with the principal organisation of North Africans in France and drew on financial support from white progressive activists in founding a new 'ecumenical' newspaper, *L'Africa*, at the end of the year.[49] It therefore seems likely that he was behind an encounter between Bilé

[44] Dewitte, *Mouvements nègres*, pp. 212–14, 299–309; Wilder, *French Imperial Nation-State*, pp. 129–85.
[45] Derrick, *Africa's 'Agitators'*, pp. 287–303.
[46] [Unnamed] to Otto (Huiswood?), 21 February 1935, RGASPI 495/155/102, pp. 2–3.
[47] Padmore to W. E. B. Du Bois, 17 February 1934, cited by Hooker, *Black Revolutionary*, pp. 39–40.
[48] Correspondence on Kwassi Bruce's repatriation application, FR ANOM 1 AFFPOL 613/1071; Helmut von Gerlach to Lehmann-Russbüldt, 6 April 1934, PAAA Inland II-A/B R99578. Gerlach died in Paris in August 1935.
[49] Dewitte, *Mouvements nègres*, pp. 360–2.

and one of his financial backers, Bernard Lecache, in early 1935; certainly Padmore had knowledge of it.[50]

Lecache was President of the Paris-based International League Against Antisemitism (LICA), whose activities had introduced the term 'antiracism' to French political discourse and which was among the leading forces lobbying in the interests of foreign workers and refugees from Nazism.[51] His contact with Bilé is documented by articles in a number of African-American newspapers that publicised Bilé's situation as an example of the conditions under which Africans were suffering in Germany. The Urban League journal *Opportunity* represented the 'African refugee from Germany' Bilé as a delegate of others in Germany who was seeking to return to Africa to raise funds for their support, and readers were asked to contribute money to pay his passage. In a letter reprinted there, Lecache remarked that the conditions of black Germans 'are even worse than the Jews, for they lack an organization of their own to arouse interest in their problems'.[52] In this case Lecache had contacted the Urban League after first writing to the Race Relations Commission of the Society of Friends. An article published in the *Chicago Defender* indicates that Lecache also wrote to the Federal Council of Churches in the United States, which in turn enquired of the League of Nations High Commission for Refugees. The enquiry prompted a statement that in Nazi Germany 'Africans are definitely considered to belong to an inferior race and the anti-racial legislation of Germany applies to them', providing authority for the article's assertion that 'the tidal wave of race prejudice in Germany, which has swept the Jews from their well established economic foundations, also threatens cruel extinction of this other racial minority whose foothold on security has ever been slight.' The article also quoted a letter from Bilé himself: 'Whenever I shall arrive in my country, I will not fail to tell my

[50] It was most likely Padmore who reported the episode to the African-American journalist Roi Ottley after the war (though Ottley's account implies that Bilé was in Germany at the time): Ottley, *No Green Pastures*, p. 154. See also Lusane, *Hitler's Black Victims*, pp. 115–17; Derrick, *Africa's 'Agitators'*, pp. 303–4.

[51] Noiriel, *Immigration*, pp. 451–3; Allali, *Contre le racisme*.

[52] 'The Hand of Hitler', *Opportunity. A Journal of Negro Life*, March 1935, p. 71. The publication of the same letter in the NAACP journal the *Crisis* provoked an exchange between an African-American reader, whose experiences in Nazi Germany had compared favourably with everyday life in Jim Crow America, and the editors, who pointed out that 'the courtesies afforded visiting American Negroes in Germany have no more relation to the treatment of German Negro residents than the courtesies extended a visiting Haitian or Abyssinian in America have to the treatment of Negroes in Alabama': *Crisis*, 42/2 (February 1935), p. 60.

countrymen that in the hour of need, our coloured brother in America came to our rescue.'[53]

For a brief period, then, Joseph Bilé embodied for an international black and white public the full scope of the 'fascist danger'. It would not have taken an intervention by Bilé to draw the attention of observers like the *Chicago Defender* editor to the situation of Africans in Germany, but the upshot of an appeal mediated through LICA, whose self-defence squads were daily confronting French antisemites on the streets of Paris, was to establish for that same audience the status of German Africans as victims of fascist violence. In late January 1934, in the run-up to the mass demonstrations by the radical right that precipitated both the appointment of a conservative government and the crystallisation of resistance on the left, meetings of the PCF's Negro Committee and Colonial Section were cancelled for fear of attacks from LICA's principal adversaries, the paramilitary Jeunesses Patriotes and Camelots du Roi.[54] All of this was a concrete reminder that Nazi 'racism' threatened both Blacks and Jews (as well as other groups). And it added 'refugee' to the many and contradictory labels that attached to Cameroonians in France.

In the following years, the situation of Africans in Germany provided a focus for the agitation of Cameroonian organisations in France, underlining the implications that Nazi racism had for the return of Germany's former protectorates that Hitler was demanding. Against the background of appeasement in Europe, British Prime Minister Neville Chamberlain's willingness to consider a revision of the mandate system in Germany's favour and the readiness of French politicians to enter into discussion of the issue provoked real anxieties among mandate subjects and their friends between 1936 and 1939.[55] Anti-colonial arguments were set aside in favour of a defensive allegiance to France or at most appeals to the League of Nations for support over the heads of the French authorities. The men who articulated these fears spoke in the name of two organisations, the National Committee for the Defence of the Interests of Cameroon (CNDIC – later CDIC) and the Cameroonian Union (UC). The CNDIC was formed in October 1936, with Gottfried Chan as president. Among the other men joining the executive committee was Harry Thomson Mandenge, who had been a member of the LzVN back in Berlin. Its founding manifesto declared it to be an 'autonomous

[53] 'African Student Tells of Hitler Tortures in Germany', *Chicago Defender*, 18 May 1935, p. 24.

[54] Report Agent Paul, 28 January 1934, FR ANOM 4002 COL 19; on the self-defence units of LICA, see the League's journal, *Le Droit de Vivre*.

[55] Callahan, *Sacred Trust*, pp. 118–48.

committee' having 'nothing to do with other black associations in Paris'. It promised to defend the general interests of Cameroonians and the well-being of the natives of Cameroon, to fight for the liberation from all dictatorship and 'to lead the masses gradually to a clear consciousness of their class interest' – combining current concerns with a language that Chan had learned in a brief association with the LDRN and the UTN. He had also attracted the attention of the police by his involvement in protests over Ethiopia. The manifesto was careful to declare however that the CNDIC was 'not in any way directed against France'.

An explicit challenge in the manifesto to the authority of native chiefs signalled the character of the CNDIC as an association whose members were not exclusively Duala. Jean Mandessi Bell was an active member, but by June 1937 the Committee had split, and a rancorous dispute developed between him and Chan. The terms of subsequent statements and discussions suggest that the ethnic divide at least exacerbated differences of personality (Chan was viewed by other Cameroonians and by the police as a thug and a schemer) and familiar disputes over funds; the CNDIC even went so far as to accuse members of the Duala elite in Cameroon of negotiating with the Germans. For his own part, Chan pursued an eloquently and resolutely anti-German line, reminding anyone who was thinking of appeasing Hitler in Africa of the genocidal war of 1904–8 in South West Africa, the judicial murder of Rudolf Duala Manga Bell and Hitler's characterisation of Blacks as 'half-apes' and of France as 'beniggered' (*vernegert*).[56] These arguments were put before a wider public at meetings to which leading politicians were invited; sometimes featuring music and dancing, the meetings could attract hundreds of attendees and did not escape the attention of the German press.[57]

Jean Mandessi Bell created the Cameroonian Union along with Léopold Moumé Étia after both had left the CNDIC in summer 1937. They took with them two-thirds of the CNDIC membership, which the police numbered at around thirty all together.[58] However, the UC seems to have made its mark primarily through personal interventions on the part of Mandessi Bell, who as the son of one of the wealthiest men in Douala had experience of dealing confidently with politicians and bureaucrats.[59]

[56] CNDIC file, FR ANOM 110COL 1003/3560; On the Subject of Gottfried Chan, 7 June 1938; Jean Mandessi Bell to Minister of the Interior, 6 May 1938: both CAC 19940437-185-17000.

[57] Flyer for and report on Grande Fête Exotique held on 2 July 1938, FR ANOM 2300 COL 31/294.

[58] On the Subject of Gottfried Chan, 7 June 1938.

[59] Mandessi Bell to Léon Truitard, 21 April 1933 and 4 September 1936. In the Ministry of Colonies it was believed that the UC too had dwindled by May 1938, as members

In October 1938 in the wake of the Munich crisis he wrote directly to Chamberlain and to King George and Queen Elizabeth of Britain to ask for assurances that the African mandate territories would not be abandoned to Hitler. At the same time he visited leading parliamentarians in Paris and wrote to Édouard Daladier, the French head of government. In his letter, which echoed a parallel submission to the League of Nations, he rejected the idea that Cameroon should become a French colony but proposed that its mandate status should be changed to match that of the historically autonomous (Mandate A) territories like Syria and Iraq; this would 'allow its gradual evolution'. And he wrote of the

> lamentable situation of the Cameroonians in Cameroon, in France and in Berlin. Regarded as Germanophiles in France, as Frenchmen in Germany, their indeterminate nationality creates the greatest difficulties for them in finding work. Yet if the mandate power is attacked they have to be mobilised for its defence. If on the other hand they are returned to Germany still more dreadful evils await them.[60]

The rescue of individuals in this predicament was a natural complement to the campaign that both Chan and Mandessi Bell were leading against German colonial irredentism. The French authorities knew about the situation in Germany. As early as 1934 the Minister of Colonies Pierre Laval put on record his concern that 'certain campaigns going on in Germany' might lead Africans to seek refuge in France, and Truitard's conversations and correspondence with refugees like Bilé and Makube would have made his office aware of their claims of discrimination and harassment.[61] The ministries remained relatively indifferent to the issue, though. In summer 1936 the new Minister of Colonies Jacques Stern prompted an inquiry into the number of Cameroonians in Germany, but his concern was to identify and if possible repatriate the Francophiles among them to counter German propaganda. The resulting correspondence exposed both the ignorance and the poor intelligence networks of the authorities in Cameroon and in Paris.[62]

By the time the results of the inquiry arrived from Yaoundé, the election of a Popular Front government had brought Marius Moutet into

distanced themselves from agitation of any kind: Deboudaud, Ministry of Colonies, to Commissioner Cameroon, 6 May 1938, FR ANOM 110COL 1003/3558.

60 Mandessi Bell to Édouard Daladier, 15 October 1938, CAC 19940437-185-1700. See also Derrick, *Africa's 'Agitators'*, p. 373; Moumé Étia, *Les Années ardentes*, pp. 46–8, 97–110.

61 Pierre Laval to Foreign Ministry, 17 July 1934, FR ANOM 2300 COL 30/277.

62 Interior Minister acting as Minister of Colonies to Commissioner Cameroon, 1 May 1936; Commissioner Cameroon to Minister of Colonies, 13 August 1936: FR ANOM 2300 COL 30/277.

the Ministry of Colonies, where he remained with one brief interruption until April 1938. Moutet, a Socialist and member of the International League for Human Rights, had strong sympathies with colonial reform movements and introduced significant improvements in the rights of colonial subjects.[63] In the National Assembly debate on the colonial budget in 1937, his Socialist colleague Jean Pierre-Bloch, an officer of LICA, put on record the character of National Socialism as 'War on the Jews. War on the Catholic Church. War on the Negroes.'[64] And black organisations in France responded by coming together in March 1937 in a Rassemblement Colonial which offered itself as an advisory group to the Popular Front government; embracing the full spectrum of political tendencies and regional interests, and including Chan's CNDIC and Ebelé, the Rassemblement did not outlast the year.[65]

The change in atmosphere may well have emboldened Gottfried Chan to undertake his own inquiries. Late in 1936 he wrote to Louis Brody asking about the situation of his compatriots in Germany. It was in response to this that Kala Kinger reported on behalf of the Berliners that their 'only' problem was getting French passports. Chan proceeded to contact the French Embassy in Paris to ask about the issue of passports to mandate subjects and then to prompt Moutet to undertake an inquiry into the situation of Cameroonians in Germany. In July 1937 Jean Mandessi Bell took up the cause, forwarding telegrams from German Africans to the Economic Agency. He later visited the Foreign Office, and in January 1939 passed on a report that mandate subjects in Germany would be arrested if found without valid identity papers. Moutet's inquiry touched off a correspondence between the Foreign Office, the Ministry of Colonies and the Consulate in Berlin, and the issues were brought into focus in spring 1938 by the submission of passport applications by Mandenga Diek, Anton Egiomue and Maria Ngambe Kaltenbach and the Togolese Bruce and Garber families. The Consul reported that these people were facing 'real difficulties'. As late as the beginning of 1939, however, the understanding in the Ministry of Colonies was that Cameroonians in Germany did not want to leave the country, but sought only the protection provided by a French passport in case of future sanctions by the German government.[66]

[63] Gratien, *Marius Moutet*.

[64] Welczeck, German Embassy Paris, to Foreign Office, 22 December 1937, PAAA Embassy Paris 584/2.

[65] Derrick, *Africa's 'Agitators'*, pp. 410–11; Report of Agent Coco, 21 October 1937, FR ANOM 4002 COL 2.

[66] Chan to Moutet, 29 March and 2 May 1937, FR ANOM 110COL 1003/3560; Jean Mandessi Bell to Deboudaud, 7 July 1937, FR ANOM 110COL 1003/3558; Telegram

The case of a Germanophone Cameroonian already in France, Paul Malapa, demonstrates the ways in which personal histories took on political weight and Africans interacted singly and collectively with state agencies in the run-up to war. Malapa's arrival in Paris in 1932 was not his first experience of French soil. Under surveillance by the police and welfare authorities since his birth, he had been identified as an undesirable alien by the Hamburg authorities following his father's expulsion in 1929. In 1928 his German papers were confiscated and he acquired a French passport. The Hamburg police fetched him from his mother's flat in late 1930 and put him on the train to Cologne, where he was escorted to another that would take him to the border and on to Strasbourg. After trekking around France for a few months he returned to Hamburg, but left again in late 1931; by his own account this was because his presence was making life difficult for his mother, who lived above a tavern frequented by Nazi brownshirts. He jobbed as a musician for a time, and headed for Paris at the beginning of 1932.[67] His request that he be allowed to join his father in Cameroon was rejected by the Commissioner; while he was uncertain himself what Malapa's official civil status was, there could be no question of a German-born *métis* (mulatto) being 'repatriated'. He also reported that Bulu Malapa was opposed to his son's 'return'. Meanwhile Malapa's circumstances took a turn for the worse when he was arrested for battery at the end of January; Malapa had attacked a young black man at Chez Boudon who propositioned him and called him a *boche* when rebuffed. Following his conviction the Parisian Police Prefect in conjunction with the Minister of the Interior initiated an order to expel Malapa as an undesirable alien. Malapa was only informed of the expulsion order in May 1935, by which time he was again in trouble with the police. He had begun to perform as a boxer, and one of the trainers on the boxing scene had reported him to the police for 'falsely claiming to be French'. He was held in La Santé prison for five months.

The exchange of letters that followed between Malapa, the police and the various ministerial agencies involved revealed how Malapa's case

Ngange na Ekombo to Jean Mandessi Bell [1937], FR ANOM 110COL 1003/3518; Director of Political Affairs, Ministry of Colonies, to Foreign Ministry, 28 April 1937; Director of Political Affairs, Foreign Ministry, to Jean Mandessi Bell, 14 May 1938; handwritten list of passport applications [May 1938]: all FR ANOM 2300 COL 31/294; Consul General in Berlin to Foreign Office, 2 May 1938, FR ANOM 1 AFFPOL 614/2; Mandel to French Consul General in Berlin, 14 January 1939; handwritten note, 17 January 1939: both FR ANOM 2300 COL 30/260.

67 'Paul Malapa Décryptage', pp. 20–2, 30–1; Police Prefecture Paris to Minister of the Interior, 2 April 1932, CAC 19940462-50-4877.

tested the question of mandate subjects' status to its limits. As far as the police were concerned, since he was born in Hamburg and spoke fluent German, he was probably German; his French passport was probably a fake and as a foreigner he could be expelled without further ado. Truitard saw the problems both personal and administrative arising from Malapa's actual status: 'What will become of him? Rejected by Germany, expelled from France, denied by his father, refused by the Commissioner in Cameroon, Malapa's situation is tragic.' Advised by the CAI that *administrés sous mandat* were in every way like French subjects *except* that they could be expelled, Truitard made efforts to find a place for Malapa in the colonial army or the Foreign Legion. This initiative, about which Malapa was unenthusiastic, failed; he could not join a regular colonial regiment because he was not a colonial, and he could not be accepted into the Foreign Legion because of his colour.[68]

The case was still unresolved when Moutet was installed in the Ministry of Colonies. In June 1937 his attention was drawn to the pending expulsions of Malapa and Vincent Moudio, who had been arrested for vagrancy. His letter to the Interior Ministry urged moral, legal and pragmatic reasons for refraining from expelling mandate subjects, and he made a direct comparison between Cameroonians and Togolese and European refugees, forced to be in permanent violation of expulsion orders because no other country would receive them: 'This situation is regrettable and painful enough for stateless foreigners, but it would be a true scandal for natives under the protection of France, one which could be all too easily exploited in the current international situation.'[69] In response the Director of the Sûreté in the Interior Ministry insisted on both the legality and the necessity of expelling undesirable mandate subjects; his answer to the question of where they should go was 'their country of origin where they would find a milieu and a climate natural to them'.[70] This was no solution to Paul Malapa's dilemma – but the situation appeared to have been temporarily resolved when Malapa left France for Switzerland in August 1937. The police were happy to let him go. When he returned the following March, though, he was rearrested within days. They charged him with breaching his expulsion order and again held him in La Santé.

[68] Truitard to CAI, 21 May 1935, FR ANOM 110COL 1003/3526; 'Paul Malapa Décryptage', p. 60.

[69] Marius Moutet to Director of the Sûreté, Ministry of the Interior, 10 June 1937, CAC 19940463-3-205.

[70] Moitessier to Marius Moutet, 7 July 1937, CAC 19940462-50-4877 (first page in CAC 19940463-3-205).

At this point the political implications of Malapa's case became critical. Malapa had been enjoying the support of a Guadeloupan lawyer, Isaac Béton, who was well known as a moderate pan-African activist and supporter of the Popular Front, and Malapa's own letters to the ministries indicate how far the question of German claims to Cameroon had become embedded in black political discourse. Penned in good French (Malapa's own French was poor) and one of them notarised, they asserted his qualities as an 'honest worker' and his sense of being French, and reminded the addressees of the effect of his expulsion on the opinions of other Cameroonians in France and in the territory.[71] Now, on 6 March 1938, Jean Mandessi Bell protested directly to the Minister of the Interior in the name of the UC. He remarked that the Minister might consider it 'opportune ... at a time when the Third Reich is revealing its hopes of seeing Cameroon become a German colony once again, to show generosity to someone from that country who has joined our Committee so that he can demonstrate alongside us his desire to see Cameroon remain attached to France.' This precipitated urgent memos and phone calls to the Sûreté from the CAI and from Moutet's office, culminating in a sharp letter with Moutet's own signature which ordered the police authorities to withdraw the expulsion order and have Malapa freed from prison. Moutet hoped this would 'reduce as far as possible the unfortunate repercussions which this regrettable incident is sure to have in Togolese and Cameroonian circles' and went on to insist on the political importance 'in the current circumstances' of completely abandoning the policy of expelling *administrés sous mandat* from France. On 17 March 1938 the expulsion order was quashed.[72] As Malapa put it many years later, 'The Cameroonians got me freed immediately; they knew my case!'[73]

Moutet had signalled his personal solidarity with Cameroon and Cameroonians by meeting with their spokesmen face to face and by speaking at meetings organised by their associations, and after leaving office he continued to support their cause.[74] It seems likely that had he remained in office action would have been taken relatively quickly to

[71] Paul Malapa to Minister, 25 October 1935; Malapa to Minister of the Interior, 29 May 1937: both CAC 19940463-3-205; Malapa to Minister of the Interior, 19 January 1936, FR ANOM 110COL 1003/3526; 'Paul Malapa Décryptage', p. 60. On Isaac Béton, see Dewitte, *Mouvements nègres*, pp. 59, 361, 368–9.

[72] Mandessi Bell to the Minister of the Interior, 6 March 1938; Moutet to the Director of the Sûreté, Ministry of the Interior, 16 March 1938; Police Prefect to the Minister of the Interior, 9 May 1938: all CAC 19940463-3-205.

[73] 'Paul Malapa Décryptage', p. 67.

[74] Flyer for a public meeting, 3 March 1939, PAAA German Embassy in Paris 584/3; Report on that meeting, FR ANOM 110COL 1003/3560.

regularise the status of Cameroonian and Togolese natives. In 1938 work began on drafting a law that would allow for the naturalisation of mandate subjects in the metropole, and in January 1939 it was made possible for them to acquire valid identity cards by applying direct to the CAI.[75] But any further progress was stalled by the developing crisis in Europe, as French politicians became preoccupied with the realities of mobilisation.

Refuge in peril: war and occupation

The threat of war seemed to offer an opportunity for Africans to demonstrate their loyalty to France by joining the armed forces, but this simple gesture, too, proved complicated. The National Service Law passed on 11 July 1938 made all male French nationals over the age of eighteen subject to mobilisation in case of war or the threat of war. It also stipulated that in a national emergency anyone not subject to mobilisation, including foreigners, could volunteer for deployment in the public service.[76] Natives of France's colonies in West Africa could volunteer for service in the colonies or in metropolitan France, and with the outbreak of war Africans in the colonies were conscripted and colonial subjects already in France and of the appropriate age were mobilised.[77] Colonial subjects present in France were also subject to labour conscription in those months. Under the terms of the mandate, however, Cameroonians could not be conscripted and French politicians shared both a lingering uncertainty about their trustworthiness and the fear that their deployment on any basis would provoke a hostile response from Germany. Moutet's successor Georges Mandel displayed sympathy for the situation of mandate subjects in the same measure as he opposed any rapprochement with Nazi Germany.[78] But he remained suspicious of them as individuals; in spring 1938 he was worrying that the Dieks, still awaiting news about their passport applications, might actually be 'collaborators' with the Germans.[79] As late as October 1939 (and in spite of Jean Mandessi Bell's apprehensions), it appears that Cameroonians in the territory were discouraged even from volunteering.[80] As the 'phoney

75 Moutet to Henri Piermé [?], 19 September 1938; Minister of the Interior to Police Prefect, Aliens Department, 6 February 1939, CAC 19940437-185-17000.

76 Ehrmann, 'The Trade Union Movement'; Flynn, *Conscription and Democracy*, pp. 53–7.

77 Echenberg, '"Morts pour la France"', pp. 364–7.

78 CNDIC flyer advertising Mandel's presence at Grande Fête Exotique, 2 July 1938, FR ANOM 2300 COL 31/294; Mandessi Bell to Édouard Daladier, 15 October 1938.

79 Mandel to Director of Political Affairs in the Foreign Office, 29 April 1938, FR ANOM 1 AFFPOL 614/2.

80 Gardiner, *Cameroon*, p. 36; Callahan, *Sacred Trust*, p. 71.

war' turned real, mandate subjects in France were invited to sign up for military service, and a handwritten list of Cameroonians in Paris which probably dates from late 1939 or 1940 shows nine as having enlisted; one of them, Kassan Ndanke, had come from Germany.[81] Another of the volunteers was the law student Jacques Moudoute Bell, nephew of the martyred Rudolf Duala Manga. His application for naturalisation had been rejected several times, but by January 1940 the propaganda value of having a citizen-officer from the Cameroonian elite persuaded Mandel to order his naturalisation.[82]

Paul Malapa remembered a less positive experience of 1940. By now a successful professional boxer with an international reputation, he was able to evade labour conscription thanks to his familiarity with Galandou Diouf, and he had no intention of fighting for France. By contrast, a group of other Cameroonians, including Vincent Moudio, Victor M'Billo, Richard Dibotto, Rodolphe Tokoto, Harry Thomson Mandenge, and probably Charles M'bonga Egiomue had made up their minds to volunteer, but only on condition that they be allowed to serve on the same terms as European soldiers, 'without the *chéchia*'. This constitutes a noteworthy statement of identity. The *chéchia* was the red cap that identified French colonial troops. Its social valence was ambivalent at best; the *chéchia* was associated with the Senegalese who were 'senior' in a hierarchy of African subjects of the French Empire and could be read as symbolising the partnership between black and white Frenchmen, but it was also a typical 'prop' in popular caricatures of the black African.[83] The refusal of Cameroonians to wear it indicates that they saw it as a marker of subaltern status, of a coloniality which they rejected for themselves. Malapa describes a debate in the rue Victor Massé, in which he warned his friends against placing themselves at the mercy of the French state, but some of them did join up. As soon as German troops crossed the border into France in May 1940 they were arrested as potential 'fifth columnists' and interned in a prison in the south of France – where Malapa brought them food parcels when he could. Charles M'bonga Egiomue died in prison in St Étienne in 1941.[84]

[81] Handwritten list of black Africans in Paris: Louis Trochon, Pierre Manga N'Gongui, Jacques Moudoute Bell, Richard Dibotto, Kassan Ndanke, Pierre N'Dongo Bouli, Thomas Makembe, Jean Lucas Womenduga and Henri Priso. Womenduga was noted as discharged, Priso as stationed with the artillery in Orléans.

[82] Jacques Moudoute Bell to Mandel, 27 December 1939; Mandel to Naturalisation Service in the Interior Ministry, 29 January 1940: both FR ANOM 1 AFFPOL 1452.

[83] Berliner, *Ambivalent Desire*, pp. 9–36.

[84] 'Paul Malapa Décryptage', pp. 70, 79–80; ITS 40588626#1. It seems likely that the prison to which Malapa refers was St Charles prison in Digne (we are grateful to Jacky Tronel, Paris, for this advice).

The 'military' career of the recent medical graduate and hospital intern Henri Duala Manga Bell underlines the continuing ambiguities of the situation of Cameroonians in the crisis. He wrote to the Minister of Colonies in September 1938 – in the middle of the Munich crisis – placing himself at the disposal of the military 'in case of need'. On that occasion he was advised that since he was not yet naturalised he was under no obligation to serve, though his offer would be considered. The following April he sought permission to apply to join the medical corps in West Africa, but was rejected because he had not been naturalised. In the summer he applied to join the French army but was rejected on account of his age (he was thirty-one), and when he applied again in September 1939 the Minister for War cited 'the current state of the legislation' as a reason for turning him down. Instead, with the outbreak of war, he was accepted as a civilian conscript in the health service and posted to Morbihan (Brittany), where the influx of refugees from Belgium, the Netherlands and other parts of France was putting acute pressure on public services. After nine months he returned to Paris to work in a hospital.[85]

When Henri had completed his service to France, the work he returned to was not the practice of medicine for which he was qualified. Following years of successful lobbying by the medical profession against the admission of foreigners and newly naturalised doctors to practice, the Vichy government introduced a new law in August 1940 that barred anyone who had not been born in France of a French father from practising medicine. This was the first step in a process of racialising 'immigration' policy that would soon find its logical conclusion in the barring of Jews as such from the professions.[86] Henri reported in January 1941 that he did not expect to keep his job long, because his employers were showing a preference for 'metropolitan French' people even in posts like his. His last recourse was to seek permission to work as assistant to his wife, also a physician; although she was black, as a native of Guadeloupe she met the nationality conditions. In soliciting the support of the police authorities for her request for a licence to practise in Paris, the Director of the Economic Agency characterised the Bells as 'a little household of natives of the colonies represented by my Agency, whose sentiments are very French and which I would be happy to be able to help out'.[87]

85 Correspondence in FR ANOM 110COL 1003/3516. See also Archives départementales du Morbihan, *Le Morbihan en guerre*, pp. 17–18.
86 Caron, *Uneasy Asylum*, pp. 322–5.
87 Director of Economic Agency to General Secretary of the Prefecture of the Seine, 30 January 1941, FR ANOM 110COL 1003/3516, and other correspondence in the same file.

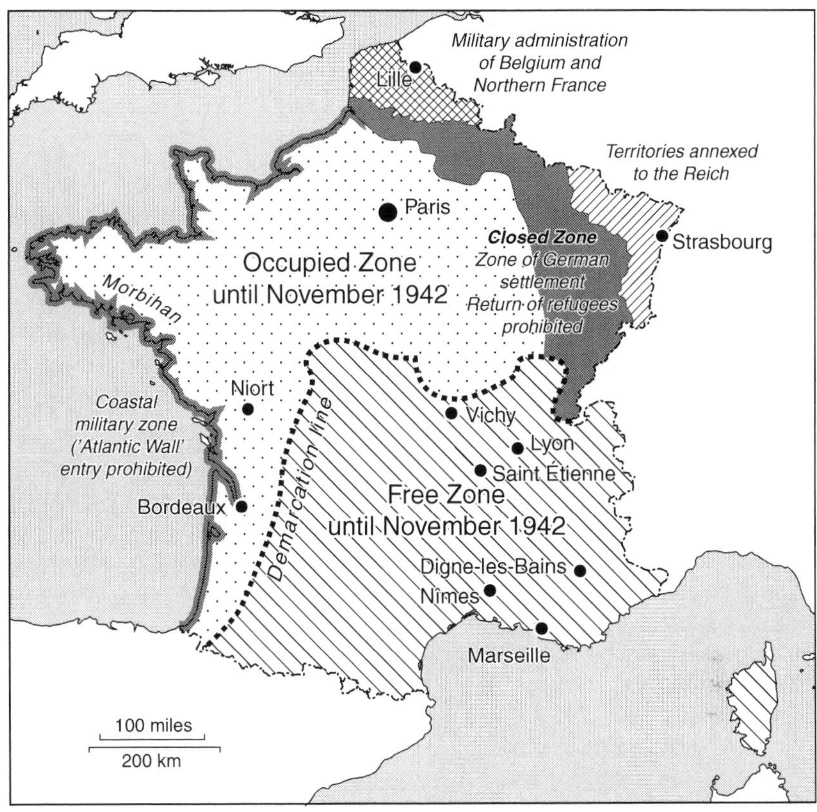

8.2 Occupied France

This episode reflects the pressures placed on black individuals and families by the defeat of France in June 1940 and the German occupation of the north and far west of the country, including Paris (Map 8.2). For a brief period Blacks were banned from performing in public.[88] A series of separate orders issued between July and September 1940 barred Jews and Blacks from crossing the line of demarcation from the 'free' to the occupied zone.[89] Africans who had fled Paris for the south with their white neighbours at the beginning of the German invasion, fearing that

[88] Ottley, *No Green Pastures*, p. 164. The Senegalese dancer Féral Benga reported that he was not allowed to dance under the German occupation: Gorer, *Africa Dances*, p. 4.

[89] Alary, *La Ligne de démarcation*, pp. 58–60, 183–4. From the summer of 1941 the Vichy government also prevented Jews from travelling from the occupied to the 'free' zone (ibid., p. 64).

the capital would be bombarded and taken by force, were unable to return home if they had travelled south, and communication between Africans settled in the far south and those in Paris and Bordeaux was cut off.[90] In November 1940 Jews and Blacks were barred from travelling first class on the Paris métro and required to ride in the rear carriages.[91] Official measures, limited though they were, provoked anxiety among the African population and created an atmosphere in which private racism could flourish. The Senegalese lawyer François-Xavier Benga remarked in November 1940 that his 'unhappy compatriots are completely disoriented at the moment, asking themselves anxiously whether France is going to deny them after they have sacrificed everything to defend her.'[92] In a set of notes apparently designed to be sent to the French puppet government in Vichy, the white industrialist Maurice Dollfus in the same month recorded the concerns of Blacks about the fate of the colonies and about not having been consulted in the armistice discussions. He also reported that the Germans were forbidding their personnel to visit shops and restaurants where Blacks worked and French employers were dismissing black workers in the hopes of ingratiating themselves with the occupiers. The last point he raised was 'the question of access to public places in Paris': '[I]t is worse than painful to see French shopkeepers refusing entry at their own initiative, even to Blacks wearing the Croix de Guerre, without being required to do so by the occupying authorities. We could cite the example of a café in Montmartre (Boudon) whose whole fortune was made by its black clientèle.'[93]

Africans and other Blacks had reason to fear more drastic consequences from German occupation. During the brief period between the German assault on 10 May 1940 and the capitulation on 22 June, over 1,500 black soldiers in the service of France were deliberately murdered by German troops both on the battlefield and as prisoners of war. As prisoners, they were brutalised and humiliated during the first months of the war.[94] Conditions improved for most of those in captivity by the end of the year, and this could have paradoxical results. Léopold Sédar

[90] For an overview of French population movements in the first year of the war, see Gemie, Reid and Humbert, *Outcast Europe*, pp. 55–131.

[91] Prefect of the Seine to Commissioner General for Jewish Questions, 10 June 1942, CDJC CXCIII_136_002. See also Schmid, Administrative Section of German Military Command in France to Head of Military Administration Paris, 10 October 1940, PAAA Paris 1275.

[92] Benga to Dollfus, 28 November 1940, FR ANOM 4003 COL 50.

[93] 'Question – Noirs et gens de couleur', FR ANOM 4003 COL 50. The attribution to Maurice Dollfus is speculative. See also Stovall, *Paris Noir*, p. 126.

[94] Scheck, *Hitler's African Victims*. For a summary history of colonial prisoners of war, see Mabon, *Prisonniers de Guerre*.

Senghor, who had been mobilised as an officer in a colonial regiment in 1939 while teaching near Paris, narrowly escaped being shot when taken prisoner in June 1940, but during the two years of captivity that followed he developed his knowledge of and affection for German language and culture.[95] But the dangers to black people inherent in the German presence were daily before their eyes during the war. It remains unclear how far French civilians white or black were aware of the atrocities of 1940, but escaped and released prisoners and white civilians like the *marraines* (nurse-social workers) who attended black prisoners would have been able to tell the story.[96] Most of the black prisoners were held in PoW camps on French soil, and after the German occupation of the south of the country in November 1942, African troops still under Vichy command were drafted for forced labour.

After the first shock of invasion and occupation, the Germans speculated on winning the hearts of the African troops in anticipation of taking over France's colonies. This was rapidly challenged by the mobilisation of some of France's African territories in support of De Gaulle's Free French; as early as August 1940 the French administration in Cameroon had turned against Vichy and hundreds of natives of the territory saw service with the Free French forces in the course of the war.[97] By the end of 1942 the American intervention, the Allied landings in North Africa and the successes of the Soviet counter-offensive made it clear that Germany had no hope of rebuilding a colonial empire in Africa.[98] This made the German authorities relatively indifferent to the situation of black prisoners, but the continued and extended occupation was clearly seen by some Frenchmen as a licence for overt racism. In May 1943 a town-hall clerk in the Auvergne reported to the Minister of Colonies that the mayor had repeatedly subjected him to verbal abuse, calling him 'dirty *nègre*' and 'coalman' before getting him sacked from his job: 'Veteran of the 1914–18 war, wounded in action, a Frenchman, I see myself as at home here. I will not accept being treated this way.' In response, the Director of the Political Section in Vichy acknowledged that this complaint was not exceptional. At the same time, his response indicates that the continuing sense of colonial mission and possibly renewed hope of fulfilling it made French administrators alert to the needs and sensitivities of Africans. He wrote of the 'inappropriateness

[95] He was released on medical grounds in February 1942 and returned to teaching: Riesz, 'Léopold Sédar Senghor'.

[96] For the latter, see de Gobineau, *Noblesse d'Afrique*; Mabon, *Prisonniers de Guerre*, pp. 68–98.

[97] Gardiner, *Cameroon*, p. 36. Félix Éboué, the native governor of Chad, also backed De Gaulle.

[98] Scheck, *Hitler's African Victims*, p. 51; Ottley, *No Green Pastures*, pp. 162–3.

of words and gestures to which our subjects and *protégés* from overseas have always shown themselves very sensitive' and of the need under the current circumstances to avoid any action that might 'ruffle their sense of attachment to France or be interpreted by them as a sign of distaste for the race to which they belong'.[99]

For educated Africans, the ambivalence and even sympathy of those in power helped to create safe spaces even in wartime. After 1942 Léopold Sédar Senghor, teaching in the Paris suburbs, formed one focus for meetings and discussions among young Africans at his flat in the rue Lamblardie. Another, more formal one was a centre for colonial students established by the Vichy authorities at 184 Boulevard St-Germain, whose comforts the students enjoyed while resisting any temptation to be sympathetic to the occupiers. The occupation of the formerly 'free' zone in November 1942 removed the barriers to travel that had existed before that, and in the last two years of the war, with the support of the French authorities, African students developed lively patterns of exchange across the metropole which one scholar has characterised as 'colonial tourism'. In 1943 they began to publish a bulletin, which was the first outlet for debates around the questions of African culture and identity that continued after the war. Alioune Diop, who would found *Présence Africaine*, played a leading role in this development.[100] This prepared the way for a shift in the centre of gravity of the African community from the Montmartre of the *maqueraux* to the intellectual and student milieu of the Left Bank in the first few years after the war, when 184 Boulevard St-Germain remained the scene of informal conversations and formal debates while Maria Diop ran her 'mini Tower of Babel' in the rue des Écoles.[101]

These freedoms were the preserve of colonial subjects like members of the Senegalese elite, who were able to circulate freely between Europe and Africa and maintain contact with family back in the colony.[102]

[99] Étienne Lebeau to Minister of Colonies, 11 April 1943; Office of Political Affairs, Ministry of the Navy and the Colonies to Prefect of Cantal, 10 May 1943: both FR ANOM 4003 COL 50.

[100] Vaillant, *Black, French and African*, p. 180; Städtler, '"Touristes coloniaux"', pp. 147–58. See also Grah Mel, *Alioune Diop*, pp. 54–5 on Alioune Diop's beginnings as a circulating intellectual on the Left Bank.

[101] See Kala Lobé, '"Ensemble" avec David Diop', pp. 62–94. He reports that by 1952, when he returned to Paris as the secretary of Alexander Douala Manga Bell after a sojourn in Cameroon, 'the negroes ha[d] deserted the Latin Quarter' (p. 89). Cf. Tyler Stovall's characterisation of the war years as producing a move 'from Montmartre to the Left Bank' for African-American intellectuals: *Paris Noir*, p. 136.

[102] For an example of this, see Diop, *À Rebrousse-gens*, pp. 161–7. The author was the brother of Alioune Diop.

Cameroonians remained at best on the margins of these developments. Andrea Manga Bell's son Manga was living in a small town on the Mediterranean in 1941. He had been working in a munitions factory in 1939, was evacuated to the south with the plant and tried unsuccessfully to flee over the Swiss border. His father, now in Senegal, sent for him and he was able to travel to Africa, where he joined the Free French army when the Vichy forces lost control of Senegal.[103] Ordinary Cameroonians had little or no access to support from families in what was now enemy territory. For them, and other Africans who were less well networked than the urban *évolués*, or of less interest to the authorities, everyday life could be a struggle. At the end of 1943 there were reportedly 1,000 African families dependent on government assistance.[104] And while a degree of normality existed for all Africans under the conditions of occupation, the everyday held constant risks and challenges, particularly as the war returned to French soil. In Joinville-le-Pont, as the Allies approached the Paris region, the sixteen-year-old David Diop and his friends formed a 'resistance group'. One day they set out on a 'mission', but were stopped by German troops who ordered them to help unload a train. When they refused, they were beaten and forced to work for the rest of the day. David returned to his distraught mother just before midnight.[105] At about the same age, Dualla Misipo's son Ekwé was first turned away when he volunteered for civil defence work with the words, 'We don't need people like you', though he was later welcomed by a more sympathetic (and politically progressive) air-raid warden.[106]

If the occupiers had reason to suspect or fear families or individuals, life could be very dangerous. By the end of 1943 there were over 2,000 German security service officers in France; they began very early to round up political enemies, among them political refugees, and they clearly had their sights on certain individuals.[107] Kouyaté fell into the hands of the Germans under circumstances that remain unclear. Sent to Mauthausen concentration camp in September 1943, he was deployed in armaments production; he died there the following July.[108] The 1942 order that all Blacks and mulattos be identified and registered

103 'Weißer Mann immer schlecht', pp. 19–22, citing a letter of Manga's to a German friend.

104 Genova, *Colonial Ambivalence*, pp. 191 and 217, citing Vichy correspondence in FR ANOM 4003 COL 50 and 97.

105 Diop, *Biographie*, pp. 22–3.

106 Misipo, *Métissages contemporains*, pp. 37–8.

107 Extract from a Report of the Reich Leader of the SS, 16 December 1943, PAAA Inland II-Geheim, R100761, frame 262431; Mitchell, *Nazi Paris*, p. 141.

108 ITS, 28559843.

applied in principle to all territories under German occupation. There is evidence, too, that ordinary Afro-Germans were under surveillance by virtue of their history in Germany. Andrea Manga Bell reported that she was watched by the German security services because of her association with Roth and other émigrés, and had to go into hiding in the country.[109] Maria Diop and her four children shared the benefits which the Vichy regime extended to the mothers of large families, and the children were able to continue their schooling in spite of the war. But once Nîmes was occupied by the Germans, she was disturbed to overhear an officer pointing her out to his companion with the words, 'That's the mother and her son.' Whether they were an object of interest simply as Africans or whether her history and that of her husband was known to the Germans, she was alarmed both at the remark and at the thought of revealing herself by responding in German (as her teenage son urged her to do).[110]

The experience of the Misipo family suggests a still more sinister pattern. In May 1939 Dualla Misipo lost his job at the pharmaceutical laboratory where he had worked since November 1937; the reasons for this are not clear. He applied for a posting back to the colonies and also sought to enlist in the army; by December 1940, having been rejected for military service because he was too old and still waiting to hear about the colonial posting, he was destitute. Ekwé Misipo later reported that the family briefly considered trying to join the Free French forces in Cameroon but abandoned the idea. Misipo managed to get work in a restaurant where, dressed in the stereotypical uniform and *chéchia* of a colonial soldier, he suffered the indignity of having to listen in silence to the racist observations of German officers. In 1944, according to Ekwé Misipo's memoir, Luise received a visit from two Gestapo officers looking for 'the black and the mulatto who live here'. Luise sent them packing, declaring in fluent German that their behaviour was unworthy of Germany, and her son remained convinced that it was only the advance of the western front and the liberation of Paris that saved them from arrest and deportation.[111]

Ekwé Misipo, like Maria Diop, records that the officers were surprised to be answered in German, but in this case it is probable that it was the fact of being German that put the family in danger. Dualla Misipo was on

[109] 'Weißer Mann immer schlecht', pp. 19–22. [110] Diop, *Biographie*, pp. 18–20.

[111] Yvon Gouet, Director of Economic Agency to Gaston Joseph, Director of Political Section, 3 December 1940; Secretary of State for the Colonies to Yvon Gouet, 6 December 1940, FR ANOM 110COL 10003/3554; Misipo, *Métissages contemporains*, pp. 28–32, 39–40.

record with the Gestapo as a troublemaker. Irrespective of his own qualities, though, the German government had begun to register all ethnic Germans and German nationals in France as early as 1938, and from mid 1942 the SS was committed to a project of repatriating all individuals of German blood.[112] In spite of her marriage, Luise Misipo remained a potential repatriate. At the end of 1941 the racial policy section in the German Foreign Office enunciated a logical corollary of the 'white wives' principle that had guided colonial administrators and their successors: any German woman abroad, irrespective of her formal nationality, represented Germany; if she had a relationship with a racial alien, she could nevertheless be 'recovered' for Germany, if necessary after a period of compulsory re-education, while any children could be sterilised.[113]

To be sure, not all German women were welcome to return to the national fold. Erna Pusch travelled to Strasbourg in 1937 to marry Peter Makembe. He had settled there after his adventures with the law and made a living as a small trader. In September 1939 they were evacuated along with most of the population of Strasbourg, in anticipation of a German invasion. They made their way to Paris and found an apartment in Montmartre. When the Germans did occupy Alsace and Lorraine, they undertook a programme of Germanisation and repatriation. But in October 1942 the Gestapo reported to the police in Strasbourg that Erna was forbidden to return – in spite of the fact that by this time her husband was dead.[114]

Theophilus Michael's son James, too, found it safer not to be a German in wartime, though for more complicated reasons. The Moroccan manager of the circus in which he had been working since 1928 decided to take the troupe to France in 1933. In 1937 James' German passport was due to expire, and when the Paris consulate refused to renew it ('You're not German any more. There are no black Germans') he was entirely without papers and forced to hide whenever the police came round. (The fact that he did not apply for French papers suggests

112 On the registration of Germans in France: PAAA Rechtsabteilung RIII, R46329. The repatriation of ethnic Germans was the responsibility of Himmler as Reich Commissioner for the Strengthening of German Nationhood, and the principal task of his deputy, the Head of the SS in Occupied France, Oberg, when he took up his post in April 1942: telegram signed Krueger, 6 August 1942, PAAA Inland II-C, R111360, frames 000167–8.

113 Rademacher, Referat DIII, to Abteilung R, 4 December 1941, PAAA Inland I-Partei, R99176, frames 00014–15.

114 File on Peter Mukuri Makembe, CAC 19949462-48-4642; file on Erna Makembe née Pusch, CAC 19940469-425-37178; household registration for Peter Mukuri Makembe, Strasbourg City Archives 603 MW 532.

that he was one refugee who remained outside of the networks of settled Cameroonians in Paris.) He had become sufficiently fluent in 'Moroccan', though, to pass for a native when the troupe visited Morocco the following year, and he managed to get a false Moroccan passport before returning to France. Back in Morocco at the outbreak of war, James was denounced as a German spy. He spent two months in jail in Casablanca before being offered the choice of joining the Foreign Legion or being interned as a foreigner: 'So I would have been German again. But they had cancelled my citizenship. If I had remained a German I would have been done for, since the Germans would have said "He's no German."' James opted for the Foreign Legion, in which he served for nearly seventeen years, rising to the rank of a non-commissioned officer.[115]

The prospect that Nazi racism would not stop at the Jews had been recognised by organisations like LICA and other early antifascists. Paradoxically, Blacks suffered first under the blanket discriminatory legislation of the early war years. The order restricting travel on the métro affected Blacks immediately, while it could not be enforced against the Jews until they were made 'visible' by the enforced wearing of the Star of David in 1942; the same is very likely true of the ban on crossing the demarcation line. In everyday life under occupation, the shared imperilment of Blacks and Jews generated paradoxes and alliances. James Michael's sister Juliana arrived in France aged sixteen in 1937, having been sent for by her older sister Christiane who had already been there for two years. After two years' work in a circus the arrival of the German armies drove her to seek work elsewhere. She found her way to a travelling menagerie, and was staying in the countryside in occupied West Central France when Gestapo officers arrived looking for 'Jews or people who look different'. Tipped off to Juliana's presence, they followed the menagerie to a fairground in Niort. At the German headquarters, Juliana was able to escape arrest by showing German identity documents that proved she was not Jewish while successfully pretending that she had forgotten all her German. For Juliana, too, the fact that she could understand German intensified the terror of the wartime situation: 'The Nazis were everywhere ... We, the circus, got around all over France. I saw a lot of things. You hear things, insulting things. Sometimes I thought: "If only you could speak...!" I mustn't. It was better, yes, better that way.'[116]

In wartime as in peacetime, Paul Malapa's story provides a particularly vivid example of the contradictory ways in which identities – German,

[115] Reed-Anderson, *Eine Geschichte von mehr als 100 Jahren*, pp. 45–6.
[116] Ibid., pp. 42–4.

Figure 8.2 Wedding of Paul and Suzanne Malapa, Paris 1941

French, black and Jewish – became entangled and shaped everyday life.[117] In the early 1930s Malapa's mother Frida was made aware that her father had been a baptised Jew, and Paul henceforth described himself as a '*Negerjude*'. In Paris, he took a job in the household of German refugees, and even applied to Jewish welfare organisations for support. He also took part in a short-lived project of organising an antifascist defence squad of black and Jewish boxers. This facilitated his introduction to the Polish immigrant Jew Leibisch Rubin, who brought his son Sam to Malapa for boxing training in the early 1930s. Malapa courted first a friend of the Rubins, and then the eldest daughter of the family, before finally marrying a younger daughter, Suzanne, in 1941 (Figure 8.2).

At this point Malapa was making a success of the war. In spite of the restrictions, he got a pass allowing him to travel back and forth across the line of demarcation by impressing the German propaganda bureau with his boxing credentials and his need to travel to international bouts. He accumulated capital by buying coffee from sailors in Marseilles and selling it on, and went on to purchase a hotel and cabaret in the port.

[117] Except where otherwise noted this account is based on 'Paul Malapa Décryptage'.

The business flourished thanks to the contacts he had established as a boxer. Malapa also became involved in some underground activities in association with the 'Liban' network of Armenian resistance fighters, and on his travels he sometimes smuggled Jews and Blacks across the demarcation line.[118] On one occasion this led to his arrest; Suzanne was also under arrest for a time. He reacted to the first news of the deportation of French Jews in 1942 by moving south with Suzanne and urging his in-laws to do likewise. Only Suzanne's youngest brother, Jules (Gilod), followed; her parents and elder sister were deported in July 1942 and perished in Auschwitz. With Malapa's help, Jules was able to acquire false papers and find work in the south of France, but he decided to risk returning to Paris. When he was picked up in April 1944 and interned in Drancy with other Jews awaiting deportation, Malapa returned to Paris to try to help. He remembered that he knew a Cameroonian who was working as foreman at the Gare d'Austerlitz, where furniture confiscated from deportees was warehoused, and who was in a position to requisition prisoners from Drancy for work there. Through the intervention of the ubiquitous Harry Thomson Mandenge he managed to arrange for Jules to be put on a work detail that would offer him an opportunity of escape. The opportunity never arose, and Jules was among the 878 men transported on 'Convoy 73' from Drancy on 15 May 1944; he was shot to death in Tallinn or Kaunas.[119]

The relative freedom of action associated with being neither French nor (actually) Jewish helped Paul Malapa to survive and flourish and to help others – up to a point. But while it might be expected that under the occupation the fact of being German would be an advantage, his testimony echoes the anxieties of others about revealing it. The last words in his interview, referring to an encounter with a Gestapo officer, are 'I don't speak German; I don't speak German.' At war's end, the fact of being or speaking German continued to be a liability, as the activists of the French Resistance engaged in a hunt for collaborators and traitors. Although the racial dimension of these early acts of reprisal and the process of *épuration* that followed remains unresearched, it is clear that it did not stop at white Europeans. The African-American journalist Roi Ottley reported seeing 'some three hundred Negroes being held at

[118] On the 'Liban Network', see Mandel, *In the Aftermath of Genocide*, p. 184. On the activity of the 'passeurs' who smuggled people across the demarcation line, and their links with the black market, see Alary, *La Ligne de démarcation*, pp. 87–150, 170–5.

[119] Rubin family papers and supporting materials, Don Alain Fillion, CDJC, CMLXXV (6)-15; [Fillion], 'Gilod Rubin'. What is documented in the CDJC and elsewhere about the management of the Austerlitz camp makes the details of the account improbable: Dreyfus and Gensburger, *Des camps dans Paris*.

Drancy as Fascist intriguers' in 1945. By contrast, it is well known that the *épuration* targeted women on various grounds. The German wives of French nationals, few as they were, were regarded with particular suspicion by the French authorities even in peacetime.[120] Ottley's account focuses on the internment of the white wife of an (unidentified) Cameroonian dancer, and as such it is a reminder of the multiple ways in which mixed couples were liminal. According to Dualla Misipo, his family also learned at the liberation the kind of challenge that a German woman married to an African of indeterminate status personified for the French sense of order as well as the German. By his account they were interned for three days because Luise was German.[121] The evidence of Misipo's own writing and his son's is that the hurts of these years stayed with him. A familiar character on the margins of the Présence Africaine group, he remained sceptical of the capacity of the Germans to overcome their racial prejudices. But he continued to write in German and to enjoy conversing (and no doubt reminiscing) in German with Maria Diop. In the memoir of his son Ekwé (which like Misipo's *Der Junge aus Duala* focuses on mixed marriage, though in celebratory mode) he appears as a figure of exile.[122]

120 Audeval, 'Une Question de catégorie?'; Genova, *Colonial Ambivalence*, p. 61.
121 Ottley, *No Green Pastures*, pp. 92–3; Dualla Misipo, Account of the Persecution, HHStAW 518/40437. This incident does not feature in Ekwé Misipo's memoir, which records liberation and the German capitulation in May 1945 in entirely positive terms, and could not be confirmed from other sources. On reprisals at liberation, see also Mabon, *Prisonniers de Guerre*, p. 129.
122 On the differences between the ways in which the two generations of Misipos processed the wartime experience, see Rosenhaft, '*Schwarze Schmach*'.

Epilogue

In 2010, Paul Malapa's son Benny (born in 1951) recounted an occasion when he and his wife stopped at a Cameroonian restaurant in Paris, carrying a bag of laundry because they were unable to afford their own place and were living with his mother. As they were eating they were approached by a stranger – 'no thing of beauty, [but] panama hat, Costas Rolland, shoes the same colour – magnificent!' The stranger had overheard the name Malapa and now made a deep bow to express his respect for a family that had been among the elite back in Cameroon. For Benny, this episode was entirely ironic. He and his brothers and sisters had been raised by their mother in the Jewish tradition and attended Jewish schools, and the first point of political and cultural identification for each of them had been the Zionist movement. At the time when the stylish stranger was saluting him as an African prince, Benny had found his way to revolutionary Socialism, and after making a career as a film-maker and music producer on the black cultural scene he attested in the 2010 interview that he identified less with Africa than with the African-American experience.[1]

Paul Malapa, by contrast, had pursued a vision of his African heritage after the war.[2] The irony here was that this had led to a recapitulation of his pre-war experience. In 1953 he returned to Cameroon hoping to claim his inheritance, with an appeal to the welfare authorities to look after his family. His wife Suzanne qualified for help from both the Jewish refugee aid agency and the state agency for refugees on the grounds that as the daughter of immigrant Polish nationals dispossessed by war and deportation she was stateless. The extent to which the children could be supported remained unclear, because they had their father's nationality. This, however, remained 'indeterminate' – or contested. Paul failed to establish himself in Cameroon, and in the event was expelled as a

[1] Interview with Benny Malapa, Paris, July 2010.

[2] Except where otherwise noted the source for Malapa's post-war experience is 'Paul Malapa Décryptage'.

troublemaker; when he was unable to find work back in Paris, he was threatened with expulsion from France. In both cases the question of where he had the *right* to remain was unresolved. When he claimed compensation for loss of property in Cameroon on the grounds that his expulsion had been illegal, the French court ruled that Malapa was not a Cameroon national; it took the view that because he was not resident in Cameroon in 1919 he could never even have been a *protégé* under the terms of the mandate, and accordingly could not have enjoyed the access to citizenship (including the status of Cameroon citizen created by decree in 1957) made available to them in subsequent years.[3] In the event he remained in Paris. Meanwhile, the welfare agencies thought that the only solution to his family's dilemma was for Paul to declare himself stateless, thus making himself and his children eligible for support. But he categorically refused to do this. He insisted that as the son of a Cameroonian native he *did* have a status and a claim to an identity as well as an inheritance. In a situation where the confusion of practices still left a space for choice, then, he chose to resist the use of a word which would have confirmed the uncertainty that had shaped his life – though in this case the cost of resistance was very high. In the draft scenario for a film, Benny writes of the years after Paul's return, when he became a chauffeur:

> There's a limousine ... parked in the street, his suits are well made and his life as the personal driver for American guests at the Plaza is played out in the best restaurants and night clubs. He clenches his teeth when they tell him to take the service entrance ... and tells himself that one day his hour of glory will come and he'll make triumphal return to Africa with his children and his white wife.[4]

Paul remains a kind of negative bellwether for the post-World War Two trajectory of our subjects. In his efforts to avoid deportation from Cameroon, he made contact with members of the Union des Populations du Cameroun, the nascent radical nationalist movement that would lead the armed struggle until Cameroon gained its independence in 1960. Paradoxically, this is the only point of contact between Germanophone Cameroonians and post-war political radicalism that has come to light. By this time Joseph Bilé had withdrawn from active politics, establishing himself as a respected family man and architect (Figure E.1); he died in Douala in 1959.[5]

Duala of the German and first French colonial generations did remain active in Cameroon's political life. Among them was Alexander Douala

[3] 'Malapa v. Public Prosecutor', 80–1.
[4] 'Chronologie Paul Malapa', unpublished MS, courtesy of Benny Malapa.
[5] Interview with Guilaume Dina Ekwe Bilé.

Figure E.1 Joseph Ekwe Bilé and daughter, Douala, around 1950

Manga Bell, who traded effectively on his paternal heritage and contributed actively to the construction of the figure of his father Rudolf as a national martyr. But as a result of shifting balances of interest and power in wartime, and not least the resistance of white settlers to the post-war reform moves, anti-colonial politics in Cameroon itself became increasingly radicalised as the centre of energy passed from the coastal elites to a new generation of up-country activists.[6] If anything, by the 1950s the period of German rule was coming to be regarded with nostalgia by those old enough to remember it, like Katharina Atangana, or the handful of former employees of the German colonial administration and pro-German activists who wrote to the government of the new Federal Republic to claim compensation or pension payments in the light of the post-war settlements.[7]

Paul Malapa, too, had pensions on his mind when he was interviewed in old age. He reported that he had got back in touch with Erika Mandenga Diek, still working in government service after the war, to get her advice about pension opportunities. In Germany, black people had begun to put their lives back together, and for them as for other survivors the disruptions and displacements of 1945 could provide opportunities for a new beginning or even for re-making oneself. In July 1945 the African-American war correspondent for the *Chicago Defender*, Edward Toles, expressed surprise on encountering black men and women walking openly through the ruins of liberated Berlin.[8] As Toles reported, some were former residents returning to the capital, whereas others had remained in the city throughout the fighting. Those he interviewed had experienced mixed fates. Gregor Kotto and the Berlin-born Paul Mierzwiack told him of their internment, while Josie Allen reported that her family had been bombed out several times and her German husband was missing. Allen and Mierzwiack had found work with the Soviet occupation administration. Elsewhere, the English skills that several Cameroonians and their children possessed helped them find at least temporary employment with the American occupiers; one second-generation man carried papers for a time that identified him as an American national, and at least two second-generation women emigrated

[6] Joseph, *Radical Nationalism*; Argenti, *The Intestines of the State*, pp. 167–72; Austen and Derrick, *Middlemen*, pp. 176–91.

[7] On Katharina Atangana, see Chapter 5. For claims for financial support from Cameroon, PAAA B 81-953, B 81-478b. On nostalgia, see Schmidt-Soltau, 'Postkoloniale Konstruktionen der kolonialen Begegnung'.

[8] Edward Toles, 'German-Born Negroes Free in Berlin', 'Reds Give Jobs to Berlin Negroes', 'Berlin Intermarriage Awaits Red OK', *Chicago Defender*, 14 July 1945, 1–2 and 28 July 1945, 1–2 and 11.

to the United States, one, Heinrich Dibonge's daughter, as a GI bride.[9] The Soviets had provided Mierzwiack and his family with a new home in a residence formerly owned by an SS officer, while in other parts of the city Cameroonian German families found refuge in nissen huts set up for bombed-out households. Toles reported that Kotto, who had found work as a doorman at Berlin's fashionable Rio Rita nightclub, was waiting hopefully for the Soviets to grant him permission to marry his German partner. This was a hope that others clearly shared. With restrictions on African-German partnerships lifted, a number of former colonial subjects and their children married within months of the end of the war.

Renewing familial and friendship ties which had been disrupted could prove to be a longer, more laborious and stressful process. Families that had been divided by war and internment, like the Egiomues and Boholles, began to search for each other as soon as they could. From a Displaced Persons (DP) camp in Frankfurt Theodor Michael began enquiring about the whereabouts of his surviving sister in 1947, but it would take fifteen years before the Michaels were finally reunited. A handful of Cameroonians and their children who had sought refuge in France during the Nazi period chose to stay there, while in the immediate post-war period others, including members of the Garber and Egiomue families, moved from Germany to France on at least a temporary basis. As Paul Malapa told it, this was because they were entitled to claim social benefits there, since in the swift sorting-out of people who were displaced or of uncertain status after the war many had been definitively assigned French nationality.[10]

At the same time, members of both generations engaged in efforts to reconstruct networks and revive community – characteristically by reviving a particular kind of performance milieu.[11] The Pinguin Bar, promoted as 'Berlin's first *Negerbar*', opened at Bülowstraße 6 in the city's West End in summer 1949. Rudolf Boholle and his brother-in-law,

9 Isaac Jones, 'Curiosity Brought Tan German Girl to America', *Baltimore Afro-American*, 4 June 1949, B3.

10 Reed-Anderson, *Eine Geschichte von mehr als 100 Jahren*, pp. 42–6; 'Paul Malapa Décryptage', p. 35. The reassignment of nationality emerges from the records of displaced persons held in ITS (and see also Chapter 3), but it was not universally the case. Andrea Manga Bell's French citizenship was denied after the war, and at least one second-generation émigré was still stateless in the 1950s and faced the familiar problems travelling with a circus.

11 The following account is based on: Interview with Herbert Reiprich, Berlin, April 2011; 'Weißer Mann immer schlecht'; 'Jack Allan und der Alex', 'Der Boden wurde zu heiß. Westerland trauert um seine "Pinguin Bar"', *Hamburger Abendblatt*, 14 February 1950, p. 8, and 21/22 October 1950, p. 1.

Figure E.2 Zoya Aqua-Kaufmann and Dorothea Diek in the Pinguin Bar, 1950

Cornelius van der Want, had already tried to start up a combo in East Berlin, where most of the survivors now lived, along with Dorothea Diek. The idea behind the Pinguin, spearheaded by Kala Kinger, was to create a nightclub in which the entire personnel were of African heritage. Financial backing came from a German couple named Gruß and Hans von Hellfeld, Zoya Aqua-Kaufmann's partner and the father of her child. Zoya was one of at least eight Cameroonians or their children associated with the bar while another dozen or so men and women of African heritage were also involved at various times (Figure E.2). The project combined elements of the pre-war African welfare associations and Bruce and Hillerkus' Afrika-Schau, and there was a degree of continuity in terms of those involved. The bar not only functioned as a sociable space in which members of Germany's black community reconvened, but it also provided employment for those involved. In the tradition of the Afrika-Schau the Pinguin played on the continued German fascination with the exotic in terms both of décor and of the live performances it featured. 'Elegant' and 'exotic' were the terms in which it was described in press reports. The walls were decorated with African masks and spears, and there was also an African throne.

In the post-war period a performance of blackness was no longer the only available survival strategy for Blacks in Germany, but for many long-term residents playing the 'exotic' had long since become a career. In the 1950s there was still some film work to be had in productions such as *Zehn kleine Negerlein* (1954) or *Tante Wanda aus Uganda* (1957) playing highly racialised roles. Within the setting of the Pinguin, however, participants could determine for themselves the musical repertoires or dance choreography they performed. The house band, which included at various times Thomas Ngambi ul Kuo and Louis Brody on drums, Herbert Reiprich (Dorothea Diek's husband) and Günter Egiomue on guitar and Kwassi Bruce on piano, frequently played samba, jazz or African-American spirituals. The classically trained Bruce also liked to include interludes of classical music during performances. Guest performances were given by touring artists such as the African-American singer Arstella Whittier and Harlem Kiddies jazz band as well as Josie Allen's brother Willi McAllen (born Wilhem Panzer), who had returned to Germany from wartime exile in Turkey.

Renewed popular enthusiasm for jazz, particularly in Berlin, helped ensure that the Pinguin enjoyed considerable success. It also proved popular with African-American troops stationed in the city. In summer 1950 the bar and personnel relocated to the holiday resort of Westerland on the North Sea island of Sylt in order to take advantage of the tourist season there. In Westerland the bar was a hit. With entrance prices starting at 50 Marks and rising to 125 Marks it remained an exclusive address. Its popularity, however, was not enough to stave off the increasing financial difficulties of its new majority backer Ernst Ring. The enigmatic Ring, a now forgotten German racing driver, ran up huge debts thanks in part to his expensive lifestyle. While he was competing in a race in East Germany the tax authorities in Westerland raided the bar and despite the protests of the personnel it was closed for good in August 1950.

Performance continued to provide a context for the maintenance of connections among Blacks across Germany, too. The post-war hunger for affordable entertainment led to a rapid revival of circuses and travelling spectacles in the provinces, and Hermann Kessern reconvened his troupe along with other veterans and some new peformers. Willi McAllen took the Pinguin sound to Kessern's home town of Crailsheim in 1957. During and after the war connections also continued among performers in Hanover, Berlin and Bavaria. Herbert Reiprich recalled that an early meeting-place for members of the black community was the autobahn service station at Helmstedt.[12] Helmstedt was the main point at which travellers crossed the dividing line between the Soviet Zone, in which Berlin lay, and the rest of Germany; after the creation of the Federal Republic and the German Democratic Republic in 1949 it was part of a heavily policed international border. The choice or memory of Helmstedt as a meeting-place signals both the geographical breadth of post-war black networks and the political conditions that would make it difficult to maintain connections between Berlin and the rest of Germany.

With the demise of the Pinguin Bar the formal ties holding the reconstructed black community together appear to have loosened. While a number of those involved chose to return to Berlin, others decided to seek their luck outside of Germany or retreated into their private lives. By this time the group of ex-German colonial subjects and their children was greatly reduced in number. By the end of the 1950s only three Cameroonians who had arrived in Germany before 1914 were still alive. A residue of informal bonds among some of their German-born children still remained, connected by genuine friendship and/or the shared experiences of the Nazi and post-war periods. These alone, however, were not enough to sustain any coherent community, particularly when one consequence of Nazi policy had been to make it impossible for some members of the second and third generations to have children of their own.

The example of another group whose members suffered substantially from sterilisation under the Nazis, German 'Gypsies', tells us how difficult that particular form of trauma made it to reconstruct personal and community life after the war – by contrast with those survivors who were able to take their 'revenge' by marrying and having children even in the DP camps.[13] Irrespective of the nature of their trauma, moreover, the lives of many other survivors were characterised by a period of silence within families. We can see signs of both of these patterns in the limited evidence we have for Afro-Germans after the war, for example Paul Malapa's comment that second-generation women preferred not to talk about *Rassenschande* cases, or in cases where individuals who suffered sterilisation chose to suppress that in their compensation claims. Most of

[12] Firla, *Der kameruner Artist*, pp. 181–9; interview with Herbert Reiprich.
[13] Krokowski, *Die Last der Vergangenheit*; Grossmann, 'Victims, Villains, and Survivors'.

the direct testimony to sterilisation on the part of the subjects themselves dates from the 1980s or later.

The question of what it was possible to say, or how far it was possible to construct a collective narrative tying together past and present, in the first decades after the war is important to understanding the trajectory of black community. Those possibilities were governed not only by processes internal to the community but also by the cultural and political conditions that prevailed in post-war West Germany. A key moment in the dialogue between the two is the process by which black men and women sought recognition and compensation for what they had suffered under the Nazis. Opportunities for this existed from a very early stage. In the immediate aftermath of the war, for example, the Berlin municipal government set up a commission whose function was to register individuals who qualified for social benefits as Victims of Fascism; Josefa Boholle, Dorothea Diek and Zoya Aqua-Kaufmann were registered with the commission by 1947, and its representatives supported them in subsequent claims. The Hamburg and Kiel municipal authorities also provided support to black victims in the first years after the war. The Basic Law of the Federal Republic promulgated in 1949 included a commitment to compensation for victims of Nazi persecution, and by 1953 each of the constituent states had passed compensation laws. Under the federal legislation that followed, compensation could be paid to individuals who had suffered persecution or abuse on political, religious or racial grounds; they could claim in respect of long-term damage to health, imprisonment, death of family members, loss of property or reduction of income, or reduction in opportunities for occupational development. Adjustments in the law after 1953 signal the problems that arose in applying its (deliberately) limited terms to the very wide range of forms of abuse enacted, licensed and encouraged by the Nazi system.[14] In particular, while it was understood that Jews had been persecuted on racial grounds and this could easily be demonstrated with reference to the Nuremberg Laws, willingness to acknowledge the victim status of other groups was delayed by a combination of ignorance of the detail of Nazi policy and prejudice on the part of the responsible administrators. The exclusion of 'Gypsies' from the category of victims was the most consistently perverse: until 1962 the official understanding was that the grounds for their persecution had only become 'racial' with the 1942 order to deport them to Auschwitz; measures of exclusion, internment, forced labour and sterilisation that took place between 1935 and 1942,

[14] See Frei *et al.* (eds.), *Die Praxis der Wiedergutmachung.*

considered on the basis of individual claims, were commonly judged to have been legitimate forms of treatment for people who had presented themselves as criminal or work-shy.[15]

Black people had more mixed success in their claims for compensation. Official records and published personal testimony have provided documentation so far for claims in respect of twenty-four members of our families, including their white partners, children and grandchildren. Of the twenty claims whose outcomes are clear, seven resulted in compensation payments, all of them to members of the first and second generations. Claims were rarely completely successful on the first application; in two cases the last payments were approved in the 1960s, in one in 1981. The most consistently successful claim was that for reduced occupational opportunities. The reasons for rejection were many: the link between incarceration or forced labour and long-term health problems was not easy to prove, and where sterilisation featured in the claim it was not always accepted that the grounds were racial. Individuals who had a criminal record or had been interned as 'asocials' made unconvincing claimants. The fact that someone had served in the army or been in employment during the war was treated as *prima facie* evidence that they had not been victims. The verbal and psychological abuse suffered by white wives was not covered by the legislation.

This mixed success is a reminder that black Germans remained ambiguously integrated in German society. The tenacity of individual men and women in pursuing their rights and entitlements is familiar from previous decades. Similarly familiar are the surprise at their very existence, uncertainty about their status and ambivalent attitudes ranging from sympathy to dismissal on the part of white Germans that recur in the compensation records. Beyond this, Zoya Aqua-Kaufmann's compensation claim, though one of the successful ones, is suggestive of the way in which Nazism and war forced a break in the already fragile public memory about the black presence in Germany. When she first applied for compensation in Berlin in 1951, action on her claim was delayed because she presented herself as a victim of antisemitic persecution, arguing that because her mother was half-Jewish and her father black she counted as a Jew. This led the authorities to focus on the question of how Jewish she was, starting with the question of how Jewish her mother was. They judged in the first instance that her claim to be Jewish was unsubstantiated because her mother had been allowed to marry an Aryan during the war, and that her claim to have been threatened with sterilisation was

[15] See most recently von dem Knesebeck, *The Roma Struggle for Compensation.*

implausible because the available documentation indicated that there had been no discussion of sterilising Jews among the Nazi leadership before 1942. As formulated, this ruling was not only internally contradictory but based on ignorance of the fine print of the Nuremberg Laws – a partial understanding of the scope and detail of Nazi policy that was characteristic of the first post-war decade. In the document recording the decision, the fact of her African heritage was acknowledged as 'clear from her Jewish-negroid appearance', but no account was taken of it in the light of the overriding question of her Jewishness. Zoya's appeal against the ruling made clear that the decision to present her as a Jewish rather than a black victim had been made by the bureaucrat handling her claim, whom she characterised as being challenged beyond his capacity by her case.

> I've come to this conclusion because of the comment which he repeatedly made to me, and which meant that every time I appeared in the office his colleagues couldn't conceal their amusement. He kept saying: 'Well, I may believe your father is a *Neger*, but the higher authorities don't have to believe it, since they can't see you!' In spite of my suggestion that . . . he could add a note that I am a mulatto, so *Negermischling*, or add some convincing pictures, he wasn't to be persuaded . . . In order to convince you of my racial background, I am adding five dated photos from various periods in my life, which prove beyond a doubt that my father was a *Neger*, and not just 'according to me'.

The appeal precipitated a review which led to the acknowledgement that Zoya was 'indubitably a *Negermischling*' – on the basis of her own and her mother's testimony but above all of her appearance. It was also acknowledged (this bureaucrat was better informed) that for this reason her relationship with her white partner would have been grounds for pursuit by the Gestapo, so that her claim to persecution was credible.

This exemplifies the way in which Nazi policy and practice had unsettled public understandings of race, without being able to enforce the Nazis' own vision of 'purity of the blood'. Making the status of Jews as victims of 'racial' persecution self-evident in terms both of law and of public and institutional awareness not only threw the victim status of other racialised groups into doubt but also tested popular and official understanding of who those others were, where they came from and what they had a right to expect. We can see the compensation officials falling back on the language of racial stereotypes – a language which Zoya herself could not avoid in 'proving' her 'racial' status. And as noted above, films of the 1950s also purveyed naive racialised images of Africans. There is a continuity here with pre-war discourses. And at the same time the portrayal of German Africans and their children, in the few examples we have available, seems curiously detached from the history of and reasons for their presence. Second-generation women feature in occasional reports in the popular press as 'the granddaughter of an African king' or visiting princesses. The 1950 article in which *Der Spiegel* reported on the background to the shooting of Manga Duala Manga Bell by his father is characteristically ambiguous. Under the rubric 'Colonies', it offers a serious and detailed account of the history of the Bells in Germany and Cameroon, and includes a sketch of the Pinguin Bar and its performers in which their German education and political views (including the membership of one of them in the official party of the GDR) are cited. At the same time its title ('White man always bad') and the issue's cover image of one of the Pinguin performers in samba costume playing a drum seem calculated to appeal to a popular taste for exoticism detached from any particular historical referent.[16] In 1959–60 Hermann Kessern stood in for a 'Togolese chief' in a small-scale Afrika-Schau that toured schools in Württemberg; what they were displaying was generic African-ness (complete with wild-animal handling).[17] And when the doughty Erika Mandenga Diek was voted Hamburg's 'most beautiful Granny' in a public competition in 1970, the same journalist who characterised her as an economist and retired civil servant could not forbear to mention that her father was 'after all a direct descendant of King Manga Bell'.[18] While this is one of the many areas which call for further detailed research, it might be suggested that these are symptoms of a break in public discourse around colonialism and its consequences, in which even nostalgic images of the colonial past had little purchase and which made the presence of a third generation of German-born Blacks inexplicable.[19] In this context, and with many pre-war allies in anti-colonial and anti-racist struggles dead or still in exile, articulating community would have meant speaking into a void.

At the same time, West Germans were developing new discourses of 'race' in response to the appearance of a new generation of German-born Blacks: the children born to German women and African-American soldiers with the occupying forces. Like the Rhineland children of the 1920s and 1930s, the roughly 5,000 *Besatzungskinder* were more numerous than other Afro-Germans and their existence carried a heavy symbolic meaning, as a signal of national defeat, as well as calling for the mobilisation of considerable moral and material resources. As part of the

[16] *Der Spiegel*, 24 August 1950, cover photo and pp. 19–22.
[17] Firla, *Der kameruner Artist*, pp. 190–200.
[18] 'Die schönste Oma darf zu Willy Brandt', *Hamburger Abendblatt*, 25 May 1970, p. 6.
[19] On the rhythms of colonial memory after 1945, see Albrecht, '(Post-) Colonial Amnesia?'; Schilling, *Postcolonial Germany*.

wider phenomenon of occupation and reconstruction under American influence, they served to further distance post-war Germans from the longer African and colonial history that they shared with black people.

Other scholars have written in depth about the experiences of the *Besatzungskinder* and their implications for West German society and culture.[20] From the point of view of trajectories of community, an aspect of that history that remains to be explored is the possibilities for contact and interchange between Germans of African descent and members of this new generation, as well as those other black people who arrived in Germany by various routes between 1945 and the 1980s. To do so here would make an already long story even longer. The authors of *Farbe bekennen*, that breakthrough text with which we began our version of the story, testified to the absence of such contacts – to their own sense of individual isolation in the early 1980s – and to the liberating effect that first finding each other, and then finding other Afro-Germans had on their imaginations and sense of self. They describe their encounter with the daughters of Mandenga Diek and Kala Kinger as deeply moving and exciting: 'Suddenly we discovered that our history hadn't begun in 1945.' In that moment a narrative linking past and present was generated of the kind that has the potential to sustain community. In the succeeding three decades of research on the first generations of black Germans, much has depended on the fact that members of the earlier generations were in contact with one another, able and willing to tell their own stories and to refer researchers to their friends and relatives. Their dialogue with activists and scholars of the post-war generations may by now mean that, as Katharina Oguntoye and May Opitz wrote in 1986, 'we no longer have to keep explaining our existence'.[21]

[20] Lemke Muniz de Faria, *Zwischen Fürsorge und Ausgrenzung*; Fehrenbach, *Race after Hitler*; Fenner, *Race under Reconstruction*; Schroer, *Recasting Race after World War II.*

[21] Oguntoye *et al.*, 'Vorwort der Herausgeberinnen', pp. 9–10.

Bibliography

ARCHIVAL SOURCES

AUSTRIA

Wiener Stadt- und Landesarchiv

BELGIUM

Rijksarchief Beveren

CAMEROON

Archives Nationales, Buea
Archives Nationales, Yaoundé

FRANCE

Archives Départementales de la Loire, Saint Étienne
Archives Nationales, Centre des Archives d'Outre-Mer, Aix-en-Provence
Archives Nationales, Centre des Archives Contemporaines, Fontainebleau
Archives Nationales, Centre des Archives Diplomatiques, Nantes
Centre de Documentation Juive Contemporaine, Paris
Strasbourg City Archives

GERMANY

Amtsgericht Charlottenburg
Archiv der Erzabtei St Ottilien
Bayerisches Hauptstaatsarchiv, Munich
Bundesarchiv, Berlin
Deutsches Exilarchiv, Deutsche Nationalbibliothek, Frankfurt a.M.
Diakoniegemeinschaft Bethel (Berlin), Archives
Diözesanarchiv Limburg
Gedenkstätte Sachsenhausen
Geheimes Staatsarchiv Preußischer Kulturbesitz, Dahlem
Hessisches Hauptstaatsarchiv Wiesbaden

Hessisches Staatsarchiv Darmstadt
Institut für Stadtgeschichte Frankfurt a.M.
International Tracing Service, Bad Arolsen
Johann Wolfgang Goethe Universitätsarchiv, Frankfurt a.M.
Kreis- und Stadtarchiv Hildburghausen
Landesamt für Bürger- und Ordnungsangelegenheiten, Abt. I – Entschädigungsbehörde, Berlin
Landesarchiv, Berlin
Landesarchiv Schleswig-Holstein, Schleswig
Ludwig Maximillians Universität, Munich, Universitätsarchiv
Mahn- und Gedenkstätte Ravensbrück
Onckenarchiv des Bundes Evangelisch-Freikirchlicher Gemeinden in Deutschland, Elstal
Politisches Archiv des Auswärtigen Amts, Berlin
Staatsarchiv Hamburg
Staatsarchiv Würzburg
Stadtarchiv Bonn
Stadtarchiv Chemnitz
Stadtarchiv Crailsheim
Stadtarchiv Darmstadt
Stadtarchiv Düsseldorf
Stadtarchiv Hannover
Stadtarchiv Kiel
Stadtarchiv Langenau
Stadtarchiv Mülheim
Stadtarchiv München
Stadtarchiv Ulm
Staatsarchiv Bremen
Thüringisches Staatsarchiv, Meiningen

NETHERLANDS

Regionaal Historisch Centrum Eindhoven

POLAND

Gedenkstätte Stutthof
State Archives Katowice/Oswiecim

RUSSIA

Russian State Archive of Socio-Political History, Moscow

SWITZERLAND

Mission 21, Basel

UNITED KINGDOM

Bristol Record Office Archive
National Archives, Kew

UNITED STATES

United States Holocaust Memorial Museum

INTERVIEWS

Emilien Joseph Manga Douala Bell, Douala, March 2006, January 2008
Grace Eyango Ekwe Bilé, Douala, March 2006
Guillaume Dina Ekwe Bilé, Douala, March 2006
Valère Epée, Douala, March 2006
Suzanne Kala Lobe, Douala, March 2006
Benny Malapa, Paris, July 2010
Theodor Wonja Michael, telephone interview, August 2009
Dr Thomas Barla Moukoko, Douala, March 2006
Suzanne Ebokulu Mukumbulan, Bonaberi, March 2006
Herbert Reiprich, Berlin April 2011
N. N., son of Zoya Aqua-Kaufmann, April 2011

FILM

Okuefuna, David, *Hitler's Forgotten Victims* (1997)

RADIO BROADCASTS

'Die erste Erfahrung war die Erfahrung der Ausgrenzung Theodor M. Aus dem Leben eines deutschen Staatsbürgers schwarzer Hautfarbe', DeutschlandRadio Cologne, 17 July 1995

PUBLISHED SOURCES

PERIODICALS

Der Abend (Berlin)
Afrika Nachrichten
Der Artist: Fachblatt für Unterhaltungsmusik und Artistik
Atlanta Daily World
Baltimore Afro-American
Berliner Börsen-Zeitung
Berliner Illustrirte Zeitung
Berliner Tageblatt
Berliner Volkszeitung
Blüthen und Früchte aus unserem Arbeitsfelde für unsere Freunde
Bulletin des Informations- und Presseamtes der Bundesregierung

Chicago Defender
Crailsheimer Heimatpost
Crisis
Daily Evening Bulletin (San Francisco)
Darmstädter Zeitung
Deutsche Juristen-Zeitung
Deutsches Kolonialblatt
Le Droit de Vivre
Echo aus Afrika
Film-Kurier
Freiburger Zeitung
Der Gemeinde-Bote. Monatliche Mitteilungen der Ersten Baptisten-Gemeinde Berlin SO
Globus: Illustrierte Zeitschrift für Länder- und Völkerkunde
Hamburger Abendblatt
Heidenkind
Hohenloher Tagblatt
Der Kämpfer
Kladderadatsch
Klinische Wochenschrift
Kölnische Zeitung
Missionsblätter St. Ottilien
National-Zeitung
Neue Zeit: Das Illustrierte Morgenblatt
New Journal and Guide
New York Amsterdam News
New York Times
Norfolk Journal and Guide
Pädagogische Blätter
Pall Mall Gazette
Philadelphia Tribune
Pittsburgh Courier
Der Spiegel
Staufener Wochenblatt
Stern der Heiden
Stern von Afrika
Teltower Kreisblatt
The Times
Unsere Heidenmission
Velhagen und Klasings Monatshefte
Verhandlungen der Berliner Gesellschaft für Anthropologie, Ethnologie und Urgeschichte
Völkischer Beobachter
Zwickauer Neuste Nachrichten

OFFICIAL PUBLICATIONS

Adressbuch für Danzig und Vororte
Adressbuch für Danzig

Adressbuch Danzig
Adressbuch Ostseebad Zoppot
Amtlicher Anzeiger: Beiblatt zum Hamburgischen Gesetz- und Verordnungsblatt
Berliner Adressbuch
Danziger Einwohnerbuch
Hamburger Adressbuch
Journal Officiel de la République Française
Ministerial-Blatt für die Preussische innere Verwaltung
Ministerialblatt des Reichs- und Preussischen Ministeriums des Innern
Neues Adressbuch für Danzig und Vororte, 1918. Gdańsk
Neues Adressbuch für Danzig und Vororte, 1919. Gdańsk
Reichsgesetzblatt
Verhandlungen des Reichstags

OTHER PRIMARY TEXTS

Abbott, Robert S., 'My Trip Abroad. VII: Sojourning in Germany', *Chicago Defender*, 21 December 1929, pp. 1 and 10

'My Trip Abroad. VIII: The Negro in Berlin', *Chicago Defender*, 28 December 1929, pp. 1 and 8

Atangana, Karl and Paul Messi, *Jaunde-Texte*, ed. Martin Heepe (Hamburg: L. Friederichsen, 1919)

Bauche, Manuela, '"Im Zirkus gibt es keine Hautfarbe – nur gute und schlechte Artisten": Die Geschichte der Familie Burkett-Dünkeloh', in Heike Schmidt (ed.), 'Mündliche Geschichte – Afrika Erinnern. Lebensgeschichten afrodeutscher und afrikanischer Berlinerinnen' (manuscript, Seminar für Afrikawissenschaften, Humboldt-Universität zu Berlin, 2004), pp. 1–108

Baum, Marie, *Rückblick auf mein Leben* (Heidelberg: Kerle, 1950)

Berger, Astrid, '"Sind Sie nicht froh, daß Sie immer hier leben dürfen?"', in Katharina Oguntoye, May Opitz and Dagmar Schultz (eds.), *Farbe bekennen: Afro-Deutsche Frauen auf den Spuren ihrer Geschichte* (1986; Frankfurt a.M.: Fischer, 1992), pp. 115–20

Böckheler, Nathanael, *Theodor Christaller: Der erste deutsche Reichsschullehrer in Kamerun* (Leipzig and Schwäbisch Hall: Buchhandlung für innere Mission, 1897)

Buchheim, Max, *Arbeitsmaterial zur Gegenwartskunde* (Hanover: Hermann Schroedel, 1964 edn)

Buchner, Max, *Aurora colonialis: Bruchstücke eines Tagebuchs aus dem ersten Beginn unserer Kolonialpolitik* (Munich: Piloty & Loehle, 1914)

'Chronologie Paul Malapa', unpublished manuscript, courtesy of Benny Malapa

Degras, Jane (ed.), *The Communist International 1919–1943: Documents*, vol. II: *1923–1928* (London: Oxford University Press, 1960)

Diop, Birago, *À Rebrousse-gens* (Paris: Présence Africaine, 1985)
Diop, Maria, *Biographie de David Léon Mandessi Diop* (Paris: Présence Africaine, 1980)
Dominik, Hans, *Kamerun: Sechs Kriegs- und Friedensjahre in deutschen Tropen* (Berlin: Stilke, 1911)
Du Bois, W. E. B., *The Dark Princess* (New York: Harcourt Brace, 1928)
Ekollo, Joseph, *Wie ein Schwarzer das Land der Weißen ansieht* (Basel: Verlag der Basler Missionsbuchhandlung, 1908)
Ekollo, Thomas, *Mémoires d'un pasteur camerounais (1920–1996)* (Yaoundé: Éditions Clé, 2003)
[Fillion, Alain], 'Gilod Rubin', at www.convoi73.org/temoignages/043_gilod_rubin/index.html [accessed 30 November 2012]
de Gobineau, Hélène, *Noblesse d'Afrique* (Paris: Fasquelle, 1946)
Goll, Claire, *Der Neger Jupiter raubt Europa* (1926; Berlin: Argon, 1987)
Gorer, Geoffrey, *Africa Dances* (Harmondsworth: Penguin, 1945)
Hauß, K., *Der Pionier der Balimission: Aus dem Leben von Ferdinand Ernst* (Basel: Verlag der Basler Missionsbuchhandlung, 1910)
Hill, Robert A. (ed.), *The Marcus Garvey and Universal African Improvement Association Papers,* vol. X: *Africa for the Africans 1923–1945* (Berkeley: University of California Press, 2006)
Hüsgen, Eduard, *Ludwig Windthorst: Sein Leben, sein Wirken* (Cologne: J. P. Bachem, 1911)
Jacob, Ernst Gerhard, *Kolonialpolitisches Quellenheft: Die deutsche Kolonialfrage 1918–1935* (Bamberg: Buchner, 1935)
Kala Lobé, Iwiyè, '"Ensemble" avec David Diop, mon frère', in Société Africaine de Culture (ed.), *David Diop: Témoignages – Études* (Paris: Présence Africaine, 1983), pp. 63–94
Karsten, Paula, 'Kamerun in Berlin und deutsche Briefe von Kamerun', *Globus: Illustrierte Zeitschrift für Länder- und Völkerkunde*, 6/72 (1897), 97–9
Kerrl, Hans, *Nationalsozialistisches Strafrecht: Denkschrift des Preußischen Justizministers* (Berlin: Decker, 1933)
Liepmann, Heinz, 'Häfen, Mädchen und Seeleute', *Velhagen und Klasings Monatshefte*, 47 (1932), 283–5
von Luschan, Felix, *Beiträge zur Völkerkunde der deutschen Schutzgebiete* (Berlin: Dietrich Reimer, 1897)
'Lydias Geheimis: Am Leben blieb der schwarze Sohn', *Der Spiegel*, 4 December 1948, pp. 6–7
Makembe, Peter, 'Duala-Texte', *Zeitschrift für Eingeborenen-Sprachen*, 11 (1920–1), 161–81
'Malapa v. Public Prosecutor, France, Civil Tribunal of the Seine, February 27, 1959', *International Law Reports*, 28 (1963), 80–1
Massaquoi, Hans, '*Neger, Neger, Schornsteinfeger!*': *Meine Kindheit in Deutschland* (Bern, Munich, Vienna: Fretz und Wasmuth, 1999)
McKay, Claude, *A Long Way from Home* (San Diego: Harcourt Brace Jovanovich, 1970 edn)

Meinecke, Gustav Hermann and Rudolf Hellgrewe (eds.), *Deutschland und seine Kolonien im Jahre 1896: Amtlicher Bericht über die erste deutsche Kolonial-Ausstellung* (Berlin: Reimer, 1897)

Meinhof, Carl, *Die Sprache der Duala in Kamerun* (Berlin: Reimer, 1912)

Ministère de la santé publique et de la population, *Liste alphabétique des personnes ayant acquis ou perdu la nationalité française par décret* (Paris: Imprimerie nationale, 1950–3)

Misipo, Dualla, *Der Junge aus Duala*, ed. Lilyan Lagneau-Kesteloot (Nendeln: Kraus, 1973)

Misipo, Ekwé, *Métissages contemporains* (Paris: Présence Africaine, 2001)

von Morgen, Kurt, *Durch Kamerun von Süd nach Nord: Reisen und Forschungen im Hinterlande 1889 bis 1891* (Leipzig: Brockhaus, 1893)

Moumé Étia, Léopold, *Les Années ardentes* (Paris: Jalivres, 1991)

bin Nasur, Amur, 'Leben des Herrn Amur bin Nasur', in Carl Gotthilf Büttner, *Lieder und Geschichte der Suaheli* (Berlin: Felber, 1894)

La Nationalité française: Textes et documents (Paris: Documentation française, 1996)

Neisser, Eugen, 'Deutschland und seine Kolonien im Jahre 1896', in Arbeitsausschuß der Deutschen Kolonial-Ausstellung, *Deutschland und seine Kolonien im Jahre 1896: Amtlicher Bericht über die erste deutsche Kolonial-Ausstellung* (Berlin: Reimer, 1897), pp. 25–42

Nejar, Marie, *Mach nicht so traurige Augen, weil du ein Negerlein bist: Meine Jugend im Dritten Reich* (Hamburg: Rowohlt, 2007)

Ottley, Roi, *No Green Pastures* (London: John Murray, 1952)

'Paul Malapa Décryptage' (transcript of an undated interview, courtesy of Benny Malapa)

Plehn, Albert, *Die Malaria der afrikanischen Negerbevölkerung, besonders mit Bezug auf die Immunitätsfrage* (Jena: Fischer, 1902)

[Reiprich, Dorothea and Erika Ngambi ul Kuo,] 'Unser Vater war Kameruner, unsere Mutter Ostpreußin, wir sind Mulattinnen', in Katharina Oguntoye, May Opitz and Dagmar Schultz (eds.), *Farbe bekennen: Afro-Deutsche Frauen auf den Spuren ihrer Geschichte* (1986; Frankfurt a.M.: Fischer, 1992), pp. 65–84

Riebow, Otto *et al.* (eds.), *Die deutsche Kolonial-Gesetzgebung: Sammlung der auf die deutschen Schutzgebiete bezüglichen Gesetze, Verordnungen, Erlasse und internationale Vereinbarungen*, 5 vols. (Berlin: Mittler, 1893–1901)

Rogers, J. A., 'Berlin – A City of 4,000,000', *New York Amsterdam News*, 21 December 1927, p. 14

'Germans Eject Negro Preacher from Pulpit', *Philadelphia Tribune*, 13 October 1932, p. 7

'Negro Colonies Lost, Germany is Fast Losing Former Interest in Negroes', *Philadelphia Tribune*, 29 December 1927, p. 9

Sadji, Uta, 'Höhere Tochter in der Kaiserstadt Berlin: Gespräche mit Maria Diop', *Études Germano-Africaines*, 5 (1987), 144–8

Scheve, Eduard, *Die Mission der deutschen Baptisten in Kamerun (West-Afrika) (von 1884 bis 1901)* (Kassel: Verlag der Missions-Gesellschaft der deutschen Baptisten, 1901)

Schnee, Heinrich (ed.), *Deutsches Kolonial-Lexikon Band 1* (Leipzig: Quelle & Meyer, 1920)

Schramm, Gert, *Wer hat Angst vorm schwarzen Mann* (Berlin: Aufbau, 2011)

Seidel, A., *Deutschlands Kolonien: Koloniales Lesebuch für Schule und Haus* (Erftstadt: Area, 2004 edn)

Statistisches Bundesamt, *Bevölkerung und Erwerbstätigkeit: Bevölkerung mit Migrationshintergrund – Ergebnisse des Mikrozensus 2010* (Wiesbaden: Statistisches Bundesamt, 2011)

Steane, Karl, *Kleine Fullah Grammatik*, Archiv für das Studium der deutschen Kolonialsprachen 7 (Berlin: Reimer, 1909)

Terkel, Studs, *The Good War: An Oral History of World War Two* (New York: Pantheon, 1984)

Vieter, Heinrich, *Les premiers pas de l'Église au Cameroun*, trans. and ed. Jean Criaud (Yaoundé: Publications de Centainaire, 1989)

'Weißer Mann immer schlecht', *Der Spiegel*, 24 August 1950, pp. 19–22

Westermann, Diederich, *Afrikaner erzählen ihr Leben* (Essen: Essener Verlagsanstalt, 1938)

PUBLISHED SOURCES: SECONDARY LITERATURE

Aitken, Robbie, 'Education and Migration: Cameroonian School Children and Apprentices in the German Metropole, 1884–1914', in Martin Klimke, Mischa Honeck and Anne Kuhlmann-Smirnov (eds.), *Germany and the Black Diaspora: Points of Contact, 1250–1914* (New York and Oxford: Berghahn, 2013)

Exclusion and Inclusion: Gradations of Whiteness and Socio-Economic Engineering in German Southwest Africa 1884–1914 (Bern: Peter Lang, 2007)

Alary, Eric, *La Ligne de demarcation 1940–1944* (Paris, Perrin, 2003)

Albrecht, Monika, '(Post-) Colonial Amnesia? German Debates on Colonialism and Decolonization in the Post-War Era', in Michael Perraudin and Jürgen Zimmerer (eds.), *German Colonialism and National Identity* (London: Routledge, 2011), pp. 188–96

Allali, Pierre, *Contre le racism: les combats de la LICRA* (Paris: Le Cherche Midi, 2002)

AntiDiskriminierungsBüro (ADB) (ed.), *TheBlackBook: Deutschlands Häutungen* (Frankfurt a.M.: IKO, Verlag für Interkulturelle Kommunikation, 2004)

Archives départementales du Morbihan, *Le Morbihan en guerre 1939–1945* (Lorient: Presses de l'Ouest, 2009)

Ardener, Edwin and Shirley Ardener (eds.), *Kingdom on Mount Cameroon: Studies in the History of the Cameroon Coast 1500–1970* (Oxford and Providence: Berghahn, 1996)

Argenti, Nicolas, *The Intestines of the State: Youth, Violence, and Belated Histories in the Cameroon Grassfields* (University of Chicago Press, 2007)

Arndt, Claus, 'Vor 70 Jahren: Jahrestag der Pogromnacht', *Gegen Vergessen – Für Demokratie*, 59 (December 2008), 36–7

Audeval, Aurélie A., 'Une Question de catégorie? Politiques du mariage mixte entre Allemandes et Français: France 1935–1940', *Le Mouvement Social*, 225 (October–December 2008), 39–51

Auslander, Leora, 'Accommodation, Resistance and Eigensinn: Évolués and Sapeurs between Africa and Europe', in Belinda Davis, Thomas Lindenberger and Michael Wildt (eds.), *Alltag, Erfahrung, Eigensinn: Historisch-anthropologische Erkundungen* (Frankfurt a.M. and New York: Campus, 2008), pp. 205–17

Austen, Ralph A., '"Ich bin schwarzer Mann aber mein Herz ist Deutsch": Germanophones and "Germanness" in Colonial Cameroon and Tanzania', in Marianne Bechhaus-Gerst and Reinhardt Klein-Arendt (eds.), *Die (koloniale) Begegnung: Afrikanerinnen in Deutschland 1880–1945, Deutsche in Afrika 1880–1918* (Frankfurt a.M.: Peter Lang, 2003), pp. 23–40

'Slavery and the Slave Trade on the Atlantic Coast: The Duala of the Littoral', *Paideuma*, 41 (1995), 127–52

Austen, Ralph A. and Jonathan Derrick, *Middlemen of the Cameroons Rivers: The Duala and their Hinterland c. 1600–c. 1960* (Cambridge University Press, 1999)

Ayaß, Wolfgang, *'Asoziale' im Nationalsozialismus* (Stuttgart: Klett-Cotta, 1995)

Badji, Bougoul, 'Itinéraire d'un homme sacrifié', in Sociéte Africaine de Culture (ed.), *David Diop: Témoignages – Études* (Paris: Présence Africaine, 1983), pp. 35–39

Balders, Günter, '100 Jahre Beteiligung deutschsprachiger Baptisten an der Mission in Kamerun', in Dietmar Lütz (ed.), *Dokumentation: Anfänge der deutschen Baptistenmission in Kamerun. Vorträge zur 100-Jahrfeier in Berlin* (Bad Homburg: Zentrale der Europäischen Baptistischen Mission, 1992), pp. 3–18

Bazlen, Gottfried, 'Die Mohren von Westheim: Vor hundert Jahren Missionsschule für Afrikaner', in Gottfried Bazlen (ed.), *Westheim am Kocher: 1200 Jahre Geschichte* (Stuttgart: Jan Thorbecke, 1988)

Bechhaus-Gerst, Marianne, 'Alexander N'Doki: Ein Opfer nationalsozialistischer Justiz', in Peter Martin and Christine Alonzo (eds.), *Zwischen Charleston und Stechschritt: Schwarze im Nationalsozialismus* (Hamburg and Munich: Dölling und Galitz, 2004), pp. 557–65

'"Hinrichtung 6.18 Uhr durch das Fallbeilgerät" – Ein Askari vor dem Sondergericht Hamburg', in Marianne Bechhaus-Gerst and Reinhold Klein-Arendt (eds.), *Die (koloniale) Begegnung: Afrikanerinnen in Deutschland 1880–1945, Deutsche in Afrika 1880–1918* (Frankfurt a.M.: Lang, 2003), pp. 41–50

Treu bis in den Tod: Von Deutsch-Ostafrika nach Sachsenhausen – Eine Lebensgeschichte (Berlin: Links, 2007)

Becker, Frank (ed.), *Rassenmischehen – Mischlinge – Rassentrennung: Zur Politik der Rasse im deutschen Kaiserreich* (Stuttgart: Steiner, 2004)

Berlin, Ira, 'From Creole to African: Atlantic Creoles and the Origins of African-American Society in Mainland North America', *William and Mary Quarterly*, 53 (1996), 251–88

Berliner, Brett A., *Ambivalent Desire: The Exotic Black Other in Jazz-Age France* (Amherst and Boston: University of Massachusetts Press, 2002)

Blanchard, Pascal, Eric Deroo and Gilles Manceran, *Le Paris noir* (Paris: Hazan, 2001)

Blasius, Dirk, *Ehescheidung in Deutschland im 19. und 20. Jahrhundert* (Frankfurt a.M.: Fischer, 1992)

Bock, Hans-Michael (ed.), *Cinegraph: Lexikon zum deutschsprachigen Film* (Munich: edition text + kritik, 1984)

Boittin, Jennifer Anne, '"Among them Complicit"? Life and Politics in France's Black Communities, 1919–1939', in Eve Rosenhaft and Robbie Aitken (eds.), *Africa in Europe: Studies in Transnational Practice in the Long Twentieth Century* (Liverpool University Press, 2013), pp. 55–75

'Black in France. The Language and Politics of Race in the Late Third Republic', *French Politics, Culture and Society*, 27 (2009), 23–46

Colonial Metropolis: The Urban Grounds of Anti-imperialism and Feminism in Interwar Paris (Lincoln NE: University of Nebraska Press, 2010)

Bourne, Stephen, *Black in the British Frame: Black People in British Film and Television, 1896–1996* (London: Cassel, 1998)

Bowersox, Jeff, 'Kolonial-Lehrling wider Willen: Bernhard Epassi in Deutschland 1896–1901', in Ulrich van der Heyden (ed.), *Unbekannte Biographien: Afrikaner im Deutschsprachigen Raum vom 18. Jahrhundert bis zum Ende des Zweiten Weltkrieges* (Berlin: Homilius, 2008), pp. 103–17

Bracher, Karl Dietrich, Manfred Funke and Hans-Adolf Jacobsen (eds.), *Die Weimarer Republik, 1918–1933: Politik, Wirtschaft, Gesellschaft* (Bonn: Bundeszentrale für politische Bildung, 1998)

Brändle, Rea, *Nayo Bruce: Geschichte einer afrikanischen Familie in Europa* (Zürich: Chronos, 2007)

Bronsen, David, *Joseph Roth: Eine Biographie* (Cologne: Kiepenheuer & Witsch, 1974)

Brown, Jacqueline Nassy, 'Black Europe and the African Diaspora: A Discourse on Location', in Darlene Clark Hine, Trica Danielle Keaton and Stephen Small (eds.), *Black Europe and the African Diaspora* (Urbana and Chicago: University of Illinois Press, 2009), pp. 201–11

Dropping Anchor, Setting Sail: Geographies of Race in Black Liverpool (Princeton University Press, 2005)

Bruschi, Christian, 'La Nationalité dans le droit colonial', *Procès, Cahiers d'analyse politique et juridique*, 18 (1987/88), 29–83

Burke, Timothy, *Lifebuoy Men, Lux Women: Commodification, Consumption and Cleanliness in Modern Zimbabwe* (Durham NC: Duke University Press, 1996)

Burleigh, Michael and Wolfgang Wippermann, *The Racial State: Germany 1933–45* (Cambridge University Press, 1991)

Callahan, Michael D., *Mandates and Empire: The League of Nations and Africa, 1914–1931* (Brighton: Sussex Academic Press, 2008)

A Sacred Trust: The League of Nations and Africa 1929–1946 (Brighton: Sussex Academic Press, 2004)

Campt, Tina M., 'African German/African American – Dialogue or Dialectic? Reflections on the Dynamics of "Intercultural Address"', in Carol Aisha Blackshire-Belay (ed.), *The African-German Experience: Critical Essays* (Westport CT: Praeger, 1996), pp. 71–88

'Family Matters: Diaspora, Difference and the Visual Archive', *Social Text*, 27/1 (2009), 83–114

Image Matters: Archive, Photography and the African Diaspora in Europe (Durham NC: Duke University Press, 2012)

Other Germans: Black Germans and the Politics of Race, Gender, and Memory in the Third Reich (Ann Arbor: Michigan University Press, 2004)

'Pictures of "US"? Blackness, Diaspora and the Afro-German Subject', in Darlene Clark Hine, Trica Danielle Keaton and Stephen Small (eds.), *Black Europe and the African Diaspora* (University of Chicago Press, 2009), pp. 63–83

Campt, Tina M. and Paul Gilroy (eds.), *Der Black Atlantic* (Berlin: Haus der Kulturen der Welt, 2004)

Caron, Vicki, *Uneasy Asylum: France and the Jewish Refugee Crisis 1933–1942* (Stanford University Press, 1999)

Centre for Contemporary Cultural Studies (ed.), *The Empire Strikes Back: Race and Racism in 70s Britain* (London: Hutchinson, 1982)

Cheddie, Janice, 'Troubling Subcultural Theories on Race, Gender, the Street and Resistance', *Fashion Theory*, 14 (2010), 331–54.

Chessum, Lorna, *From Immigrants to Ethnic Minority: Making Black Community in Britain* (Aldershot: Ashgate, 2000)

Ciarlo, David, *Advertising Empire: Race and Visual Culture in Imperial Germany* (Cambridge MA: Harvard University Press, 2011)

Clifford, James, *Routes: Travel and Translation in the Late Twentieth Century* (Cambridge MA: Harvard University Press, 1997)

Cohen, Anthony, *The Symbolic Construction of Community* (London: Tavistock, 1985)

Comaroff, John L. and Jean Comaroff, *Of Revelation and Revolution: The Dialectics of Modernity on a South African Frontier*, 2 vols. (University of Chicago Press, 1997)

Conklin, Alice L., *A Mission to Civilize: The Republican Idea of Empire in France and West Africa, 1895–1930* (Stanford University Press, 1997)

Coquery-Vidrovitch, Catherine, *African Woman: A Modern History*, trans. B. B. Raps (Boulder CO: Westview, 1997)

Czarnowski, Gabriele, *Das kontrollierte Paar* (Weinheim: Deutscher Studienverlag, 1991)

Debrunner, Hans Werner, *Presence and Prestige, Africans in Europe: A History of Africans in Europe before 1918* (Basel: Basler Afrika Bibliographien, 1979)

Dennis, Mike, 'Asian and African Workers in the Niches of Society', in Mike Dennis and Norman LaPorte (eds.), *State and Minorities in Communist East Germany* (New York: Berghahn, 2011), pp. 87–123

Derrick, Jonathan, *Africa's 'Agitators': Militant Anti-Colonialism in Africa and the West, 1918–1939* (London: Hurst, 2008)

'Free French and Africans in Douala, 1940–41', *Journal of the Historical Society of Nigeria*, 10 (1980), 53–70

DeWitte, Philippe, *Les Mouvements nègres en France 1919–1939* (Paris: L'Harmattan, 1985)

Döring, Hans-Joachim and Uta Rüchel (eds.), *Freundschaftsbande und Beziehungskisten: Die Afrikapolitik der DDR und der BRD gegenüber Mosambik* (Frankfurt a.M.: Brandes & Apsel, 2005)

Döscher, Hans-Jürgen, *Das Auswärtige Amt im Dritten Reich. Diplomatie im Schatten der 'Endlösung'* (Berlin: Siedler, 1987)

Douala Manga Bell, René, *Le Prince Alexandre* (Berlin: Exchange & Dialogue, 2007)

Dreyfus, Jean-Marc and Sarah Gensburger, *Des camps dans Paris: Austerlitz, Lévitan, Bassano, juillet 1943–août 1944* (Paris: Fayard, 2003)

Eberhardt, Martin, *Zwischen Nationalsozialismus und Apartheid: Die deutsche Bevölkerungsgruppe Südwestafrikas 1915–1965* (Berlin: LIT, 2007)

Echenberg, Myron, '"Morts pour la France": The African Soldier in France during the Second World War', *Journal of African History*, 26 (1985), 363–80

Eckert, Andreas, '"Der beleidigte Negerprinz": Mpundu Akwa und die Deutschen', *Etudes Germano-Africaines*, 91 (1991), 32–8

Die Duala und die Kolonialmächte (Hamburg: LIT, 1991)

Edwards, Brent Hayes, *The Practice of Diaspora: Literature, Translation and the Rise of Black Internationalism* (Cambridge MA: Harvard University Press, 2003)

Ehrmann, Henry, 'The Trade Union Movement in the Framework of French War Economy, 1939–1940', *Journal of Politics*, 6 (1944), 263–93

El-Tayeb, Fatima, *Schwarze Deutsche: Der Diskurs um 'Rasse' und nationale Identität 1890–1933* (Frankfurt a.M. and New York: Campus, 2001)

Epprecht, Marc, *Heterosexual Africa? The History of an Idea from the Age of Exploration to the Age of Aids* (Athens OH: Ohio University Press, 2008)

Eyoum, Jean-Pierre Félix, Stefanie Michels and Joachim Zeller, 'Bonamanga: Eine Kosmopolitische Familiengeschichte', *Mont Cameroun*, 2 (2005), 11–48

Fehrenbach, Heide, *Race after Hitler: Black Occupation Children in Postwar Germany and America* (Princeton University Press, 2005)

Fenner, Angelika, *Race under Reconstruction in German Cinema: Robert Stemmle's Toxi* (University of Toronto Press, 2011)

Feuchert, Sascha, Erwin Leibfried and Jörg Riecke (eds.), *Die Chronik des Gettos Lodz/Litzmannstadt 1943* (Göttingen: Wallstein, 2007)

Fieldhouse, D. K., *Unilever Overseas: The Anatomy of a Multinational* (London: Croom Helm, 1978)

Firla, Monika, *Der kameruner Artist Hermann Kessern: Ein schwarzer Crailsheimer* (Crailsheim: Baier, 2010)

Fletcher, Yael Simpson, 'City, Nation and Empire in Marseilles, 1919–1939', (PhD thesis, Emory University, 2000)

'Unsettling Settlers: Colonial Migrants and Racialised Sexuality in Interwar Marseilles', in Antoinette Burton (ed.), *Gender, Sexuality and Colonial Modernities* (London: Routledge, 1999), pp. 79–94

Flynn, George Q., *Conscription and Democracy: France, Great Britain and the United States* (Westport CT: Greenwood Press, 2001)

Frei, Norbert, José Brunner and Constantin Goschler (eds.), *Die Praxis der Wiedergutmachung: Geschichte, Erfahrung und Wirkung in Deutschland und Israel* (Frankfurt a.M.: Campus, 1997)

Friedlander, Henry, *The Origins of Nazi Genocide: From Euthanasia to the Final Solution* (Chapel Hill: University of North Carolina Press, 1995)

Frost, Diane, *Work and Community among West African Migrant Workers since the Nineteenth Century* (Liverpool University Press, 1999)

Fryer, Peter, *Staying Power: The History of Black People in Britain* (London: Pluto, 1984)

Führer, Karl Christian, *Mieter, Hausbesitzer, Staat und Wohnungsmarkt* (Stuttgart: Steiner, 1995)

Gardiner, David E., *Cameroon: United Nations Challenge to French Policy* (London: Oxford University Press, 1963)

Geary, Christraud M., 'Political Dress: German-Style Military Attire and Colonial Politics in Bamum', in Ian Fowler and David Zeitlyn (eds.), *African Crossroads: Intersections between History and Anthropology in Cameroon* (Providence RI and Oxford: Berghahn, 1996), pp. 165–92

Gellately, Robert and Nathan Stoltzfus (eds.), *Social Outsiders in Nazi Germany* (Princeton University Press, 2001)

Gemie, Sharif, Fiona Reid and Laure Humbert, *Outcast Europe: Refugees and Relief Workers in an Era of Total War 1936–48* (London and New York: Continuum, 2012)

Genova, James E., *Colonial Ambivalence, Cultural Authenticity and the Limitations of Mimicry in French-Ruled West Africa, 1914–1956* (New York: Peter Lang, 2004)

Gerhard-Sonnenberg, Gabriele, *Marxistische Arbeiterbildung in der Weimarer Zeit (MASCH)* (Cologne: Pahl-Rügenstein, 1976)

Gerlach, Christian, 'The Wannsee Conference, the Fate of German Jews, and Hitler's Decision in Principle to Exterminate all European Jews', in Omer Bartov (ed.), *The Holocaust: Origins, Implementation, Aftermath* (London: Routledge, 2000), pp. 106–61

Gilroy, Paul, *The Black Atlantic: Modernity and Double Consciousness* (London: Verso, 1993)

'*There Ain't No Black in the Union Jack*' (1987; London: Routledge, 2000)

Gosewinkel, Dieter, *Einbürgern und Ausschließen: Die Nationalisierung der Staatsangehörigkeit vom Deutschen Bund bis zur Bundesrepublik Deutschland* (Göttingen: Vandenhoeck & Ruprecht, 2001)

Gouaffo, Albert, 'Prince Dido of Didotown and "Human Zoos" in Wilhelmine Germany: Strategies for Self-Representation under the Othering Gaze', in Eve Rosenhaft and Robbie Aitken (eds.), *Africa in Europe. Studies in Transnational Practice in the Long Twentieth Century* (Liverpool University Press, 2013), pp. 19–33

Wissens- und Kulturtransfer im kolonialen Kontext: Das Beispiel Kamerun – Deutschland (1884–1919) (Würzburg: Königshausen & Neumann, 2007)

Grah Mel, Frédéric, *Alioune Diop, le bâtisseur inconnu du monde noir* (Abidjan: Presses Universitaires de Côte d'Ivoire, 1995)

Graml, Hermann, *Antisemitism in the Third Reich,* trans.Tim Kirk (Oxford: Blackwell, 1992)

Gratien, Jean-Pierre, *Marius Moutet. Un socialiste à l'Outre-mer* (Paris: L'Harmattan, 2006)

Green, Jeffrey, *Black Edwardians: Black People in Britain, 1901–1914* (London: Frank Cass, 1998)

Grosse, Pascal, 'Koloniale Lebenswelten in Berlin 1885–1945', in Ulrich van der Heyden and Joachim Zeller (eds.), *Kolonialmetropole Berlin* (Berlin Edition, 2002), pp. 195–201

Kolonialismus, Eugenik und bürgerliche Gesellschaft in Deutschland 1850–1918 (Frankfurt a.M.: Campus, 2000)

'Zwischen Privatheit und Öffentlichkeit: Kolonialmigration in Deutschland, 1900–1940', in Birthe Kundrus (ed.), *Phantasiereiche: Zur Kulturgeschichte des deutschen Kolonialismus* (Frankfurt a. M.: Campus, 2003), pp. 91–109

Grossmann, Atina, 'Victims, Villains, and Survivors: Gendered Perceptions and Self-Perceptions of Jewish Displaced Persons in Occupied Postwar Germany', *Journal of the History of Sexuality*, 11 (2002), 291–318

Gruchmann, Lothar, '"Blutschutzgesetz" und Justiz: Zu Entstehung und Auswirkung des Nürnberger Gesetzes vom 15. September 1935', *Vierteljahrshefte für Zeitgeschichte*, 31 (1983), 418–42

Gründer, Horst, '"Neger, Kanaken und Chinesen zu nützlichen Menschen erziehen": Ideologie und Praxis des deutschen Kolonialismus', in Thomas Beck, Horst Gründer, Horst Pietschmann and Roderick Ptak (eds.), *Überseegeschichte: Beiträge der jüngeren Forschung* (Stuttgart: Steiner, 1999), pp. 254–66

Günther, Jürgen, 'Mission im kolonialen Kontext: Beiträge zur Geschichte der Mission der deutschen Baptisten in Kamerun 1891 bis 1914' (Masters Thesis, University of Hamburg, 1985)

Hagemann, Karen, *Frauenalltag und Männerpolitik: Alltagsleben und gesellschaftliches Handeln von Arbeiterfrauen in der Weimarer Republik* (Bonn: Dietz, 1990)

Hay, Margaret Jean, 'Changes in Clothing and Struggles over Identity in Colonial Western Kenya', in Jean Marie Allman (ed.), *Fashioning Africa: Power and the Politics of Dress* (Bloomington: Indiana University Press, 2004), pp. 67–83

Hebdige, Dick, *Subculture: The Meaning of Style* (London: Methuen, 1979)

van der Heyden, Ulrich, 'Afrikaner in der Reichs(kolonial)hauptstadt: Die Kolonialausstellung im Treptower Park 1896 sowie die Transvaal-Ausstellung auf dem Kurfürstendamm 1897', in Marianne Bechhaus-Gerst and Richard Klein-Arendt (eds.), *Die (koloniale) Begegnung: Afrikanerinnen in Deutschland 1880–1945, Deutsche in Afrika 1880–1918* (Frankfurt a.M.: Peter Lang, 2003), pp. 147–59

'Die Kolonial- und die Transvaal-Ausstellung 1896/97', in Ulrich van der Heyden and Joachim Zeller (eds.), *Kolonialmetropole Berlin* (Berlin Edition, 2002), pp. 135–42

Hochstadt, Steve, *Mobility and Modernity: Migration in Germany, 1820–1989* (Ann Arbor: University of Michigan Press, 1999)

Hohorst, Gerd, Jürgen Kocka and Gerd Ritter (eds.), *Sozialgeschichtliches Arbeitsbuch II* (Munich: C. H. Beck, 1978)

Holzbach, Alexander, 'Kamerun, Limburg und die Pallottiner', *Information für Religionslehrer*, 1 (1988), 10–11

Hooker, James R., *Black Revolutionary: George Padmore's Path from Communism to Pan-Africanism* (London: Pall Mall Press, 1967)

Hopkins, Leroy, 'Einbürgerungsakte 1154: Heinrich Ernst Wilhelm Anumu, African Businessman in Imperial Germany', in Marianne Bechhaus-Gerst and Reinhard Klein-Arendt (eds.), *Die (koloniale) Begegnung: Afrikanerinnen in Deutschland 1880–1945, Deutsche in Afrika 1880–1918* (Frankfurt a.M.: Peter Lang, 2003), pp. 161–70

Huggan, Graham, *The Postcolonial Exotic: Marketing the Margins* (London: Routledge, 2001)

von Joeden-Forgey, Elisa, 'Nobody's People: Colonial Subjects, Race Power and the German State 1884–1945' (PhD thesis, University of Pennsylvania, 2004)

(ed.), *Mpundu Akwa: The Case of the Prince from Cameroon. The Newly Discovered Speech for the Defense by Dr M. Levi* (Berlin and Münster: LIT, 2002)

Johnson, E. Patrick, *Appropriating Blackness: Performance and the Politics of Authenticity* (Durham NC: Duke University Press, 2003)

Johnson, Samuel D., *Schwarze Missionare – Weiße Missionare! Beiträge westlicher Missionsgesellschaften und einheimischer Pioniere zur Entstehung der Baptistengemeinde in Kamerun (1841–1949)* (Kassel: Onken Verlag, 2004)

Joseph, Richard A., 'The German Question in French Cameroon, 1919–1939', *Comparative Studies in Society and History*, 17 (1975), 65–90

Joseph, Richard A., *Radical Nationalism in Cameroun: Social Origins of the U.P.C. Rebellion* (Oxford: Clarendon, 1977)

'The Royal Pretender: Prince Douala Manga Bell in Paris, 1919–1922', *Cahiers d'Études Africaines*, 14 (1974), 339–58

Kala Lobé, Iyé, *Douala Manga Bell: Héros de la résistance douala* (Paris: ABC, 1977)

Karwelat, Jürgen, 'Bitte einsteigen und Türen schließen: 150 Jahre Berliner Schienenverkehr', in Dampfergruppe der Berliner Geschichtswerkstatt (ed.), *Landgang in Berlin: Stadtgeschichte an Landwehrkanal und Spree* (Berlin: Dirk Nishen, 1987), pp. 91–113

Kater, Michael, *Different Drummers: Jazz in the Culture of Nazi Germany* (Oxford University Press, 1992)

von Kempis, Franziska and Oliver das Gupta, 'Gert Schramm: Der Schwarze, der Buchenwald überlebte', *Süddeutsche Zeitung*, 5 June 2009

Kerker, Arnim, 'Du liebes Deutschland', in Hans-Jürgen Heinrichs (ed.), *Abschiedsbriefe an Deutschland* (Frankfurt a.M.: Qumran, 1984), pp. 45–57

'Ende einer Koloniallegende', *Die Zeit*, 10 October 1980

Kesting, Robert W., 'Forgotten Victims: Blacks in the Holocaust', *Journal of Negro History*, 77/1 (1992), 30–6

Killingray, David (ed.), *Africans in Britain* (Ilford: Frank Cass, 1994)

'Africans in the United Kingdom: An Introduction', in David Killingray (ed.), *Africans in Britain* (Ilford: Frank Cass, 1994), pp. 2–27

von dem Knesebeck, Julia, *The Roma Struggle for Compensation in Post-War Germany* (Hatfield: University of Hertfordshire Press, 2011)

Krokowski, Heike, *Die Last der Vergangenheit: Auswirkungen Nationalsozialistischer Verfolgung auf deutsche Sinti* (Frankfurt a.M.: Campus, 2001)

Kuck, Dennis, '"Für den sozialistischen Aufbau ihrer Heimat"? Ausländische Vertragsarbeitskräfte in der DDR', in Jan C. Behrends, Thomas

Lindenberger and Patrice G. Poutrous (eds.), *Fremde und Fremd-Sein in der DDR: Zu historischen Ursachen der Fremdenfeindlichkeit in Ostdeutschland* (Berlin: Metropol, 2003), pp. 245–57

Küttner, Sibylle, *Farbige Seeleute im Kaiserreich: Asiaten und Afrikaner im Dienst der deutschen Handelsmarine* (Erfurt: Sutton, 2000)

Kundrus, Birthe, 'Von Windhoek nach Nürnberg? Koloniale "Mischehenverbote" und die nationalsozialistische Rassengesetzgebung', in Birthe Kundrus (ed.), *Phantasiereiche: Zur Kulturgeschichte des deutschen Kolonialismus* (Frankfurt a.M.: Campus, 2003), pp. 110–31

Laburthe-Tolra, Philippe, *Vers la Lumière? ou le Désir d'Ariel. A propos des Beti du Cameroun: Sociologie de la conversion* (Paris: Karthala, 1999)

Lake, Marilyn, and Henry Reynolds, *Drawing the Global Colour Line: White Men's Countries and the International Challenge of Racial Equality* (Cambridge University Press, 2008)

Lawless, Richard L., *From Ta'izz to Tyneside: An Arab Community in the North-East of England during the Early Twentieth Century* (University of Exeter Press, 1995)

Lawrance, Benjamin, *Locality, Mobility and 'Nation': Periurban Colonialism in Togo's Eweland, 1900–1960* (Rochester NY: University of Rochester Press, 2007)

Lemke Muniz de Faria, Yara-Colette, *Zwischen Fürsorge und Ausgrenzung: afrodeutsche 'Besatzungskinder' im Nachkriegsdeutschland* (Berlin: Metropol, 2002)

Lewerenz, Susann, *Die Deutsche Afrika-Schau (1935–1940): Rassismus, Kolonialrevisionismus und postkoloniale Auseinandersetzungen im nationalsozialistischen Deutschland* (Frankfurt a.M.: Peter Lang, 2006)

Lewy, Guenter, *The Nazi Persecution of the Gypsies* (Oxford University Press, 2000)

Lindfors, Bernth, 'Introduction', in Bernth Lindfors (ed.), *Africans on Stage: Studies in Ethnological Show Business* (Bloomington: Indiana University Press, 1999), pp. vi–xiii

Lindsay, Lisa A. and Stephan F. Miescher, 'Introduction', in Lisa A. Lindsay and Stephan F. Miescher (eds.), *Men and Masculinities in Modern Africa* (Portsmouth NH: Heinemann, 2003), pp. 1–30

Linne, Karsten, *Deutschland jenseits des Äquators? Die NS-Kolonialplanungen für Afrika* (Berlin: Links, 2008)

Lotz, Rainer E., *Black Entertainers of African Descent in Europe and Germany* (Bonn: Birgit Lotz, 1997)

Luchterhandt, Martin, *Der Weg nach Birkenau: Entstehung und Verlauf der nationalsozialistischen Verfolgung der 'Zigeuner'* (Lübeck: Schmidt-Römhild, 2000)

Lusane, Clarence, *Hitler's Black Victims: The Historical Experiences of Afro-Germans, European Blacks, Africans, and African Americans in the Nazi Era* (New York: Routledge, 2003)

Lyonga, Nalova, Eckhard Breitinger and Bole Butake, *Anglophone Cameroon Writing* (Bayreuth: Breitinger,, 1993)

Mabon, Arnelle, *Prisoniers de Guerre 'Indigènes': visages oubliés de la France occupée* (Paris: La Découverte, 2010)

Majer, Diemut, *Non-Germans under the Third Reich: The Nazi Judicial and Administrative System in Germany and Occupied Eastern Europe, with Special Regard to Occupied Poland, 1939–1945* (Baltimore: Johns Hopkins University Press, 2003)

Malzahn, Manfred, 'The Black Captains of Köpenick: A Story of 1920s Berlin', in Susanne Marten-Finnis and Matthias Uecker (eds.), *Berlin-Wien-Prag: Moderne, Minderheiten und Migration in der Zwischenkriegszeit* (Bern: Peter Lang, 2001), pp. 91–106

Mandel, Maud, *In the Aftermath of Genocide: Armenians and Jews in Twentieth-Century France* (Durham NC: Duke University Press, 2003)

Martin, Peter, 'Der Afrikanische Hilfsverein von 1918', in Peter Martin and Christine Alonzo (eds.), *Zwischen Charleston und Stechschritt* (Hamburg: Dölling & Galitz, 2004), pp. 73–80

'Anfänge politischer Selbstorganisation der deutschen Schwarzen bis 1933', in Marianne Bechhaus-Gerst and Reinhardt Klein-Arendt (eds.), *Die (koloniale) Begegnung: AfrikanerInnen in Deutschland 1880–1945, Deutsche in Afrika 1880–1918* (Frankfurt a.M.: Peter Lang, 2003), pp. 193–206

'Die "Liga gegen koloniale Unterdrückung"', in Ulrich van der Heyden and Joachim Zeller (eds.) '*... Macht und Anteil an der Weltherrschaft*': *Berlin und der deutsche Kolonialismus* (Berlin: Unrast, 2005), pp. 261–9

'Schwarze Sowjets an Elbe und Spree?', in Peter Martin and Christine Alonzo (eds.), *Zwischen Charleston und Stechschritt* (Hamburg: Dölling & Galitz, 2004), pp. 178–93

Schwarze Teufel, edle Mohren: Afrikaner in Geschichte und Bewußtsein der Deutschen (Hamburger Edition, 2001)

Martin, Peter and Christine Alonzo, *Im Netz der Moderne: Afrikaner und Deutschlands gebrochener Aufstieg zur Macht* (Hamburg: Kovac, 2012)

(eds.), *Zwischen Charleston und Stechschritt* (Hamburg: Dölling & Galitz, 2004)

Martin, Phyllis, *Leisure and Society in Colonial Brazzaville* (Cambridge University Press, 1995)

Maß, Sandra, *Weiße Helden – schwarze Krieger: Zur Geschichte kolonialer Männlichkeit in Deutschland 1918–1964* (Cologne: Böhlau, 2006)

McClellan, Woodford, 'Africans and Black Americans in the Comintern Schools, 1925–1934', *International Journal of African Historical Studies*, 26 (1993), 371–90

'Black *Hajj* to "Red Mecca": Africans and Afro-Americans at KUTV, 1924–1938', in Maxim Matusevich (ed.), *Africa in Russia – Russia in Africa: Three Centuries of Encounters* (Trenton and Asmara: Africa World Press, 2007), pp. 61–84

McCormick, Dorothy, 'Women in Business: Class and Nairobi's Small and Medium-Sized Producers', in Kathleen Sheldon (ed.), *Courtyards, Markets, City Streets: Urban Women in Africa* (Boulder CO: Westview Press, 1996), pp. 193–212

McElligott, Anthony, *Contested City: Municipal Politics and the Rise of Nazism in Altona, 1917–1937* (Ann Arbor: University of Michigan Press, 1998)

McGowan, Moray, 'Black and White? Claire Goll's *Der Neger Jupiter raubt Europa*', in Eric Robertson and Robert Vilain (eds.), *Yvan Goll – Claire Goll: Texts and Contexts* (Amsterdam: Rodopi, 1997), pp. 205–18

McMeekin, Sean, *The Red Millionaire: A Political Biography of Willi Münzenberg, Moscow's Secret Propaganda Tsar in the West* (New Haven and London: Yale University Press, 2003)

Mehnert, Wolfgang, 'Schulpolitik im Dienste der Kolonialherrschaft des deutschen Imperialismus' (PhD thesis, Karl Marx Universität, Leipzig, 1965)

Messina, Jean-Paul and Jaap van Slageren, *Histoire du christianisme au Cameroun: Des origins à nos jours* (Paris: Éditions Karthala, 2005)

Meyer-Bahlburg, Hilke and Ekkehard Wolff, *Afrikanische Sprachen in Forschung und Lehre: 75 Jahre Afrikanistik in Hamburg (1909–1984)* (Berlin and Hamburg: Reimer, 1986)

Michels, Stefanie, 'Askari – treu bis in den Tod? Vom Umgang der deutschen mit ihren schwarzen Soldaten', in Marianne Bechhaus-Gerst and Reinhold Klein-Arendt (eds.), *Afrikanerinnen in Deutschland und schwarze Deutsche – Geschichte und Gegenwart* (Münster and Berlin: LIT, 2004), pp. 171–86

'Mülheim an der Ruhr: Der kleine schwarze Prinz. Das Grab von Moses Equalla Deido', in Ulrich van der Heyden and Joachim Zeller (eds.), *Kolonialismus hierzulande: Eine Spurensuche in Deutschland* (Erfurt: Sutton Verlag, 2008), pp. 417–21

Schwarze deutsche Kolonialsoldaten: Mehrdeutige Repräsentationsräume und früher Kosmopolitismus in Afrika (Bielefeld: transcript, 2009)

Miller, Christopher L., *Nationalists and Nomads: Essays on Francophone African Literature and Culture* (University of Chicago Press, 1998)

Miller, James A., Susan Pennybacker and Eve Rosenhaft, 'Mother Ada Wright and the International Campaign to Free the Scottsboro Boys', *American Historical Review*, 106 (2001), 387–403

Miller, Monica L., *Slaves to Fashion: Black Dandyism and the Styling of Black Diasporic Identity* (Durham NC: Duke University Press, 2009)

Mitchell, Alan, *Nazi Paris: The History of an Occupation 1940–1944* (New York and Oxford: Berghahn, 2008)

Möhle, Heiko, 'Betreuung, Erfassung, Kontrolle – Die "Deutsche Gesellschaft für Eingeborenenkunde"', in Joachim Zeller and Ulrich van der Heyden (eds.), *Kolonialmetropole Berlin* (Berlin Edition, 2002), pp. 243–51

'Von Duala nach Altona: Vornehme Handwerkslehrlinge aus Kamerun', in Heiko Möhle, Susanne Heyn and Susann Lewerenz (eds.), *Zwischen Völkerschau und Kolonialinstitut: Afrikanerinnen im kolonialen Hamburg* (Hamburg: Eine Welt Netzwerk Hamburg e.V. und St Pauli Archiv e.V., 2006), pp. 16–21

Moses, A. Dirk and Dan Stone (eds.), *Colonialism and Genocide* (London: Routledge, 2007)

Moumé Étia, Léopold, *Histoire de Bona Ebele Deido* (Douala: Press-Union, 1986)

'La Révolte des femmes en 1931', *Wife*, 13 (1985), 12–16

Mudimbe, V. Y., (ed.), *The Surreptitious Speech: 'Présence Africaine' and the Politics of Otherness 1947–1987* (University of Chicago Press, 1992)

Mukherji, S. Ani, '"Like Another Planet to the Darker Americans": Black Cultural Work in 1930s Moscow', in Eve Rosenhaft and Robbie Aitken (eds.). *Africa in Europe: Studies in Transnational Practice in the Long Twentieth Century* (Liverpool University Press, 2012), pp. 120–41

Nagl, Dominik, *Grenzfälle: Staatsangehörigkeit, Rassismus und nationale Identität unter deutscher Kolonialherrschaft* (Frankfurt a.M.: Peter Lang, 2007)

Nagl, Tobias, '"Sieh mal den schwarzen Mann da!" – Komparsen afrikanischer Herkunft im deutschsprachigen Kino vor 1945', in Peter Martin and Christine Alonzo (eds.), *Zwischen Charleston und Stechschritt* (Hamburg: Dölling & Galitz, 2004), pp. 81–91

'"... und lass mich filmen und tanzen bloß um mein Brot zu verdienen": Schwarze Komparsen und Kinoöffentlichkeit in der Weimarer Republik', in Marianne Bechhaus-Gerst and Reinhard Klein-Arendt (eds.), *Afrikanerinnen in Deutschland und schwarze Deutsche Geschichte und Gegenwart* (Berlin: Lit, 2004), pp. 139–54

Die unheimliche Maschine: Rasse und Repräsentation im Weimarer Kino (Munich: edition text + kritik, 2009)

Nathans, Eli, *The Politics of Citizenship in Germany: Ethnicity, Utility and Nationalism* (Oxford and New York: Berg, 2004)

Naumann, Christine, 'African American Performers and Culture in Weimar Germany', in David McBride, Leroy Hopkins, and C. Aisha Blackshire-Belay (eds.), *Crosscurrents: African Americans, Africa, and Germany in the Modern World* (Columbia SC: Camden House, 1998), pp. 96–105

Neliba, Günter, *Wilhelm Frick, der Legalist des Unrechtsstaates: Eine politische Biographie* (Paderborn: Schöningh, 1992)

Noiriel, Gérard, *Immigration, antisémitisme et racisme en France* (Paris: Fayard, 2007)

O'Donnell, Krista, 'Home, Nation, Empire: Domestic Germanness and Colonial Citizenship', in Krista O'Donnell, Renate Bridenthal and Nancy Reagin (eds.), *The Heimat Abroad: The Boundaries of Germanness* (Ann Arbor: University of Michigan Press, 2005)

Oguntoye, Katharina, *Eine Afro-Deutsche Geschichte: Zur Lebenssituation von Afrikanern in Deutschland von 1884 bis 1950* (Berlin: Hoho Verlag, 1997)

Oguntoye, Katharina, May Opitz and Dagmar Schultz (eds.), *Farbe bekennen: Afro-Deutsche Frauen auf den Spuren ihrer Geschichte* (1986; Frankfurt a.M.: Fischer, 1992)

'Vorwort der Herausgeberinnen', in Katharina Oguntoye, May Opitz and Dagmar Schultz (eds.), *Farbe bekennen: Afro-Deutsche Frauen auf den Spuren ihrer Geschichte* (1986; Frankfurt a.M.: Fischer, 1992), pp. 9–15

Oltmer, Jochen, *Migration und Politik in der Weimarer Republik* (Göttingen: Vandenhoeck & Ruprecht, 2005)

O'Neil, Robert, 'Imperialisms at the Century's End: Moghamo Relations with Bali-Nyonga and Germany, 1889–1908', in Ian Fowler and David Zeitlyn (eds.), *African Crossroads: Intersections between History and Anthropology in Cameroon* (Oxford: Berghahn, 1996), pp. 81–100

Orosz, Kenneth J., 'The *Affaire des Sixas* and Catholic Education of Women in French Colonial Cameroon, 1915–1939', *French Colonial History*, 1 (2002), 33–49

Religious Conflict and the Evolution of Language Policy in German and French Cameroon, 1885–1939 (New York: Peter Lang, 2008)

Ottley, Roi, *The Lonely Warrior: The Life and Times of Robert S. Abbott* (Chicago: Henry Regnery, 1955)

Owona, Adalbert, 'A l'aube du nationalisme camerounais: la curieuse figure de Vincent Ganty', *Revue Française d'Histoire d'Outre-Mer*, 56/204 (1969), 199–23

Pennybacker, Susan D., *From Scottsboro to Munich: Race and Political Culture in 1930s Britain* (Princeton University Press, 2009)

Perraudin, Michael and Jürgen Zimmerer (eds.), *German Colonialism and National Identity* (London: Routledge, 2011)

Petershagen, Henning, 'Afro-Aristokrat in Aalen ausgebildet', *Südwest Presse*, 31 May 1997

Peukert, Detlev J. K., *Inside Nazi Germany: Conformity, Opposition and Racism in Everyday Life* (Harmondsworth: Penguin, 1989)

Pommerin, Reiner, *Sterilisierung der Rheinlandbastarde: Das Schicksal einer farbigen deutschen Minderheit, 1918–1937* (Düsseldorf: Droste, 1979)

Przyrembel, Alexandra, *'Rassenschande': Reinheitsmythos und Vernichtungslegitimation im Nationalsozialismus* (Göttingen: Vandenhoeck & Ruprecht, 2003)

Pugach, Sara, *Africa in Translation: A History of Colonial Linguistics in Germany and Beyond, 1814–1945* (Ann Arbor: University of Michigan, 2012)

Quinn, Frederick, 'Charles Atangana of Yaounde', *Journal of African History*, 21 (1980), 485–95

In Search of Salt: Changes in Beti (Cameroon) Society 1880–1960 (Oxford and Providence RI: Berghahn, 2006)

Ramm, Gerald, *Als Woltersdorf noch Hollywood war* (Woltersdorf: Bock & Kübler, 1996)

Ray, Carina E., '"The White Wife Problem": Sex, Race and the Contested Politics of Repatriation into Interwar British West Africa', *Gender & History*, 21 (2009), 628–46

Reed-Anderson, Paulette, *Eine Geschichte von mehr als 100 Jahren: Die Anfänge der Afrikanischen Diaspora in Berlin* (Berlin: Die Ausländerbeauftragte des Senats, 1995)

Reiter, Raimond, *Psychiatry in the 'Third Reich' in Lower Saxony* (Hanover: Hahn, 2008)

Rheinisches Journalistinnenbüro, *'Unsere Opfer zählen nicht': Die Dritte Welt im Zweiten Weltkrieg* (Berlin: Assoziation A, 2005)

Riesz, János, 'Léopold Sédar Senghor in deutscher Kriegsgefangenschaft', in Peter Martin and Christine Alonzo (eds.), *Zwischen Charleston und Stechschritt: Schwarze im Nationalsozialismus* (Hamburg: Dölling & Galitz, 2004), pp. 596–603

Röblitz, Michael Thomas and Ralf Schmiedecke (eds.), *Berlin-Schöneberg: Nicht nur 'wie einst im Mai'* (Erfurt: Sutton Verlag, 2005)

Römer, Gernot, *Die grauen Busse in Schwaben: Wie das Dritte Reich mit Geisteskranken und Schwangeren umging. Berichte, Dokumente, Zahlen und Bilder* (Augsburg: Wißner, 2009)

Rosenberg, Clifford, *Policing Paris: The Origins of Modern Immigration Control between the Wars* (Ithaca: Cornell University Press, 2006)

Rosenhaft, Eve, 'Afrikaner und "Afrikaner" im Deutschland der Weimarer Republik: Antikolonialismus und Antirassismus zwischen Doppelbewusstsein und Selbsterfindung', in Birthe Kundrus (ed.), *Phantasiereiche: Zur Kulturgeschichte des deutschen Kolonialismus* (Frankfurt a.M.: Campus, 2003), pp. 282–301

'Blacks and Gypsies in Nazi Germany: The Limits of the "Racial State"', *History Workshop Journal*, 72 (2011), 161–71

'*Schwarze Schmach* and *métissages contemporains*: The Politics and Poetics of Mixed Marriage in a Refugee Family', in Eve Rosenhaft and Robbie Aitken (eds.), *Africa in Europe: Studies in Transnational Practice in the Long Twentieth Century* (Liverpool University Press, 2013), pp. 34–54

Rosenhaft, Eve and Robbie Aitken, 'Edimo Wilhelm Munumé und Peter Mukuri Makembe', in Ulrich van der Heyden (ed.), *Unbekannte Biographien: Afrikaner im deutschsprachigen Raum vom 18. Jahrhundert bis zum Ende des Zweiten Weltkrieges* (Berlin: Kai Homilius, 2008), pp. 153–62

'"König der Abenteurer": Joseph Soppo Muange', in Ulrich van der Heyden (ed.), *Unbekannte Biographien: Afrikaner im deutschsprachigen Raum vom 18. Jahrhundert bis zum Ende des Zweiten Weltkrieges* (Berlin: Kai Homilius, 2008), pp. 179–87

Rudin, Harry, *Germans in the Cameroons, 1884–1914: A Case Study in Modern Imperialism* (New Haven: Yale University Press, 1938)

Rüger, Adolf, 'Der Aufstand der Polizeisoldaten (Dezember 1893)', in Helmuth Stoecker (ed.), *Kamerun unter deutscher Herrschaft. Band 1* (Berlin: Rütten und Loening, 1960), pp. 97–147

'Die Erste Internationale Konferenz der Neger-Arbeiter (Hamburg 1930)', *Beiträge zur Geschichte der deutschen Arbeiterbewegung*, 9 (1967), 782–97

'Imperialismus, Sozialreformismus und antikoloniale demokratische Alternative. Zielvorstellung von Afrikanern in Deutschland im Jahre 1919', *Zeitschrift für Geschichtswissenschaft*, 23 (1975), 1293–308

Ruppenthal, Jens, 'Die Kolonialabteilung im Auswärtigen Amt der Weimarer Republik', in Ulrich van der Heyden and Joachim Zeller (eds.), "*. . . Macht und Anteil an der Weltherrschaft": Berlin und der deutsche Kolonialismus* (Berlin: Unrast, 2005), pp. 22–8

Saada, Emmanuelle, *Les Enfants de la colonie* (Paris: Découverte, 2007)

Sadji, Amadou Booker, 'L'Héritage germanophile de la négritude en Afrique francophone', *Études Germano-Africaines*, 20–1 (2002–3), 242–53

Sadji, Uta, 'Les racines de la germanophilie de Senghor', *Études Germano-Africaines*, 20–1 (2002–3), 254–73

von Saldern, Adelheid, 'Gesellschaft und Lebensgestaltung: Sozialkulturelle Streiflichter', in Gert Kähler (ed.), *Geschichte des Wohnens Band 4: 1918–1945 Reform, Reaktion, Zerstörung* (Stuttgart: Deutsche Verlags-Anstalt, 1996), pp. 45–183

Sammartino, Annemarie, 'Culture, Belonging and the Law: Naturalization in the Weimar Republic', in Geoff Eley and Jan Palmowski (eds.), *Citizenship and*

National Identity in Twentieth-Century Germany (Stanford University Press, 2008), pp. 57–72

Scheck, Raffael, *Hitler's African Victims: The German Massacres of Black French Soldiers in 1940* (Cambridge University Press, 2006)

Schilling, Britta, 'Memory, Myth and Material Culture: Visions of Empire in Postcolonial Germany' (DPhil thesis, Oxford University, 2010)

Schler, Lynn, 'Bridewealth, Guns and other Status Symbols: Immigration and Consumption in Colonial Douala', *Journal of African Cultural Studies*, 16 (2003), 213–34

'Writing African Women's History with Male Sources: Possibilities and Limitations', *History in Africa*, 31 (2004), 319–33

Schmelz, Andrea, *Bildungsmigranten aus Afrika und Asien* (Frankfurt a.M.: Iko-Verlag, 2004)

Schmidt, Christoph, '"Die kolonialen Sklaven sind erwacht...": Der "Kongress der Negerarbeiter" in Hamburg', in Heiko Möhle (ed.), *Branntwein, Bibeln und Bananen: Der deutsche Kolonialismus in Afrika – Eine Spurensuche* (Hamburg: Assoziation A, 1999), pp. 93–7

Schmidt-Soltau, Kai, 'Postkoloniale Konstruktionen der kolonialen Begegnung: Die deutsche Kolonialzeit im Blick des anglophonen Kamerun', in Marianne Bechhaus-Gest and Reinhard Klein-Arendt (eds.), *Die (koloniale) Begegnung: Afrikanerinnen in Deutschland 1880–1945, Deutsche in Afrika 1880–1918* (Frankfurt a.M.: Peter Lang, 2003), pp. 269–82

Scholder, Klaus, *The Churches and the Third Reich*, vol. I: *Preliminary History and the Time of Illusions* (London: SCM Press, 1987)

Schröder, Hans Eggert, *Ludwig Klages: Die Geschichte seines Lebens*, 2 vols. (Bonn: Bouvier, 1966)

Schröder, Heribert, *Tanz- und Unterhaltungsmusik in Deutschland 1918–1933* (Bonn: Verlag für systematische Musikwissenschaft, 1990)

Schröder, Martin, *Prügelstrafe und Züchtigungsrecht in den deutschen Schutzgebieten Schwarzafrikas* (Münster: LIT, 1997)

Schroer, Timothy L., *Recasting Race after World War II: Germans and African-Americans in American-Occupied Germany* (Boulder CO: University Press of Colorado, 2007)

Setkiewicz, Piotr, 'Ausgewählte Probleme aus der Geschichte des IG Werkes Auschwitz', *Hefte von Auschwitz*, 22 (2002), 7–147

Shack, William A., *Harlem in Montmartre: A Paris Jazz Story between the Great Wars* (Berkeley: University of California Press, 2001)

Sippel, Harald, 'Rassismus, Protektionismus oder Humanität? Die gesetzlichen Verbote der Anwerbung von "Eingeborenen" zu Schaustellungszwecken in den deutschen Kolonien', in Robert Debusmann and János Riesz (eds.), *Kolonialausstellungen – Begegnungen mit Afrika?* (Frankfurt a.M.: IKO, 1995), pp. 43–64

Smalls, James, 'Féral Benga's Body', in Eve Rosenhaft and Robbie Aitken (eds.), *Africa in Europe: Studies in Transnational Practice in the Long Twentieth Century* (Liverpool University Press, 2013), pp. 99–119

Sonnenberger, Dietrich, 'Der Prinz von Holthausen hat wieder Familie – neue Erkenntnisse rund um ein "rätselhaftes" Grab', *Nachrichten der evangelischen Kirchengemeinde Holthausen* (April/May 2005), 10–11

Sparing, Frank, 'Hilarius Gilges – Ein von der SS ermordeter Arbeiter und Kommunist', in Peter Martin and Christine Alonzo (eds.), *Zwischen Charleston und Stechschritt: Schwarze im Nationalsozialismus* (Hamburg: Dölling & Galitz, 2004), pp. 549–56

Städtler, Katharina, 'Léopold Sédar Senghor und die Deutschen', in Ulrich van der Heyden (ed.), *Unbekannte Biographien: Afrikaner im Deutschsprachigen Raum vom 18. Jahrhundert bis zum Ende des Zweiten Weltkrieges* (Berlin: Homilius, 2008), pp. 274–82

'"Touristes coloniaux" dans la France occupée', in Romuald Fonkoua (ed.), *Les Discours de voyages* (Paris: Karthala, 1998), pp. 147–58

Stoecker, Holger, *Afrikawissenschaft in Berlin von 1919 bis 1945: Zur Geschichte und Topographie eines wissenschaftlichen Netzwerkes* (Stuttgart: Steiner, 2008)

'Sprachlehrer, Informant, Küchenchef: Der "preußische" Afrikaner Bonifatius Folli aus Anecho (Togo) im Dienste der Berliner Afrikanistik', in Ulrich van der Heyden (ed.), *Unbekannte Biographien: Afrikaner im deutschsprachigen Raum vom 18. Jahrhundert bis zum Ende des Zweiten Weltkrieges* (Berlin: Kai Homilius, 2008), pp. 217–37

Stoler, Ann Laura, *Carnal Knowledge and Imperial Power: Race and the Intimate in Colonial Rule* (Berkeley: University of California Press, 2002)

Stovall, Tyler, 'Harlem-sur-Seine: Building an African American Diasporic Community in Paris', *Stanford Electronic Humanities Review*, 5/2 (1997), www.stanford.edu/group/SHR/5-2/stoval.html [accessed 30 November 2012]

Paris Noir: African Americans in the City of Light (New York: Houghton Mifflin, 1996)

Strachan, Hew, *The First World War in Africa* (Oxford University Press, 2004)

Tabili, Laura, *'We Ask for British Justice': Workers and Racial Difference in Late Imperial Britain* (Ithaca NY: Cornell University Press, 1999)

Tate, Shirley Anne, 'Translating Melancholia: A Poetics of Black Interstitial Community', *Community, Work and Family*, 10 (2007), 1–15

Thode-Arora, Hilke, '"Charakteristische Gestalten des Volkslebens": Die Hagenbeckschen Südasien-, Orient- und Afrika-Völkerschauen', in Gerhard Höpp (ed.), *Fremde Erfahrungen: Asiaten und Afrikaner in Deutschland, Österreich und in der Schweiz bis 1945* (Berlin: Das Arabische Buch, 1996), pp. 109–34

'Völkerschauen in Berlin', in Ulrich van der Heyden and Joachim Zeller (eds.), *Kolonialmetropole Berlin* (Berlin Edition, 2002), pp. 149–54

Torpey, John, *The Invention of the Passport: Surveillance, Citizenship and the State* (Cambridge University Press, 2000)

Tower, Beeke Sell, '"Ultramodern and Ultraprimitive": Shifting Meanings in the Imagery of Americanism in the Art of Weimar Germany', in Thomas W. Kniesche and Stephen Brockmann (eds.), *Dancing on the Volcano: Essays on the Culture of the Weimar Republic* (Columbia SC: Camden House, 1994), pp. 85–104

Tracey, Donald R., 'The Development of the National Socialist Party in Thuringia', *Central European History*, 8 (1975), 23–50

Vaillant, Janet G., *Black, French and African: A Life of Léopold Sédar Senghor* (Cambridge MA: Harvard University Press, 1990)

Volkov, Shulamit, *The Rise of Popular Antimodernism in Germany: The Urban Master Artisans, 1873–1896* (Princeton University Press, 1978)

Wachsmann, Nikolaus, *Hitler's Prisons: Legal Terror in Nazi Germany* (New Haven: Yale University Press, 2004)

Wagner, Patrick, 'Kriminalprävention qua Massenmord: Die gesellschaftsbiologische Konzeption der NS-Kriminalpolizei und ihre Bedeutung für die Zigeunerverfolgung', in Michael Zimmermann (ed.), *Zwischen Erziehung und Vernichtung: Zigeunerpolitik und Zigeunerforschung im Europa des 20. Jahrhunderts* (Stuttgart: Steiner, 2007), pp. 379–91

Weber, Eugen, *The Hollow Years: France in the 1930s* (London: Sinclair-Stevenson, 1995)

Wei, Ebele (Valère Epée), *Le Paradis tabou: Autopsie d'une culture assassinée* (Douala: Editions Cerac, 1999)

Weiss, Holger, 'Glimpses of African Political Engagement in Weimar Germany – The Berlin Section of the *Ligue de la Defense de Race Negre*', www.abo.fi/institution/media/7957/komintern.pdf [accessed 4 April 2013]

Wiegräbe, Paul, *Pastor Robert Kwami: Ein Zeuge und Zeugnis des Evangeliums in Westafrika* (Bremen: Anker, 1948)

Wildenthal, Lora, *German Women for Empire, 1884–1945* (Durham NC: Duke University Press, 2001)

Wilder, Gary, *The French Imperial Nation-State: Negritude and Colonial Humanism between the Two World Wars* (University of Chicago Press, 2005)

Wildt, Michael, *Generation des Unbedingten: Das Führungskorps des Reichssicherheitshauptamtes* (Hamburger Edition, 2003)

Wilson, Edward T., *Russia and Black Africa before World War Two* (London: Holmes and Meier, 1974)

Wimmelbücker, Ludger, *Mtoro bin Mwinyi Bakari* (Dar es Salaam: Mkuki na Nyota, 2009)

Wright, Michelle M., *Becoming Black: Creating Identity in the African Diaspora* (Durham NC: Duke University Press, 2004)

Wulf, Josef, *Musik im Dritten Reich: Eine Dokumentation* (Frankfurt a.M./Berlin: Ullstein, 1989)

Zeller, Joachim, 'Das Deutsche Kolonialhaus in der Lützowstraße', in Ulrich van der Heyden and Joachim Zeller (eds.), *Kolonialmetropole Berlin* (Berlin Edition, 2002), pp. 84–92

Zeller, Joachim and Stefanie Michels, 'Kamerunischer Nationalheld – treuer Diener und Soldat: Mebenga m'Ebono alias Martin Paul Samba', in Ulrich van der Heyden (ed.), *Unbekannte Biographien: Afrikaner im deutschsprachigen Raum vom 18. Jahrhundert bis zum Ende des Zweiten Weltkrieges* (Berlin: Kai Homilius, 2008), pp. 128–34

Zimmerman, Andrew, *Alabama in Africa: Booker T. Washington, the German Empire, and the Globalization of the New South* (Princeton University Press, 2010)

Anthropology and Antihumanism in Imperial Germany (University of Chicago Press, 2001)

Zimmermann, Michael, 'Die Entscheidung für ein Zigeunerlager in Auschwitz-Birkenau', in Michael Zimmermann (ed.), *Zwischen Erziehung und Vernichtung: Zigeunerpolitik und Zigeunerforschung im Europa des 20. Jahrhunderts* (Stuttgart: Steiner, 2007), pp. 392–424

Index